For the Love of Murphy's

A KEYSTONE BOOK®

A Keystone Book® is so designated to distinguish it from the
typical scholarly monograph that a university press publishes.
It is a book intended to serve the citizens of Pennsylvania by
educating them and others, in an entertaining way, about as-
pects of the history, culture, society, and environment of the
state as part of the Middle Atlantic region.

THE PENNSYLVANIA STATE UNIVERSITY PRESS, UNIVERSITY PARK, PENNSYLVANIA

For the Love of

MURPHY'S

THE BEHIND-THE-COUNTER STORY OF A GREAT AMERICAN RETAILER

JASON TOGYER

Published with the assistance of a grant from the
G. C. Murphy Company Foundation.

Library of Congress Cataloging-in-Publication Data

Togyer, Jason.
    For the love of Murphy's : the behind-the-counter story of
a great American retailer / Jason Togyer.
            p.   cm. — (A Keystone book)
Summary: "Presents a detailed history of the G. C. Murphy
Company, headquartered in McKeesport, Pennsylvania. Ex-
amines the larger context of the origins and evolution of five-
and-ten-cent stores"—Provided by publisher.
Includes bibliographical references and index.
ISBN 978-0-271-03370-9 (cloth : alk. paper)
1. G. C. Murphy—History.
2. Variety stores—United States—History.
3. Stores, retail—United States—History.
I. Title.

HF5465.U6M878 2008
381′.14909748—dc22
2008010470

Copyright © 2008
The Pennsylvania State University
All rights reserved
Designed by Regina Starace
Printed in the China
Published by The Pennsylvania State University Press,
University Park, PA 16802-1003

The Pennsylvania State University Press is a member of the
Association of American University Presses.

It is the policy of The Pennsylvania State University Press to
use acid-free paper. Publications on uncoated stock satisfy
the minimum requirements of American National Standard
for Information Sciences—Permanence of Paper for Printed
Library Material, ANSI Z39.48–1992.

contents

illustrations

foreword

Sixteen-year-old Tom Messner drove the big car carefully, fully aware both of the importance of his passenger and that his new job as his male secretary was at stake. Male secretaries were not uncommon in 1920 since the job often also involved serving as driver and traveling companion. Young Tom's passenger, Walter C. Shaw Sr., one of the two men who had taken over the G. C. Murphy Company after its founder's death, was a tall, slender gentleman with an imposing presence and a gentle demeanor. Tom enjoyed his trips to visit many of the forty-six stores of the young company and learned much by listening to Mr. Shaw's instructions to store managers. Shaw must have liked Tom as well—after a few years he promoted him to the position of hardware buyer, a position Tom held until his retirement in 1968 after forty-eight years of service.

I am Tom's son. In 1965, after Dartmouth College, University of Pennsylvania Law School, and a tour of duty in Korea with the U.S. Army, I joined a large Pittsburgh law firm specializing in corporate law. Three years later, in 1968, through a series of coincidences, first Ken Paxton, Murphy's vice president of personnel, and then board chairman and CEO Jim Mack invited me to join Murphy's as its first inside legal counsel. Shortly after I joined the company, Jim Mack died unexpectedly. Ken Paxton became chairman and CEO, and I became the company's general counsel and corporate secretary. Seventeen interesting and challenging years later, in 1985, it was my responsibility to record the minutes of the Murphy board of directors meeting at which, having been "in play" on Wall Street for some time, Murphy's was acquired in a "bear hug" hostile takeover by Ames Department Stores of Connecticut—the saddest day in Murphy's history. Perhaps because my father and I accounted for sixty-five of the company's seventy-four years of independent existence and were privileged to witness much of it personally, I have been asked to write this foreword.

In 1985, as the company was in the process of being acquired, it dawned on a few of us that the G. C. Murphy Company Foundation was not really part of the company, having been required by the Internal Revenue Code to be a separate and distinct entity. We realized how important the foundation had been to many Murphy communities and how critical it could be in the future to those communities that had also recently been devastated by the collapse of the American steel industry. We are pleased to report that since that time, the G. C. Murphy Company Foundation has made grants totaling millions of dollars to local communities and deserving causes. Those who served on the foundation's board of directors during that time include Charles W. Breckenridge, William T. Cullen, Edwin W. Davis, Alice J. Hajduk, Thomas F. Hudak, Martha Mack Lewis, Charles H. Lytle, Clair A. McElhinny, C. E. Palmer, S. Warne Robinson, Philip W. Rogers, and Walter C. Shaw Jr.

With the closing of so many Murphy's variety stores, the renaming and closing of Murphy's Marts, as well as the subsequent Ames bankruptcy, those of us on the foundation's board realized it might not be long before this important retailing institution, G. C. Murphy Company, passed from the public's memory. We did not want that to happen. At this point, it was our good fortune to encounter Jason Togyer, who combined excellent research and writing talents with a unique sense of the company's history and its importance to the communities it served.

Since then, Jason has devoted thousands of hours to interviewing hundreds of former Murphy employees and customers throughout the eastern half of the United States, to exhaustive historical research, and to writing and editing this wonderful book. It exceeds the foundation's fondest hopes. We hope you enjoy it. We also hope it will preserve the memory of Murphy's.

ROBERT T. MESSNER
President, G. C. Murphy Company Foundation

preface and acknowledgments

There will soon be a generation of Americans that has never set foot in a "five-and-ten" store—that doesn't even know what a five-and-ten was. They never marveled at the rows of thread and buttons, goggled at the racks of toy cars or doll beds, or cooed over the hamsters and parakeets in the pet department. Sure, F. W. Woolworth Company kept a dwindling number of five-and-tens open until 1997, and McCrory soldiered on for a few years after that, but their remaining locations were a pale reflection of variety stores in their heyday from the 1920s through the 1970s, when they were a staple of American life.

Wal-Marts and Targets tend to run 100,000 square feet and more, but the typical dime store was built on a human scale of perhaps 10,000 or 20,000 square feet. A small child could safely walk around a five-and-ten and mom could keep an eye on him the whole time, but any parent who allowed a youngster to roam Wal-Mart would soon be questioned by the child-welfare authorities. Unlike the "big boxes," dime stores were woven into the fabric of downtown shopping areas—you could walk to the five-and-ten. (Try to walk to a Target across a four-lane interstate highway and a busy parking lot and you're taking your life into your hands.) A few independent variety stores still exist, but they lack the sense of showmanship the big chains had; and while there are a number of "dollar stores" around, they stock only a fraction of the inventory that was carried by Woolworth, McCrory, or G. C. Murphy Company five-and-tens.

If you grew up on the West Coast or in a major city such as New York or Chicago, you probably never heard of the G. C. Murphy Company. For most of its existence, the G. C. Murphy Company and its more than five hundred stores flew under the national radar. While Woolworth was slugging it out in Manhattan, Murphy's was opening stores in small towns to serve the miners of West Virginia, the steelworkers of Pennsylvania, and the farmers of Indiana. In many of these communities where the only retailers were owned by the mines or the mills, workers often did "owe their souls to the company store." The G. C. Murphy Company store brought name-brand merchandise at low prices to these towns, liberating them from the tyranny of company stores and allowing even the poorest residents to splurge on perfume, candy, or a rare meal out at a restaurant.

That's why people in Appalachian and midwestern communities were fiercely loyal to the G. C. Murphy Company for decades until its takeover by Ames Department Stores in 1985. But because G. C. Murphy Company avoided the national spotlight, almost nothing was written about it, except for a few articles in trade and business publications. In fact, although a few books have been written about the F. W. Woolworth Company, there has been no comprehensive examination of the five-and-ten business since perhaps the 1960s. In its small way, this book seeks to rectify those omissions and maybe even educate a new generation on why the five-and-ten was so special. I hope that people looking to recapture the fun they had shopping or working at the five-and-ten find plenty here to make them nostalgic. I also hope that people interested in business history can learn how a company with its roots in the nineteenth century adapted itself to every major American trend and crisis only to perish in the freakish economic climate of the 1980s.

It's said that "history is written by the victors," and when Ames and McCrory dismembered the G. C. Murphy Company between 1985 and 1990, they cared little for preserving its heritage. No official "corporate archive" exists, which made writing this book somewhat more difficult. So, I'm deeply indebted to two groups: the Society of Murphy Employees Retired and Fired, maintained for nearly twenty years by Alice Hajduk, former editor of the mail at Murphy's home office; and the G. C. Murphy Company Foundation, the charitable arm created in 1952 and spun off in 1985. Members of both groups spent countless hours helping me track down former Murphy's employees throughout the United States.

Many members of the Murphy's family, in turn, consented to lengthy interviews or contributed employee handbooks, photos, personal reminiscences, and other memorabilia. I cannot thank them enough for their help. If this book is accurate, they deserve the credit, but any errors are mine alone. Several people helped fact-check the text, but a few mistakes have undoubtedly crept in.

Because of space constraints, I could only use a fraction of what I received, but it was all appreciated and enjoyed, and everything is being donated to the McKeesport Heritage Center, a museum, historical society, and genealogical library in Murphy's headquarters city of McKeesport, Pennsylvania. Letters, interviews, and other items will be preserved and eventually put on display for future generations to learn about the legacy of the people behind the G. C. Murphy Company.

Only a relative handful of the tens of thousands of employees who worked for Murphy's between 1906 and 1985 are mentioned by name in this book. I did not mean to slight anyone who is not mentioned and I do not want to minimize their contributions; instead, I hope that the experiences of the people who are quoted reflect those of their former co-workers as well.

As G. C. Murphy Company closed its doors, longtime employees saved as much material as they could, which was donated to the heritage center where it fills most of two file cabinets. Heritage center volunteers and staff, including Gail Waite and the late Cynthia Neish, were extraordinarily helpful throughout my more than two years of research. In the heritage center's collection are many long memos about the company's history written in the 1940s and 1950s by former Murphy chairman Walter Shaw Sr. These, along with John Sephus Mack's annual letters to shareholders—and speeches delivered by Mack, Shaw, Murphy president Paul Sample, and others—were vital in reconstructing the company's early years. Little remains in McKeesport of the founder, George C. Murphy, who died in 1909. Thankfully, his granddaughter Betty Rehfeldt loaned me an entire file of his personal papers and correspondence. Using these papers, census records, and a few memoirs from Murphy's contemporaries, I was able to shed some light on the life of this neglected retail pioneer.

In the interest of full disclosure, I should mention that although I did not receive any compensation or remuneration to work on this book, my travel, telephone, and photo-copying expenses were funded by the McKeesport Heritage Center through a grant from the G. C. Murphy Company Foundation. However, the foundation did not attempt to censor or alter the text in any way, even when some passages reflected poorly on certain individuals. This required a great deal of patience and trust on their part, and I am forever grateful to the board of directors: Charles W. Breckenridge, William T. Cullen, Edwin W. Davis, Alice Hajduk, Thomas F. Hudak, Clair A. McElhinny, and Robert T. Messner. In alphabetical order, I would like to single out three for particular kudos: Edwin Davis, who fielded many late-night phone calls and e-mails when I had "just one more question"; Clair "Mac" McElhinny, who loaned hundreds of documents and opened many doors for me; and Robert Messner, whose vision and persistence pushed this project (and me) forward.

Finally, I am grateful to my family and friends, who put up with my countless side trips to former G. C. Murphy Company stores and my purchases of Murphy memorabilia. For three years, they have listened to innumerable (and interminable) Murphy anecdotes and have been told over and over again that I could not do one thing or another because I was "working on the book." I'll now have to come up with a new excuse or start working on another book.

This book is dedicated to the men and women who made the G. C. Murphy Company a beloved institution in more than five hundred American communities and to all of the "five-and-ten girls" who worked for Murphy's, Kresge's, Woolworth's, and other chains. In fact, the title of the book comes from something that several former Murphy employees said when I asked them why they put up with various hardships. "They did it because they loved the company," Wayne Potter's wife Lil told me. "They loved Murphy's." Memories of these men and women and their hard work have endured long after the stores closed. Two former five-and-ten girls are very near to my heart and provided much of the inspiration for this work. They are my grandmothers Charlotte Makatura, former floor supervisor at H. L. Green Company Store No. 29, and Lena Togyer, former waitress at G. C. Murphy Company Store No. 1, both in McKeesport.

BETHEL *Park*

CHAPTER 1

1970

The preparations had gone right down to the wire, but the G. C. Murphy Company's newest store in the Pittsburgh suburb of Bethel Park, Pennsylvania, was as ready as it was going to get. True, the construction workers hadn't finished up until late the night before, but it didn't matter because Store No. 802 was going to open on time. Outside, the thousand-car parking lot was freshly paved and striped. Inside, two hundred employees were ready for work under manager C. W. "Chuck" Henderson, who'd recently transferred to Pittsburgh from one of Murphy's big flagship stores—the massive five-and-ten in Washington, D.C., known within the company as No. 166. Some of Henderson's employees were new hires, but most were experienced, having worked at other G. C. Murphy stores.

Stacked just inside the front entrance were plastic laundry baskets and women's raincoats—giveaways for the first customers through the door. The laundry baskets were an appropriate (and a little bit ironic) feature, though few people realized it at the time. Back in the early 1900s, Mr. George C. Murphy himself had featured cheap laundry baskets at the grand-opening sales of his first five-and-tens around Pittsburgh. He had been dead now for a little more than sixty-one years, but somewhere, maybe, George Murphy was chuckling.

Inside Store No. 802, the shelves were stacked high with specials. The automotive department had oil going for 40¢ a quart; hardware had gallons of paint for $2; and leather gloves cost $3.44 in ladies' wear. There was a shiny new cafeteria waiting, too, with 114 seats and a New Orleans Bourbon Street motif. The opening-day specials would include a full-course turkey dinner for $1 and strawberry pie for 44¢ a slice.

And, thank goodness, the notoriously fickle spring weather in Pittsburgh seemed to be cooperating on that Wednesday before Memorial Day in 1970. The morning was cool but clear, and temperatures were expected to hit the mid-seventies by that afternoon.

The only question remaining: Would any customers be there? The executives of the G. C. Murphy Company had plenty of reasons to worry. The chain, based in the nearby steel mill town of McKeesport, had 520 variety stores (most people still called them five-and-tens, though few, if any, items were still available for a nickel or a dime) from Connecticut to Florida, including some large locations in shopping malls and major cities. But it had never operated a store this big—just a shade more than 150,000 square feet.

Nor had the company ever been in the high-volume, low-margin discount business. Until recently, employees had been forbidden to even use the word "discount." The late Jim Mack, son of the man who helped rescue the G. C. Murphy Company from bankruptcy in 1911 and the former company president who died unexpectedly two years before, had insisted that all stores present a "premium" image.

Most Murphy executives and even many store managers knew what had happened a few years earlier when a photographer for the magazine *Chain Store Age* snapped a picture of an innovative display at a Murphy store in upstate New York. In the background was a sign with the word "discount" on it. Mack hit the roof, first threatening to fire the store's manager, and then demanding the negative from the publisher so that the photo could be destroyed.

He wasn't the only one who disliked discount stores. Walter C. Shaw Sr., who with Mack's father had bought the Murphy chain out of insolvency, "was very much against those big stores," says Bob Beyer, who worked in the company's architectural department. "He did not like them at all." Shaw had died in 1962, but his influence still loomed large over the G. C. Murphy Company, and his son remained on the board of directors. Murphy's was a tradition-bound company, and one of these traditions was helpful service. It had been a wrenching decision for Murphy's to move its salesgirls out from behind their counters, install checkout lines, and allow customers to serve themselves; executives were convinced the changes would harm the company's image as "The Friendly Store."

Elsewhere in the industry, some old-time full-price retailers also looked on the upstart discount chains with scorn. "Do you know what discounting is?" one old-time retail executive told a reporter. "It's nothing more than selling inferior merchandise on Sundays." True, with their barn-like interiors, bare fluorescent light fixtures, and clothing displayed on plain pipe racks, early discount stores had none of the class or elegance of department stores such as Pittsburgh's Joseph Horne Company or even the showmanship and razzmatazz of big variety stores such as Murphy's. But in their hearts, most Murphy executives knew that the chain had to move into discounting. They were being passed up by their old five-and-ten rival, Michigan-based S. S. Kresge Company, whose namesake had been a business partner of Mr. Murphy and a personal friend of former Murphy president Paul Sample.

In 1961, the rundown old Kresge company, whose small, downtown variety stores were lagging behind those of competitors such as Murphy and F. W. Woolworth Company, changed its entire direction by closing many of those locations and opening big, suburban discount stores called Kmarts. Their success was instant and phenomenal—Kresge, which did $419 million in sales in 1960, was doing more than three times that volume in 1970. It had three hundred fewer Kresge dime stores but three hundred big new Kmarts, including seven right on the G. C. Murphy Company's home turf in Pittsburgh.

Murphy executives studied the new Kmarts with admiration and a little jealousy. They saw things they wanted to copy and things they wanted to improve on, and they knew they could learn from Kresge's mistakes. Blueprints and proposals for Murphy discount stores were even drawn up in the mid-1960s, but in secret for fear of bringing down Jim Mack's wrath. When Mack died, one executive remembers, "The plans came out of the desk drawers the next day."

Still, despite all the preparation, dealing with a high-volume discount operation was uncharted territory for Murphy's, remembers Paul Hindes, who started his forty-three-year career with the company in 1942 as a stock boy in a five-and-ten south of Pittsburgh. By 1970, he was buying infants' and children's wear for the chain. "I'm not sure we knew how much [merchandise] we were going to need in that Bethel store," says Hindes, one of the scores of employees from the Murphy headquarters, or home office, who stayed all night Tuesday to get the building ready. "We were working with types of displays we had never worked with before."

Murphy's advertising and sales promotion departments were considered among the best in the field—the company had pioneered variety store advertising and was the first five-and-ten chain to run television commercials in the 1940s—and it was running flat out to promote the new store. Twelve pages of advertising ran in the city's biggest newspaper, the *Pittsburgh Press*, on Tuesday afternoon, guaranteeing that about a quarter million people were aware of the new store.

The newspaper further obliged by running several stories about the G. C. Murphy Company's new venture. In the process, some unknown editor made a mistake that would be repeated for the next fifteen years by newspapers and customers alike and would grate on Murphy employees every time they heard it. The *Pittsburgh Press* had referred to the new store as the "Murphy Mart." It was supposed to be "Murphy's Mart," though, just as

FIG. 1
The G. C. Murphy
Company's first discount
store, Murphy's Mart
No. 802 in Bethel Park,
Pa., south of Pittsburgh,
did nearly a half million
dollars in sales during
its first four days in
operation in 1970,
more than some of
the company's variety
stores sold in a year.
Lucille Crow, assistant
buyer of infants' wear
for Murphy's, fights her
way through crowds in
the wig department on
opening day, May 27, 1970.

everything else about the new store, the name had been the subject of a protracted debate at the home office.

Marketing studies indicated that, thanks to Kmart's popularity, the word "mart" now meant "bargain" to consumers, and some executives insisted that the new Murphy discount stores have the name "mart" in them. Other retailers had reached the same conclusions when they launched their own discount chains; for example, Federated Department Stores called its stores Fed-Marts. Inside Murphy's, many people felt their company's name had high recognition, so "Murphy" had to be included, says Luther Shay, who was managing the merchandise investment control department. That ruled out one contender, "M-Mart," which in retrospect was probably too imitative of "Kmart." In any event, M-Mart "didn't get to first base," Shay says.

Hindes remembers that the clothing buyers wanted to capitalize on Murphy's popular line of work clothes. "We wanted to call the stores 'Big Murph,'" he says. "We had a drawing of a big lumberjack guy holding a sign that said 'Big Murph.' They didn't go for it." Bill Kraus, another home office buyer, suggested "Murphy's Merchandise Marts," evoking the famous Merchandise Mart in Chicago. He suggested the name be abbreviated "M-M-M" or

"Three-M's." The fear of provoking a lawsuit from the other 3M in Minnesota squelched that proposal. Thus, the Bethel Park store, and all its progeny, would be christened "Murphy's Mart," a compromise name that never pleased some in the company and confused customers for years to come. "We were stuck with it," Kraus says.

Even the location, which wasn't an entirely auspicious place to launch a new business venture, was a compromise. The first Murphy's Mart was supposed to be a brand-new store north of Pittsburgh in the semi-rural community of Harmar Township, but Murphy's sharp-eyed real estate men were able to secure the Bethel Park building, which had been occupied by a failed shopping complex called The Mayfair. Murphy's construction division quickly converted the location for the company's needs, and the store was ready to open months before the Murphy's Mart in Harmar.

Yet it begged the question: If The Mayfair had flopped in that spot, why would Murphy's succeed? Sure, Murphy's had a long and honorable history in more than twenty states. In Pittsburgh, four generations had grown up with the company. But it was known for five-and-ten stores—the kind of places where kids shopped for candy, mom bought lipstick and thread, and dad bought pipe tobacco and fishing lures. Those were low-volume, low-price items, not the higher-priced lines of clothing, appliances, and housewares that were the lifeblood of discount houses.

It wasn't a given that Murphy's even knew how to sell fashion apparel and automotive supplies, much less that the public's warm, nostalgic feelings for the Murphy name would be enough to draw customers away from Kmart, which incidentally had also placed several pages of advertising in Tuesday's *Press*, possibly to combat the publicity Murphy's Mart was receiving.

If Murphy employees still had serious doubts Wednesday morning, they evaporated along with the dew. At 10:00 A.M., Ed and Ken Paxton—brothers and the company's president and chairman, respectively—helped cut the ribbon at the Murphy's Mart entrance. By then, the thousand-car parking lot that had seemed so vast a few hours before was filled to capacity and customers were crowding the doors. For the next four days, employees of the new Murphy's Mart sold everything they could get their hands on: more than $140,000 in merchandise the first day. "Opening day, you couldn't get near it," recalls Fred Speidel, who was an assistant manager. "Every road to the place was blocked off. The volume was so much! . . . Up to that point, the biggest volume store I had ever been in was doing $200,000 a year." By Saturday night, the Murphy's Mart on Route 88 had done $455,215 in sales, including $10,000 at the restaurant, which translated into quite a number of 44¢ slices of pie.

Perhaps the Murphy name had some magic in it after all. Although they'd previously never run a discount house, there apparently was magic in those Murphy's employees, too. After all, they'd been through the company's rigorous in-house training program, which was the envy of the retail industry. Bob Bishop, a zone manager at the Bethel Park store,

FIG. 2
Murphy's Mart No. 801 in Harmar Township, Pa., north of Pittsburgh, was the first designed and constructed by the G. C. Murphy Company from the ground up. It opened on July 22, 1970. The new discount stores required Murphy's to learn how to sell more expensive and fashionable merchandise, including jewelry, shown here.

remembers that when the books closed on its first full year of operations, it had done $18 million in sales, "and that was a lot of money a long, long time ago."

The impact on the community became humorously evident to Bishop a few months later. One of the hot items at the Bethel Park Murphy's Mart was ladies' polyester pantsuits. Murphy's Mart was such a hit in the communities south of Pittsburgh, Bishop recalls, that "every corner I went to for the next month, I saw those pantsuits because we sold so many of them."

The Bethel Park store would have problems to overcome, as would the next two Murphy's Marts in Harmar and Connellsville. Murphy's would have to streamline its procedures, some of which had been in place for more than sixty years. It would have to shake off its dime-store mentality, which stressed high profit margins and low sales volume, to instead go for low profit margins and high sales volume. Murphy's fervent desire to catch up with Kmart by opening dozens of Murphy's Marts would eventually threaten to sink the company. New management closed the money-losing locations, trimmed some of the bureaucracy, and turned the company into a Wall Street darling in the early 1980s. That, ironically, would sow the seeds for the G. C. Murphy Company's eventual destruction—the surprising success of the humble retail chain in McKeesport, Pennsylvania, attracted the attention of corporate raiders.

Nobody knew that in 1970, of course. Instead, the exciting new Bethel Park store seemed to be the dawn of a great new era for a venerable old company, which was much beloved by customers and employees. The first Murphy's Mart "was the turning point for the company," says Ed Davis, Murphy's longtime public relations man, who, as had so many executives, started his career in the stockroom of a small-town five-and-ten.

Bill Kraus had been discouraged by the company's conservatism and had watched Kresge's runaway success with increasing dismay. At one point, he even entertained a job offer from an Arkansas five-and-ten operator, Sam Walton, who had recently opened his own Kmart-style discount stores called Wal-Marts. In the end, Kraus couldn't tear himself away from Murphy's, which he, as did so many employees, viewed as a family.

So when the Bethel Park store opened and the sales division started reporting the unprecedented volume of merchandise it was handling, Kraus felt his pride in Murphy's swelling. He didn't think of leaving again. "When it opened, it was dynamic," Kraus says. "I thought, 'Man, we have finally hit it.' We were on our way."

A Revolution IN RETAILING

Those teenagers milling around your local shopping mall owe a debt of gratitude to a nineteenth-century boy from upstate New York who hated life on the farm. By abandoning his rural roots and creating the five-and-ten store, Frank Winfield Woolworth practically invented the modern-day pastime of recreational shopping.

Before Woolworth's then-shocking decision to put merchandise out on counters with clearly marked prices and allow customers to pick them up and inspect them before they bought, shopping could be an unpleasant affair. There were no Better Business Bureaus, money-back guarantees, or consumer protection laws in the 1800s. Goods were kept behind the counter where clerks brought them out upon request. Prices were flexible (haggling was expected) and it wasn't uncommon for dishonest shopkeepers to put their thumb on a scale or deliberately measure a bolt of cloth incorrectly to short the buyer. "The law of trading was then the law of the jungle," said John Wanamaker, founder of one of the first great department stores in the United States. "Look out for number one."

Woolworth's invention of the five-cent counter was practically the only thing he did right during his early career in retailing. One of his early bosses called him the worst salesman he'd ever seen; about the only talents evident were his head for figures (Woolworth, who had taken some business courses after grammar school, was a demon for bookkeeping) and his skill at arranging window displays. He was working for William H. Moore's dry-goods store in Watertown, New York, in 1878 when a business downturn hit the region. A former clerk from a competing store who was passing through the area stopped for a visit and suggested that Moore build traffic by offering "special bargains" on old and discontinued merchandise. Moore traveled to New York City and ordered $100 worth of trinkets—costume jewelry, hairpins, needles, and thimbles—which arrived just before the county fair. As the most artistic member of Moore's staff, Woolworth lined two tables with bright red cloth, arranged the bargain merchandise, and painted a nice, large sign: "Any Article On This Counter Five Cents."

The next day, families poured into Watertown on their way to the fair, having saved up a few nickels to spend on games and food. Many wound up spending their nickels at Moore's store instead. By the end of the night, the five-cent counter was empty, and Woolworth ran to the telegraph office to place a rush order for more merchandise. The experiment set off a craze around the region—customers liked the plainly marked prices that eliminated haggling—and Woolworth wondered what would happen if an entire store was organized the same way.

He convinced Moore to loan him $300 worth of merchandise and rented a small storefront on a side street in the nearby city of Utica where he opened The Great Five-Cent Store on Saturday, February 22, 1879. The crowds were underwhelming. Curiosity attracted customers for a few days, but there was a limit to the kinds of merchandise he could profitably sell for a nickel, as well as little repeat business. After paying his debt to Moore (netting about $252 in profit), Woolworth closed the store and opened another store in Lancaster, Pennsylvania, the heart of Pennsylvania's Amish country. This time when business went slack, Woolworth added ten-cent counters, doubling both the variety of his goods and his profit margins. The store was a roaring success. He leased a store in Pennsylvania's capital, Harrisburg, and asked his brother Sumner to run it, but the location was a flop, as was another in York. In November 1880, the Woolworth brothers leased a storefront in Scranton, which did the trick—it was soon netting $1,000 per year. To justify volume purchasing and bigger discounts, Woolworth needed more locations. So, after refining his selection to include more everyday staple items, he returned to Harrisburg and Utica and also opened stores in Wilmington, Delaware; Elmira, New York; Trenton, New Jersey; and Easton, Pennsylvania. When Moore's store failed in 1885, Woolworth bailed him out and set him up with a five-and-ten. The Woolworth syndicate now had annual sales of more than $100,000 and an annual profit of more than $10,000.

That was a lot of nickels and dimes, and Woolworth's success attracted a raft of imitators across Pennsylvania, including another former farm boy, John Graham McCrorey. Born in Indiana County, Pennsylvania, in 1860, McCrorey was working in the company store owned by the Cambria Iron Works in Johnstown when he heard of Woolworth's bustling business in Lancaster. He moved to the coal-mining town of Scottdale, Pennsylvania, south of Pittsburgh, and with $350 he'd saved and another $200 he borrowed, opened his own five-cent store. It lasted only two years, but by then McCrorey had already added stores in the burgeoning oil field and mining towns of Bradford, Oil City, DuBois, Lock Haven, and Clearfield, Pennsylvania. "WAKE UP!" read the headline of one of his early handbills. "Everyone can readily see that by running five stores, I have every advantage in buying goods, getting low prices and big discounts. . . . You will wonder how the goods were got for the money." McCrorey's "fantastic bargains" included two-quart buckets for 7¢ each; "a thousand harmonicas" for a nickel each, Turkish bath towels for 10¢ ("the best I ever saw for the money"), "fine colognes," and kid-leather gloves at a range of prices ("cheap at twice the price").

Before the century was out, McCrorey had dropped the "e" from his name to save space on his signs and opened three new stores, including one in Jamestown, New York, where one of his first employees was a confident young man named George Clinton Murphy. Born in 1868 in Indiana County, Murphy met his wife, Ella, in Jamestown as well. There is no historical record of when Murphy was hired into J. G. McCrory's Jamestown store or when McCrory named the handsome lad with the handlebar mustache the store's manager, but at least one fact is evident: everything in Murphy's life, and in retailling history, changed when a traveling salesman from Scranton went to work in the store. His name was Sebastian Spering Kresge, he sold pots and pans for a New York manufacturer, and he was intrigued by the five-and-ten stores that kept popping up in his territory. He tried to invest in the Woolworth chain, but the company was closely held by Frank Woolworth's family and friends, who turned Kresge down flat. Not discouraged in the least, Kresge called on McCrory, offering an $8,000 investment in his chain of eight stores. McCrory readily accepted and in 1897 sent Kresge to Jamestown to learn the variety store business from George Murphy.

Kresge's son Stanley credited Murphy with teaching his father much of what he knew about retailing. Sebastian Kresge must have been a quick study because within a few months he and Kresge had opened a new five-and-ten in Memphis, Tennessee. Murphy went there as the manager. When McCrory and Kresge opened another store on Woodward Avenue in Detroit in 1898, Murphy followed. But in March 1899, just after the birth of his only daughter, he decided to strike out on his own. No one knows now why Murphy chose McKeesport, Pennsylvania, for his new venture, but it was a logical selection. Located south of Pittsburgh on the Monongahela River, McKeesport was the heart of the region's steel industry, home to large mills and foundries, and was bisected by busy railroad lines; its population was growing daily, fueled by immigrants from southern and eastern Europe. Recently elevated from a borough to a city, McKeesport had three newspapers, four street-car lines, and many working-class residents who would find much to like in a dime store that would help them stretch their meager wages and liberate them from purchasing at stores owned by the steel companies.

FIG. 3
George C. Murphy began his dime-store career in Jamestown, New York, working for a fellow native of Indiana County, Pa., John G. McCrorey. McCrorey (he later dropped the "e" from his last name to save space) opened his first five-and-ten-cent store after seeing the runaway success of Frank W. Woolworth.

The Murphys rented a house at 324 Shaw Avenue, and George opened a store at 301 Fifth Avenue, the city's main commercial street. Years later, M. F. Bowers of the McKeesport *Daily News* recalled one of Murphy's "first big sales" offering large clothes baskets for 10¢ each. Though several off-duty policemen had been hired to control the crowds, the sidewalks were thronged with customers. When the doors "were opened by frightened clerks, there was a mad rush of female humanity," Bowers wrote, adding that Murphy made two tactical errors: "First, he underestimated the crowd and failed to get enough baskets. Next, he purposely placed the basket counter in the extreme rear of his good-sized store. The rush of women scattered quantities of articles other than baskets all over the place, some to be damaged underfoot." Unable to carry the baskets at their sides, happy shoppers carried them over their heads and trampled new hats and dresses as they fought their way out the door.

Early riot scenes notwithstanding, Murphy was on his way to cornering the five-and-ten business in the Pittsburgh area. Within a few years, he had additional stores in nearby communities such as Braddock, Homestead, and Wilkinsburg. The resulting income didn't make his family wealthy, but they were certainly comfortable living in an eight-room house at 626 Madison Avenue valued at $7,100. Murphy hired an English-born maid to help Ella with the housework and employed a chauffeur and groomsman to take care of his wagon, stable, and two dappled gray horses. He also had enough money to invest in a number of other busi-

ness ventures. Some were ill advised, including several western gold mines that were never more than a hole in the ground; others were more successful, including the D. L. Clark Candy Company—makers of the famous Clark Bars, the first successful mass-marketed candy bars—and the Pittsburg Coaster Construction Company, which operated a roller coaster at the nearby Kennywood amusement park.

The growing success of the G. C. Murphy Company attracted the interest of Frank W. Woolworth's confidant and second-in-command, Carson C. Peck, who came to McKeesport in the summer of 1904. The Woolworth syndicate of seventy-six five-and-tens was expanding into larger cities by buying existing chains whenever it could. Peck knew Murphy's fourteen stores would give Woolworth a solid base in the booming Pittsburgh region. The sale was effected in August and by the end of the year G. C. Murphy's name had been scrubbed from the stores. As part of the sales agreement, Murphy promised not to open any five-and-tens in any town where Woolworth had a store. He also told the *Daily News* he intended to concentrate on real estate investments.

But a young, ambitious man like Murphy wasn't content to sit still for long, nor would he allow a contract to stand in his way. The agreement with Woolworth didn't prevent him from operating stores that sold items for more than a dime. In February 1906, Murphy rented a store at 545 Fifth Avenue—only a few doors away from one of the locations he had sold to Woolworth—and he opened the doors at 8:30 Saturday morning, July 1, selling items for 5¢, 10¢, and 25¢. Within a few months, Murphy was running another chain of twelve Pittsburgh-area stores and giving Woolworth's all the competition it could handle—in its first year of operation, the new G. C. Murphy Company did more than $210,000 in sales. Besides McKeesport, Murphy soon had stores on Fifth Avenue in downtown Pittsburgh and in the nearby towns of Greensburg, New Kensington, Turtle Creek, Latrobe, Rochester, Wilmerding, Kittanning, and Ellwood City.

Little information about George Murphy's personality survives, but Betty Briggs Rehfeldt, who grew up in the Madison Avenue house, says her grandmother frequently talked about her late husband. "I have a feeling from what she said of him that they were very much alike," she says. The Murphys were strict, church-going Methodists and teetotalers—until her death in 1961, Ella Murphy would tolerate neither drinking nor smoking, says her granddaughter, and "you did not go to a movie on Sunday." Ella Murphy described George Murphy as very disciplined but also kind and gentle with children. Many years later, as the G. C. Murphy Company prepared for its seventy-fifth anniversary, an anonymous letter writer who described herself only as "an old lady in her middle 80s" sent in her memories of the founder. Her family had attended McKeesport's First Methodist Episcopal Church with the Murphys and she remembered him as "a good Christian man in every detail . . . a business man, and well thought of by all who knew him."

Unfortunately, the business world never learned what Murphy might have achieved in the retail industry. On Sunday morning, April 18, 1909, as the family dressed for church, George Murphy felt a sharp pain in his side. A doctor was called, diagnosed the problem as constipation, and administered an enema. But Murphy had an inflamed appendix, which ruptured as a result of the doctor's ill-advised actions. He lived in agony for about a week before dying at home on April 26 at age forty-one. His will, dated only two months earlier, directed that his stocks and investments be sold to provide annuities for his mother, wife, and children, along with substantial gifts for the Methodist church and the McKeesport YMCA. Unfortunately, as a probate judge noted, Murphy "undoubtedly contemplated a much larger estate" and surely hadn't expected to die so young. It would take the courts and the executors of Murphy's estate until 1920 to settle all his debts.

Among his assets were 388 of the 789 outstanding shares of the G. C. Murphy Company. A public auction of the stock in December 1910 found no takers, and there apparently was no thought of turning the stores over to his widow, Ella. "I think my grandfather, shame on him, never told her anything about the business," Betty Briggs says. "And she was no dummy." On January 11, 1911, the trustees of the Murphy estate and the managers of the G. C. Murphy Company made their final annual report. The company had more than $150,000 in assets (mostly in the form of merchandise) and liabilities of nearly $118,000. The previous year, the ten Murphy stores had done about a quarter million dollars in sales. After marking down the merchandise and the value of the Turtle Creek store to account for depreciation, the trustees reported that the G. C. Murphy Company had ended 1910 more than $24,000 in the black and with $1,240 in the bank.

But rumors were spreading that the company was failing. The receivers had now closed four locations and the board of directors was complaining that the remaining stores were carrying the wrong merchandise and had too much money tied up in inventory. There were even reports that one or more of the bank appointed managers had a drinking problem. J. G. McCrory sent his general manager, John Sephus Mack, to McKeesport to inspect the G. C. Murphy Company for a possible acquisition. Mack returned and urged McCrory to purchase the chain as soon as possible. McCrory exploded. "Young man, I make the decisions around here," he said.

It wasn't the first time McCrory rejected one of Mack's proposals. Mack wanted to pay bonuses to store managers to motivate them to break their sales targets; McCrory turned him down flat, saying that only top executives were entitled to extra compensation. Mack wanted to invest his own savings in the McCrory chain; McCrory refused. McCrory was grooming his only son, Van, to take over the company, and perhaps he was worried that rewarding Mack's initiative might make that more difficult, or maybe he just wanted to show the younger man his place. Whatever the reason, Mack was getting frustrated at having his ideas rejected time and time again.

Mack, another Indiana County native—at least one reference claims he was a cousin of George Murphy—had been working for McCrory for eight years. The son of farmer John M. Mack, whose father immigrated to Pennsylvania from Ireland in 1803, and Sarah Ellen Murphy, he grew up on a farm in Brushvalley Township, Pennsylvania, where he might have remained if he hadn't developed health problems—probably allergies. The family doctor advised the Macks to send the boy they called "Seph" to stay with relatives until his attacks subsided. At age eleven he was packed off to stay with an aunt whose son ran a general store. When Seph Mack felt better, he began waiting on customers and passing out advertising circulars. He discovered that he loved the retail business.

At age eighteen, Mack was hired as a stockroom clerk in the Johnstown store owned by his cousin John McCrory at the munificent sum of one dollar per day. Though he had just a few years of formal schooling, Mack's mind was quick, as was his rise through management—he was quickly promoted to assistant manager, manager, district superintendent, construction supervisor, and in 1908 general manager of the McCrory Company. While visiting McCrory's store in York, Pennsylvania, Mack caught sight of the windows at the C. H. Bair Company department store across the street and went inside to find out who had designed them. A supervisor introduced him to a twenty-year-old from the nearby town

FIG. 5
Indiana County native John Sephus Mack was the general manager of another five-and-ten chain, the J. G. McCrory Company, when he split with the founder over what he viewed as old-fashioned business practices. He and fellow employee Walter Carlysle Shaw used their savings and money borrowed from relatives to purchase control of the G. C. Murphy Company from Murphy's estate.

of Stewartsville named Walter Carlysle Shaw. The youngest of nine children, Shaw's father, John, was a talented carpenter who bought derelict homes, remodeled them, and sold them for a profit—by the time Walter was born, John Shaw and his wife, Lidia, had moved fourteen times. Shaw inherited his father's talent for woodworking and made trains, boats, and other toys from scrap lumber and sold them to other boys at school; one of his specialties was a mechanical wind-powered "whirligig" that depicted two men boxing. When he grew older, Walter joined his father's building crew. But, despite his gift for working with his hands, he had no interest in the construction business. He took a job at a dairy, then at a general store, and finally at Bair's for $6 per week, putting his carpentry experience to work designing window trim and displays. Mack and Shaw quickly became friends, and Shaw joined McCrory's in 1902, working his way up from the stockroom to manage stores in Hagerstown and Cumberland, Maryland; East Liverpool, Ohio; and the Memphis, Tennessee, location that George Murphy had helped to open.

Shaw had been promoted to district superintendent of McCrory's when Mack told him that McCrory had rejected his proposal to take over the G. C. Murphy Company. "We're not going to be able to get to the top of this company," Mack said in frustration. An idea began to germinate. Mack had saved up a few thousand dollars. Their families might be able to loan them some money as well. If they sold everything they had and borrowed the rest, couldn't they buy the G. C. Murphy Company themselves? They offered the executors of the Murphy estate about $100 each for the 789 outstanding shares (a little bit less for some, more for others) and in February 1911, Mack and Shaw obtained control of the failing McKeesport dime-store chain. Years later, Shaw couldn't remember exactly how much he and Mack had paid but said it was enough, "the business not being worth much at the time."

Official G. C. Murphy Company histories eventually reported that their severance from McCrory's was "very pleasant." That wasn't necessarily true, says Joe Mack, whose father was Seph Mack's brother Edgar McCrorey Mack. "There was bad blood there," Joe Mack says, and for years, J. G. McCrory refused to speak to his cousin Seph. Mack and Shaw agreed not to open any new Murphy stores in a town where McCrory's was already operating. They also agreed—perhaps to preserve harmony in the Mack and Murphy families—not to remove George C. Murphy's name from the stores. Shaw's daughter, Betty Shaw Gamble, says her father and Mack at some point tried to invent a new name for the company by combining their last names but couldn't come up with anything they liked. "So they kept the name 'Murphy's,' which was a good idea," Gamble says. "'Murphy's' was a catchy name." (Eventually, the G. C. Murphy Company's real estate arm, launched in 1919, would bear the Mack family name. It was called, appropriately enough, Mack Realty Company.)

Mack was the senior partner in age and finance, owning more than 450 of the 789 outstanding shares. He and Shaw reported for work in McKeesport on March 4, 1911. The challenge must have seemed overwhelming at times—John Sephus Mack had turned thirty-one only five days earlier; Walter Carlysle Shaw was thirty—and, according to legend, the attorney who handled the sale hated to see them buy the G. C. Murphy Company. "Those two nice young men are going to lose their shirts," he said. And, in a way, he was right. Between the coal smoke belched from the locomotives of the Baltimore & Ohio Railroad on the other side of the street and the red iron soot blown into the sky from the Bessemer converters at the nearby National Tube Company, it was a cinch that Mack and Shaw were going to lose their shirts—or would at least have to change their collars—by lunchtime. McKeesport was booming with impressive new buildings on every corner, but the headquarters of the G. C. Murphy Company was not one of them. Its offices were on the second floor of the dime store Murphy opened in 1906, which shared the block with a livery stable, a barbershop, and some other merchants. Streetcars passed under the front window, freight trains rattled back windows, and, three times daily, steelworkers—many of them recent immigrants or first-generation Americans—streamed in and out of the tube plant, then the largest manufacturer of steel pipe in the world.

All this commerce, while dirty, should have augured well for the company's success, and it probably would have if George Murphy had been alive for the past two years. But in the hands of his estate, various creditors, and attorneys, the G. C. Murphy Company that Mack and Shaw had just purchased was very sick. Among their first orders of business was to close money-losing stores in Pittsburgh's East Liberty neighborhood and another in Youngstown, Ohio. By the end of the year, the G. C. Murphy Company had lost $19,136 on sales of $251,699. Neither man was a stranger to manual labor, which was a good thing since there would be a lot of it in the first few years. From building their own counters to trying to make sense of the helter-skelter merchandise mix in the Murphy stores, "the work was hard and back-breaking, but we did get things done, and we progressed," Shaw said, recalling the nights that he and Mack worked until 2:00 A.M., lay down on a counter and slept for a few hours, then got up and started again. "We used to look at those stores and wonder, 'Will they ever succeed?'"

After a few months, Mack and Shaw had hired away McCrory's advertising manager, R. H. Callahan, who joined Murphy's as merchandise manager, secretary, and treasurer. Callahan was in charge of buying all the merchandise except candy, which was supervised by Shaw himself, who also managed Store No. 2 in downtown Pittsburgh. From the beginning of the partnership, Mack's and Shaw's talents proved complementary, with the former watching the company's financial side and the latter overseeing sales and promotions. Mack, who had a knack for making long-term plans, set the policies and procedures; Shaw, with his strong attention to detail, made sure they were implemented correctly. Years later, an article in *Chain Store Age* called Mack the "architect" of the G. C. Murphy Company and Shaw the "engineer."

Their personalities were complementary, too. While Shaw was quick to smile and crack jokes, Mack was stern and brooked no nonsense. "He was totally authoritative," says his grandson, Sephus. "Henry VIII could not have been more extreme. If anyone wanted to see him, including his wife and children, they had to have an appointment. He did not tolerate dissent." He instilled a demanding work ethic in his sons, James Stephen and John Gordon Mack; the former once disappointed his father severely when he earned a "B" grade at McKeesport High School. "Whatever he did, his father would always say, 'Why did you do this?' or 'What's taking so long?'" recalls Jim Mack's wife, Barbara Mack Reister. "With the family, [Sephus] Mack was very, very strict." She learned that the hard way. In later years, Sephus Mack spent weekends at the family farm in Indiana County where he raised and bred horses and eventually set aside one for her to ride. When she didn't visit for three weeks, Mack gave her horse to the president of Grove City College. "Next time, don't stay away so long," he said.

Mack was as tough on himself as he was on family and subordinates. "He was not a terribly affectionate man, and yet he was brilliant," Sephus Mack says. "Totally organized and extraordinarily structured. He also had a very deep sense of responsibility." That sense of obligation may have stemmed from Mack's deeply held Christian faith. No matter where he traveled, he found time to attend church. Mack even decorated the main assembly room

FIG. 6
Born in Stewartsville,
York County, Pa., Walter
Shaw met Mack while
working at a department
store in Johnstown,
Pa. Because of his skill
at forward planning,
employees called Mack
"the architect" of the
G. C. Murphy Company
and Shaw "the engineer."

at the home office in McKeesport with his favorite Bible verses, starting—appropriately enough—with the first four words of the Old Testament: "In the Beginning, God." But his faith didn't stop Mack from speaking his mind. "He always knew more than the minister," Reister says, laughing. "He would talk back to the minister—in the service! If I was sitting next to him, I'd say, 'Shh, you're supposed to listen!'"

Shaw was by far the more personable of the pair. Indeed, he was never happier than when visiting the stores and talking to customers and employees—usually, he could greet the clerks by name. "On birthdays, if he would get one hundred cards, he would respond to every one of them, which I think was lovely," Betty Gamble says. A writer for the *Pittsburgh Press* in the 1950s said Shaw bore something of a resemblance to the pioneer automaker Henry Ford with his lean frame and twinkling eyes. There was also some of Ford's frugality in Shaw, perhaps because both grew up poor. Shaw drove himself everywhere, ate his lunch—rarely more than a sandwich—in inexpensive restaurants, and spent what free time he had poking through antique and second-hand stores.

Though he was reluctant to spend a dollar on himself, McKeesporters of a certain age remember fondly that Shaw often carried a pocketful of silver dollars with him to pass out to any children he might meet. Adults who met him were likely to receive a reprint of a magazine or newspaper article that he had enjoyed—Shaw was a voracious reader—usually some editorial that supported his rock-ribbed Republican beliefs. People of any age would find themselves gently teased, or if Shaw was in the mood, he might tell them a story or a joke. "He had a wonderful sense of humor," Gamble says. "I just idolized him."

There wasn't much time for humor in the early days. The "architect" and the "engineer" had to stifle their creative impulses while they first straightened up the mess that the G. C. Murphy Company had become. Though the assortment was mainly down to five- and ten-cent items, Murphy's was still selling a selection of goods for 25¢, but they were stocked with little rhyme or reason. Having dealt primarily with five-and-ten items at McCrory's, Mack was dead set against selling anything for a quarter, but Shaw convinced him to develop a list of seventy-five good 25¢ items. "If we added a 25¢ item, we took off a poor 25¢ item," he said. Nevertheless, nickel and dime merchandise composed most of the inventory until 1922.

Working methodically to bring some order to the chaos, the two "cleaned out all undesirable merchandise during the first couple of years," according to Shaw. Some of the firm's thirty full-time employees were cleaned out as well. After two years without strong leadership, there was a firm hand on the tiller again and shirkers were told to start pulling their own weight or find work elsewhere. From now on, Mack and Shaw informed them, they were required to show a 34 percent profit on sales. "We fear the majority of our managers are operating on a 'hit or miss' plan, placing orders week after week without any close tab on profit," read a May 12, 1911, memo to the stores:

> To conduct a successful business and produce net profits, a manager must at all times know the profit on the kinds of goods he is buying. Most managers think they know this and will tell, when asked, that they are doing business on profitable merchandise, yet when pinned down to a statement of facts, it is found that they don't know. . . . It should not be necessary for this office to insist that you must do a reasonable thing. We are simply laying before you common business facts, and trust you will fall in line and do your best to heed these facts.

Conditions were tightened up at the home office as well; forbidden were "loud talking, laughing, whistling, or smoking" during office hours.

The new owners asked no more of employees than they asked of themselves. "Every one of us worked," Shaw said. "If top management works, others can't very well refuse or neglect to work. But you can't get anything done unless you have guts enough to work." The manager of Store No. 6 in Latrobe, John L. Widmeyer, one of the few retained by Mack and Shaw from the old crew, had the dedication the new owners demanded. Shortly after the takeover, Mack decided to remodel the Latrobe store and hired a contractor to build a new entrance. He started by demolishing the old one. Unfortunately, the store remained open during the work. Because the interior (and thus the merchandise) couldn't remain unprotected, Widmeyer slept on a counter at the front of the store until new windows and doors were installed. He would eventually be promoted to a buyer for the company, purchasing hardware, enamel-plated and tin housewares, and wooden articles, first from a Murphy office in the Empire Building in Pittsburgh, then from McKeesport after the home office was expanded.

G. C. Murphy stores expanded, too, and eventually became known for a complete array of merchandise—something for everyone, from penny candy to riding lawn mowers—but it's instructive to see what wasn't carried in a typical Murphy store before 1920. There were no ladies' accessories, dress patterns, or loose bolts of fabric or "oilcloth." There was no pet department, though things such as dog collars and chains were carried in the hardware aisle. Murphy's carried no clothing, other than hosiery, and no paint, other than a small assortment of brushes. What Murphy's did carry was a lot candy. In 1921, the earliest year for which figures are available, Murphy's did 21 percent of its sales in sweets. For good reason, Shaw issued detailed instructions to his managers on which candy to stock and which to avoid, especially during the summer. "You must be very careful the kinds you carry or it will be a case of big shrinkage in this department," he wrote in July 1913. Because there was no mechanical refrigeration, cream wafers, coconut squares, and jellied candies could be sold, but chocolate was to be avoided, as were nut-filled candies. "[They] will get wormy at this season of the year," Shaw said, "so you want to be very careful in buying any of them." Salted peanuts were fine, but managers were to buy them in small quantities, not by the keg, "as they become stale very quickly. . . . [P]ay a little more and have fresh goods." The names of the candies, some of which would be unacceptable today, speak of a simpler time. Hardie Brothers was supplying Murphy's with something called "chocolate pickaninnies," while the D. L. Clark Company named one of their candies after an even worse racial slur. Candy counters later added cake, cookies, and pastry.

Besides candy, Murphy's offered a complete line of "notions" (thread, thimbles, buttons, hair nets), though, at 11 percent, they ran a distant second to candy in sales volume, followed by "dry goods" (lace, ribbons, handkerchiefs) at 9.3 percent and "hardware" (curtain rods, shoe cleats, cup hooks) at 8.5 percent. Though counted in separate categories, housewares, kitchen utensils, glasses, and pots and pans together accounted for more than 10 percent of Murphy's sales in the early days. By 1912, the end of Mack and Shaw's first full year of ownership, the G. C. Murphy Company had turned a small profit of $1,405 on sales of $370,616—a poor return but better than the previous year's loss. Some of the money that could have been booked as profit was instead reinvested in six new stores Murphy's opened that year in Charleroi, Meadville, and Grove City, Pennsylvania; Elkins and Wellsburg, West Virginia (the first West Virginia stores in what became a long and prosperous association with the Mountaineer State); and Ashland, Kentucky.

Murphy's also moved one store that year in a most unusual way. In the fall of 1912, Shaw learned that the owners of the Thompson Restaurant next to Store No. 2 in downtown Pittsburgh wanted to expand. Shaw sold the lease to Thompson's and conducted a final clearance sale in December. The remaining stock, counters, and fixtures were carted by wagons to the edge of the Monongahela River where he made a deal with a packet boat captain to carry the entire load 270 miles down the Ohio River to Gallipolis, Ohio, for the magnificent sum of $120. "It was quite a sight to see that packet pull out, as the counters were hanging out over the sides of the packet, and it made a very peculiar-looking sight going down the Ohio River," an early company history notes. The new Gallipolis store became the next "Store No. 2," starting a G. C. Murphy tradition of relocating store numbers from town to town, often to the confusion of employees and nonemployees alike. Eighteen years passed before Murphy's returned to downtown Pittsburgh.

The following year, Murphy's opened five locations, mainly in West Virginia and Ohio. In 1914, it added four more—three around Pittsburgh and one in Erie, Pennsylvania. Murphy's looked for locations along major rail lines or rivers—all the better to ship from McKeesport by packet boat or express train. What couldn't be supplied from a small storage room at the home office was shipped directly from the manufacturers to the stores by parcel post or railway express. Unlike the F. W. Woolworth Company, which was expanding as rapidly as possible by gobbling up smaller companies and opening new stores in every town where a lease could be negotiated, Murphy's grew incrementally. Just as army generals don't want the front lines of a battle to go farther than their communications and transportation lines can reach, Mack and Shaw didn't want to tax the company's ability to keep its stores connected. They built clusters of Murphy stores in adjacent towns to keep dpwn advertising and distribution expenses. "Mack thought of expansion in vertical terms—strengthening volume through present locations, rather than adding new stores," says the undated company history.

Also unlike Woolworth, which was drawn to major urban areas, Murphy's purposely avoided large cities and their higher rents, concentrating on smaller communities. When Woolworth reached thirty stores in 1897, it had locations in Philadelphia, Boston, and New York. In contrast, Murphy's thirtieth store was in the coal-mining town of Brownsville, Pennsylvania—a city between the Murphy store in Charleroi and several West Virginia locations. Once installed in Brownsville, Monessen (Store No. 31), or Beaver Falls (Store No. 32), Murphy's focused on becoming the number one store in town. Perhaps the sales "pie" in Brownsville was smaller than in Boston, but Murphy's got the entire thing—not just a small slice. As *Chain Store Age* wrote in 1950, "in the big downtown shopping areas, 'dime stores' were novelty appendages to the basic retail structure. Not so with Murphy. In Turtle Creek, Pa., Murphy's was the store."

With Shaw running the sales department, Murphy's would fight for every last nickel and dime. "The trouble with most of us is that we don't think right—our ideas are too small," he wrote in a memo to store managers in 1915. "Certainly you want increased sales—who wouldn't—yet some of our boys put ounces of ginger [into] work which requires pounds of steam." Display related items together, Shaw told managers—someone buying mixing spoons might also want measuring cups—and put out "big, bold" displays of the best-selling items in each department. Forty years before Vance Packard wrote *The Hidden Persuaders*, Shaw had developed an inherent understanding of ways to motivate shoppers.

In the meantime, Mack developed his own philosophy of selling. As a boy in Indiana County, he'd accompanied his father on trips to the gristmill and sold produce to other farmers as they waited for their grain to be ground. "The successful farmer," Mack wrote years later, "must be able to provide what his people want, must be able to provide at a price that will meet competition, and at a price his customer can afford to buy." He refined that lesson into what became "The Three Fundamentals" of the G. C. Murphy Company:

> Have What the People Want
> Let Them Know You Have It
> Organize to Serve Them Quickly, Courteously, and Satisfactorily

In one form or another, these three fundamentals were drummed into the head of every Murphy employee for the next eighty years. Mack had one more fundamental concept that soon made Murphy's the operator to beat in the dime-store industry. Perhaps remembering his own frustration during his last few years at McCrory's, Mack decided not to impose rigid, top-down control on his stores. Instead, he set sales targets and expected managers to meet them; how they met them was their own business. Managers were expected to learn about their communities and adapt their merchandise mix and promotional ideas to suit.

The best Murphy personnel thrived under this autonomy, developing creative solutions to problems. For instance, an assistant manager named Harry Rich revolutionized counter displays in five-and-tens across the country, not just at Murphy's. The early counters had been crude at best, with red-stained boards, wooden shelves on T-shaped stands, and signs hung on bent wires. Merchandise was laid on top of the counters, with salesgirls—they were almost all "girls"—stationed behind each to assist customers. To separate different items on the top of the counter, managers salvaged scraps of wood and made dividers. It was effective but not very attractive. In those days, cars, trucks, and trolleys had windows made of plain-old plate glass, which could be shattered by nearly any errant stone. As the number of cars increased throughout the decade, hardware stores did a booming business making replacement windows and windshields, but they invariably had a lot of leftover odd-shaped pieces of glass.

One day in 1916, Rich, then working at Store No. 3 in Greensburg, learned that a nearby paint and glass dealer had an entire roomful of these odds and ends. He bought the entire supply for $10. Rich and manager E. J. Bartlett then busied themselves replacing all their scrap-wood dividers with glass ones. They had enough left over to put a band of glass around the edges of the counters as well. The glass reflected the light, made the merchandise more visible, and generally made their store more attractive. Bartlett and Rich were feeling pleased with themselves until Walter Shaw arrived on one of his inspection trips the following week. The "extravagance" of glass-trimmed counters nearly sent him into orbit until the two men explained that they had paid $10 for an entire roomful of glass. Shaw spread the word to all of the Murphy stores to copy the idea. Soon, all of the competing dime stores were also trimming their counters in glass.

Although Murphy's could control it's own merchandise mixes, display techniques, and personnel practices could all be refined, but other problems were developing beyond the company's control. The war raging in Europe cut off silks, toys, flatware, dishes, and other imported goods from England, France, Italy, and Germany. One buyer, E. E. Holmes, estimated that inability to get merchandise in 1916 cost the company $100,000—the lack of Swiss and German chocolate cost Murphy's $5,000 in sales in October alone. On the other hand, the demand for American armaments and steel, manufactured in the cities where Murphy's was strongest, was good for the company's core customers. "Business was good in the towns," Mack said. "Pay rolls were big and money was being spent." In McKeesport, for instance, sales were strong enough for Murphy's to open a second store—No. 33—in the city's old opera house a few blocks from Store No. 1. At Mack's direction, Murphy's continued to shrink its 25¢ departments, some of which were losing money. By the end of 1916, only stores in McKeesport, Rochester, Kittanning, and Elkins were still selling goods for more than 10¢ .

In his annual letter to stockholders the following February, Mack was sanguine about the upcoming year: "Our sales aim for this year is $1 million, and unless unusual conditions develop, we will get it. . . . For the year 1917, we can express about the same sentiments as we expressed in 1916—we are still better organized. Each year finds us better organized." But in April 1917, the United States ended its official policy of neutrality and entered World War I on the side of the Allies.

The American contribution to the war effort was smaller than those of Britain and France, yet the toll on American business was significant in terms of personnel. "We were badly crippled in our managerial work, as many of our men were subject to the draft," Mack said. "When the new draft requirements—'18 to 45'—went into effect, I think [we] only had about two men, including managers and officers, who were not subject to the draft." There were higher operating expenses and more "leakage" (losses due to damaged or stolen merchandise) as well, Mack said, "caused by disturbing our well-trained store managers and having to substitute with assistant men who did not have the necessary training."

As American manufacturers converted their plants from making civilian goods to producing material for war, merchandise became scarce as well. "The continued increase in

the cost of merchandise crippled our gross profits," Mack said. "We kept many items on our lists that were costing us our full sales value and some items in excess." Some items—he gave flour sieves as an example—were actually selling for less than Murphy's paid. "Our aim was to keep the people shopping with us and make as much money as we could, but not to suffer a slump in business by lack of merchandise. Our sales speak for themselves. Our net profits tell the story of less profits on our merchandise, and higher operating expenses." While total sales passed $1 million in 1917 and rose another $320,000 in 1918, profits actually dropped $8,000 from 1917 to 1918. In spite of "the high cost of everything," as Mack put it, Murphy's opened new stores in Piqua and Sidney, Ohio, and Greenville and Braddock, Pennsylvania. The first three were farming towns; the fourth was a steelmaking community in the heart of Murphy's territory around Pittsburgh. Mack told stockholders he hoped that he would "never experience another year such as we have just passed through . . . for the sake of humanity" and for the good of the company.

In the last year of the decade, Murphy's made its biggest gamble yet. Until then, the company had financed its growth strictly by reinvesting its profits and taking out bank loans, but that had its limits. Paul Sample, who later became the company's president, joined Murphy's in 1919. In his opinion, despite the "spirit of progressiveness and determination" that Mack and Shaw had infused, the G. C. Murphy stores of that era were still "very incomplete. . . . Most of our stores were shabby little rooms, and we had only a half-dozen stores at that time which would have been considered modern, according to the accepted standards of that day."

Mack reached a fateful decision in September of that year. Since Mack and Shaw had purchased control of the G. C. Murphy Company in 1911, another 211 shares of stock had been issued, bringing the total to the maximum one thousand allowed by the corporation's charter. Mack proposed that those shares be split four ways and converted to "preferred" status and another ten thousand shares of stock be sold to outside investors to raise about $100,000. A small competing chain called the Callahan Stores would also be absorbed. "It is [my] intention to utilize this new capital to add stores as fast as good locations at fair rentals can be obtained, securing long leases on these sites," Mack said. "The policy will be to open stores in larger cities than we now have. This will mean increased sales volume, which will decrease our overhead operating expenses." With the additional stores he envisioned, Mack predicted that Murphy's existing system would generate another $1 million in sales "practically without additional expense."

The board of directors approved the changes on December 20, 1919. Murphy's closed the books on the year with forty-six stores, $1.4 million in sales, and $45,000 in profits—more than double the previous year's—and $100,000 in new capital. "Your management had this in mind in their promotion for the last eight years," Mack said, adding "the increase in sales in profits will be quick and substantial." In fact, though Mack was a visionary, the G. C. Murphy Company's successes in the 1920s and '30s were going to surpass even his most optimistic predictions. And keeping things under control was going to take every bit of skill the architect and the engineer possessed.

As for the attorney who predicted that Mack and Shaw would soon "lose their shirts," Shaw later calculated that a single share of G. C. Murphy Company stock that was virtually worthless in 1911 was worth more than $30,000 in the 1940s. In 1951, when the G. C. Murphy Company was one of the nation's largest variety store chains, Betty Briggs Rehfeldt worked for a few weeks in Store No. 1 in McKeesport to help with the Christmas rush. Did her co-workers know that she was the granddaughter of the founder? Yes, and it didn't make "a hooting bit of difference after all of those years," she says, laughing. "I think sometimes about what could have been."

CHAPTER 3

THE Macy's of APPALACHIA

They weren't called the "Roaring Twenties" for nothing. "Never had there been a better time to get rich, and people knew it," wrote popular historian and economist John Kenneth Galbraith. Credit was "plentiful and cheap," spurring both business expansion and consumer buying. The stock market seemed to have no limits in sight—the *New York Times* index of leading industrial stocks shot from 106 points in 1924 to 245 in 1927. The American public, flush with money, suddenly discovered that shopping could be a leisure-time activity.

"During these years people were indeed being supplied with an increasing volume of goods," Galbraith said, "but there is no evidence that their desire for automobiles, clothing, travel, recreation, or even food was sated. On the contrary, all subsequent evidence showed (given the income to spend) a capacity for a large further increase in consumption." And few businesses could satisfy that need to "consume" better than five-and-ten chains, with their ability to buy large volumes of mass-produced items and then sell them at low prices. "Many a U.S. inhabitant has furnished his home at five-cent and ten-cent stores," said *Time* magazine. "To these emporiums he has also hastened for Christmas presents and such luxuries of life as teacups, cookies, ribbons, bottle openers, pins, whatnot."

Variety chains had grown quickly in the first part of the century, but even that was barely a prologue to the explosion that would come in the 1920s. From 1920 to 1925, Woolworth added more than three hundred locations, while W. T. Grant Company and S. S. Kresge Company doubled in size. Godfrey Lebhar, editor of *Chain Store Age,* surveyed twenty "leading" companies, including G. C. Murphy Company, several grocery chains, and a few specialty retailers, such as Kinney Shoes. The firms, which together had nearly ten thousand stores in 1920, had more than twenty-five thousand five years later.

Murphy's had ended the previous decade with a front office staff that company president and chairman John Sephus Mack felt was fairly extravagant and "top heavy" (he told the board of directors in 1919 that operating expenses were still "abnormally high"), but he was determined to use that to the company's advantage. "When we secure the capital we wish, it will not be necessary to build up this organization," he said. "We have gotten our stocks in excellent condition, [and] we have given our men some rigid training in merchandising."

In preparation for the expected growth, Murphy's moved the home office and Store No. 1 in McKeesport the vacant Cumberland Presbyterian Church one door away on Fifth Avenue. A new two-story annex along Fifth disguised the church's heritage somewhat, though the buttresses along the roof could still be seen from the side alley. The old sanctuary was carved into two floors and Store No. 1 moved into the street-level space.

Then, in 1920, Mack and Shaw decided to put the new G. C. Murphy Company to the test. After several years of restricting prices to either five or ten cents, Murphy's finally started adding more higher-priced items again in 1920. It would take Woolworth another fifteen years to officially drop its rigid nickel-and-dime limits. By then, the larger company had resorted to ridiculous subterfuges, such as pricing a hammer's handle and head separately. A committee of five people—Walter Shaw, two merchandise "buyers," and two sales personnel from the field—met every two weeks to review the list of twenty-five-cent items. Mack insisted that no more than one hundred quarter items could be carried at a time; if a new one was added, something else had to come off.

As Paul Sample said years later, Shaw and Mack also were realizing that the existing stores were "entirely too small" to become dominant in their towns. In a few cases, Murphy's relocated smaller stores to bigger, nearby buildings, but often the company merely leased a neighboring storefront, knocked down the interior adjacent walls, and remodeled the entire space. (This practice came back to haunt Murphy's decades later. Landlords often entered into long-term leases with the company only on the condition that Murphy's would restore any missing walls before it vacated the premises. By the 1980s, some small locations acquired six decades earlier had long since become unprofitable, but it was cheaper to keep them open than trying to repair the walls that had been destroyed years before.)

Where other chains were growing "horizontally," adding "store after store," Mack "thought of expansion in vertical terms, strengthening volume through present locations rather than adding new stores," as an early company history put it. The strategy wasn't promising at first. In 1921, Murphy's lost nearly $27,000 on sales of $2.2 million, the first time since 1912 the company hadn't shown a profit, and the first since 1911 it didn't pay a dividend to investors.

Still, the directors were confident enough about the prospects for the future to give all employees a Christmas bonus of $5 in gold for one year of service, $10 for two years, and $15 for three or more. The board of directors also decided to offer paid vacations for the first time. The votes of confidence in their employees were rewarded. Though Murphy's added only one new store in 1922, sales were up nearly a half-million dollars and the company posted a $178,000 profit at the end of the year.

The 25¢ limit (or "quarter top," in variety store jargon) helped boost Murphy's sales, but Walter Shaw, as sales manager, decided he wanted more. Tired of watching Murphy's customers buy only inexpensive items in his stores and then purchase bigger-ticket merchandise from nearby department stores, he convinced Mack to allow him to add items priced up to a dollar in eight stores on a trial basis, starting with Store No. 3 in Greensburg, Pennsylvania. Then, New Kensington, Latrobe, and other stores got the new, higher-priced items, which Murphy's called its "B" division.

It was a radical notion at the time, which some people both inside and out thought would confuse shoppers and wreck their conception of Murphy's as a place for low-priced bargains. So the new 25¢ to $1 items were confined to separate floors in the selected stores—usually the second floor, though the "B" division wound up in the basement in No. 1 (McKeesport) and No. 10 (Ellwood City). The "dollar stores" had separate managers and even their own store numbers, clerks working the 5¢ to 25¢ floor were not to mingle with the clerks on the 25¢ to $1 floor. Even individual departments were duplicated, with 10¢ cold cream on the ground floor and more expensive cosmetics upstairs.

Suddenly, Murphy's was selling fine, woven dresses for children at less than a dollar and patterned aprons for 59¢. Miners and steel mill laborers who were paying $1.29 for work shirts could now buy them from Murphy's for less. The McKeesport *Daily News* called the new 25¢ to $1 basement at Store No. 1 "most startling . . . all classes of merchandise usually found in department stores will be sold for under a dollar. The company's buyers have scoured the market far and wide for desirable merchandise." The addition of more expensive items also allowed Murphy's to feature products from the newly emerging chemical industry of the 1920s—products made of things such as rayon (an artificial silk spun from wood pulp) and early plastics. Women who needed purses had been paying $1.95 at department stores; Murphy's brought out handbags made of an imitation "leatherette" for 98¢. Colored in bright pastel shades, they were a sensation. So were rayon lingerie and hats for $1.

FIG. 8
Seph Mack was reluctant to add higher-priced merchandise up to $1, Shaw recalled years later. As an experiment to test the public's acceptance, Murphy's "dollar stores" were put on upper or lower floors of the existing five-and-tens, such as Store No. 40 in Sidney, Ohio, shown here in 1925.

The quality of merchandise Murphy's sold could now be improved as well. Most clothing items had been simply too expensive to sell at 25¢ or less. "Outside of hosiery, all the textiles we did carry were listed under the dry goods department" prior to 1921, Shaw said. Murphy's volume in "dry goods" that year amounted to less than 10 percent of sales.

But with a $1 limit, the company could offer ladies' cotton dresses and other furnishings. As with everything Mack and Shaw tried, clothing was tested slowly at first—rolled out in only a few stores—with folded dresses displayed on top of a few counters. When customer response proved that the experiment was working, Murphy's began adding better-trimmed dresses and established its first New York buying office on Broadway at West Twenty-fifth Street, not far from the city's "Garment District." In 1924, men's, women's, and children's clothing was added to all but the smallest stores. By the end of the decade, many Murphy's stores had cleared space for free-standing dress racks. These so-called "soft lines" became an increasingly important part of the company's offerings.

"In the twenties the small Murphy communities were merchandise poor," said *Chain Store Age*. "Between conventional 'five-and-10s' and the big city department stores was a merchandise desert which Murphy hoped to irrigate."

A typical "merchandise desert" was Keyser, West Virginia, where G. C. Murphy Store No. 22 was the only variety store in a town of six thousand people. "It was a good, good Murphy town," remembers Luther Shay, whose father, Jim, managed the Keyser store. "West Virginia in general was one of the best states we had for Murphy's." Located at the foot of a seventeen-mile grade on the Baltimore & Ohio Railroad, Keyser became home to a locomotive repair facility and a switching yard and was an important community for railroad workers and their families. Still, the store was a small affair, with a double-wide entry door, an aisle down the center, and counters on both sides, says Shay, who later went to work for Murphy's himself. Despite its size, the store loomed large in the lives of Keyser residents. "We always had these high-backed chairs at the front of the store with cloth over the backs that said 'Meet Your Friends at Murphy's—The Friendly Store,'" Shay says. "They all came in on Saturday night and sat around and talked. It was kind of the social center."

Years later, Walter Shaw Sr. told Shay that his father was "the best salesman" Murphy's ever had. Shaw said he was visiting the Keyser store when a customer came in looking for a three-quarter-inch bolt. "He didn't have any, so he sold him a one-and-one-quarter-inch bolt," Shaw remembered. "The man said, 'I don't have anything to cut it with.' So he sold him a hacksaw. He said, 'But I don't have anything to hold it with.' So he sold him a vise!"

Besides providing a local meeting place, Murphy's was also bringing small towns like Keyser a variety of consumer goods they'd previously never seen in their small towns. Although big department stores such as Macy's and Gimbels were out of reach for Keyser, Charleroi, or Brownsville, Murphy's was now bringing a little taste of their merchandise into the valleys and hollows of Pennsylvania and West Virginia. It would be the Macy's of Appalachia. "We were beginning to step out a little bit," said Paul Sample, who in the mid-1920s was superintendent of Murphy's Erie, Pennsylvania, district. "We were just starting to feel our way with merchandise priced higher than 25¢." Take silk hose, for instance. In the fall of 1928, a manufacturer offered silk stockings to Murphy's that could be sold for $1 per pair. Walter Shaw examined and reluctantly agreed to take sixty dozen, sending the entire shipment to Store No. 91 in Stamford, Connecticut, as a test. The manager put them out before the store opened in the morning. Before the home office closed, he was on the telephone to McKeesport—could they ship more silk stockings? He had sold fifty dozen in one day. Silk hose were soon available in all Murphy's stores.

Not even Shaw grasped how important that single item was to boosting Murphy's image until he was on a trip through the Allegheny Mountains where his car broke down. Knocking on the door of a farmhouse, he introduced himself to the woman who answered as the sales manager of G. C. Murphy's. She was delighted. "Why, look at these wonderful silk hose I bought at your store in Ligonier!" she said.

FIG. 9
Unlike many of its competitors, Murphy's bypassed large cities and targeted small towns such as Weston, W.Va., where stores such as Store No. 21, shown here, could dominate the market. Offering a wide selection of merchandise at low prices won Murphy's quick acceptance among Pennsylvania's steelworkers, Ohio's farmers, and West Virginia's miners. The local G. C. Murphy Company outlet functioned as the de facto department store in many communities.

The new range of merchandise also left Murphy's well positioned to take advantage of fad items. When Westinghouse in 1920 opened the world's first commercial radio station, KDKA, on the roof of its East Pittsburgh plant—within sight of Murphy's Store No. 89—a national radio craze erupted. By 1926, Murphy's had added "radio departments" where "radio bugs" could purchase electron tubes, wires, coils, and other gadgets to build their own sets. Within two years, the company was selling $140,000 of electrical gadgets. Rather than destroying Murphy's image, selling higher-priced merchandise had clearly enhanced the company's position. In Greensburg and New Kensington, the "B" division "was so hot," Shaw said, "we opened the basement [stockrooms] and transferred the 'B' lines to there."

"It was evident that store separation by price lines was artificial and awkward to the customers," *Chain Store Age* said. "Tacks on the main floor, but tack hammers upstairs." Inside a few stores, the separate 25¢ floors and $1 floors were finally merged and reorganized. The advantages were obvious. By 1928, all the Murphy stores were operating as united operations. And there were more of them—Murphy's began the decade with 53 locations and ended it with 166, many obtained through shrewd acquisition of smaller companies. The Stamford store, for instance, was one of five added in 1924 through the purchase of the J. R. Evans Company for $225,914. Shaw later mused that the acquisition had been "a bad one" since it took the locations more than a decade to earn back their purchase price. Other additions were more successful. In 1927, Murphy's bought twenty-one stores in Pennsylvania, New York, and New Jersey from the Steele's Consolidated chain. Other stores were picked up that year from the Index Notions Company and several small, local operators.

One of the company's biggest bargains came in Ligonier, Pennsylvania, where a little five-and-ten on the town square was being sold for $3,200 by the estate of its former owner. A mountain hideaway east of Pittsburgh, Ligonier was the weekend playground of many of the city's millionaires, including the heirs of the Mellon banking fortune. Under Murphy's management, the store grossed more than $41,000 its first year, and Shaw later estimated that each dollar Murphy's invested in Ligonier returned $13 to the company. Eight new stores—six in the Pittsburgh area, one in northern Pennsylvania, and one in Logan, West Virginia—also opened in 1927, while the two Turtle Creek stores were merged and Store No. 16 in Meadville was moved at a cost of $662,209 according to construction division reports. The following year brought more acquisitions, including five stores in central Pennsylvania from the R. B. Fleisher Company.

Perhaps the G. C. Murphy Company's most important purchase came in May 1928 when it acquired four stores in the Midwest from Trick Brothers 5, 10 & 25 Stores Inc. for $27,041. Those stores in Greencastle, St. Joseph, and Indianapolis, Indiana; and Van Wert, Ohio, brought in $198,442 in sales their first year, or about seven times what Murphy's paid, making the purchase a neat "trick" for Mack and Shaw. More than the volume the Trick stores added to Murphy's line, the merger also brought the company two surprisingly good assets that didn't come with a price tag assigned: "a spindly kid and his stocky brother" from Putnam County, Indiana, named Kenneth and Edgar Paxton, respectively. Ed was managing the store in Greencastle, their hometown, while Ken was working at the busy store in Indianapolis's Fountain Square. Omar Trick, who liked the brothers, asked Murphy's management to keep them employed, so they were retained, though Ed was sent to Indianapolis.

The new manager appointed by Murphy's, George McCormick, decided he wanted the two kids—dressed in their Sunday suits—out of his busy store in the city and back to their farm in Greencastle as soon as possible. He decided to stick them with the dirtiest, sweatiest, most back-breaking job he could find: unloading eight thousand pounds of pottery from the big kegs, or "hogsheads," in which it had been shipped, marking the price on each piece, and stocking them on the shelves. "It was the toughest job in the store, for hardly just one hogshead was about as much as any experienced man could be expected to accomplish in one day," wrote Stewart Monroe in a profile of the Paxton brothers for the *Indianapolis Star*. "When the manager returned, he fully expected to find the Paxton boys ready to quit. . . . Instead, he found eight empty hogsheads with all of the goods they had contained marked and stashed neatly away."

Within two years, both Paxtons were managing stores of their own—Ed in Pittsburgh; Ken in Buffalo. The Buffalo store was then known a "dog" in the company, with poor morale and poorer performance. According to Monroe, Ken Paxton knew the names of every employee in the store by the end of his first week. "Within a month, he knew their personal backgrounds and their home problems," Monroe wrote. Morale went up and it wasn't long before sales also improved. Eventually, both would rise to the very top management ranks of the G. C. Murphy Company. "Horatio Alger would have loved them," Monroe said.

In 1928 and '29, Murphy's made a big move into the Washington and Baltimore markets with the purchase of seven stores from the J. W. Tottle Company for $568,557. Murphy's also took over the lease to an unbuilt Tottle location in Baltimore, which became Store No. 138. Shaw groused that the company paid about $1.60 for every $2.00 in sales it got from Baltimore in the first few years ("entirely too high," he said), but the purchase helped Murphy's dominate the variety store business in the nation's capital and much of Maryland for years to come.

In addition to the stores Murphy's purchased, a few new locations were constructed or remodeled to the company's specifications. Beginning in 1925, they were designed by Murphy's in-house architect, Harold E. Crosby, who became the first and only employee of the newly created construction division on July 8. A graduate of Iowa State College, the twenty-six-year-old architect was hired on the basis of his plans for the new McKeesport YMCA around the corner from the home office. Crosby would oversee the construction of Murphy's flagship stores while also designing two new wings for the McKeesport Hospital, including one donated in 1948 by Walter Shaw and his wife, Virginia.

FIG. 10

Another Murphy location, Store No. 32 in Beaver Falls, Pa., with 25¢ items on the second floor. When customer response to more expensive merchandise was overwhelming, the "five-and-ten" and "25¢ to $1" floors were merged. The largest U.S. dime-store chain, F. W. Woolworth Company, didn't follow Murphy's into higher-priced items until 1932.

It's unclear whether Crosby or that inveterate sales promoter Walter Shaw were responsible for another aesthetic improvement, this one inside the Murphy stores. The colorful new silk-screened signs—printed in Murphy's very own sign shop in McKeesport, supervised by V. F. O'Brien—that popped up inside all Murphy variety stores in 1927 were the first used by any of the dime-store chains. The printing process, called "serigraphy," wasn't cheap and wouldn't be copied by competitors for another five to ten years, but it sure made Murphy stores brighter and more attractive than rivals' stores. At Shaw's insistence, all stores also began printing their own price tags for the counter bins instead of buying them from outside vendors. The printing machines cost the company $20,000, but Shaw estimated they saved Murphy's about $60,000 per year.

Surprisingly, this bustling Murphy network of dime stores was fed for many years without a proper warehouse. In the early years, most merchandise was shipped directly from manufacturers to the stores, with a few small items being handled by a "wareroom" at the home office above Store No. 1. At the end of 1919, Murphy's finally bought McKeesport's old opera house where Store No. 33 was located, and soon the empty stage and auditorium were being used for storage as well. (Mack grumbled that the $135,000 purchase "crippled" the company's earnings that year.) The opera house was actually built on both sides of an alley, with the upper floors continuing across the street. In the days of live theater, a block and tackle were used to lift sets and props into the building via a door above the alley. Now Murphy's used the same arrangement to unload wagons (and, increasingly, motor trucks).

By 1923, the jury-rigged system of direct shipments and the make-do storage in McKeesport were being outstripped by the company's sales volume, and Murphy's finally established a "Warehouse Department," opening its first real warehouse in a rented building on Market Street on May 1. By the end of the 1920s, that warehouse was too small, so Murphy's moved in 1929 to a seven-floor, 39,800-square-foot rented facility on Thorne Alley in the city—only to reacquire the Market Street building a few years later when the new facility also became overcrowded.

For a time, the stores were supplied mainly by train (a Baltimore & Ohio Railroad siding went directly to the Market Street building), but in 1925, Murphy's persuaded a young truck driver to buy his own rig and make local deliveries. E. J. Lowery bought a second-hand truck for $150 and started making runs from McKeesport to the stores in East Pittsburgh, Wilmerding, and Irwin and made pickups or deliveries to trains or packet boats. His second truck cost $500 and could carry about seven thousand pounds at a time—enough for eight or nine stores—and Lowery's company was soon supplying thirty-six stores per week over the often narrow, winding roads around Pittsburgh. To reach the store in California, Pennsylvania, for example Lowery's drivers took the road to Brownsville, turned off at Newell, and crossed the Monongahela River on a ferryboat. The little E. J. Lowery Company grew along with Murphy's to eventually became one of the company's main freight carriers, supplying stores across the Eastern Seaboard through the very end of the G. C. Murphy Company.

More stores meant more people at the home office, which also grew in those years and became too crowded for comfort at times. When longtime Murphy's secretary Agnes Whalen started at the home office in 1924, there were no desks or chairs available, so she was forced to sit on an upended crate to take dictation. Adding a third-floor to the old church building helped some, as did the purchase of the neighboring Wernke livery stable and carriage works.

Once connected to the church, the second floor of the Wernke building was remodeled for Murphy's executive offices. The "executive floor" was treated to paneling recently removed from Pittsburgh's Frick Building, supposedly from the private suite of Henry Clay Frick, Western Pennsylvania coal magnate and a business partner of Andrew Carnegie until the two had a bitter falling-out in the late 1890s. During the infamous strike at Carnegie's Homestead, Pennsylvania, steelworks in 1892, an anarchist named Alexander Berkman attempted to assassinate Frick in that very same office. One of the bullets from Berkman's revolver went wild and became embedded in the paneling. The handsome wood paneling was one of the few extravagances that Mack tolerated around the home office, and Murphy officials liked to show visitors the scar supposedly made by Berkman's wild third shot.

All this expansion came at a price, of course, even though sales had been phenomenal. Swelled by all those new $1 items, Murphy's volume had exploded to $8.6 million in 1926, a better than 400 percent increase since the start of the 1920s. But the company's rapid rate of growth couldn't be sustained indefinitely by its operating profits. After twenty-one years of private ownership, the G. C. Murphy Company decided to sell stock to the general public. The timing was perfect. "It was a good time to raise money for general corporate purposes," John Kenneth Galbraith wrote years later. "Investors would supply capital with enthusiasm and without tedious questions."

On May 6, 1927, Murphy's directors received permission to increase the number of shares in the corporation from 10,000 to 120,000. Existing shares of stock were split nine for one, and an additional 5,000 shares were sold to employees and officers (Mack bought more than a tenth of them). That left 25,000 shares of "common" stock available to the general public, which the New York brokerage firm of George H. Burr & Company was retained to sell at $27.50 each. As with most new stock issues of the era, Murphy common was listed on the New York Curb Exchange, a predecessor of today's American Stock Exchange, and the entire offering was snapped up within two weeks. Murphy's put the capital to good use, adding forty new stores between 1927 and 1929.

The promise of quick dividends and the availability of low-interest loans to purchase stock were attracting many unqualified speculators to the market, and Murphy's was suddenly caught in the "great boom." Chain stores were particularly attractive stocks, Galbraith said, because investors had concluded that "central direction and control" enabled quick growth and steady profits. "Montgomery Ward was one of the prime speculative favorites of the period," he said. "It owed its eminence to the fact that it was a chain and thus had a particularly bright future. The same was true of Woolworth, American Stores, and others." Newspaper financial pages that had long ignored the little dime-store company in McKeesport were suddenly speculating on Murphy's sales figures. "Everyone, it seemed, talked stocks," wrote economist Robert Patterson. "It was considered easy to make money." It was certainly easy for people who had Murphy stock—those who bought G. C. Murphy common during the initial public offering in May doubled their investment by August. A year later, Murphy shares were selling on "the Curb" for $81 each, and they topped $100 in 1929.

Here and there, financial writers and a few college professors complained about "inflated values" on the stock market or "overcapitalized companies," but in the summer of 1929, prices were hitting new records. Still, there were signs that something was going wrong. Stock prices were moving erratically. Interest rates were getting tighter. Investors who had borrowed heavily against future stock market gains—so-called "margin" accounts—were suddenly being faced with demands to cover those loans with cash. They dumped their stocks into the market, and other investors, stretching their own credit to its limits, snapped them up; frantic waves of selling were followed by frantic waves of buying. Yet, in September and October, the markets seemed to rally. Murphy stock hit a new high of nearly $107 per share, $17 more than its Pennsylvania-based rival, the J. J. Newberry stores. Murphy's directors voted to pay a 28¢ dividend to holders of the common shares and $2 to holders of preferred.

By October 23, the price of Murphy common had declined some, but it was still strong at just under $100 per share. The following day, more than 6 million shares of stock changed hands on the Curb, shattering the previous record volume of 3.7 million shares. When the stock tickers finally caught up with the trading frenzy almost three hours after the exchange closed, Murphy's stock was listed at $96 per share. One year later, brokers were asking $50 for G. C. Murphy Company stock. They had few takers.

Murphy Memories

As a resident of Wilkinsburg, Pennsylvania, it was often the custom to "get cleaned up," which was different from getting "dressed up." "Dressed up" meant Sunday church clothes. "Cleaned up" meant your good Keds and freshly washed and ironed play clothes. Then you went "down street" to the business section of Wilkinsburg and G. C. Murphy's.

I remember the counter where you could look up at the candy in the glass display containers. The saleswoman in the center would watch you as you walked around and around until you decided what to buy. You could then say to her, "Five cents' worth of 'such-and-such,'" and she would weigh it out and put it in a bag for you. On Sundays nothing was open due to the Blue Laws, but it was a big deal to walk down street and window shop at Murphy's.

—Anonymous

When my sister Marcie turned sixteen, she began working at the G. C. Murphy Company in Irwin, Pennsylvania. She would get off the bus from school, run in the house for a snack, and be out waiting for the next bus in less than twenty minutes.

Five-and-ten-cent stores are pretty much a thing of the past, but I guess you could call them the predecessors to today's Wal-Mart. They sold everything from clothes to school supplies to tools. Marcie started in the department that sold material and sewing needs. She didn't have much experience, but her charm and learning skills quickly made her the top salesperson.

For her efforts, she was rewarded with an ivy plant that grew and grew, taking up way too much space in the house, so my mother planted it outside along the steps to our backyard. If you know the Pennsylvania winters, they can be quite fierce, but come spring that ivy plant not only survived, it flourished. In fact, we had to keep trimming it to keep the vines from growing over the steps!

My sister is now sixty-seven years old and living in Florida, but she recalls the days she worked at G. C. Murphy with pride and excitement. She was diagnosed with non-Hodgkins N-cell lymphoma five years ago, and she recently underwent chemotherapy treatment. Yet, just like the ivy, she remains strong and a dear friend to many.

—Karen Dygan Inglese
Greenwood, S.C.

Located next to Pine Alley in Washington, Pennsylvania, G. C. Murphy's had swinging doors, as did the other stores on the block. Several check-outs were up front with candy displays and gumball machines. Later came ones with small toys and trinkets instead of gum.

Straight ahead from the front doors was a double-wide staircase of maybe thirty steps, about ten feet across, that led to the basement where shelves held boxes and boxes of shoes and kitchenware. Display bins were set up along the three sides of railing on the first floor, preventing anyone from accidentally falling into the staircase.

On the first floor they sold fresh popcorn, candy, and other things at the counter, and the smells wafted through the store all the way out to the front sidewalk, especially in the summer when the doors were propped open. The long plank flooring that ran from front to back was oiled regularly, but it still creaked, squeaked, and groaned with every footstep. In places the floor slanted slightly downward and children could often be seen trying to slide in those sections until mom or dad admonished them to "stop doing that!"

Our Murphy's carried just about "everything under the sun" except furniture. Boxy counters held the merchandise with wood partitions separating various small items, while stacks of neatly folded clothing were held in deep bins. Behind the displays was a center island, and inside each, a saleswoman was ready to help and to restock merchandise almost immediately as it was removed by customers.

As a young child, I could barely see the salesclerks. The first time I remember realizing there was a person "back there" was catching sight of her between two packages and I was startled! She made me jump about three feet!

Housewives depended on finding what they needed at Murphy's, and the housewares section was generously stocked. Men could find almost anything in the hardware area. Children loved the toys, many of which were under $1. While J. C. Penney's across the street had fancy silk dresses, women could find long-wearing cotton dresses and dusters on Murphy's racks.

It was a sad day when Murphy's closed. People almost felt guilty for buying at their going-out-of-business sale since everyone knew the last merchandise represented the loss of a fine old store, as well as the end of a tradition of family shopping trips.

—Judith Florian
Girard, Ohio

I used to love the G. C. Murphy five-and-ten in Greensburg, Indiana, the town where I was born and raised. It had wood floors, a candy counter with the smell of popcorn popping, balls of yarn, potholder makers, fish tanks full of goldfish that you could take home in little Chinese food take-out cartons, rows of inexpensive toys, a mechanical horse you could ride for a dime, one of the first photo booths (four for a quarter), a lunch counter with hamburger platters and club sandwiches, plaid mackinaws, car coats with buttons that looked like root beer barrels, Roy Rogers holster and handgun sets, 45-rpm records, colored glass you could look through at the world, snow globes, and cows painted on small round boxes, which when turned upside down and righted again would make the lowing sound of a cow. (I once took one of them apart to see if there was a cow inside.)

Once when I was not paying attention, my mother got out of sight and I thought I was lost. I was about seven, I think. I walked to the front of the store and looked up and down the long street but no sign of her. I started to cry. A nice man in a fedora and a suit came up and said, "Can I help?" I told him I was lost. He asked if I knew where I lived, and I said yes and pointed and said, "That way."

He took my hand and we walked toward the fire department and the Tree Theatre; then we crossed the street, turned left, walked past the *Greensburg Daily News* and the bank, past The Fashion Shop and Grenner's Blue Plate Specials, and crossed the street again, past the A&P and the Republican headquarters with a big poster that said "I Like Ike." We walked by the tavern and Mr. Grennell's store where we bought penny candy and magazines and soda pop, past Mr. Clemen's hardware store and Goodyear's and the Gulf station, and then I pointed to a two-story white house on South Michigan Avenue and said, "There is where I live."

The man asked if I could make it home now by myself and I said, "Yes, thank you." He was very tall and stood over me now in his fine suit and his beautiful hat. I'll never forget his face. He smiled and touched my shoulder and said, "Bye now." I crossed the street and ran home but stopped to turn and look back at my friend who had helped me home. I waved, but he didn't turn around.

When I got home (our doors then were always unlocked) I went in but my mother was not there. Then I laid down on our green couch and went to sleep. When my mother got home, the first thing she said was, "Thank God!" I told her about the tall man who had helped me find my way home.

Murphy's was also the store where I bought my Cub Scout uniform with the yellow scarf and gold necktie clasp. It was where I bought my first Miller Waxy Figures (aliens from eight other planets), which were very colorful and, unfortunately, broke very easily; where my sister Mary Ann bought her copy of Pat Boone's hit "April Love"; where our mother purchased our Christmas lights and trimmings; where my brother, Mike, then five, bought his first 45-rpm recordings of Mr. Greenjeans singing "The Erie Canal" and Fabian Forte singing "Turn Me Loose"; Mary Ann bought all her Elvis Presley RCA recordings; and where I bought my very first record, "All American Boy," by Bill Parsons (Bobby Bare), in 1958!

—Nicholas Campbell
Atascadero, Calif.

A cherished memory of growing up in rural Fayette County was the Saturday shopping trip to downtown Uniontown, and the highlight was the visit to G. C. Murphy on Main Street where the enticing smell of freshly made popcorn filled the air. My brother and I immediately headed to the candy counter and stared at the seemingly endless glass cases filled with every variety imaginable. We pressed our hands against the warm nut counter and watched, mesmerized, as cashews spun around on a dish.

After a long and boring winter, we knew spring would soon arrive when we saw tables filled with hyacinths at Murphy's. To this day, there have never been hyacinths as fragrant as those were!

A big step in my life was entering California University of Pennsylvania. One of the first things my parents and I noticed when we entered town was the G. C. Murphy store on Wood Street. As an old friend would, it was there to greet me in a new and uncertain environment. Although the California Murphy's was much smaller than the Uniontown store and lacked hot food service, it was nonetheless a lifeline for both academic and personal needs. As a poor college student, I could depend on Murphy's for necessities as well as affordable luxuries.

Looking back, it wasn't considered cheap to buy a girl something from Murphy's. The various holidays brought unique gift ideas. We still have Christmas items purchased from college days—from the California store, as well as from the "big" Murphy's in Charleroi and the Murphy's that curved along Market Street in Brownsville, Pennsylvania.

—Anonymous

The G. C. Murphy Company was our Woolworth's (is that a dirty word?) in the Ohio Valley, and the connection of Murphy with our family is a bit of a soap opera. My father, Andrew Clooney, married a beautiful girl, Annie Elsie Ennis, when he was twenty and she was eighteen. The result was young Andrew Clooney, born, I believe, in 1921. Not long thereafter, his mother died. Annie's family thought the elder Andy Clooney was derelict in his duties. They took custody of young Andy and denied any contact with his father and any Clooneys.

In 1927, the elder Andy married my mother, Frances Guilfoyle. In 1928, my sister Rosemary was born. Then in 1931 it was my sister Betty. In 1934, I came along. Throughout this period, my mother tried to establish contact so that we could have a relationship with our older half-brother. They refused. I don't blame them. Their loss was excruciating. Still, in the way of small towns, contact between children was made anyway. Andy was a handsome, popular boy who looked a great deal like Rosemary. When World War II came along, he enlisted and did his duty—he was a superior young man, a leader. When the war ended, he came home to Maysville, all of twenty-four. He connected with G. C. Murphy Company and within a surprisingly short time was made manager of the Maysville store. There was talk of his advancing through the system and moving to other, larger cities.

At this moment, fate intervened. On an outing on one of the many sandbars of the Ohio River, young Andy waded into the current, hit a "step-off" and in an instant was gone, dead before he was thirty.

We remembered his smile, his gift of laughter. At the store we remembered the glass cases of endless candy—silver-tops, caramels, bonbons, fudge, mints. An endless cornucopia of sweets, much like our memories of our mysterious but always accessible older half-brother, Andy Clooney. I put flowers on his grave every Decoration Day.

—Nick Clooney
Journalist and television personality
Cincinnati, Ohio

My dad died on the job (as manager of the Keyser, West Virginia, store) when he was sixty-two. He'd had two heart attacks, and he was off after the first one for maybe six weeks or so. Someone in the McKeesport office asked W. C. Shaw Sr., "Why don't we retire him and get someone else to run the store?" He said, "He will have a job with Murphy's as long as he wants it." Corporate loyalty worked both ways then.

I went with Murphy's right out of college. Foolishly, I didn't even go on any interviews—I knew I wanted to work for Murphy's. People couldn't believe it: "You graduated from Princeton and you want to work in a stockroom at Murphy's?" But growing up around the stores, it must have stayed with us—I had no particular aspirations, I just thought I might like to work for Murphy's.

—Luther Shay
Retired vice president of administrative services,
G. C. Murphy Company
Edgewood, Pa.

CAN YOU SPARE *a* Dime?

It must have looked like a scene out of *Babbitt* when the McKeesport Rotary Club met in the 1920s. The city of fifty-four thousand was bustling and its prosperous businessmen gathered monthly for dinner and cigars in its newest and finest hotel, the Penn-McKee. The featured speaker at the Rotary's September 27, 1929, meeting was a fitting representative of the city's success—an executive from the fast-growing G. C. Murphy Company, whose offices were just a few blocks away.

"McKeesport should be proud to have a chain store company's headquarters located here," clothing buyer George Raikes told the Rotarians. "I believe it does more than any other agency to advertise the city." Murphy's had seven thousand employees and, he said, would soon top $17 million in sales and 160 stores. One of the newest locations was going up just about two blocks from the hotel. After twenty years of operating out of a cramped sales room on the first floor of the home office, the company would finally have a location worthy of its headquarters city. Murphy's was spending about $200,000 to build Store No. 33, which included two floors of sales area spanning 16,800 square feet, a restaurant seating more than one hundred people, and fixtures worth $125,000.

FIG. 11

"Old No. 1" was the G. C. Murphy Company's original store, shown here in 1934. Located in the former Cumberland Presbyterian Church, the new storefront along Fifth Avenue concealed the original entrance to the sanctuary but couldn't hide the buttresses visible in the alley. Murphy's home office was located upstairs. The company's rapid growth and need for more office space finally forced Store No. 1's closure in 1938. Though the home office eventually expanded to incorporate several neighboring buildings, the old "corner store" remained part of the company's headquarters until it ceased operations in 1989.

One of twenty-four new locations Murphy's completed or acquired in 1929, construction on Store No. 33 was finished in November and the store opened its doors on January 2 of the following year. Three weeks later, the G. C. Murphy Company reported the most successful year in its history, with sales approaching $16 million (shy of Raikes's estimate but up nearly 30 percent over 1928) and profits of $849,000. The new year, 1930, promised great things to come, including twelve new stores—two of them massive flagships in Pittsburgh and Washington, D.C. John Sephus Mack set the company's sales goal for the year at $19 million. "Our possibilities are in excess of our aim," he said. "We have great opportunities to increase sales in our stores."

It would be the last time for nearly a decade that anyone at Murphy's could express that kind of optimism. A worldwide financial calamity would soon put millions of Americans out of work and wipe out thousands of banks and companies, including some of Murphy's competitors. The F. & W. Grand, I. Silver, and Metropolitan chains were forced into receivership and wound up in the hands of the Chase National Bank. McCrory, McLellan, and Schulte-United plunged into bankruptcy as well.

The G. C. Murphy Company weathered the Great Depression better than most retailers—in large part thanks to Mack's cautious expansion program of the 1920s—and even took advantage of its rivals' misfortunes. And despite the October 1929 stock market crash, 1930 didn't seem that bad at first, although Murphy common plunged from a high of $107 per share to only $65 at the end of January and $54 by the middle of the year. Sales in January 1930 were up 15 percent, and in May the board of directors voted to authorize another 20,000 shares of preferred stock (Mack expected to sell about 7,500 shares at $100 each). Murphy's used the proceeds to fund several big remodeling projects and eleven new stores, including the Pittsburgh and Washington locations, which Mack said would be "worth in sales volume and [profit] many times the smaller units we have been adding" but would not "require much more work from our construction and sales forces." Once again, the Indiana County farm boy was right on the money—the Washington and Pittsburgh stores were soon generating millions of dollars in sales.

Yet, by the end of the year, what *Time* magazine was calling the "shadow of panic" had settled over Wall Street. The storied Manhattan brokerage of Prince & Whitely failed in October 1930, causing traders to dump blue chip stocks and shaking markets around the world. Two other brokerages withdrew from the New York Stock Exchange. The talk among investors was that "all mankind is doomed to a steadily decreasing standard of living until poverty, perhaps starvation, is the rule of life," an anonymous *Time* magazine reporter wrote archly, noting that despite the gloom, "commodity prices rose slightly [and] a definite rise was reported in homebuilding."

Time's writer was whistling through the graveyard, for conditions were steadily deteriorating, although no one quite understood what was happening at the time. Explosive sales growth at Murphy's and other chain stores through the 1920s concealed a troubling fact about the American economy: their sales went up, in part, because factories were producing consumer goods even when they had no buyers for the inventory. That was good for consumers because the excess supply reduced demand, but it also meant glutted inventories. Free-flowing credit allowed lower- and middle-class Americans to borrow money to make ends meet, but when sales of consumer goods stalled, workers were laid off and unable to make their payments.

For a while, Murphy's and other stores held their own. When Merrill, Lynch & Company analyzed sales at grocery, apparel, and variety chains, they reported that sales increased for the first nine months of 1930 by 1.65 percent, and newspapers were quick to point to evidence of economic recovery. But a closer reading of the statistics showed that sales in September 1930 were sharply down compared to sales in September 1929—J. C. Penney was off 12.5 percent; Sears, Roebuck, 14.1 percent; and Montgomery Ward, 18.3 percent. Of major grocery chains, only A&P was reporting a sales increase. Ken Paxton, then a Murphy store manager, joked years later that "folks were fighting for the better street corners where they could peddle apples or pencils." Still, Murphy's was holding it's own. In early 1931, the G. C. Murphy Company reported that 1930 sales had topped $17 million—up nearly 9 percent—while Woolworth and McCrory were both down. On March 4, employees gathered at the home office to celebrate the firm's twenty-fifth anniversary and Mack and Shaw's twentieth year with the company. A little booklet issued to commemorate the event listed employee benefits, including free life insurance coverage, two weeks of paid vacation, and Christmas bonuses of up to $15 in gold. An accompanying history reported that the first employee hired by Mack was still with the company and the second had stayed until 1927. Eighty percent of Murphy stock was held by employees or the board of directors, it said, and the company was paying the highest dividends of any variety store chain, "matched in percentage only by such concerns as General Motors."

Although the booklet's text isn't attributed, its philosophical and spiritual tone strongly suggests that Mack wrote it:

> By the age of man, your company is just in early manhood. Man does not seem to reach his best in mental ability until he nears the fifty-year mark. Henry Ward Beecher said that a man did not attain unto wisdom until he reached sixty. If that is so, then as a company, we are mere youngsters. With that in mind we will strive earnestly to develop and to improve our service. We will sit at the feet of the older companies. We will study histories and biographies. If we do this consistently and work faithfully, we will succeed.

In a speech that morning, Mack told employees the G. C. Murphy Company was dedicated "to serve our fellow men. With a worthy aim of such high character, we can courageously solicit the endeavors of the very highest type people." Lest anyone think Murphy's

FIG. 12
With the opening of its new Store No. 33 in McKeesport, Pa., in 1930, the G. C. Murphy Company finally had a location worthy of its headquarters city. The store, shown here in the late 1930s, also had a large restaurant and cafeteria on its second floor.

was strictly an altruistic enterprise, he noted that Murphy's was "in business to make a profit," but added, "to make money it must serve its community. If it serves well, it will be paid well. As it makes money, this money is distributed among the employees with a portion left for the common stockholders and for surplus." Murphy's would bank on men of "high ideals and a firm purpose" with "courage and stamina," Mack said, "We have these men with us. They are working and your chief is strongly optimistic on the further development of the Murphy Company."

It's easy to dismiss Mack's words as a mere pep talk, but the employees Murphy's was attracting did seem to have something special. Though the company encountered "many heart-breaking problems" during the Depression, "we were still adding stores and girding our loins for greater progress," said Paul Sample, who years later became Murphy's president. "It is in adversity that true character is displayed. We realized, more than ever, how fortunate we were in having such a loyal, hardworking group of men and women . . . pushing and fighting for their company in those trying days."

They became much more trying as economic conditions continued their freefall. When Merrill Lynch surveyed chain store sales in September 1931, practically everyone was losing

ground except the G. C. Murphy Company. Sales at Woolworth, Kresge, McCrory, and F. &
W. Grand were all down and McLellan had plummeted 23.7 percent. Kress, Newberry, and
W. T. Grant showed modest sales gains, but the G. C. Murphy Company was up more than
11 percent, and its sales continued to increase even as competitors saw theirs slip. For the
year, Murphy's sales increased $1.7 million as Woolworth's dropped $7 million and Montgomery Ward recorded a staggering loss of $19 million. Mack credited Murphy's conserva-
tive expansion policies with enabling it to take advantage of falling commodity prices and
pass the savings onto customers. "We are in a splendid position to take advantage of every
market fluctuation," he said.

Murphy's was not going to pull off a similar miracle in 1932. Sales dropped (for the
first time under Mack and Shaw's management) by 3.7 percent. The Depression hit the
company's loyal customer base particularly hard, and they simply didn't have money to
spend. "Many of our stores are located in the industrial sections, in the coal regions, and
in railroad terminal sections," Mack said. "When business in the steel and manufacturing
industries is bad, the coal industry suffers, and railroad employment drops below normal."
By 1932, labor writer Robert R. R. Brooks said, "Real desperation stalked the steel towns."
As demand for automobiles and appliances dried up and new construction slowed to a
crawl, steel production went from 58 million tons in 1929 to 15 million in 1932. In Pittsburgh,
some families reported eating potatoes at every meal. Within a few months, U.S. Steel
had laid off two-thirds of its workforce and was operating at 9 percent of capacity. From
McKeesport to Donora to Duquesne, Murphy's stores were within walking distance of
every U.S. Steel facility in the Pittsburgh area, and those mills had fallen eerily silent; plants
that produced 14.3 million tons of steel in 1929 shipped only 3.8 million tons four years
later. The Depression hit the region "much harder than other areas" where a single industry wasn't as dominant, said historian Stefan Lorant, as mill workers were dismissed
"overnight. Those who kept their jobs were forced to take large cuts. Wages declined by 60
percent, salaries by 40 percent."

Soup kitchens opened alongside Murphy's big new Store No. 12 in downtown Pittsburgh, and shantytowns sprung up in the city's Strip District, home to railroad yards and
wholesale produce dealers. One study estimated that in 1933 more than 200,000 people in
the Pittsburgh area were unemployed and most of the rest were working only part time.
Recovery was slow, according to Lorant, with one-third of Pittsburgh's working class still
unable to find a job in 1934. In Baltimore, which was fast becoming a vital market for Murphy's, the situation was no better. Bethlehem Steel laid off more than 14,000 men and cut
the wages of the remaining 3,500 workers by 15 percent. Families subsisted on a sort of soup
made from fish heads, day-old vegetables, and boiling water. "When steel was disabled, grocers on Dundalk Avenue sold less food; when paychecks of eighteen thousand steelworkers
dried up, fewer families could meet their monthly house mortgages," Mark Reutter wrote
years later in his history of the city's Sparrow's Point section. "Among the row houses of

East Baltimore, repossession agents stalked relentlessly with their bank papers and moving trucks."

The mining communities that Murphy's served in Pennsylvania and West Virginia were also hard-pressed. With less steel being made, mills needed less coal for their furnaces. Rural families were already suffering because agricultural prices had been artificially low for years; now, as grocery sales plummeted, farmers let fields go fallow or killed livestock that was no longer worth its feed. Foreclosures spread and employment continued spiraling down. On the Curb Exchange, G. C. Murphy Company stock plunged from its 1929 high of $106 per share to $18 in 1932—less than its par value of $25—representing losses to investors of more than $11 million. Earnings were less than $3 per share for only the second time since Mack and Shaw had taken over the company.

In later years, Murphy veterans were proud to note that their company never let go any store employees, even in the Depression's most crippling hours, but there were sacrifices to be made. At the home office, controller John Krut eliminated overtime pay, began docking employees for absences, and cautioned them that they should be grateful to be working at all. "When we consider what Mr. J. S. Mack is doing for this office by maintaining salaries and reducing office hours, I believe every employee should show his or her appreciation by increased effort," Krut said. "Now, let's dig in and put this job across in such a way that the officers of the company can readily see that we appreciate what they are doing for us and that we are really doing our best."

With capital drying up, Murphy's was opening only four stores per year, and the construction division laid off all its employees except manager J. L. Hoyt and superintendent H. L. Fulkrod. New locations in Erie, Waynesburg, and Bedford, Pennsylvania, and Bellefontaine, Ohio, were outfitted with used fixtures scavenged from failed stores operated by competitors. One of those was F. & W. Grand, which slid into bankruptcy and was merged with two other chains to form H. L. Green Company. A young management trainee at a Grand store in Baltimore, William Anderson, became friendly with the manager of a competing Murphy's store and was enticed to change companies in 1933.

"He said, 'Why don't you go to work with a good store?'" says Anderson, who eventually spent more than forty years with Murphy's. "I looked around and said, 'Well, this doesn't look as good as the store I'm working in.'" Grand had a larger, more impressive-looking operation, but Anderson decided after talking to G. C. Murphy employees that it offered something besides flashier fixtures. "The whole quality of Murphy's was better— that's what made the Murphy Company," says Anderson, who was hired into Store No. 149 in Annapolis, Maryland.

While he and many other employees were in good spirits, the year was one of "nerve-wracking suspense" for G. C. Murphy Company executives, according to Mack. A brief rally on Wall Street in 1933 stalled when banks began failing. Bank closures drained $102,000 in cash from Murphy's in 1933, forcing the company to set up a $39,000 emergency fund. An "unexpected surge in industrial activity" was followed by another nosedive in September, Mack said, and "new doubt and uncertainty arose." They were "dreary and discouraging" days, Ken Paxton said later. "We were all mighty happy just to have a job." Yet sales recovered and 1933 was the company's best year ever, with average profits per store nearly doubled, giving Mack reason to be optimistic about the future and vowing to leave "no stone unturned" in the coming year. Rather than rapidly adding stores—which was sinking the competition further in debt—Murphy's continued expanding existing locations and broadening their selection of merchandise. That added volume while keeping payrolls low because additional staffing requirements were minimal. And since the real estate market was soft, Murphy's picked up additional sales space at bargain prices.

In fact, against all odds, the G. C. Murphy Company was becoming healthier during the Depression. By 1936, Murphy's nearly two hundred stores averaged sales of almost $195,000, more than Woolworth, Newberry, and McLellan and within a few thousand dollars of industry leaders Grant, McCrory, and Kresge. Within four years, Murphy's passed them all. Though the company was affected by the so-called "Roosevelt recession" of 1937–38, which caused earnings to dip from $5.84 to $4.77 per share, Murphy's still added twenty-five locations and tripled its sales while competitors were laying off workers and closing stores. Not surprisingly, Wall Street noticed. Thomas Foristall, who wrote the *Wall Street Journal*'s "Inquiring Investor" column, singled out the G. C. Murphy Company for special praise. "Not only was [Murphy's] able under the worst depression influences to retain the major portion of its best previous earning power, but it has since been displaying an exceptional measure of profits resiliency," Foristall said. By 1935, Murphy stock had shot to $154 per share—a nearly 50 percent increase over its precrash high—and split three for one. On May 1, 1936, after issuing another 15,000 shares, the company's stock moved from the smaller Curb to the larger, more prestigious New York Stock Exchange where it was traded alongside the nation's biggest railroads, automakers, and oil companies. The G. C. Murphy Company had arrived among the blue chips.

Mack used the new capital from the stock issue to launch what he called "the most ambitious expansion program we have ever had," a three-year, $4.75 million capital improvement plan. For the next several years, twenty or thirty locations were remodeled each year, often by acquiring neighboring buildings, knocking down connecting walls, and expanding sales floors horizontally. Though it didn't add to the raw number of stores Murphy's operated, Mack knew it provided the opportunity to carry more expensive merchandise and sell existing lines in greater volume. "Our experience proves the addition of new stores in moderation and the improving of old stores to meet more modern standards of operation is needed," he said.

Not everything Murphy's was trying worked. In October 1934, Anderson was sent to what was billed as "the third-largest store in the Murphy Company" on Salina Street in Syracuse, New York. It turned out to be a flop. "It was in the wrong location, on the wrong side of the street, next to the railroad track," he says. "When the 20th Century Limited came through, it would block the intersection for ten or fifteen minutes" as it stopped at the nearby depot. There were other snags. The store was so large that the stockroom wouldn't fit in the same building and was located across the street. Salesgirls from Store No. 166 in Washington, D.C., ordered the initial inventory, but no one told them that winters along the Potomac are very different from those in central New York. The new Syracuse store had no gloves or toboggans, but it did get a lot of warm-weather gear, says Anderson. Worst of all, with few other Murphy's stores nearby—the only stores in western New York were between Buffalo and Rochester, more than two hours away—the "G. C. Murphy" name was unknown in the market and the Syracuse store couldn't share the cost of advertising with any other stores. The store struggled for years before finally closing in 1951. "To this day, I don't know why they picked that location," Anderson says.

Depression conditions forced some time-honored practices to give way. Murphy's was doing a solid business on selected items priced up to $1, including men's dress shirts, ladies' handbags, clocks, and certain fabrics, and pressure from Murphy's and a few other variety chains that broke the 5¢ and 10¢ limit eventually forced mighty F. W. Woolworth to add items for 20¢. It also helped that deflation had reached nearly 10.5 percent in 1932 and lower commodity prices made better-quality items profitable at a quarter. But when wholesale and commodity prices went back up, the profit margin went down on items that Murphy's had capped at 98¢. Though managers dropped some low-margin items, they were forced to carry others because they pulled traffic into the stores. Inflation finally led Murphy's to relax its $1 cap in 1937 and it added better-quality ladies' dresses for $1.98 and $2.98. Woolworth reluctantly followed Murphy's lead again, finally adding 40¢ items in 1935 and $1 items in 1936, though the bigger firm still lagged far behind in per-store profits, averaging only $9,580 versus Murphy's $15,103.

Other merchandise also was improved as employment picked up. In 1933, Murphy's established its own laboratory to test prospective merchandise and investigate complaints about faulty products. Newspaper advertisements promoted the new "Bureau of Standards" to customers, saying "all lines of merchandise are being carefully analyzed for *your* protection." At first, the entire laboratory staff amounted to newly hired employee Sam Cooper and some rudimentary test equipment. In February 1936, the Bureau of Standards needed bigger quarters, so Murphy's rented a building around the corner from the home office for the lab, printing department, and sign shop.

Many of the new products being tested were paints and varnishes. While Murphy's and other dime stores had long sold small cans of paint and a few brushes, shoppers who were working on bigger jobs went elsewhere. After experimenting in a few stores with a larger variety of paints and stains in the early 1930s, the company gave the products their own department and a big investment, teaming up with Tex Products Company, based in Newark, New Jersey, to create a special line of "Super-Tex" paints for Murphy stores. By

1937, nearly every store was selling indoor and outdoor paints and varnish in a variety of colors, and some larger locations handled paint in sizes up to five-gallon drums. Paint and accessories became a large part of Murphy's business, especially when the company began running "paint contests" that pitted managers against one another to see who could sell the most. By the end of the decade, Murphy's was doing $600,000 in paint sales, on its way to more than $1 million during World War II.

"Long ago Murphy's executives figured out that [the] Depression would accelerate the growing function of their five-and-ten-cent chain as a cheap-commodity department store where middle-class Americans are shopping more and more," wrote Pittsburgh's *Bulletin Index* magazine in a 1935 profile of Sephus Mack. Murphy's stores were becoming known not just for candy and notions but for "low-priced clothing necessities like hats, shoes, hosiery, lingerie, ties, etc.," the *Bulletin Index* reported. "Murphy's ventured out to get this business by emphasizing such articles in window displays and even advertising clothing bargains in handbills, something no other five-and-ten store has ever done."

As a minor sideline, the G. C. Murphy Company even entered the publishing business. Woolworth's sold a series of fiction, romance, crime, and celebrity magazines printed on cheap pulp paper, which were the supermarket tabloids of their day. The "Tower Magazines," named for the Woolworth skyscraper in New York City, sold more than 1.3 million copies each month of titles such as *Illustrated Detective* and *Illustrated Love*. Murphy's and several smaller competitors banded together to sell 500,000 copies per month of two new magazines, *Love Mirror* and *Movie Mirror*. The hope was that women who "never patronize a newsstand will buy 10¢ love fiction, Hollywood chit-chat, etc., where they buy their merchandise," *Time* said, adding that stories were illustrated with photographs "of ravishing young females ravishing young males."

In the meantime, something more important than paint, pantyhose, and "Hollywood chit-chat" was happening off Murphy's sales floors. When Paul Sample joined Walter Shaw's sales department in the mid-1920s, he was asked to develop training manuals for practically every part of store operation, from stockrooms to window trims. In 1927 and '28, Murphy's began issuing little booklets of thirty or forty pages on various subjects and then giving managers and assistant managers written quizzes on their content. One year later, John Harkless, a professor of education, was hired to create a formal training program, and the home office surveyed personnel in seventy-five stores to find out if the lessons were sticking. The answers depressed Shaw, Sample, and the others, who found "weak selling efforts," "inconsistent methods," and "poor communication from home office to salesgirls." The latter problem was addressed immediately with a new "weekly sales school" for all clerks, a program of hour-long lessons on techniques, tools, and new merchandise. Addressing the other fundamental problems required more work, and, in 1934, Sample, who had become the sales manager, and Harkless, the director of personnel, created the Murphy "School of Instruction." Part on-the-job training, part correspondence school, the training program was the first of its kind at any retail chain and was widely imitated by other variety-store companies. The School of Instruction (later renamed the Executive Training Program) eventually included textbooks edited and published by the G. C. Murphy Company and classes on management and leadership skills, merchandise selection and promotion, designing displays and advertising, and dozens of other topics.

From the 1930s forward, nearly all new male employees in the stores were hired as "student assistants," started in the stockroom, and worked their way up to the sales floor where they eventually became assistant managers. Each promotion, whether to a new job or a larger store, required them to complete another step of the training program until they were ready to take the final series of quizzes to determine whether they received a G. C. Murphy Company diploma—and a store of their own to manage. Even Walter Shaw Jr., who graduated from Westminster College in New Wilmington, Pennsylvania, in 1934, and Sephus Mack's son Jim, who earned a Harvard MBA in 1936, began their Murphy careers unloading merchandise, mopping floors, and trimming windows. Admittedly, they rose through the ranks more rapidly than most—Mack was elected to the board of directors in 1940 and Shaw in 1942. But the training program was one reason Murphy's Depression-era sales remained under what *Chain Store Age* called "forced draft," with the stores drawing a "powerful suction" and the merchandise buyers "pouring on the coals."

"Without the highly trained professionals in the stores, the whole merchandise program might have bogged down of its own weight," *Chain Store Age* concluded.

Other pressures besides the economy pressed Murphy's in the 1930s. In response to Depression conditions, voters swept president Herbert Hoover and many of his fellow Republicans out of office in 1932. The new Roosevelt administration and Democrats in Congress launched an ambitious slate of federal programs designed to stimulate the economy and put Americans back to work.

For Murphy's, one of the most problematic of the New Deal regulations was the National Industrial Recovery Act, signed into law on June 16, 1933. The law gave the federal government authority to set minimum wages, working conditions, and prices for practically all industries in the name of encouraging fair trade and full employment. Workers were guaranteed a minimum wage of 20¢ to 40¢ per hour and maximum work weeks of thirty-five to forty hours; businesses were required to keep their prices above minimum "floors" and provide overtime pay and certain job protections. A new agency, the National Recovery Administration (NRA), negotiated the rules with industry trade groups. Businesses that stayed in compliance were allowed to display the NRA emblem—a blue eagle with the slogan "We Do Our Part." G. C. Murphy Company advertisements were soon sporting blue eagles and Murphy girls wore celluloid buttons with the NRA slogan on their uniforms.

As did so many New Deal agencies, the NRA had noble aims and good intentions. But in practice, it became one of the nation's most infuriating bureaucracies, issuing ten thousand pages of regulations containing some three thousand different orders between 1933 and

1935. Mack grumped because Murphy's could no longer easily cut wages as sales fell and the company's costs increased. However, the NRA didn't prevent Murphy's from taking occasional shortcuts. Anderson, for instance, started at a salary of $120 per month, but when the NRA mandated overtime pay, the company wound up owing him more than eighty hours in back wages. Murphy's responded by giving Anderson a $5 raise, which delighted him until he learned that the promotion made him an "executive" and exempt from overtime pay. Though the Supreme Court struck down the National Industrial Recovery Act as unconstitutional in 1935, many of its regulations were incorporated into other agencies.

Another controversial Roosevelt reform was the federal Social Security Act, the pension program created after 50 percent of the nation's elderly slipped below the poverty line. Most working Americans were subject to the new tax and employers were ordered to collect it for the government. At Murphy's, calculating Social Security payments became the job of the eleven women who maintained the company's two automatic tabulating machines—primitive mechanical ancestors of modern electronic computers. The twelfth woman hired was Minnie Beckman, a newly graduated honors student from McKeesport High School who eventually spent three decades at Murphy's. When a personnel interviewer asked Beckman if she wanted to work "in the tabulating department," she was nonplussed. "I guess you can work anywhere if you have to," replied Beckman, who had no idea what a tabulator was. She still didn't know after they took her to visit the tiny, cramped tabulating office above Store No. 1. "You have to sit down for a minute," the supervisor told her. "The machine is on fire."

"I thought, 'What kind of a department am I getting into?'" Beckman says. And at home that night, her mother asked what she would be doing for Murphy's.

"I did the dumbest thing you ever saw," Beckman told her mother. "I sat and punched holes in cards all day."

She quickly learned that each hole corresponded to numbers that could be counted electrically by the tabulators. Using special keyboards to enter data from handwritten invoices and ledgers, the women of the tabulating department punched holes in the cards (the fastest operators could punch about three hundred cards per hour). The tabulators, which could add but not subtract, then read the cards; multiplication required a different machine.

Another workplace innovation championed by Roosevelt, collective bargaining, came to the G. C. Murphy Company in 1937. On March 20, 150 clerks and 25 stock boys went on strike in Murphy stores in East Pittsburgh, Wilmerding, Turtle Creek, and Pitcairn, Pennsylvania. Inspired by the sit-down strikes that won union recognition, higher wages, and better conditions for auto workers, steelworkers, and other laborers, they stayed at their posts and refused to work. But because there were no chairs behind the counters, they couldn't sit down; they called it a "fold-arms" strike instead. Customers wished the strikers good luck before the store managers locked the doors, and striking clerks told the *New York*

Times they wanted 50¢ per hour and a five-day week instead of the flat $9 salary many were earning for six days of work. Harkless responded that Murphy's was already paying better wages than other chain stores and that the company offered many perks, such as Christmas bonuses. The strike lasted only a few days, and only a few Murphy stores were ever organized by unions, partially because of intense antiunion campaigns mounted by management, but, more importantly, because many of G. C. Murphy's twenty-three thousand employees didn't feel the need for protection from a company they viewed as benevolent and even generous despite wages that seem penurious by today's standards. Murphy's had begun offering paid vacations for all full-time employees in 1922. Staff with one year of service received one week with pay, while those with two or more years received two weeks. By the end of the 1930s, vacation pay had been extended to all employees with at least six months of continuous service and expanded to five weeks off for employees with twenty-five years at Murphy's. In addition to the life insurance program, group hospitalization was added in February 1940 along with paid sick leave of up to 60 percent of a worker's salary for twenty-six weeks. Though white-collar employees have come to expect those kinds of perks, they weren't common at the time in any industry. It took more than a year of work stoppages and bare-knuckle negotiating before the newly formed United Steelworkers union got a contract from U.S. Steel in 1937 that provided one week of paid vacation, and it took another twelve years and two more strikes for the Steelworkers to secure health insurance from all the major American steel companies.

No wonder Murphy employees didn't feel compelled to unionize—their company was providing benefits that had required bloodshed by workers at other big American corporations. A genuine sense of collaboration between employees and management that was unique among chain stores was developing at the G. C. Murphy Company. "Variety chains of those days were probably second only to the army in their passion for obedience to home office regulations," *Chain Store Age* said. "This military style concept of personnel relations was offensive to [Sephus] Mack." By the 1930s, said the *Pittsburgh Press* in a profile of Walter Shaw Sr., Murphy's was treating its employees "as more important than 'merchandise and mortar.' Bosses were to be guides, not masters, at every level." Murphy's was also known for exercising compassion in ways never recorded in any rulebooks. One clerk of the 1930s remembers the home office sending the company nurse every day to check on her mother, who was dying of cancer.

For all that, home office employee Howard Q. Milar still didn't know what to make of Mack's proposal for a "veterans' club" in 1939. "My office was next to his, and several times he came to my desk to discuss plans," Milar remembered years later. "He visualized a group of two thousand or more members, a goal which I confess seemed to me at that time almost unattainable." Mack had been thinking for more than a year about ways to reward veteran Murphy employees. "The longer faithful and loyal service continues, the more precious it becomes," he said, deciding that there would be no "gold watch" or other

FIG. 13
Clerks at G. C. Murphy Store No. 69 in Pitcairn, Pa., look glum as they pose for a photo sometime in the early 1930s. Workers at this store and several others went on strike for a brief period of time in 1937; however, most clerks and managers felt they were treated well by Murphy's, which offered then-rare benefits such as pensions, paid vacations, and sick leave.

trinket to reward employee faithfulness. Instead, Mack would treat Murphy employees with fifteen years of service to a banquet, with all travel and entertainment expenses paid by the company. A new "class" would be inducted into the "G. C. Murphy Veterans Club" every year, and those classes could attend subsequent banquets every five years. The board of directors approved the plan on November 7, 1939. When controller Krut finished looking over the personnel records, he found ninety-one employees who were eligible for the "Class of 1940," including Mack and Shaw. Among them were three Murphy employees who had been hired by "the architect and the engineer" right after they had taken over the company: Christine Knodel, assistant corporate secretary and treasurer; John L. Widmeyer, who had risen from store manager to hardware buyer; and Agnes Felding, a home office employee. Two other employees had been with Murphy's since 1912. The clerk with the longest tenure was Stella Robinson of Store No. 2 in Gallipolis, Ohio, who joined the company in February 1913. In all, twenty-three "Murphy girls" were eligible.

The invitations were duly mailed, and the new Class of 1940 gathered in McKeesport on the morning on May 15. For some attendees, it was their first overnight trip away from home. They boarded chartered buses for a trip to Youghiogheny Country Club, just south of the city, where the G. C. Murphy Veterans Club held its first meeting and elected candy buyer Ralph Blank as its first president. From there, it was back onto the buses for a sightseeing tour of Pittsburgh's "Golden Triangle," a visit to Buhl Planetarium on the North Side, a drive along the city's scenic overlook on Mt. Washington, and a look at the Allegheny County Airport. Then the buses headed back to McKeesport where the veterans trouped to the restaurant at Store No. 1 for a meal of either filet of sole or broiled filet mignon.

Sales manager Paul Sample served as toastmaster, but Mack gave the keynote address. "We are appreciative that the heavenly father has prospered us," he said. "During depressed times, we have added to our force instead of laying off. For this, we are thankful. We are thankful for you, our dear friends, who have assisted us in our development, so that this business belongs to no single one of us, but rather to all of us, and especially to our good customers, whose money has made the business possible and pays you and me."

After encouraging the veterans to take to heart the motto displayed in the home office auditorium—"In the Beginning, God"—Mack urged employees to return to work "determined to render to our good customers and our associates a bigger, broader, and kinder service than we have ever given—a service prompted by love." They closed by singing a song written for the occasion by Frances Frum of Store No. 197 in Morgantown, West Virginia:

> We'll be loyal throughout the coming years,
> To our G. C. Murphy Veterans Club and give our rousing cheers.
> Now that we are here, we're proud to say, we're happy as can be,
> And we'll all be looking forward to our next big jamboree.

The veterans club held "big jamborees" year after year for the life of the G. C. Murphy Company, eventually inducting thousands of employees, including a few who marked their forty-fifth and fiftieth anniversaries of loyal service. Of the original ninety-one charter members of the veterans club, forty-seven were still working for Murphy's in 1965 and attended the twenty-fifth-anniversary gathering. For the short term, however, upcoming banquets were going to be less elaborate and the bus tours not as extensive as food and gasoline became scarce as America went onto a war footing. Personnel and merchandise in the stores became scarce for a few years, too.

"The G. C. Murphy Company appreciates the loyalty and faithfulness of all of its employees," Mack said in 1940. "A company, like a chain, is no stronger than its weakest link." Murphy's exited the Depression stronger than ever, but coping with a world at war again put the chain to another severe test.

A Million-Dollar Baby from the Five-and-Ten

For two years during the Great Depression, a former Murphy girl from McKeesport, Pennsylvania, was among the most famous women in the world.

Henrietta Leaver went from selling cosmetics at Store No. 1 to worldwide fame as "Miss America" and then to tabloid headlines and Hollywood screen tests before sinking back into obscurity (but happiness) as a wife and mother in Columbus, Ohio.

She was born in Monongahela, Pennsylvania, in 1916 to a teenaged tin mill worker and his wife. But the marriage didn't last, and the infant they called "Hen" was soon living with her grandmother. Her mother, Celia, married another mill worker, George Leaver, but that marriage fell apart, too, as he moved from town to town looking for work. Celia Leaver's mother had gone to McKeesport where she cleaned an office building in exchange for free use of an attached apartment, so Celia Leaver and her daughters followed, living in a few shabby third-floor rooms within sight of the smokestacks at the city's pipe mills.

Dreaming of a career as a model or actress, Henrietta entered McKeesport High School but lasted only one year before dropping out to take a job at Murphy's and help pay the family's expenses. As with other "Murphy girls" she might have stayed at the company for many years had several local businesses not sponsored a "Miss McKeesport" beauty contest across the street at the Liberty Theater. When Leaver, a five-foot-six, blue-eyed brunette, went home on the night of August 1, 1935, she had the crown, the right to enter a "Miss Greater Pittsburgh" contest the following week, and a nagging feeling that she was in deep trouble.

Leaver had a secret that would have disqualified her from competing in the pageant or working for the G. C. Murphy Company: several months earlier, she had married her sweetheart, twenty-four-year-old John Mustacchio, in a civil ceremony in Wellsburg, West Virginia. Mustacchio, whose parents owned a McKeesport tavern, had met Leaver a few years earlier during a picnic at a local amusement park. When the truth was revealed later, the happy couple admitted it was "a mistake" to lie about their nuptials, but neither thought Henrietta would win the McKeesport pageant or the Pittsburgh contest a week later. By the time Leaver went to Atlantic City to compete for the Miss America crown, they were too afraid to confess their deception. On September 3, Leaver was crowned "Miss America" after singing and tap dancing to the Dorothy Fields–Jimmy McHugh song "Living in a Great Big Way," a hit that year for Benny Goodman and His Orchestra.

For several months, Henrietta toured the country making personal appearances and performing on stage, pausing in Pittsburgh long enough to pose for a statue by local sculptor Frank Vittor, who chose the former cosmetics clerk as his ideal of "American female beauty." When the statue was unveiled, Leaver was upset and scandalized—Vittor had depicted her in the nude. As newspapers dubbed her the new "American Venus," Leaver protested that she was "a modest girl" and had worn a bathing suit during her modeling sessions. Threatening a lawsuit, Leaver's manager demanded Vittor clothe or drape the statue before displaying it, but juries of local art critics and students convinced the angry beauty queen that her attitudes were "foolish and old fashioned." During what the McKeesport *Daily News* described as a "long and voluble discussion," Henry Hornbostel, head of the College of Fine Arts at Pittsburgh's Carnegie Institute of Technology, told Leaver, "If you are not proud of your body, you might as well close up shop."

In January 1936, Leaver went to Hollywood where she was named "Miss Model America" by a group of department store fashion experts, and in February she took screen tests at Twentieth Century Fox and Warner Brothers. In later years, her family sometimes claimed that Leaver was the model for the woman holding the torch in the Columbia Pictures logo, but the studio has no records to back up the assertion and other women also claimed to have been the inspiration. Leaver did make it onto celluloid with a small, uncredited appearance in a Dick Powell film called *Stage Struck,* but she was turned down for a role in *Poor Little Rich Girl* with Shirley Temple. Her nascent film career came to end in May when the Mustacchio family and Leaver's mother announced that Henrietta was "awaiting the stork's visit." Henrietta and John confessed that not only had they wed in secret, they had later returned to Wellsburg and convinced a records clerk to change the name on their marriage license to hide the evidence. "Hen had a chance to go to an acting school and continue in her career, if she wanted to do that," said John Mustacchio, "but she figured that I had given up enough for her while she was Miss America, and that she ought to give up something for me. So we decided that she would announce that we were married and then settle down to making a home."

After raising two daughters and marrying twice more, Leaver took a job in retailing again, but not with G. C. Murphy Company. Instead, she worked as a merchandise buyer for a women's clothing store in Columbus, Ohio, where she died of cancer on September, 18, 1993, at age seventy-five—a star who shone brightly but briefly after rising from behind a counter at a G. C. Murphy store.

FIG. 14
Henrietta Leaver was working as a cosmetics clerk at G. C. Murphy Store No. 1 in McKeesport when friends urged her to compete in a local beauty pageant. In September 1935 she was crowned "Miss America" but didn't tell officials that she had married in secret.

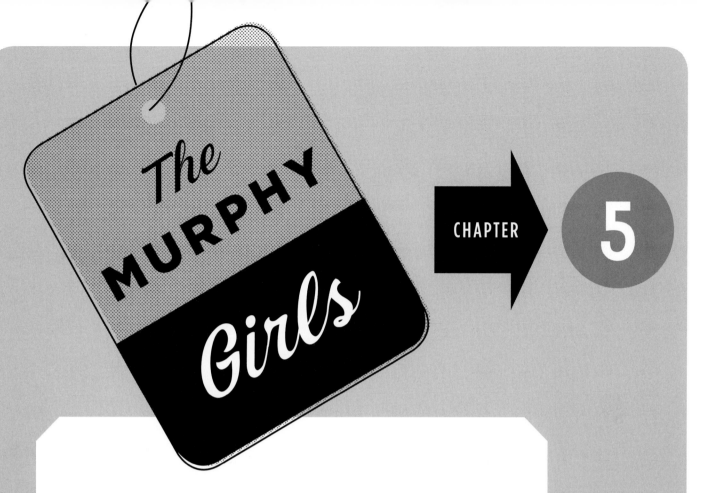

The MURPHY Girls

You are the contact between the Murphy Company and our customers. If you please the customer, you are creating good will for the company. Likewise, if you displease, through inattention, lack of merchandise, errors, etc., you hurt your company.

—*Service with a Smile (1929)*

These days, the average retail store replaces 64 percent of its employees every year, according to surveys by the National Retail Foundation, while a study by a leading industrial research firm indicates that half of all cashiers in the United States are under age twenty-four. Taleo Corporation reports that the constant turnover at retail stores leads "directly to lost sales and poor customer service."

Times have changed, of course, since G. C. Murphy Company could forbid its "salesladies" or "girls" from chewing gum, smoking, or even marrying. For one thing, women have more opportunities to pursue careers than they did in the 1920s when chances to work outside the home were mainly limited to teaching, nursing, running a telephone switchboard . . . or clerking in a store.

But it says something about the kind of employees that worked in Murphy stores that it was not uncommon—even after Ames Department Stores purchased the Murphy Company in 1985—to find clerks in G. C. Murphy variety stores with thirty or forty years of service. In 1959, more than 10 percent of Murphy employees had worked for the company for more than fifteen years.

"They were a wonderful breed that worked for me at the Elizabeth store," says Marianne Molnar, a former Murphy girl at Store No. 321 in Belle Vernon, Pennsylvania, who later managed Store No. 46 in nearby Elizabeth, Pennsylvania. When she transferred to the Elizabeth store in 1980, she was one of the youngest clerks there. "Everyone else was sixty-five years old and above," Molnar says.

Most of the longtime clerks were "sweet" and dedicated, she says, but decades of employment in the same store had left a few set in their ways.

"It was the same routine, day after day after day," Molnar says. The Elizabeth store, which had opened in the 1920s (and hadn't changed much since then) was still running on a system of bells that told employees when to open the doors, when to take breaks, and when to close.

Molnar was used to arriving at 8:00 A.M. to unlock the office, and then rang the bell at 8:55 A.M. to signal the start of work. "Even when there were only three people on the sales floor, they would march down there like little soldiers," she says. "I always thought there should be music playing." One day, Molnar became preoccupied with paperwork and forgot to ring the 8:55 bell. When she looked out onto the floor, the clerks were still sitting behind the counters, patiently waiting for the signal to open the store. "I said, 'Oh, come on!'" Molnar says, laughing.

Still, they were loyal employees. So was Betty Moats, who retired after forty-three years—first with Murphy's, then Ames, and finally with McCrory Stores after they purchased the G. C. Murphy variety-store division from Ames. She spent much of her career in Store No. 217 in Mercersburg, Pennsylvania, rising from cashier to become one of the company's first female store managers. Indeed, the picture of Moats's graduating class from the Murphy School of Instruction has forty-two faces—forty men and two women. At her first regional meeting as a store manager, she was the only woman in the room with sixty men who worried that she might be mugged or assaulted in the "big city."

"They treated me like an old mother hen—they told me 'don't you dare go out of that room without one of those guys,'" Moats says.

Most of the employees in the Mercersburg store—she calls them "my girls"—had long careers with Murphy's, Moats says. "They liked their work, and there wasn't anything except factories to work in around Mercersburg," she says, "unless they wanted to drive out of town a good piece to Chambersburg."

Sally Porterfield was typical of the "farm girls" and other female employees who were attracted to jobs in G. C. Murphy stores. The oldest of nine children living near Connellsville in Fayette County, Pennsylvania, she knew that if she wanted to buy anything for herself, she'd have to get the money. "If you live on a farm, you don't have an income coming in every month, unless you sell milk to a dairy," she says, "so I needed a job."

Employment options for young women in Connellsville in 1937 were limited, especially for women without a college degree. Porterfield could have taken a job as a domestic, cleaning houses or watching children. Or she could have taken a job with Bell Telephone as an operator. In fact, the telephone exchange in the coal-mining town was the first place she applied.

Porterfield hadn't heard from the phone company when she stopped at Store No. 201, which was not yet open, to put in her application. She was on her way out when the personnel director, Hazel Humbert, called her back to the office. "I can use you right now up in the stockroom," she said, hiring Porterfield on the spot.

The telephone company called a few days later, offering fill-in work for operators who were sick or on vacation. Porterfield turned them down.

"Operators had to sit in one spot for eight hours, and I decided that wasn't for me," she said. "I was never sorry I turned that job down."

Murphy's was among the last of the dime-store chains to adopt supermarket-style checkout counters and self-service. Until the introduction of hanging "pegboard" displays and "gondolas"—free-standing movable shelving units—in the 1960s, almost all merchandise was displayed on mahogany counters trimmed in glass, just as it had been since before World War I. Extra merchandise, or "understock," was concealed behind sliding doors underneath the counters. Murphy girls were expected to count their understock regularly and place their orders for the following week.

There was no computer-aided "just-in-time" delivery and no point-of-sale tracking at the cash register. The Murphy salesclerk stored all that data in her list books and used her brain to run the calculations.

"I'd inventory nylons one week, maybe next week children's socks, maybe next week men's socks, and by then it would be time to start all over again," says her former clerk Emmeratta McDonough, "and then you'd kind of have to watch your merchandise and place more orders."

Counters weren't just display areas. Each served as a base of operations for a specific Murphy girl. Through the 1950s, a salesgirl staffed nearly every counter in a Murphy store. The salesgirls were responsible for every aspect of operations at their counters—they ordered the merchandise, kept the counters clean and sorted, rang up sales, wrapped purchases, and turned in their cash receipts at the end of the day.

With few exceptions, salesgirls didn't move from counter to counter. A clerk responsible for one group or department was not supposed to drift to the other side of the store and help at another counter unless specifically told to do so.

Besides investing clerks with a sense of ownership in their departments, assigning Murphy girls to specific counters enabled them to build up a trade with their customers. "I got to know my regular customers," says Millie Reiland, who started working at Store No. 25 in East Pittsburgh in 1941 and stayed there for twenty-one years. "There were some people who would only buy things from me. I worked down there for so long that occasionally someone will come up to me, still, and say, 'You worked at the five-and-ten in East Pittsburgh.'"

In fact, one of Reiland's steady customers became her husband. John Reiland worked at the Westinghouse Electric plant in East Pittsburgh and would stop at the store with his co-workers in the afternoon. Eventually, he asked her out. "I always teased him that he found a million-dollar baby in the five-and-ten-cent store," she says.

Some claerks became institutions in the communities they served. Esther Weatherton became so identified with the Latrobe store by it's customers—including Winnie Palmer, wife of famed golfer Arnie, a native of Latrobe—that some of them called her "Mrs. Murphy."

Yet, staffing so many counters was labor intensive. When the Connellsville store opened on November 26, 1937, it had one hundred clerks and six female sales supervisors, or "floor girls." Another twenty-eight men worked in the stockroom. Even a relatively small store like the one in East Pittsburgh had fourteen girls behind counters on the main floor at all times and another five in an annex.

On the other hand, labor costs were low. Depression-era Murphy clerks were paid $8 per week in 1937, or a little more than $100 in 2006 dollars. For that money, Murphy girls were expected to work from 9:00 A.M. to 5:00 P.M., Monday through Saturday. Salesclerks in stores that stayed open late on Saturday were sometimes expected to work from 9:00 A.M. to 9:00 P.M., says Weatherton, who started working for Store No. 3 in Greensburg, Pennsylvania, in 1936 before moving to nearby Latrobe.

Gertrude Geisler, who started working at Store No. 64 in Tarentum, Pennsylvania, in 1933 for $7 per week, was one of those who worked twelve hours on Saturdays. "I remember the girls getting together, making signs," she says. "We were going to go out and picket, but we chickened out because we knew we would get fired." Most girls were happy just to have a job during the Depression, says Alberta Onaitis, who was hired at Store No. 51 in McKees Rocks, Pennsylvania, in 1932 at $9 per week. "When I worked on Saturdays, I worked ten hours and made an extra dollar and a half," she says. As with many other Murphy clerks, she thought she was being treated royally—better than her other friends who had jobs outside the home. "I remember that after working there a year, I got a week's vacation because I went to Washington, D.C.," Onaitis says. "I didn't expect it because I didn't know anyone else who got a [paid] vacation."

Nostalgia aside, *Time* magazine called the working conditions of five-and-ten girls "deplorable." A survey by Mary Elizabeth Pidgeon, a longtime economist for the U.S. Department of Labor who specialized in women's issues, concluded that the average weekly wage of six thousand dime-store clerks was about $12, or half of what women earned in other jobs. Most of the girls Pidgeon studied worked at least nine hours per day six days per week, and only one in ten had been able to move away from home.

"To the extent that the employed girl is unable to maintain herself entirely, she becomes dependent upon her family," Pidgeon said. Rather than improving the family's financial situation, she concluded, the average clerk in a five-and-ten was making it worse. The introduction of minimum-wage laws and mandatory-overtime laws helped the plight of the Murphy girl, as did the Roosevelt administration's creation of the National Recovery Act, which attempted to place more people on the employment rolls during the Depression by restricting the number of hours clerks could work in any given week.

More help came from events beyond the control of even Roosevelt's New Deal as social and economic pressures forced Murphy's and other chains to increase pay for female clerks. When World War II broke out and men enlisted or were conscripted into military service, defense plants suddenly needed women to fill many positions. The author's grandmother, Lena Togyer, quit her job at Store No. 1 in McKeesport in 1942 to take a position at a nearby U.S. Steel plant. "I just couldn't afford it. I was taking care of my mother and she had doctor's bills," says Togyer, who was making $16 per week when she left Murphy's. "If I got a job in the mill I made three times that, and I didn't [have to] work on Saturdays."

Years later, such penury would come back to haunt longtime Murphy girls, says Earl Rehrig, a store manager and district manager. "Some of the ladies were old maids, and where else were they going to go?" he says. "It was a shame. I had one lady come up to me when she was ready to retire and she said, 'Do you know how much I'm going to get when I retire? Forty-nine dollars a month.' She had been there almost fifty years. She was bawling, and I was ready to bawl with her."

Wartime experience also convinced businesses that women could make a valuable contribution outside the home, opening millions of new employment opportunities and further improving conditions. By 1948 when Emmeratta McDonough began working at Store No. 65 in Bellaire, Ohio, girls were down to five days—four and a half days from Monday through Friday and a half-day on Saturday.

Although the hours may have been many and the days were long, they weren't empty. "Be [as] busy as a little bee and see how fast the time flies," admonishes 1947's *The Spirit of Service*, a guide for Murphy clerks that went through many printings and revisions. "Thinking of ways to improve your department, filling up and improving displays without being told to do so, are a few of the many ways you can show initiative. . . . It's your business to keep signs straight and clean, to take care of counter displays and understocks. If you do all this, you'll find it easy to keep busy."

Porterfield's first counter in Connellsville was in "Department 8," which included purses, gloves, and men's and ladies' handkerchiefs. "Head squares were one of our more expensive items," she says, at about 39¢. More commonly known around Pennsylvania as

FIG. 15
The Spirit of Service,
an employee handbook
issued to all new Murphy
girls in 1947, offered
them practical informa-
tion about the company,
though the tone seems
a little patronizing by
today's standards. "Be
[as] busy as a little bee
and see how the time
flies!" the book advises.

"babushkas," a Russian word meaning "grandmother" or "old lady," "head squares" were colorful scarves that women used to keep their hair clean and free of the soot and dirt that characterized mining, mill, and railroad towns in the days of coal-fired furnaces, boilers, and locomotives.

Service with a Smile, a pocket-size training manual for Murphy clerks printed in 1929, urged Murphy girls to practice "suggestive selling" or "related item suggestion," for exam- ple, recommending a new toothbrush to a customer who purchases toothpaste, or a knife sharpener to a customer who purchases a paring knife. Porterfield practiced a little sugges- tive selling of her own. She couldn't understand why men's handkerchiefs were being sold in a ladies' department, so she took some downstairs in the Connellsville store where men's furnishings were available.

Porterfield was ahead of the times. It wasn't until the 1960s that Murphy stores began grouping merchandise by "themed" areas, putting hardware, paint, and sporting goods next to auto accessories, for instance. Until then, merchandise was assigned to departments based on which buyers at the home office purchased it for the company. Thus, since men's handkerchiefs were bought by the same person who bought ladies' hankies, they went on the same counter.

An old nursery rhyme says that "woman's work is never done." Besides waiting on customers, Murphy girls had many responsibilities. "When you were given a department like that, you were expected to do everything," says Gert Geisler, who was first assigned to a hardware counter in Tarentum. "Things weren't just dumped out on the counters—they wanted the stores to be orderly and clean and neat," Onaitis adds.

FIG. 16
Duties of a Murphy girl occasionally brought her out from behind the counter. Here clerks at Store No. 165 in Harrisburg, Pa., are pressed into service for a fashion show in 1949.

Service with a Smile directed "salesladies" to dust their counters daily and suggested a schedule of other duties:

> MONDAY—Fill counters and shelves. Straighten merchandise and wait on trade, as Monday is usually a good sales day and stocks are somewhat depleted from Saturday's selling.
>
> TUESDAY—Clean and straighten counter. Check merchandise and efficiency.
>
> WEDNESDAY—Take order inventories.
>
> THURSDAY—Clean and dust understocks. See that merchandise is in boxes or covered to prevent soil.
>
> FRIDAY—Make feature displays out of fast-selling items for Saturday on advice of manager. Prepare for a big Saturday trade.
>
> SATURDAY—See that all stocks are complete. See that all displays are kept filled during the day and especially so before closing time. Monday is usually a busy day.

It was no exaggeration to say that Saturday had a "big trade" in many of the factory towns Murphy's served. Bellaire, Ohio, on the Ohio River across from Wheeling, was typical of the mill towns that Murphy's served. The city was home to four glass factories, several foundries, and an enamel plant, and workers and their families poured into downtown on a Saturday night, McDonough says. "We'd have four people on a counter on weekends to take care of the customers," she says.

In Tarentum, home to Allegheny Steel Company, plate glass and bottle factories, and other industries, Saturday night "was like Old Home Week," Geisler says. "Everybody came downtown and met everybody in Murphy's. People would just walk around in there and stand around in little groups and talk. The idea was just to be down there."

For many of the small towns that Murphy's called home, social life revolved around the store and the Murphy girl was at the center. "It truly was 'The Friendly Store,'" says Barbara Sue Livingston, who was hired as a clerk at Store No. 189 in Shinnston, West Virginia, in 1947 and later became a personnel director at Shinnston and other stores. "When you entered the main door, there were chairs on both sides of the stairway and also people sitting and talking, and everyone knew everyone [else] by name."

A few customers got more than the merchandise. Sandra Wilson was a part-time clerk at the jewelry counter at Store No. 155 in Washington, Pennsylvania, in 1957–58 when a big seller during Christmas was a "costume" diamond ring with a fake stone that was the equivalent of a two-and-a-half-karat gem.

"My boyfriend came to pick me up one evening and appeared at my counter shortly before I got off," Wilson says. "He stood there trying on the paste diamond. When he found one he thought was the right size, he purchased it."

FIG. 17
Until the 1960s, nearly every counter in a G. C. Murphy Company store was staffed by a salesgirl who was responsible for displaying and reordering merchandise, waiting on customers, and collecting money for sales. For many years, cash registers rang only to $5; bigger purchases required a supervisor's approval. This is Store No. 29 in Pittsburgh's East Liberty neighborhood, circa 1950.

And then he offered the ring to Wilson and asked her to marry him. She accepted on the spot.

On Christmas Day, of course, he gave her a real diamond engagement ring. Sandra Wilson—now Cramer—was married six months later.

Not all of a Murphy girl's duties were on the sales floor. Larger Murphy stores had stock boys to carry bulky items out from the stockroom, but in smaller stores, such as the one in Elizabeth, clerks were often on their own, wrestling hand trucks up the stairs or

FIG. 18
The Murphy girls, stock boys, and assistant managers at the Charleroi, Pa., store gather for a group portrait on May 21, 1942. Long-time manager Frank Miller is in the center of the back row. As able-bodied men went off to war, defense plants began hiring women to work on assembly lines. The G. C. Murphy Company lost many clerks to higher-paying war work.

even unloading delivery trucks from the warehouse. "Some of the drivers were nice," and would help, says Cece Gallagher, an employee in Elizabeth. "Some of them didn't care if there were three or four women trying to unload those pre-fab entertainment centers." After one such experience, Molnar says she "threatened to send one Murphy driver back to the warehouse in a body bag."

Other everyday activities could be equally unpleasant. The author's grandmother started her career as a Murphy girl at the old Store No. 1 in McKeesport on the candy counter and stationery counter before moving to the lunch counter. "I was the first one in there and the janitor would let me in," she says. "There were so many rats there we had wooden racks to walk on. Before I'd go down there I used to take pop bottles and [roll] them down there to scare out the rats."

Even the first floor of the rickety old store wasn't safe from vermin, however. Once, while drawing a glass of root beer from an old-fashioned keg under the counter, a rat ran across her hand. "You couldn't scream—you couldn't do anything to let the people know about it," she says.

Geisler says that going to the stockroom was her least favorite activity, but it had nothing to do with the merchandise or any rodents. It seems that although female employees were forbidden to "fraternize," that didn't stop the younger male employees from trying. "I've laughed about this so often," she says. "The girls today make such a fuss if boys say something that offends them, but if we didn't get chased around the stockroom, we thought we were losing it."

It wasn't live employees but a dearly departed one who made the stockroom at the Elizabeth store an adventure, Molnar says. Employees thought it was haunted by a former Murphy girl named "Myrt" who had died only three or four months after her retirement.

"Say what you will about her, she was there," Molnar says. "You never went down there unless you had a damned good reason." She and Cece Gallagher swear that lights in the basement would turn themselves on and off at random. Molnar had to go to the basement each morning and check the boiler to make sure it had water in it. "I'd say, 'Good morning, Myrt. How are you? I hope you have a good day.'"

Many jobs were unpleasant simply because they were tedious or messy. Before the introduction of preprinted price signs, girls in smaller Murphy stores were expected to print their own. "You'd have black ink everywhere," Molnar says. "When they went to the blank signs with the stick-on numbers, that was the best thing they ever did."

Mary Rooney went on to have a long career at the home office as a toy buyer, but her very first job for Murphy's was in Store No. 12 counting "penny balloons," says her son, Tom Glenn. "Being new to the business world, she went over and started picking up the balloons one at a time and counting them, one, two, three," he says.

An assistant manager watched Rooney for a minute and stormed over in a huff.

"What are you doing?" he demanded.

"Counting balloons," she said.

The assistant thrust his hand into the pile, grabbed a bunch, and shouted, "Ten!" Then he tossed them to one side and grabbed another handful. "Twenty!"

"That's how you count balloons!" he said, before storming off.

"My mother said it was a lesson well learned," Glenn says.

Because Murphy managers and assistant managers changed so often—roughly every three years, sometimes less—Murphy girls often wound up knowing more about a particular store's operation than their nominal bosses. Smart managers and assistants learned to keep their clerks, especially their "floor girl," happy. "The floor girls were the backbone of the Murphy Company," says longtime store manager Fred Speidel. "If you were a young assistant, you could learn more from the floor girls than you could from the manager."

Floor girls set work schedules, made change, and supervised clerks either for an entire store or several departments in a large store. "The worst thing you could do as a young assistant was to go in and buck that floor girl," Speidel says. "She could make your life hell. But if you came in and were decent, you could learn a lot." Because female Murphy employees—at least until the 1960s and '70s—tended to stay at the same location for most of their careers, floor girls had the upper hand in most disputes, too. "If it came to the manager sticking up for you or the floor girl, he's going to side with the floor girl because she's going to be there for a long time—the assistant is going to be transferred," Speidel says.

Murphy floor girls had to be able to go from "one extreme to the other," Gallagher says. "I was trying to schedule and appease sixty-five- and seventy-five-year-old women, but yet I've got a twenty-five-year-old kid [manager] I'm supposed to work for." She remembers telling one particularly young manager: "I've only got two guidelines. I will not make you coffee and I will not put down the seat when you're done."

If the clerks had their peculiarities, managers could be strange, too. Harold McNeish, who managed the Latrobe store for a time, was a former army officer who started every day by playing a march over the public address system, Weatherton says. "It wasn't a pretty song—it was an army song," she says.

Though it wasn't quite the army, Murphy girls were expected to abide by high standards of conduct and appearance. Until the 1950s, Murphy girls wore uniforms—pink or blue at first, maroon later, with white buttons, cuffs, and collars. "All right, so you don't look like Hedy Lamarr," says *The Spirit of Service*. "That's no excuse for not being as neat and well groomed as you possibly can. . . . Customers will notice whether you keep your uniform pressed and fresh looking, your hair neat, and your makeup at its best. A nice appearance combined with a pleasing personality will win friends for the store and increase your own chances for recognition."

"We grumbled about having to keep those collars clean," says Pat Potter, who worked in the Connellsville store while attending college. "After a while, the company said, 'Okay, wear white blouses and black skirts.' That was almost as bad, but at least we could change blouses."

Behavior standards were even more stringent than appearance protocols. In the 1920s, any purchases totaling more than $1 had to be approved by a supervisor. As Murphy's began carrying more expensive merchandise, the limits were raised to $3 and then to $5, but Molnar says that even into the late 1960s, there were a few older cash registers around that only rang to $5.99.

The registers also didn't automatically calculate the customer's change. "We actually had to be able to do math and figure out the correct change," says Adrienne Kapisak, who clerked at Store No. 1 in McKeesport during her high school and college years. Her father was a private secretary to Walter Shaw Sr. and Walter Shaw Jr. at the home office. She met her best friend, Betty Clair O'Brien, at the store, and they still laugh about some of the rules that were taught to Murphy girls. "Murphy's insisted that all of our currency had to go in the same direction in our [cash] drawers," Kapisak says. "You don't even see that in a bank any more. To this very day, both [Betty] and I keep the currency in our wallets arranged in the 'Murphy' way."

Years later when Kapisak became a schoolteacher, she applied the lessons she was taught at Murphy's to her dealings with students. "Those of us who clerked learned to deal with the public and to always have a positive approach, even when the customer was less than pleasant and very demanding," she says. "That was certainly worthwhile experience.

FIG. 19
More liberated attitudes eventually forced Murphy's to relax old work rules such the one forbidding female clerks to marry. Women were finally allowed to take management training in the 1960s. An unidentified saleswoman at a Murphy's Mart helps a customer in the 1970s.

. . . I taught for thirty-three years and had to many times accept the verbal abuse delivered by students and parents when they thought I had been unfair."

At Store No. 217 in Mercersburg, Pennsylvania, Wanda Wood learned how to pack a box of loose candy. "You do not just scoop candy into a box," she says. "You count it out by pieces, and then weigh it for a price." Girls working the candy counter were also advised to make sure the same number of pieces went into each box in case two siblings bought candy at the same time and decided to compare them, Wood says. "That was customer service," she says.

When Wood began working for Murphy's in 1949, candy bars, gum, and rolls of Life Savers were 5¢ each. At Easter time, cream-filled eggs were 1¢, marshmallow rabbits were 2¢, and molded chocolate bunnies or birds were 25¢. "We usually cooked cashews and peanuts on Friday or Saturday, and the aroma would entice customers to buy," Wood says.

Dorothy Everetts, another Mercersburg employee, started her twenty-three-year career as a Murphy girl in 1964 and says clerks were still weighing out bulk candy and gumballs then, but not for long. "All the candy started to come in bags," she says. Some customers complained when the bulk candy disappeared. Wooden counters and floors vanished at about the same time, as did mechanical cash registers, which were replaced by electric ones. But mechanical registers had one feature that the electric ones couldn't match, Everetts says. When the electricity went off, clerks could still complete sales by hand-cranking the machines.

Despite all the rules, Murphy salesladies were not expected to be mindless drones—far from it. They were expected to answer questions thoroughly and be prepared to demonstrate merchandise—even "men's" items such as tools. In the Greensburg store, the manager stuck Weatherton with the "electric" counter, selling items such as wire, sockets, and switches, "and I didn't know too much about electricity," she says. Eventually, she was moved to infants' wear. But in Latrobe, she ended up with hardware.

"I had to make keys, and I hated to make keys," Weatherton says, "especially those double [sided] keys. They were terrible to make, but we made them." Onaitis wanted to work a candy, cosmetics, or stationery counter, but she wound up in the hardware department selling hammers and screwdrivers and cutting wire screens for windows and doors each summer. "You learned on the job," she says. "I learned a lot." At the Bedford, Pennsylvania, store, Eva Miller was put to work selling fishing tackle and flats of bedding plants, but she found an unexpected fringe benefit. After all the plants were sold, she was allowed to take home the extra potting soil in the bottom of the flats. "I spread it in front of my home, and that's how I got my lawn," Miller says.

"Anyone can put merchandise in a paper bag," says *The True Spirit of Service*, issued by Murphy's in 1959. "You're different. You know your items. You know how they are made and of what material. . . . From the customer's standpoint, the preference is to do business with the store whose employees know their merchandise and who are intelligent, honest, and trustworthy. They'll come back again and again to the store where the salesperson knows what she's talking about."

With that in mind, store managers conducted "Sales School" for clerks on Friday mornings. "We'd have a little meeting and the manager would talk about what new merchandise was coming in," says McDonough. Each girl also was expected to pick one item from her counter and tell the other clerks about it as practice for selling the items to customers. Sometimes, written lessons would be supplied or training films would be shown and, occasionally, the sales demonstrations became audience-participation events. "You will enjoy the little playlets which are presented at [sales] school from time to time, and the enthusiastic song fests and quiz programs," says *The Spirit of Service*, adding "you will like taking part in these Sales School meetings," though it's not clear whether that was a prediction or an order. "I'm not sure what we learned," Gallagher confides.

Murphy girls were sure to find fun where they could. At Store No. 130 in Bedford, Pennsylvania, in 1954, trainee Barbara Allison was put to work scrubbing counters for the more experienced employees, who started calling her "Scrub Lady." One finally altered Allison's name tag to display the nickname, and everyone had a good laugh—until her supervisor, Grace Richey, saw it. "[She] had some choice words for us," Allison says, but "she was just doing her job, and we went on with ours, laughing." There was a sisterhood of Murphy girls, and clerks bonded together as a family, Onaitis says, though there wasn't much socializing away from work in the 1930s and '40s. "Most everybody lived in walking distance of the store," she says. "Where would we go?"

FIG. 20

Long hours and demanding work bonded Murphy store employees into a close-knit family, and social functions were an important part of off-hours. M&L Discount was a Murphy's Mart–type store operated by the company's Morgan & Lindsey division in West Monroe, La. Store employees relax at a store picnic in 1975.

Everetts misses getting the type of service she provided to Murphy's customers: "When you ask a clerk now about an item, they look at you as if you are talking a foreign language. When I see that, I tell them to forget it." It's just a sign of the times, she says. Murphy girls "knew what you should be doing and what was expected of you," and were proud of their work, Everetts says. Today's clerks are "just there for the paycheck." Onaitis misses those days, too. "At Murphy's, the customer was always right," she says. "You never gave them a hard time, and if it got too bad, there was someone else who took over for you. The motto was supposed to be 'Service with a Smile,' and someone from the main office was always trying to put that across. For a while we even had that printed on our tally sheets. When I see what goes on today, I just say, 'Oh, my!'"

More Murphy's Memories

As young teenagers in the early 1970s in Duquesne, my good friend Tim and I used to deliver newspapers and look for interesting ways to spend our money. One way was to take the [bus] to McKeesport and enjoy many Saturdays at the G. C. Murphy lunch counter.

Tim and I could travel to McKeesport and back and enjoy a hot roast beef sandwich and a Coke, all for less than $3 each including bus fare. Then we always checked out all the fish and other pets, browsed the toy section for a nice model, or simply walked around.

Those were good days. As a competitive retailer, G. C. Murphy helped two boys understand the value of a dollar and the many ways we could dispose of one.

—David Marks
Duquesne, Pa.

The Sewickley, Pennsylvania, store was small and did not have a lunch counter. It did have the creaky wooden floors, though, and the wooden display cases and bins, too. I remember that they sold just about everything. Toys were in the back of the store, right corner. Toward the front, they sold stationery and paper products and, in the front left corner, a small selection of music tapes and cassettes. Sometimes, they also had a small black-and-white television for sale. The checkout counter was in the front of the store between the two entrance doors.

After the store closed, it was rebuilt to house an optician along with three offices. They carpeted over the original floor, I believe, because the same creaky wooden floors could be heard when you walked on it!

—Brian Limbach

Mount Lebanon, Pa.

Murphy's was responsible for many priceless childhood memories. I grew up in Fayette City, a little Mon Valley town. Although we didn't have our own Murphy's, Charleroi was only a bus ride away. My mother and I would walk down from our home in Brownstown to the bus stop at the post office in Fayette City. For a five-year-old, that was quite a walk—more than a mile up and down an incredibly steep hill—but it was certainly worth it because of the treasures that awaited at Murphy's.

I am forty-seven years old now but can remember those trips like it was yesterday. Although there were many stores in Charleroi, to me there was only Murphy's. I can remember the lunch counter to the left with the red-topped stools and how the lady sliced the hot dog in half, lengthwise, before she put it on the grill. I wondered why my mother never did that for me (although I never asked).

The toy department was on the lower level, and I remember the rows of yellow and blue Matchbox cardboard boxes (before the blister packaging of today). You could actually open the boxes and check out all the features: opening doors, trunks, and hoods, drivers in the car, etc. One of my favorites was a blue Studebaker station wagon with a retractable roof that had a separate man with a hunting rifle and an English pointer dog. I never made the connection until just now, but my favorite pet was an English pointer.

There were so many I could never decide, and my mother always asked, "Are you sure that's the one you want?" Of course, I now had to reevaluate my choice. I still know what my first Matchbox car was: a bronze-colored motorcycle with sidecar. If I had that today, in the original box, it would be worth a few hundred dollars. But then I would not have had the endless hours of enjoyment I had playing with all those cars.

—Frank Berna

In New Castle, Pennsylvania, everyone went to Murphy's for just about anything from soap to stereos. It was right in the center of the shopping district and had a front and a back door, so you could cut through on your way from J. C. Penney's to Strouss's, a local department store chain from Youngstown. You'd always run into someone you knew.

Prices were low, which is why kids didn't feel intimidated shopping there. A couple of dollars could get you a 45-rpm record, a hot dog, and a Coke.

We'd meet friends at Murphy's, which had a great record department (I remember I bought LPs by the Archies, the Monkees, Cream, and Three Dog Night there for $3.99, as well as "American Pie" and many others). They also sold musical instruments like guitars and drum sets for kids who wanted to be like The Monkees or The Beatles.

The woman who staffed the music department was there for years and had really red hair, heavy makeup, and held her glasses in a chain around her neck. She always treated us well, even though we hung out looking at records more than we bought.

Murphy's at that time had a small pet department in the basement where they sold peeps, turtles, birds, and fish. At Easter, the peeps would all be dyed different colors. The turtles were very small, and Murphy's sold little terrariums with plastic palm trees to house them. My brother and I had two turtles named "Skipper" and "Gilligan." Of course, pets like these did not reach full maturity, which is why they are probably not sold any more. One thing I remember is the smell of the place when you walked in. As I remember, the New Castle Murphy's didn't have a lunch counter, but it did have a stand-up counter where you could buy hoagies, hot dogs, and drinks. We knew the woman who worked the counter because she went to our church. We bought a hoagie from her every Saturday.

It was a fairly large store, with a set of wide stairs in the front and another set in the back, but there was no elevator or escalator, so I don't know what people in wheelchairs did. (This was way before the Americans with Disabilities Act.)

In the early 1970s, Murphy's opened a second store in downtown New Castle at the Towne Mall, but the mall Murphy's didn't have the ambience of the old one.

—George Hazimanolis
Pittsburgh, Pa.

John Sephus Mack called himself "a farmer by birth and a five-and-ten-cent man by adoption," and true to form, he continued to maintain the family farm, Old Home Manor, in Indiana County, Pennsylvania throughout the 1930s. As the third generation of the Macks to work the land, which would eventually grow to more than 1,700 acres, he frequently spent his weekends tending to his collection of prize-winning show horses and Black Angus cattle. He even erected a small hospital on the grounds for the convenience of his neighbors in Brushvalley Township.

But if Mack was at the farm during the last week of April 1936, he must have been grinding his teeth in frustration over the front page of the *Indiana Weekly Messenger*—the oldest newspaper in the birthplace of John G. McCrorey, George C. Murphy, and John Sephus Mack—which was declaring war on "the evil influence and effect of the chain store system," such as G. C. Murphy Company Store No. 126 on Philadelphia Street in downtown Indiana. If the *Messenger* and thousands of other anti-chain-store campaigners had their way, the nation would soon abolish what one Indiana County resident called "the parasitical invaders of the local field."

The campaign launched by the *Indiana Weekly Messenger* was typical of the breed, sounding many familiar themes—that chains were owned by far-off companies in "big eastern cities" (G. C. Murphy Company was located an hour away in McKeesport, no one's idea of a metropolis) and controlled by "Wall Street bankers" (Indiana County native Mack was by far the biggest Murphy shareholder) who were destroying the Main Street business districts of small towns such as Indiana (though Murphy's Store No. 126 had been praised a few years earlier by the *Indiana Evening Gazette* as "a beautiful new building" presenting "a fine appearance").

Farmers were among the first Americans to complain about the spread of chain stores such as Kroger and The Great Atlantic & Pacific Tea Company (A&P) when those grocery retailers began demanding lower prices on produce and dairy products, while independent businessmen found sympathetic ears at small-town newspapers that needed their advertising. One expert estimated that newspapers and civic groups launched four hundred "shop-at-home" campaigns across the country during the 1920s and '30s, and the anti-chain band-wagon gained momentum during the Depression, when "hardships for numerous small retailers, wholesalers, manufacturers, and other groups" left them "embittered" as Alfred Buehler wrote in the *Journal of Marketing*.

Several early anti-chain-store bills (including one in Allegany County, Maryland, home to Murphy Store No. 179) were struck down as unconstitutional because they set arbitrary limits on the number of locations a chain could operate. But in 1931, the U.S. Supreme Court upheld a chain-store tax in Indiana, and opposition forces gained strength. Murphy's and thirteen other variety chains together spent $175,000 annually to fight legislation, though their efforts didn't seem to make much of a dent at first. Twenty-seven states followed Indiana's lead by enacting chain-store taxes during the 1930s. *Chain Store Age* editor Godfrey Lebhar blamed the "combined effects of sustained anti-chain propaganda and the widespread need for additional state revenue."

Many of the taxes were on "sliding scales" that increased with the number of stores each company operated. In Pennsylvania in 1937, for instance, Governor George Earle proposed taxing each chain store location between $1 and $500. With ninety stores in its home state, Murphy's faced a $22,500 tax bill, yet the company was more fortunate than most. The grocery companies took a real beating. The first supermarket didn't open until 1936 (an A&P in Braddock, Pennsylvania) and chains were still operating many small neighborhood grocery stores. More than four thousand of those in Pennsylvania were netting less than $500 per year, and the tax would likely put them out of business. Though Pennsylvania's law passed the state general assembly, a circuit court judge struck it down as unconstitutional later that year and the state Supreme Court unanimously upheld the decision.

Far more serious challenges to Murphy's and other chains came from Washington, led by colorful U.S. Representative Wright Patman of Texas, who sought what the *New York Times* called "a chain-store death sentence." Patman biographer Nancy Beck Young speculates he was motivated by good, old-fashioned Texas chauvinism. During his first campaign for Congress in 1928, Patman railed against the "money barons of the East" who controlled the chains and, in his view, threatened the small-town way of life.

Patman got a national platform for his anti-chain crusade after the stores themselves made a colossal blunder. On April 16, 1935, the Limited-Price Variety Stores Association (of which G. C. Murphy Company was a charter member) and twelve other trade organizations announced plans to create the American Retail Federation (ARF), with former Kroger executive and Cincinnati city manager Clarence O. Sherrill as president. The organizers confidently told reporters the ARF would represent "one million merchants" with $20 billion in sales. Though Murphy's wasn't involved in the planning, S. S. Kresge Company, S. H. Kress Company, and W. T. Grant Company were.

But the people behind ARF hadn't actually talked to the members of the thirteen trade groups, and many of them balked—including drug and hardware retailers, which competed directly against the variety stores in many lines of merchandise. When they announced they were staying out of the new federation, the retail grocers followed. Worse, the idea of "one million merchants" coordinating policies sounded like collusion to Congress, and the House Ways and Means Committee launched an investigation headed by Patman. The eventual result was 1936's Robinson-Patman Act, which restricted the "quantity discounts" that manufacturers could extend to chain stores.

Patman had no intention of stopping there. In the fall, he went on a speaking tour comparing chain stores to the fascist governments taking control in Europe, claiming that business had been "Hitlerized by a few absentee owners." It was as inaccurate as it was inflammatory—*The Nation* magazine pointed out that the Nazis had actually tried to stamp out chain stores—but Patman's economic populism found many enthusiastic listeners. And it didn't help big retailers in 1938 when he released a list of America's highest-paid business executives compiled from U.S. Treasury Department tax records. Widely reprinted in newspapers, the list revealed that Murphy's had paid Sephus Mack $113,000 in 1936, almost twice what the presidents of the Pennsylvania Railroad, Alcoa, and Koppers had made, while Murphy vice president Walter Shaw Sr. earned $65,000, more than most of the top executives of Pittsburgh Plate Glass. Among other major chains, Woolworth's president earned $216,000, while Sewell Avery of Montgomery Ward and four executives of A&P pulled in $100,000 each.

By 1938, Patman had seventy-five cosponsors for his legislation, the most punitive measure yet proposed against variety and grocery store chains. Each company operating stores in more than one state would have been taxed $1,000 per location, multiplied by the number of states in which they operated. G. C. Murphy Company's bill would have come to $11,000 per store, or more than $2 million, completely wiping out its 1938 profits, while Woolworth faced an $81 million levy (versus profits of $28 million) and A&P (with 12,000 stores in forty states) faced a staggering $471-million bill on profits of $9 million. An escape clause allowed chains to defer the tax for two years if they liquidated themselves. "In other words," Lebhar noted wryly, "they could escape the death penalty by committing suicide."

Now the tide started to turn. Secretary of Agriculture Henry Wallace blasted the legislation, arguing that "sound public policy requires that we promote efficient methods of marketing and distribution," while an economist from Colgate University estimated that Patman's legislation would wipe out a half-billion dollars in economic benefit in Pennsylvania alone. Professor Charles Phillips said the state's consumers saved nearly $69 million shopping at chain stores, which paid more than $24 million in rent and $74 million in salaries. Taxing the companies out of business would put many people on relief rolls, he said, adding, "such a measure is nothing short of economic suicide."

In Indianapolis, where Murphy's was fast becoming the city's leading variety store operator, the *Indianapolis Times* blasted the Patman legislation: "We'll take the grocery chains, the five-and-ten stores, the assembly-line automobiles, and the store-bought clothes in preference to the one-horse, two-holer economy for which Patman seems to yearn." Newspapers in other G. C. Murphy Company towns such as Monessen, Pennsylvania, began speaking out as well. "Not even the supporters of the bill have denied that the mass distribution of merchandise . . . has resulted in tremendous savings to the consumer," said the Monessen *Daily Independent*. "There is another argument used against chain stores. It is that they neglect their community responsibilities, and to a certain extent that is a valid objection. But so do many independent merchants neglect their community responsibilities, and we rather imagine that in proportion to their numbers, the chain stores are as active in civic and social life as are their independent competitors."

In fact, few chains were as active in their communities as a matter of corporate policy as was Murphy's. In a series of letters issued during 1934, sales manager Paul Sample laid out what he called "The Murphy Company Philosophy of Community Service." Since coming into the home office in 1926, Sample, Walter Shaw's nephew, had quietly and persistently become an important behind-the-scenes force at the G. C. Murphy Company. As one of the principal designers of the company's training program, he was shaping the views of its key managers. And, as one of Shaw's most trusted associates, Sample made sure that front-line sales personnel implemented home office policies. Part of what made Sample so effective was his personal warmth and ability to relate to employees, and it was hard to find anyone inside or outside Murphy's who didn't think well of him. He counted among his personal friends James Cash Penney and Sebastian S. Kresge, founders of the chain stores that bore their names. As a result, possibly no one outside of Mack and Shaw had a bigger role than Sample did in shaping the corporate character of the G. C. Murphy Company, and the tight-knit family atmosphere he fostered no doubt helped propel the company's success during the difficult 1930s and '40s.

Sample now called on each of his managers to be "a gentleman . . . just, considerate, and helpful . . . quick to think, but slow to act." Quoting Jesus' admonition in the Gospel according to Mark that "he who would be the greatest among ye, let him be the servant of all," Sample said, "The 'big shot' idea has no place in that honorable, dignified, self-respecting service which the Murphy Company desires to personify." In one memo, he instructed employees that the primary mission of the G. C. Murphy Company would be "that of servants to the community . . . in merchandise, in alert, courteous, pleasant attention, in considerate thoughtfulness for the customers' comfort and care."

Sample instructed Murphy managers to build relationships with "important industries and institutions" such as the Salvation Army, churches, hospitals, and schools. In every city where the company had a store, civic groups from the Boy Scouts to the chamber of commerce soon learned that the Murphy manager was a "soft touch" when a community event or charity campaign needed to be organized. Many threw themselves into the work with zeal. Gertrude Geisler, a clerk at Store No. 64 in Tarentum, Pennsylvania, remembers when her manager was tapped to lead the YMCA's membership drive. "Mr. Waldron told us, 'Now girls, you all are going to join the Y,'" she says. "He didn't say 'You can join the Y,' he said, 'You are *going* to join the Y.'"

A few managers went overboard. When the borough council in Gettysburg, Pennsylvania, decided to install parking meters in 1938, local farmers recruited M. B. Frazee, who ran Murphy Store No. 129, to organize their protest. He was circulating petitions throughout the area until someone complained to the home office. Seph Mack shot off a telegram to Frazee telling him to "go slow," then followed up with a letter to Gettysburg council assuring them that G. C. Murphy Company "is in favor of any and all civic improvements" and was willing to contribute toward them. "I can appreciate [Frazee's] getting the farmers' slant on this, for we have quite so many of them as our friends and customers, but he must remember that he is living in the city of Gettysburg," Mack said.

As for the Patman bill, opposition continued to mount. Labor unions argued that chains paid higher wages and were easier to organize than independent stores, while consumer organizations produced voluminous studies showing that chain buying drove down food and clothing prices. A spokeswoman for the Washington, D.C., federation of women's clubs called the legislation "the most vicious, inhuman bill ever to come before Congress." Perhaps no one was as effective at destroying it as Congressman Patman himself, who went out on another national speaking tour to drum up support. His trip was funded by a major drug wholesaler, McKesson & Robbins, but investigators probing a stock swindle discovered that the company had been a front for a bootlegging operation during Prohibition and that its president had spent six months in federal prison for falsifying U.S. Customs records. Patman's support evaporated. When Congress finally opened hearings on the chain-store legislation in March 1940, more than two hundred witnesses were called—virtually all of them in opposition. On June 17 the subcommittee considering the bill decided not to put it to a vote before the full House of Representatives. The chain store "death sentence" had been commuted.

In the meantime, the G. C. Murphy Company continued to expand even where its competitors were struggling. Two stores were closed for good in 1938 but not through economic pressure. One was the Lawrenceville, Illinois, store, which moved to Linton, Indiana, while the other closure was a real milestone for the company. Store No. 1 in McKeesport, which George Murphy himself had opened in 1906, rang up its last sales on February 26, 1938, and employees were transferred to the larger, more modern Store No. 33 a few blocks away. Murphy's home office, which by now occupied the entire building above old Store No. 1 along with space in the neighboring buildings, needed more room to grow. Store No. 33, which took Store No. 1's number, was enlarged slightly to compensate and the restaurant was remodeled. "We believed with this additional space we could maintain our sales in McKeesport," Seph Mack told the board of directors, adding "sales have been justifying our belief."

With the new space in what had been Store No. 1's first-floor sales room and lunch counter, the company's headquarters now occupied more than 42,000 square feet. Additional work on upper floors created an auditorium, work areas for buyers, and other amenities. Of course, the always-frugal Mack was quick to point out that the renovations were hardly an extravagance. "We were in congested quarters and the remodeling was necessary," he said. "This will take care of our needs for some time in the future, although we are not overbuilt to any great extent."

Murphy's opened its two-hundredth store in 1939 on Belair Road in Baltimore and remodeled sixteen others, while sales were up 12 percent and earnings went to $6.47 per share. In retrospect, perhaps the year's most important event was the fire that destroyed one of the company's two cramped, overcrowded warehouses in McKeesport. The old Market Street facility burned on November 5, 1939. Since the other warehouse on Thorne Alley was bulging at the seams, Murphy's quickly erected a 100-by-200-foot temporary building so that it could continue operations. Although a few offices in the Thorne Alley warehouse were moved elsewhere to relieve some of the pressure, the company clearly needed a long-term solution, and Murphy's paid nearly $56,000 for fourteen acres of land along the Baltimore & Ohio Railroad tracks south of McKeesport. The construction department began drawing up plans for a beautiful new brick and steel warehouse on the site.

With all of this progress, it was natural for Murphy's president, chairman of the board, and majority stockholder to want to share part of his own windfall. John Sephus Mack's health was failing, and perhaps, as had Andrew Carnegie, he decided that a man who "dies rich, dies disgraced." It's not surprising, given Mack's fervent Protestantism, that one of his first beneficiaries was the church—specifically the ministry of fundamentalist southern preacher Reverend Dr. Bob Jones Sr. Saved at a revival meeting when he was eleven years old, Jones was one of the most prominent evangelists of the 1920s, "second only to Billy Sunday," according to a later profile in the *Washington Post*. Traveling the country preaching in revival tents, Jones condemned the evils of liberal thought, strong drink, jazz music, loose sexual morals, and movies, among other things. When a group of prominent McKeesport clergymen and business leaders invited Jones to the city, he staged a month-long revival at the high school football field during January 1927. It was a roaring success—eleven thousand people turned out during the first day of services, including a nine-hundred-person choir, and a school board meeting had to be canceled a few weeks later for lack of a quorum. (The school directors were at the football field listening to Jones.)

Mack loaned Jones a Peerless touring car for his personal use during his four-week stay in McKeesport. The evangelist and the merchant became fast friends, possibly because Jones viewed himself being in the retail business, too, selling religion rather than dry goods. "I am a salesman and the type work I have always done has schooled me in putting propositions over quickly," he told Seph Mack.

Jones had founded a Christian college in Florida, hoping that an affiliated real estate venture would keep it afloat, but the market for both Florida property and higher education collapsed during the Depression. Flirting with bankruptcy, Bob Jones College moved to Cleveland, Tennessee, and the pastor called on Mack for help. At first, Mack chided Jones for being too optimistic and overspending, but then he promised to help the pastor keep the doors open no matter what. "I am going to put my shoulder to the wheel and help you in a big way," Mack wrote back, telling Jones, "construct your buildings and send me the bill." It's not clear how much money Mack extended over the years, but from every indication the gifts were substantial. Mack "was very, very fond of that school," says Barbara Mack Reister, who married Seph Mack's son Jim in 1936. "Dr. Bob was a very, very fine person." In gratitude, the college trustees awarded Mack an honorary doctorate, and Bob Jones University (now located in Greenville, South Carolina) still has a library named in his honor.

Other gifts were made closer to home. In 1935, Mack donated 1,500 shares of G. C. Murphy stock, valued at $200,000, to the hospital in Indiana, Pennsylvania, to establish a trust fund to care for indigent patients. Four years later, Mack gave Indiana Hospital another $115,000 to erect a maternity wing in honor of his parents, John and Sarah Mack. His wife, Margaret, personally selected the furnishings. At the dedication on September 21, 1939, one local pastor called it "Indiana's Bethesda" and compared Mack to the hero of James Henry Leigh Hunt's poem *Abou Ben Adhem* about a man who "loves his fellow men" so well that his name is placed atop heaven's list of "those who love the Lord."

McKeesport Hospital was another regular recipient of Mack's generosity. In addition to an annual $5,000 donation, in 1932 Seph Mack took personal control of the hospital's fund-raising after the extraordinary crush of charity cases pushed it into financial difficulty. Within a few months, Mack collected $165,000—$65,000 more than administrators needed—and pledged another $5,000 annually toward retiring the hospital's mortgage. Mack later gave $2,500 to help pay for meals for indigent patients, donated two hundred shares of G. C. Murphy Company stock to create a $40,000 endowment, and paid for the construction of two dormitories for male employees.

Another recipient of Mack's generosity was Westminster College in New Wilmington, Pennsylvania, a liberal arts school affiliated with the Presbyterian Church. In May 1935, Mack gave the college $20,000 in memory of a boyhood friend and distant relative, Reverend Ralph Gibson McGill, a missionary who drowned in Egypt in 1926 while trying to save a local woman. Mack also created a student loan fund to pay for the education of needy students. Westminster thanked him in 1938 with an honorary doctorate in humanities. At the College of William and Mary in Williamsburg, Virginia, where his son Jim earned a bachelor's degree in business administration, Mack's money endowed a professorship, while in Indiana County, Mack and his cousin Edgar McCrorey Mack (then vice president of Murphy's real estate and construction division) purchased the fairgrounds that had fallen into disrepair and opened them as a public park.

All told, G. C. Murphy Company entered the 1940s in fine form. It closed the books on the 1930s by reporting another year of record sales ($47 million, a 12 percent increase over 1938) and earnings of more than $6 per share. Ground was broken for large new stores in York and Brentwood, Pennsylvania. In his February 1, 1940, message to shareholders, Sephus Mack noted that the economy was expanding rapidly as American factories ramped up production to supply the war in Europe. A few days later, McKeesporters gathered at Youghiogheny Country Club to pay tribute to Mack's right-hand man and junior partner, Walter Shaw Sr. As the G. C. Murphy Company's major stockholder, Sephus Mack had always been the chain's public face, but that didn't make Shaw's contributions less important—and as was Mack, Shaw was sharing his newfound wealth with the community. In the past few years, Shaw had donated more than $45,000 to his church and became a driving force behind the McKeesport YMCA, the hospital, and other organizations. A proclamation heralded Shaw as the city's "most cheerful giver" and McKeesport Hospital's superintendent praised his "kind heart, his cheery smile, and fine sense of humor."

Each of the speakers was warmly applauded, but none so loudly as Mack, who received a standing ovation as he approached the podium. The ailing G. C. Murphy Company president, who had not left home at night since the previous May, called his "warm friendship" with Shaw "a priceless possession. Walter has always taken the Great Teacher seriously. He has always followed His instructions that 'it is better to give than to receive,' and that 'to give is happier than to get.'"

Their "warm friendship" didn't stop Mack from cracking the whip on occasion. Many of Murphy's successes were possible, after all, because of its conservative cash management (it had $3 million in the bank and little long-term debt). When Shaw returned from a Florida vacation in April, he received a blistering memo from Mack regarding the sales department's telephone and telegram expenses, which called Shaw's staff a group of "swivel chair majors" who "gabble and gossip":

> Look at Baker with his $35.00 for telegrams—better than a dollar a day.
> $9.30 for telephone calls. Why, he is crazy! Charlie Green is no piker! Be-

fore we got that boy from the farm, he didn't know the whole Western Union Company took in that much money. Look how fast he learns! He must have been sitting at Baker's feet. When John Getty was working in Indiana, I doubt if the whole telegraph office took in more than $9.00. Yet, he showed that much for telegrams in the month of January. And, he wasn't satisfied with that, he put in that many toll calls. What for? Saving him from writing a few letters. Tell John to use his head a little bit.

Telephone expenses aside, 1940 was another good year, with sales and profits up again and seventeen stores remodeled, including Store No. 12 in downtown Pittsburgh, where the Fifth Avenue frontage grew significantly after the company leased a neighboring six-story building, expanding the first floor and basement sales area while adding stock space above. In November, ground was broken on the new Murphy warehouse, which would be a monster—295,000 square feet of storage and 8,000 feet of office space under a 3.5-acre roof. It would handle practically everything the stores sold, except for apparel, because a few months earlier Murphy's had opened its new "Style Center" on Seventh Avenue in New York City just outside the Garment District.

Only one event spoiled what would otherwise have been a perfect year for the G. C. Murphy Company. On Friday morning, September 27, "the architect" of the company's success suffered a stroke at Old Home Manor and died later that afternoon. John Sephus Mack's body was returned to McKeesport and for three days mourners filed through the family home on Union Avenue to pay their respects. Four colleges sent their choirs—Westminster, Bob Jones, William and Mary, and Indiana State Teachers College in Indiana County—and Reverend Bob Jones Sr. canceled his speaking engagements to attend. On Sunday night, hundreds gathered in a pasture at Old Home Manor for a memorial service led by Jones and two local pastors. A male quartet from Indiana's First Presbyterian Church led them in singing "Lead Kindly Light," "One More Day's Work for Jesus," and "Jesus Savior, Pilot Me."

Two days later, the Murphy home office closed at noon and McKeesport's Store No. 1 closed all day so employees could attend Mack's funeral, held at the family home. Though the furniture was removed from the first and second floors, it still wasn't large enough to handle the crowd, so the auditorium at nearby Central Presbyterian Church was opened and its public address system connected to the house so all the mourners could participate in the service. Jones delivered the eulogy: "His faith in the Almighty is expressed by his many noble deeds and virtues. The smile that was so quick, his genial and delightful personality, his joy in living, his pride in his family—all contributed to the character that we loved."

More than one hundred students from the McKeesport Hospital School of Nursing filed past Mack's casket, each placing upon it a single red rose. At the end of the service, as state troopers riding motorcycles led a motorcade back to Indiana's Greenwood Cemetery, all of McKeesport's businesses closed for two minutes in silent tribute. The following day, Murphy's board of directors elected Edgar McCrorey Mack chairman and Walter Shaw president and an editorial in the *Daily News* drew a sharp contrast between John Sephus Mack's life and the events unfolding in Europe:

> [The] career of Mr. Mack is a stirring example of the opportunities and progress inherent with the democratic way of life—a system whose very essentials are endangered now by the moves of the dictators on the chessboard of international war and politics. . . . Perhaps the most fitting tribute that can be paid to him is that he lived the life of the true American, that he gave us all new courage to maintain a society which makes possible such careers as that of John S. Mack.

The United States remained officially neutral in the conflicts in Europe and Asia, but Americans were watching them with increasing alarm. Though industrial plants were bustling while the federal government refitted the ill-equipped army and navy, consumer goods were becoming scarce. The war in the Pacific started taking its toll on the variety-store business in 1937 when Imperial Japan's brutal invasion of the Chinese city of Nanking and its bombing of the USS *Panay* and three Standard Oil tankers triggered U.S. boycotts against Japanese products. Japan was exporting up to $100 million worth of goods—mainly pottery, toys, and silk—to the United States, but Woolworth, Kress, and Kresge announced they would no longer purchase Japanese merchandise, and the rest of the industry followed. Domestically, production lines were being converted to lucrative defense contracts while commodities such as tin, copper, rubber, and cotton were being diverted for government use. Murphy architect Harold Crosby reported that Murphy's was unable to add any locations during 1941 due to "inability to obtain building material." New stores in Butler, Pennsylvania, and Wheeling and South Charleston, West Virginia, were the last constructed until 1945.

Luckily, the company's most important construction project—the new Murphy warehouse—continued on schedule. The new distribution center was largely complete when the Japanese bombed Pearl Harbor on December 7, 1941, triggering the United States to enter World War II. The $725,000 warehouse opened three weeks later and by the end of its first full year had handled nearly 6,023 different product lines valued at nearly $18 million. The crew had emptied and refilled the building eight times. The first floor was dedicated to unloading merchandise from train cars and sorting it by departments (130 new flat trucks and three electric tractors helped speed the work), while the basement level was used for shipping orders to stores. When a store ordered merchandise, crews picked the items out of inventory on the first floor and slid them down chutes to the shipping area below.

One of the early employees was Dave Backstrom, a seventeen-year-old from West Newton, Pennsylvania, hired in 1942 to help fill orders. While the stores dealt with the public and a certain amount of decorum was expected of clerks and managers, life in the warehouse among the mostly young, male workforce was laid back. At lunchtime, janitor

FIG. 21
The G. C. Murphy Company opened its first modern warehouse in McKeesport, Pa., in December 1941, just a few weeks after the Japanese bombing of Pearl Harbor triggered the United States to enter World War II. The facility handled $18 million worth of goods in its first full year of operation.

Eric Anderson would cut the fire in the incinerator so that workers could toast sandwiches over the flames. Afterward, if the weather was nice, there might be a touch football game outside or guys might head for the baseball diamond that Murphy's built at one end of the complex. Eventually, Murphy's warehouse fielded its own fast-pitch softball team, Backstrom says. "George Komer—who was a high-lift operator—was the pitcher, and I want to tell you, he could really pitch."

A little horseplay wasn't uncommon either. Komer, who weighed only 140 pounds, once hid inside an empty packing crate while stationery buyer Ralph Henry was in the building. When a warehouse employee told Henry that no one could figure out what was in the box, Henry announced confidently, "I'll find out," and stuck his hand inside. "George grabbed it," Backstrom remembers, "and Ralph liked to have died."

The carefree days didn't last. Along with thirteen of his classmates from West Newton High School, Backstrom joined the army air forces and wound up as a gunner on a B-24 bomber. Many of his co-workers were enlisting or being drafted as well. Paul Hindes began working at the Brentwood, Pennsylvania, store while still attending Carrick High School. A week after his graduation in 1943, he joined the navy. By then, 486 Murphy employees were in military service; within a year, the number would double, and in 1945 more than one thou-

FIG. 22
Labor shortages allowed women employees to take traditionally male jobs in the McKeesport distribution center during World War II. After the war, pay disparities between men and women eventually triggered a federal civil rights lawsuit against the G. C. Murphy Company and one of its unions.

sand were in uniform. Many Murphy men gave their lives as well, including seven in 1943, thirteen in 1944, and twenty-four in 1945 when the war in the Pacific reached its bloody climax.

They went with the company's blessing, vice president of sales Paul Sample told the *Washington Post*. He assured them "their jobs will be waiting for them on their return." The personnel office did its best to boost the spirits of Murphy employees with regular letters from home, gifts (including $5 money orders and subscriptions to *Reader's Digest*), and holiday cards. "According to the news we hear, the year won't be so old before you're back to hear us cheer because you've knocked the Axis cold," said one card sent to servicemen. "So carry on the Murphy Spirit, no matter where you are today, the spirit that will win you friends from Philly to Bombay. But until the fight is over, and you're back just let us say, 'A very merry Christmas, Pal, and a happier New Year's Day.'"

Men weren't the only ones leaving the G. C. Murphy Company. Murphy girls were deserting counters in droves. Some of them joined military services such as the Women's Army Corps or the navy's WAVES (Women Accepted for Volunteer Emergency Service), but many others took high-paying jobs in defense plants as factories short on manpower opened industrial jobs to women for the first time. Competition for female labor soon forced Murphy's to boost wages (adding $2.2 million in new payroll costs) and scrap its long-standing rule forbidding women store employees from marriage.

Those who stayed at Murphy's didn't let the war effort pass them by. Employees sold war bonds (more than $9 million in 1943 alone) and clerks created a novel and successful fund-raising campaign to purchase blood-donor vehicles and other supplies for the American Red Cross. It was the brainchild of Catherine McElhinny, a secretary in the home office, and several of her colleagues to set a goal of $10,000 and encourage women employees in all of the company's 207 stores and the New York office and Style Center to contribute their "dimes and dollars." When the final results came in four weeks later, ten thousand Murphy girls had collected $20,000, enough to purchase eleven vehicles, including ambulances and field canteens that were used by Red Cross chapters in Miami, Florida; Newport News, Virginia; Mobile, Alabama; and other cities. The trucks were delivered to the Red Cross's eastern regional director following a parade through McKeesport a few days before Christmas. "This gift is tangible evidence of the faculty of women for dreaming great dreams and seeing them come true," the director told the *Daily News*.

Among those in uniform was architect Crosby, who enlisted in the Army Corps of Engineers and was commissioned as a captain in the 343rd Engineer Regiment building bridges, landing strips, and roads as the Fifth Army chased the Nazis out of North Africa. On May 1, 1942, Edgar Mack's brother Paul, a building contractor from Indiana, Pennsylvania, took over Crosby's duties temporarily, vowing "to keep our stores in as good physical condition as possible." He kept crews busy washing and painting walls, but there wasn't much to buy in the stores anyway as staple items either disappeared or were replaced by ersatz imitations—stamped metal toys were replaced by wooden or cardboard versions, for instance. An April 20, 1942, letter from Shaw to store managers outlined some of the problems. Radio and phonograph manufacturing was ending in two days, he wrote, and vacuum cleaner production had "virtually ceased." No nylon stockings were available, and because cloth was being diverted to make uniforms, Murphy's could get only half the blankets, rugs, and bolts of fabric it usually sold. Goods that required silk (needed for parachutes and no longer available from Japan) and rubber (largely imported from Dutch colonies in the Pacific that were now under Japanese control) were virtually impossible to purchase. Even light bulbs were hard to get: With steel, bronze, and other metals going to war work, production was curtailed by 75 percent. Metal was banned from bedsprings, too. Shaw instructed stores to return any unsold typewriters by order of the War Department. Murphy's couldn't even get cellophane to wrap products, but he rallied employees to make the best of the situation: "We all want to do our part to help win this war."

When there was merchandise available, Murphy's had to be careful not to run afoul of price controls aimed at preventing stores from gouging consumers on scarce items. In late 1943, Murphy's and nine other chains, including J. C. Penney and Montgomery Ward, were accused by the federal Office of Price Administration (OPA) of violating regulations that capped the prices of women's dresses, coats, and suits at 1942 levels. With material costs going up, many manufacturers found themselves unable to make a profit selling to Murphy's and either dropped lines of inexpensive dresses or forced them to buy higher-priced versions. "The big retailer or chain that never carried higher-priced goods before is high and dry," *Time* magazine said. If a store's top price on dresses in 1942 was $5.98 and no dresses were being made in 1943 that could be sold at that price, OPA regulations effectively required the store to stop selling them altogether. Forced into federal court by Murphy's and its competitors, the OPA raised "ceiling prices" on some clothing lines while the War Production Board allocated more low-cost fabric to keep prices down.

Still, it was tough to keep stores filled with items to sell, and receiving deliveries of stock was as if "opening a surprise package," says Bill Anderson, who managed Store No. 15 in Elkins, West Virginia, and No. 33 in Wheeling during the war. (The new Wheeling store reused the number of the old McKeesport store.) "Sometimes you didn't know what you were selling until the warehouse truck arrived," says Anderson, who once received five hundred boxes of chocolate and marshmallow candy bars without warning. For a town starved of sweets, it was like manna from heaven: "I sold every damned one," he says. Sometimes a little fancy horse trading was needed to keep the shelves stocked, and chocolate figured into one of the best swaps Anderson ever made. Since most chocolate was going overseas for soldiers' rations, Murphy's could rarely get any. But Anderson learned that a nearby ice cream factory had more than it could use and was willing to sell some to him. However, Anderson knew if he let the home office find out, they'd take the chocolate from him and divvy it up among bigger locations. Finally, he hit on an idea. Anderson told the ice cream plant he'd be happy to take the chocolate if they sold some to the nearby Kresge five-and-ten, too. When the home office found out the Wheeling store had chocolate and complained, Anderson pointed out that he had to be able to compete with Kresge's.

Stockings were in heavy demand, but each Murphy's store got just a few each month, which Anderson held until he accumulated enough to stock a display. Then he'd put an ad in the paper. The next morning, women tired of painting seams on their legs to make it look as if they were wearing hose would line up on the sidewalk outside, and the small pile of stockings would be gone in less than a half-hour. Rationing and shortages meant that Murphy's was unable to stock counters systematically and couldn't even refuse poor-quality items. Paul Sample said in 1944: "We take as much as can be had of such merchandise that is available, and are very happy to get it." Bill Kraus, who worked as a stock boy at Store No. 12 in downtown Pittsburgh before he turned eighteen and joined the army air forces in 1944, remembers receiving bulk loads of strange sugar candy from Cuba and odd-looking brown soap packed in large bins. It was as good as the store could get in those days. During his two years of service, Kraus received two furloughs from the air forces—one for ten days and one for thirty days. Both times he came home to Pittsburgh and was put to work in the stockroom at Store No. 12 to the amusement of buddies who wanted to carouse during leaves.

"When I got back to the base, they were all laughing at me," Kraus says. "But working at No. 12 was fun for me, and besides, I didn't really know anyone else back home at the time."

Despite the trying conditions, many within the G. C. Murphy Company were preparing for the future—the sales division was planning a big new store in Richmond, Virginia, and work was underway to expand stores in Fort Wayne, Indiana, and Erie and York, Pennsylvania. But the optimism wasn't universal. Edgar Mack, reluctantly thrust into the chairmanship by the death of his cousin, urged a "go slow" policy, earning him a sharp rebuke from Shaw. "We have been known as an aggressive concern in the past," Shaw said. "We cannot continue to do nothing or practically nothing like we are today and still be known as an aggressive concern. . . . For us to stop dead in our operations is the [worst] thing that can happen to an organization. You begin to die of dry-rot, and no business can survive that stands still."

Murphy's did add a few locations during the war by buying existing five-and-tens, including a store in Oakmont, Pennsylvania, north of Pittsburgh, and Shaw urged the real estate division to lock up leases on other promising sites as soon as possible. "This war will not last forever, and certainly we don't want to stop dead," he said. Yet Shaw, as did most

FIG. 23
Fabric, metal, plastics, and other materials were diverted to war production in 1942, making consumer goods scarce long after hostilities ended. When Store No. 99 in Clinton, Ind., ran a small ad in the *Daily Clintonian* promoting "hard-to-get" items such as nylon stockings, customers began lining up before 9:00 A.M. on September 13, 1947. The day's sales were nearly $1,500, or three times the usual volume.

Americans, expected the war to drag on if a land invasion of Japan became necessary, and with the unconditional surrender of Germany in May 1945, all Allied military manpower and materiel shifted to the Pacific.

Only a handful of American scientists and officials knew the United States had built and perfected the two atomic bombs that were dropped on the Japanese cities of Hiroshima and Nagasaki in August. When a rumor spread on August 13 that Japan had surrendered, pandemonium erupted. In McKeesport, locomotive and factory whistles shrieked, scrap paper fluttered from windows, traffic ground to a halt, and clerks from Murphy's home office poured into the street. News of the actual surrender was greeted with no less enthusiasm. Outside Store No. 166 in Washington, D.C., sailors, soldiers, marines, and civilians danced and sang, jamming F and G streets and stalling trolley cars in their tracks. In Wheeling, West Virginia, employees at Store No. 33 set up a table on the sidewalk to sell any left-over Halloween and New Year's Eve noisemakers they could find along with other items (including pots and pans) that could be banged or clanged in jubilation. There was bedlam outside Store No. 3 in Greensburg, Pennsylvania, where employees couldn't even open the front doors, so they watched through the windows as shoulder-to-shoulder crowds made their way down streets strewn with confetti. "Our town was a mess," says clerk Esther Weatherton. "I don't think anyone was in the store—they were all in the streets."

Airman Kraus was on leave in Pittsburgh when Japanese Emperor Hirohito ordered all forces to lay down their arms. He sent a wire to his commanding officer in Kearney, Nebraska: "YOU CAN SEE THE SUN IN SMOKY OLD PITTSBURGH FINALLY. CAN I HAVE MORE TIME?" Back came the answer like a rifle shot: "NO."

Kraus and other Murphy employees would be home for good soon enough and working for a revitalized G. C. Murphy Company under the leadership of Walter Shaw Sr., who was finally emerging from behind John Sephus Mack's imposing shadow. With his handpicked sales staff and a loyal right-hand man in Paul Sample, Shaw would reshape the G. C. Murphy Company. In the booming postwar economy, the sun was going to shine on Murphy's, too.

Meals AT MURPHY'S

CHAPTER 7

Today, we'd call the kind of meals served at G. C. Murphy Company's restaurants "comfort food." Savory casseroles, hot beef sandwiches with gravy, burgers and fries, banana splits, pies, cakes, and fresh coffee. But what about lobster tails?

No, it wasn't normal fare, but for a while you could indeed get a complete lobster dinner on Thursday nights at G. C. Murphy Store No. 165 in Harrisburg, Pennsylvania, says Ed Kinter, who managed the store's restaurant in the 1960s. "Of course, you must remember now, this was 1966," he says. "I think they were like $3.50 for two small lobster tails. It was a good deal, and we even got a nice write-up in the paper." Located in the heart of Pennsylvania Dutch country, nearly two hours from the nearest saltwater, Harrisburg would seem to be an unlikely place for fish lovers, but Murphy's in the Keystone State's capital "sold a lot of seafood," Kinter says. Perhaps it was because of all the legislators, lobbyists, and lawyers from eastern Pennsylvania who worked for the state government, but each week Murphy's in Harrisburg sold sixty pounds of crab meat and twelve to fifteen gallons of oysters, shipped in ice-packed wooden drums direct from Crisfield, Maryland's self-proclaimed "seafood capital."

"We'd feature three fried oysters with French fries, coleslaw, roll, and butter," Kinter says. "We also had a half-fry, which gave you three extra oysters on it. I don't remember what the price was now—probably $1.35."

At its height, the G. C. Murphy Company had 266 restaurants, cafeterias, snack bars, and lunch counters in its more than five hundred stores. When the company was taken over by Ames in 1985, chain restaurants were cutting into Murphy's food-service business, yet the remaining 126 Murphy restaurants collectively turned a $202,000 profit in their last full year of operation. Most of the fare sold at Murphy's was prosaic—the ubiquitous burgers, hot sandwiches, and casseroles—but it was some of the first "fast food" that many diners ever tasted. Before the McDonald brothers opened a hamburger stand in California, before Dave Thomas had a daughter named Wendy, and before gas-station owner and fried-chicken cook Harland Sanders was named an honorary Kentucky colonel, Murphy's food-service operations could wait on a customer, serve the meal, and have the check ready in less than ten minutes. That left satisfied, happy diners with plenty of their lunch hours available to shop in the store, of course.

Various Murphy histories indicate that the first restaurant opened in 1931, but Store No. 1 in McKeesport began serving food as early as 1927, when Lena Togyer began working at the small lunch counter at Store No. 1 in McKeesport. "I was about seventeen years old—and it wasn't my first job," she says. "I worked in the YMCA cafeteria when I was sixteen, maybe for a year and a half. The Murphy men used to come there to eat, and one of them asked me if I wanted to come to work for Murphy's." For a short period of time, she sold stationery and candy, but because of her YMCA experience she was moved to the small lunch counter, which employed three waitresses and a cook. One suspects that the lunch counter in McKeesport was opened as much as a convenience for home office employees as it was for customers because Murphy management became some of the steadiest patrons. "J. S. Mack always called me 'handsome,' and when he'd buy a Coke from me, he'd always try to grab my hand," Togyer says. "I'd drop it in his hand and pull my hand back, and he'd laugh like heck. He didn't mean anything by it. Walter Shaw was a nice man—friendly. Some were friendly, some weren't."

Food at the first Murphy lunch counter was simple: hamburgers, salads, creamed chicken, Salisbury steak. "Sometimes we had a special on a [roast] chicken dinner for 35¢," Togyer says. "Chicken, stuffing, mashed potato, a vegetable, and a piece of toast for 35¢—boy, we were rushed when we had that." The counter opened at 8:00 A.M., before the store, and breakfast was a busy time. The waitresses doubled as cooks, frying bacon and eggs on electric hot plates as they took orders. Workers from nearby offices waited three deep at the counter for seats, and a few quickly became regulars. The owner of a McKeesport department store had a bad stomach and placed the same special order each morning. "You had to make him two pieces of toast, put hot water on it, sprinkle it with sugar, and put two eggs in the water and poach them," Togyer says. "That's what he ate every day." A woman

FIG. 24
One of the company's busiest lunch counters was at Store No. 12 in downtown Pittsburgh, where employees remember seeing people waiting three deep at the counter for seats. In this 1955 scene, customers crowd the aisles to purchase submarine sandwiches for 20¢ cents, about $1.55 in 2007 dollars.

who worked in the city attorney's office came daily for lunch and always ordered a salad and toast. "I'd try to make it a little bit different for her every day," Togyer says. "She also got two pieces of toast for a nickel, but she'd only eat one—she'd save the other one for the next day."

The restaurants were originally a "loss leader" for Murphy's to draw traffic into the stores, Kinter says. The monster of the variety-store industry, F. W. Woolworth Company, started opening "refreshment rooms" in 1910 as an enticement to shoppers. But the arrival of restaurants in Woolworth's, Murphy's, Kresge's, and the other five-and-tens also was a godsend for many small towns since getting an inexpensive meal in a restaurant could be a dicey proposition in the early twentieth century. Bars and taverns served cheap food, but they didn't admit children and respectable adults were loath to enter them. Hole-in-the-wall "luncheonettes" or "lunch wagons" were available, but there were no guarantees as to the quality of the food or the sanitation in the kitchens—they weren't called "greasy spoons" for nothing.

Not until 1921 when two entrepreneurs in Wichita, Kansas, made consistency and cleanliness selling points for their hamburger restaurant, which they called "White Castle," and offered franchises to businessmen in other cities, did the modern concept of "fast-food"

FIG. 25
Waitresses at Store No.
166 in Washington, D.C.,
get ready for the morn-
ing rush in 1937. Restau-
rants in G. C. Murphy
Company stores were
originally intended as
loss leaders to attract
customers. The demand
for inexpensive break-
fasts and lunches soon
made the food-service
operations attractions of
their own.

chains appear. The idea, though much copied, took time to catch on—fast-food chains
didn't became a juggernaut in the restaurant business until the 1960s. In the meantime,
until the day when nearly every town had a McDonald's, nearly every town between Pittsburgh and Baltimore had Murphy's five-and-tens, which had developed reputations for offering quality, low-cost merchandise. Why couldn't they offer quality, low-cost meals, too?

Perhaps to combat the "greasy spoon" image, Murphy's took great pains to empha-
size that it offered wholesome food made from first-quality ingredients, printing a lengthy
manifesto right on the front of a menu in 1934:

> Murphy Company "serves only the best." This is not a "catch" phrase, but
> an actual statement of our high standard of food quality. Our policy is to
> serve you with the best foods available at the lowest possible price. . . . In

the restaurant, as in all other departments of the store, our slogan is "Not how much we can get, but how much we can give." The low prices on our menu do not indicate low quality. Quality is never sacrificed for price. . . . All food is prepared in our spotlessly clean, modern, sanitary kitchens by expert cooks, under the personal supervision of the restaurant manager, who is specially trained and qualified to hold to the high Murphy Standard.

Waitresses and busboys were expected to uphold "the high Murphy Standard," too. A 1940s handbook for restaurant employees called *Eating at Murphy's* cautions that the correct greeting for customers is "May I serve you, please?" and not "Can I wait on you," "What's yours," "What'll you have," or "What's it gonna be?" "Say it with a *smile*," the book says. "Not a grin, grimace, or smirk, but *a real smile*. . . . The customer is doing us a favor by eating with us. We are not doing customers a favor by waiting on them." Before waiting on a diner, waitresses were to remove old dishes, wipe the counter, hand the customer a menu, and serve a glass of water. "Be sure the glass is wet on the inside only," the manual cautions. Another chapter of the handbook admonishes cooks to forget "kitchen tricks and short cuts. Our aim is to serve food that tastes as near like home-cooked food as possible." Waitresses were authorized to refuse any plate from the cooks that was drippy, running over, or otherwise unappetizing.

Upholding those spotlessly clean and wholesome standards was expensive, and as the price of restaurant equipment accelerated, Murphy management decided the company had better start making money on the food-service division. An executive named Russ Jennings from Cleveland's Stouffer restaurant chain was recruited to head the effort, which operated in a parallel universe to Murphy's retail stores. The restaurants received separate store numbers, managers, and personnel and were expected to make a profit on their operations. Usually, Murphy stores and restaurants operated smoothly together, as two cogs in a well-oiled machine, but there were turf wars and tensions at times. "The [sales] executives didn't want the restaurants to raise prices," says Ellison "Al" Boggs, who started in the restaurant division in 1940 and spent nearly twenty years as its head until his retirement in 1984. "If the stores wanted to raise prices, they raised prices, but the restaurants couldn't. I remember when we went from nickel coffee to 7¢ coffee. First, all of the executives in the company had to approve it, and then we had to give a second cup if someone asked for it. So what good did it do us to raise prices?"

With some store personnel, the idea that the restaurants were loss leaders persisted into the 1960s and '70s. "That's why you always put the restaurant at the back," Kinter says. "You brought [customers] in past the merchandise and they walked out past the merchandise." But Boggs, knowing that the restaurants had to succeed on their own merits, "pushed for a long time" to get them moved to the front of the store: "My argument was that people were not going to go past Pizza Hut and McDonald's and Burger King to get to Murphy's."

Some Murphy's restaurants did have their own customers who came to eat, specifically in downtown, urban locations. Restaurants located in some Murphy's Marts, particularly in rural Appalachia, also developed separate customers from the stores—Boggs cites Ashland, Kentucky, Mart No. 828 as an example. "But in general, I can't say that our food service really drew people in," he says. "They were there to serve the people in the store." If a customer is shopping and gets hungry, "they're going to leave, and they're never going to come back," Kinter says. "If you entice them to stay and they eat in the store, they're refreshed and they'll do more shopping."

Most Murphy restaurants were set up similar to the classic diners or soda fountains of the 1940s and '50s. Customers sat on twenty or thirty leather- or vinyl-topped stools along Formica counters with chrome or aluminum trim. Larger stores usually had a few booths as well. The waitresses patrolled behind the counter, keeping the coffee fresh, warming up soups in electric plug-in kettles, and preparing many items, especially ice cream treats and other desserts, on the spot in full view of the customers.

Little was left to chance as Murphy's made portion control an exact science. A 15¢ sundae, for instance, came in a tulip-shaped glass dish with "two No. 30 scoops" (about two ounces total) of ice cream and one spoonful of topping. Triple-decker sandwiches got three slices of bread evenly spread with butter, two leaves of lettuce, and two layers of cold cuts or other sandwich fillings. Waitresses were then to cut them diagonally "from corner to corner, making four pieces," spear each quarter with a toothpick, and stand them up on edge, with a scoop of salad or coleslaw in the center of the plate. More complicated meals were prepared by short-order cooks like George Smillie, who worked in sixteen Murphy's restaurants during his twenty-two-year career with the company, starting in Store No. 3 in Greensburg, Pennsylvania, in September 1973 fresh out of high school. As a county seat, Greensburg had a thriving downtown business district. "The courthouse helped us quite a bit—people who had to come to court, people who were having cases tried," he says. The breakfast rush started at 8:30 and didn't slack off until 10:00, and employees had just enough time to catch their breath and clean before the lunch rush started at 11:00. Smillie started his day at 7:30 A.M. making twelve to fifteen dozen submarine sandwiches, or "hoagies." There was only one variety (cold cuts, sold for 79¢), but it "truly kept me busy," he says. "It was basically all carry-out. In downtown Greensburg, it was so 'rush-rush-rush.' They wanted something quick and fast, but they wanted something good." The meat, bought fresh from a local butcher, included bologna, salami, and the Pittsburgh-area specialty known as "chipped ham" (pressed meat sliced paper thin). On top of that, Smillie added lettuce, tomato, and thin ribbons of American cheese. "When customers came up, we'd squirt on Italian dressing or mayo, or serve them plain," he says.

Lunchmeat wasn't the only sandwich filling bought fresh and local—so was ground beef for hamburgers. "We never had frozen patties," says Smillie, adding with pride, "the Greensburg Murphy's was known for its hamburgers." Everything was prepared "right in front of the customers' eyes—if you ordered a hamburger, they put the hamburger right on the grill there." Burgers were a perennial favorite at all G. C. Murphy restaurants, and the biggest sellers were "Murphyburger platters," Boggs says. "You got a quarter-pound hamburger with lettuce and tomato and French fries and coleslaw. It was probably $1.09, $1.19 in 1957. When I retired in '84 it was probably $2.49." Breakfasts were another strong feature at Murphy's restaurants, including the "1-1-1"—one slice of toast, one strip of bacon, and one egg—originally priced at 29¢. In the mid-1980s, a Murphy 1-1-1 still cost less than a dollar (just barely) at 97¢.

While official menus were printed at the home office, restaurant managers were allowed to create special features that changed daily and were inserted on mimeographed sheets. Some specials were simple—for example, at Greensburg, George Smillie invented one called the "Smillieburger," with lightly fried chipped ham and cheese—but most were stews, roasts, and casseroles that could be kept warm on a steam table. "If they had a recipe that their grandmother used that they wanted to try, we would let them try it," Boggs says. "They could put anything on that insert they wanted as long as it was food. We gave our local manager the permission to do his or her own thing."

Some Murphy restaurants sampled regional cuisine as well. When the company began opening stores in Texas, "we included some Mexican items on the menu," Kinter says. "Burritos, tacos, enchiladas. It was the first time I had seen them—I wasn't familiar with that stuff at all." Murphy stores in the South also were more likely to have a cafeteria instead of a sit-down restaurant. "Cafeteria units really went better in the South," Boggs says. "In Texas, we tried 'all you could eat' for 99¢ in several stores—we still had that in several units when I retired. Another big thing down South was catfish—all the catfish you can eat for a price. People would stand out in the parking lots waiting to get in."

Still, Kinter, who helped open Murphy's first store in Fort Worth, Texas, in 1962, says it took a while for Murphy's northern managers to learn the local customs. "They wanted us to run the standard menu, and that was the first problem I ran into," he says. "A man ordered a hamburger, and lettuce and tomato were 5¢ extra. He said, 'Extra! A hamburger's not a hamburger unless it has lettuce and tomato!' In Texas, a hamburger came with lettuce and tomato. The second thing was fish—we were using precut, formed fish. People complained: 'Fish isn't square.'" Within two months, Murphy's corporate menu had separate prices and items for Texas.

The Fort Worth store opened with a six-foot-long snack bar, six booths, and a thirty-three-seat counter, but not all Murphy restaurants were such simple affairs. One of the grandest restaurants, naturally, was in Murphy's headquarters city of McKeesport at Store No. 33, which eventually merged with the old Store No. 1 and took its number. The restaurant opened in

September 1935 as a fairly mundane affair, with lunch counters on both the first floor and in the basement, but it was heavily damaged when fire swept the building during World War II. Wartime rationing meant that restaurant and construction supplies were scarce, and Murphy's might not have been able to rebuild if local defense plants hadn't needed someplace for their employees to eat lunch. When the store reopened in 1944, a lunch counter remained on the first floor to serve snacks and "short-order" meals, but the basement restaurant was relocated to the second floor. Accessed via a tall, narrow staircase between Murphy's and the adjoining J. C. Penney store, it's still remembered fondly by employees and McKeesporters for the elegant decoration it received during a 1949 remodeling. "At one time, it was the premium eating place between Greensburg and downtown Pittsburgh," Kinter says. Customers could choose their meals in a cafeteria line or order from a menu in the five-hundred-seat dining room; an adjoining private suite seated another forty guests. Into the 1970s, some of the region's most important banquets and receptions were hosted at Murphy's restaurant, when guests could dine on broiled black Angus steak at $3.30 per person, prime rib for $3.00, or filet mignon for $3.55.

The daily menu was typical American cuisine such as hot sandwich platters, soups, and pasta dishes. Diners were often lined up for seats. "They served a lot of meals," remembers Lloyd "Del" Davis, who for many years worked for McKeesport real estate broker T. J. Lewis, husband of G. C. Murphy Company director Martha Mack Lewis. "There was always very courteous service, and the food was good." The steadiest customers were from the nearby Murphy home office—executives, managers, and even secretaries had regular tables, and woe betide any newcomer who unwittingly sat in one of those hallowed seats. But many other local employers also had regular tables. "From Kelsey-Hayes [a wheel manufacturer] we knew were going to get ten or twelve people every day, so we'd set up a table for them," says Boggs, who managed the restaurant for a time. "Payday at Kelsey-Hayes was one of our busiest days." Two tables were set each day for the "Three-C Club" and the "Three-M Club," he says. The former comprised bankers and financial people (the "Cs" were "crabbing, credit, and corruption"), while the latter were attorneys ("Murphy's Midday Moochers").

At its height, the McKeesport operation had forty-five full-time employees, including two bakers, and averaged $5,000 in weekly sales during the 1940s, Boggs says. "Remember, these were the 'nickel coffee' days. And during Christmas we did double that." The crowds in McKeesport thinned in the 1960s; by 1969, the restaurant was no longer making a profit. The self-service cafeteria line closed in the mid-1970s and the space was converted into offices. The remainder of the dining room hung on for a few more years before closing for good on February, 28, 1980.

The restaurant at Store No. 103 in Fort Wayne, Indiana, lacked the elaborate banquet facilities of McKeesport but offered another distinction—Murphy's only full-service, in-house bakery. "We had a complete doughnut shop with two automatic doughnut machines right up in the front window," says Kinter, who managed the Fort Wayne restaurant in the 1970s. "We made pies, four or five different kinds of bread, fourteen kinds of sweet rolls,

seven kinds of cookies—and also party cookies, about fourteen varieties of those. We had three different types of rolls. We made all kinds of cakes, up to $75 wedding cakes." The main restaurant in Fort Wayne seated more than 128 people and featured a one-hundred-foot-long snack bar and a delicatessen. Another busy Murphy's restaurant was located in the store on Indianapolis's Lafayette Square. As did the Fort Wayne operation, it featured a complete deli, but it also sported a conveyor belt that allowed waitresses to automatically send dirty dishes back to the kitchen. "It broke down the day it opened, and they never did get the damned thing working right," Kinter says.

At the other end of the spectrum was the restaurant at the G. C. Murphy store in Montgomery, West Virginia, now home to West Virginia University Institute of Technology but then a sleepy railroad town of 3,400 people. Kinter was there from 1953 to 1957. Hurting for business in such a tiny community, he began a catering service. "I catered dinners at the country club out of a Murphy's store," Kinter says, laughing. "I catered the Elks club, the Civitan club."

Through the 1960s, most downtown Murphy variety stores closed with the rest of the business districts in which they were located—typically 5:00 P.M. That meant the restaurants

FIG. 26
G. C. Murphy Company restaurants ranged from the elaborate banquet facilities at Store No. 1 in McKeesport, Pa., to straight-line lunch counters, such as this one at Store No. 197 on High Street in Morgantown, W.Va.

FIG. 27
By the 1970s, the development of fast-food chains such as McDonald's and Pizza Hut made it hard for Murphy restaurants to compete. Although Murphy's Mart No. 901 on Liberty Road in Randallstown, Md., featured a snack bar near the checkout counters, some of the company's new discount stores didn't have food service at all.

did a strong trade at breakfast and lunch but little or nothing for dinner. But Murphy's Marts, which began opening in 1970, were located exclusively in suburban areas and stayed open until 9:00 or 10:00 P.M. That forced the restaurants to think more in terms of larger, evening meals and to cater to families as never before.

"It was a completely different concept," says Smillie, whose first Murphy's Mart restaurant was at Store No. 807 in North Huntingdon, Pennsylvania, between Greensburg and Pittsburgh. Instead of waitresses taking orders at the counter, meals were served from steam tables, with busboys (and girls) walking around the dining room refilling drinks and taking dessert orders. "You were to make sure that [customers] never had to get up a second time," Smillie says. "If someone wanted a piece of pie, you were to get up and get them a piece of pie." Thursday nights became "family night," with two complete meals—veal cutlet, meat loaf, baked chicken, ham steak—for one price. Fridays meant "all-you-can-eat fish," with girls carrying hot pans full of fish filets around the tables to make sure "everyone got their fill," Smillie says. "On any normal Friday, you sold eighty to one hundred [fish] dinners, but during Lent, you sold 150-plus on a good Friday night." Saturday was "all-you-can-eat spaghetti day" in Murphy's Marts.

The company's shifting focus in the 1970s from downtown variety stores to suburban Murphy's Marts was symbolic of a serious problem facing the restaurant division. "We'd be building a new store out in the shopping center, and before we got our store opened there'd be a Pizza Hut or a McDonald's sitting on the corner," Boggs says. When the company was planning a new Murphy's Mart in Boardman, Ohio, outside Youngstown, he made a survey of the area and found nineteen restaurants at the same intersection where the store was going to be built. "We didn't put food in that location—it didn't make sense," Boggs says. Kinter was in Harrisburg when that city got its first McDonald's. "Their hamburgers were 15¢, and ours were a quarter, I'm guessing," he says. "We used to joke that McDonald's sold forty million hamburgers, and then they killed the second cow." But McDonald's national television advertising and lower prices—even if the burgers were smaller—put Murphy's at a competitive disadvantage. "Of course, our [sales] people started hollering for 15¢ hamburgers: 'How come McDonald's can do it and Murphy's can't do it?' Well, because we can't!" Boggs says. Many of Murphy's restaurant employees had spent five, ten, or twenty years with the company and were making more money than the part-time help the fast-food chains employed. Murphy's was often paying higher rent as well.

The G. C. Murphy Company almost entered the fast-food business on at least one occasion. A regional hamburger chain called "Winky's" had a location in the parking lot of Murphy's Mart No. 802 in Bethel Park, Pennsylvania, a Pittsburgh suburb. When Winky's folded, the restaurant division tried to get Murphy's to take over the lease. "The company wouldn't let us," Kinter says. "We would have made a fast-food [operation] out of it. We could have done a lot of things in the food division, but we were always a little bit of a stepchild."

On the other hand, some of Murphy's most successful restaurants were located inside enclosed malls. The Monroeville Mall restaurant "was one of the best restaurants we ever opened," Boggs says. "It started making money from the day we opened and it never stopped." The restaurant actually opened before the mall was complete to feed employees of other stores and train new Murphy personnel. When the store was thoroughly remodeled in the early 1980s, the front of the restaurant was set up to emulate a mall food court, with different snack bar counters offering hot pretzels, popcorn, hot dogs, pizza, ice cream, and cotton candy. "The snack bar did more in sales than the restaurant did," Kinter says, "but oh boy, did I have to fight to get that thing in—no one wanted to spend any money."

After the G. C. Murphy Company was taken over in 1985, the restaurant division was divided between the marts, which Ames Department Stores kept, and the variety store division, which was spun off to the McCrory Corporation in 1989. Neither Ames nor McCrory expressed much interest in keeping the food operations, and former Murphy restaurant managers were soon closing several restaurants a month. Ironically, some of the restaurants were the only operations keeping their associated stores in the black. "We had a store in Indianapolis where our restaurant was carrying the store for ten years," Boggs says. "Fort

Wayne was the same way." Restaurants inside a retail store are probably passé now, he admits. "Notice Wal-Mart today puts McDonald's in the store. They don't have a food division. People don't come into a variety store to eat." But for generations of Americans who grabbed a Murphy 1-1-1 breakfast on their way to work, stopped in for a Murphyburger at lunchtime, or enjoyed an ice cream sundae with their sweetie after a Saturday movie, memories of G. C. Murphy restaurants will never go out of style.

Boggs has no regrets: "In fact, it's really the only job I had in my life—forty-five years. People couldn't believe that. A lot of salesmen would look at me and ask about that." And Smillie put his experience to work by opening a restaurant of his own outside Mount Pleasant, Pennsylvania, where he's still serving up some of the same features he first made at the G. C. Murphy store in Greensburg, Pennsylvania, more than thirty years ago. "A lot of the things I do today, I learned at Murphy's," he says.

Murphy Tastes, Sounds, and Smells

From 1958 to 1964, my mother and I were regulars at the Murphy lunch counter in the downtown McKeesport store every Saturday morning following my ballet lesson. The waitresses had pretty uniforms with their name tags prominent. Some of them had beautiful handkerchiefs arranged in the breast pocket.

I usually ate a hot dog right from the rolling grill. The fries were outstanding as well. Occasionally, we had lunch upstairs—it was a bit more formal—but the counter with the word "luncheonette" above its wall-length mirror was my favorite place.

One day near Easter, I wandered past the peeps as my mom was shopping farther down the aisle. It turned out they were free that day, as long as there was an adult present. The pet clerk knew me and mom from all the other visits, so she packaged up the peep and I carried it to where mom was. Needless to say, it chirped all the way home on the streetcar!

—Cynthia Corey
West Mifflin, Pa.

As a kid in the 1960s and '70s I shopped (and cut through) Murphy's in the Manoa Shopping Center in Havertown, Pennsylvania, nearly every day of my life. On my way home from school I would park my bike in the rack and stop and buy a bag of popcorn in a long paper bag. It was almost impossible to be in that store and not buy a bag due to the smell of freshly popped corn wafting through the entire place. Many lunches and milkshakes were eaten by me, my family, and my friends at the luncheonette that operated in the store. It was also where I bought my first 45-rpm record!

I live in the Chicago suburbs now but I still pass that shopping center when I am in Pennsylvania on business and I always remember the old Murphy's store fondly.

—Jack Taddeo
Park Ridge, Ill.

My mother was an Orthodox Jew, so I had never tasted a "gentile" hot dog until I got my first one at Murphy's, and I think I liked them better because they were "forbidden fruit"! It cost me 5¢, and I made it a ritual every week. I can almost taste them now, including the steamed buns!

—Arthur N. Rupe
Founder of Specialty Records and
President of the Arthur N. Rupe Foundation
Santa Barbara, Calif.

I grew up in Beckley, West Virginia, in the 1960s, and Murphy's was the first "big" store I remember. My father and I would go downtown and somehow always end up in Murphy's. The smell of popcorn and sweeping compound (it was red and sprinkled on the floors to help collect dirt) always greeted you at the front entrance.

There was a large lunch counter and that is where my first love affair started. Fried oysters! I begged dad to take me downtown so we could stop there and I'd order a big plate of the greasy, steaming things. With a Coke and lots of ketchup for the fries, life didn't get much better.

In '76, I was graduating high school and had my own car. Several malls were open and there was a large Murphy's Mart as an anchor at one of them. The downtown location had closed along with everything else, so the "gang" would pile into our cars and meet at "The Mart."

There was a Murphy's Mart jingle on the local radio station for a short time that was sung to the tune of "bad, bad Leroy Brown, baddest man in the whole damn town." The station changed the words to "the biggest store in the whole damn town." Boy! What an uprising! It wasn't long before the local "holier than thou" crowd created such friction that the radio station changed the jingle to "darn" town.

I miss the days of the five-and-ten. Now it's a trek to find parking at a Super Wal-Mart and walk up and down aisles to find two items, stand in line to pay, and then remember where you parked. Life with the fried oysters was much simpler and better!

—Rick Woodrum
Redmond, Wash.

My very favorite thing to do at G. C. Murphy's in Tarentum, Pennsylvania, was to go to the peanut counter, and if I was lucky, I could talk my mom or dad into buying me some of those peanuts that were kept warm in the display case. My favorite was Spanish peanuts—you could get so much more due to the fact that they cost less than the other types of nuts, and a 10¢ bag of them was huge. I can close my eyes right now and see that counter and smell those hot Spanish peanuts as if I were there today. If I were not so committed to my diet I would rush out right now and buy some Spanish peanuts, heat them up, and eat them with my eyes closed to make my stroll down memory lane complete.

I also remember the sound of walking on the wooden plank floors—and the store in Tarentum had an upstairs and downstairs. Because toys were downstairs, I made an untold number of trips up and down those stairs. Heck, as kids, we just liked going up and down those stairs for fun—usually with mom in hot pursuit, trying to get us to stop and stand still (with little success, of course).

My mom used to go almost every day to the lunch counter to have coffee and occasionally lunch, but mostly she went there to socialize with other moms.

Our doctor and dentist were right next door to Murphy's, and any time my brother or sisters or I had a tough visit, we were taken to G. C. Murphy for a toy or treat to help ease our pain. Hey, mom . . . more hot Spanish peanuts for me, please!

—Michael Warriner
Plano, Texas

I grew up in McKeesport, Pennsylvania, during the 1950s and '60s and remember Murphy's during the late '50s when I was working at Cox's Department Store. It's hard to forget the delicious grilled pecan rolls at Murphy's takeout counter that I couldn't do without in the morning—you could smell that nutty buttered aroma outside. I remember Jean, who worked at the take out counter, which opened early to accommodate other people who could not begin their day without a pecan roll and a hot cup of coffee. (I haven't had grilled pecan rolls like those since.) I remember Betty, who also worked at the counter, and see her from time to time. She hasn't changed much. Still very assertive and sassy—she was one of my favorites there. Those ham barbecue sandwiches on buttery toasted buns with relish made your mouth water while you waited.

I can also remember wooden chairs lined up around the stairs going to the basement where weary shoppers could relax. All of these were great memories.

There is also one negative memory that stayed with me. During the '50s, blacks were not welcome to dine in the upstairs dining room. This changed in the coming years, but I can remember asking my parents why we could not eat up there, when my friends who were white could. It was a sign of the times, I guess.

—Yvonne Urquhart
Pittsburgh, Pa.

John Sephus Mack would be forever admired by old Murphy hands and residents of McKeesport and Indiana alike for his hard work, vision, and philanthropy. Yet, outside his family, few would have described him as "beloved"—and it seems likely that the taciturn, no-nonsense businessman would have wanted it that way. "My grandfather was not a nice guy," his grandson, Sephus Mack, says. "I can say that. But he was brilliant."

With Mack's death, the management style at the G. C. Murphy Company changed radically. Technically, Seph Mack's cousin Edgar was chairman of the board, but "E. M." was in poor health and died in 1946 at age sixty-eight, just a few months before his planned retirement. The resulting power vacuum was filled by Murphy president Walter Shaw Sr. Racing around Murphy territory in his Cadillac sedan, Shaw seemed to be everywhere at once—dropping into Murphy stores unannounced, asking questions, and giving managers a tongue-lashing.

One morning Shaw popped into Store No. 4 in New Kensington, Pennsylvania, but the manager, Bucky Moore, was nowhere to be found.

He decided to wait. A half-hour later, as Moore entered the store, Shaw was on his feet, demanding to know where he'd been. "I got a haircut," Moore replied.

"Don't tell me you got a haircut on company time!" Shaw said.

"Sure, it grew on company time," Moore said. That was an old joke and Shaw was ready for it: "It didn't all grow on company time!"

But Moore had a response ready, too: "I didn't get it all cut off," he said.

Emery Fannin of the construction division was supervising the installation of a new air conditioner at Store No. 431 in Bucyrus, Ohio, one morning when Shaw walked in. The store manager had gone home to eat, which sounded like a fine idea to Shaw, who asked Fannin, "Where do you like to go to lunch?"

"There's a little hotel around the corner with a pretty nice restaurant," Fannin replied, with visions of a free meal dancing in his head. When the checks came, however, Shaw picked up his and left Fannin's sitting on the table. "You're on expenses, you can pay your own," Shaw retorted.

"Boy, I thought he could spend a buck and a half," Fannin remembered years later.

Shaw's grandniece Dorothy Sample Hill says the man she knew as "Uncle Walter" always "had a kind of a twinkle in his eye. He was a tough old guy, sure . . . but he was a grand great-uncle to have around. I always felt like he had the old Nick in him. He had a playful side, like my dad did." And in her father, Murphy vice president of sales Paul Sample, Shaw also had a strong and skilled ally who had literally come of age in the variety-store business. When Edgar Mack died, Murphy's board of directors elevated Shaw to the chairmanship and his nephew Sample to the presidency. Together they transformed the G. C. Murphy Company from a regional dime-store operator into a retail chain capable of serving the greatest consumer market the world had ever known—the American postwar baby boom.

Sample had big plans for Murphy's after the war—replacing small stores with larger operations, adding display area, increasing promotion and advertising, and introducing more higher-priced merchandise. For the first few years, however, Murphy's was selling anything it could get. Four years of rationing had driven the public into a buying frenzy, and through 1946 the newspapers reported so-called "nylon riots" as women tried to purchase stockings. When Store No. 123 in Indianapolis received three hundred pairs of nylon hose, women began lining up more than two hours before the doors opened. Men showed no more restraint. "Dress shirts, undershirts, shorts, and all types of underwear are quite scarce," the home office counseled Murphy employees still in uniform. "Civilian suits and topcoats are almost impossible to get in some towns. . . . If you intend to leave the service soon and happen to see civilian clothes to your liking, you should buy them and send them home." Hoarding became common and government inspectors worked fruitlessly to stop the black market from selling merchandise outside legal channels. Not until 1949 could Shaw and Sample report that wholesale prices were declining as "the buying public has become more

FIG. 28
Customers line up outside brand-new Store No. 214 in Arlington, Va., in 1950. Aggressive promotions and a first-class training program made G. C. Murphy Company the variety-store chain to beat in the 1950s. Though it had fewer outlets than Woolworth, Murphy's per-store sales average was two to three times that of the larger firm.

conservative in its shopping habits." In the meantime, although Murphy's added only three stores between 1944 and 1950, sales increased 41 percent to $136 million.

As had the Mack-Shaw partnership of 1911, the Shaw-Sample pairing worked well because the two had different but complementary personalities. Shaw was quick with a quip and never shy about sharing his opinion—or stirring up trouble. Because the Samples had forbidden their daughters to chew gum, Walter Shaw always made sure he had some in his pockets to give to his grandnieces. "I think he did it just to bedevil us," Dorothy Sample Hill says.

Just as Mack had been, Shaw was a political conservative and fired off letters about the Communist menace to President Eisenhower, Vice President Nixon, and other figures of national importance—and received responses. Store managers were also queried by Shaw, who wrote out detailed instructions with stubby double-ended red and blue pencils he carried in his pockets, and he usually knew the answers before he asked any questions. Since before the Depression, most Murphy stores had chairs where customers could just sit and talk—even noncustomers were welcome to "meet their friends at Murphy's." "You had steady customers who were in that store every day, without fail," says Fred Speidel, who started with Murphy's in 1952. "I was in a store in Wilmington, Ohio, when Mr. Shaw came in, and he didn't come to the manager first—he went up there and sat with all of those old people before he came back. Those old people told him what was good and what was bad about the store." And Shaw could still greet many longtime Murphy clerks by name, even if he hadn't visited their store for several years. Bill Kraus was an assistant manager in Store No. 1 in McKeesport, a few blocks from the home office, when Shaw visited one afternoon and decided he wanted the dress racks moved. Taking some cleats and a hammer from the hardware department, Shaw, then in his late sixties, rolled up his sleeves, got down on his knees, and began pounding the cleats into the floor to mark the spots where the racks were to be installed. "He finally looked up at me and said, 'What's wrong with this picture? Get down here and put these cleats in!'" Kraus says. "He also had a thing about framed pictures. The landscapes had to be hung with the landscapes and the portraits had to be hung with the portraits." If the pictures on sale were mixed up, Shaw would tug Kraus by his ear and drag him down the aisle, saying, "How many times do I have to tell you about this?"

By comparison, Sample practically snuck into Murphy stores on his own unannounced inspection tours. A Murphy girl would see a smiling, well-dressed gentleman approaching the counter. "May I help you?" she'd ask, only to be astonished when the man replied with a long string of gibberish and double-talk. Was it a mental patient? A foreigner? No, it was just Paul Sample testing a clerk's reaction to being confronted with a difficult customer.

Born in 1898 in Manteo, North Carolina, a tiny village on the Atlantic coast, Sample's father ran a general store until his death at age thirty-two; his wife, Mae (Shaw's sister), was left to raise the children alone. She moved the family to Elizabeth City, North Carolina, where she opened a millinery shop, and it fell to Paul and the other children to keep the household together. Despite his hectic childhood, which included many long hours at his mother's shop, Sample graduated from high school—an accomplishment in those days—and enrolled in what was then called Trinity College (present-day Duke University), paying his own way by operating a variety of enterprises (including a bookstore) and saving money to send home to his mother and sisters. Upon graduation in 1919, Sample went to McKeesport to ask his Uncle Walter for an executive position with the growing G. C. Murphy Company.

Shaw said no. Instead, he offered his nephew a lowly position as a stock boy. If young Paul applied himself, Shaw said, perhaps he could advance. Sample agreed to stay in McKeesport, writing his mother that, although he had left North Carolina, "rest assured that I will always take care of you." In later years, Sample claimed that Shaw's directive was the best thing that ever happened to him because his experience gave him insight into employees' problems: "I was there. I can relate."

As was Seph Mack, Sample was a religious man who was not averse to quoting "the Golden Rule"—Jesus' admonition to his followers to "do unto others as you would have them do unto you." He also became friendly with competitor James Cash Penney, who ran the J. C. Penney Company along the same principle; in fact, Penney's first shops had been called "Golden Rule Stores." After the Samples built a summer cottage at Chautauqua, New York, near the famed Chautauqua Institution, Penney came for a visit. Before his arrival, Helen Sample impressed upon her daughters that he was a great man who "taught the Golden Rule." By the time Penney arrived, little Becky Sample could only stare in awe: "In my mind, I thought that Mr. Penney had invented the Golden Rule."

Paul Sample's own principled approach to life shone through a dozen little incidents. Once, while very young and on a trip with her father to visit Murphy's stores, his daughter Tilda slipped a piece of merchandise into her coat. "What do you have in your pockets?" Paul Sample asked.

"My hands," she replied. Dad wasn't amused, and he was even less happy when she finally showed him the offending item.

"Well, we have to go back and talk to the manager," he said. Tilda Sample was "terrified," but her father insisted that she confess what she had done and apologize.

On the other hand, Sample could be a prankster and a rebel like his uncle when the mood struck him. Strict Methodists, the Samples didn't work on Sundays. But when Dorothy Sample desperately wanted to see a monster movie, her father snuck her down to McKeesport's Memorial Theater on the Sabbath, cautioning her not to tell her mother or sisters.

Though fond of sporting spats over his shoes, he also favored long, dark Packard sedans instead of flashier Cadillacs or Lincolns. The drab cars resembled hearses to his teen-aged daughters, and they hid on the floor when they passed their friends. Sample drove himself everywhere, often wearing a captain's hat—and sometimes people mistook him for the chauffeur.

"Whose car is this?" they'd ask.

"Paul Sample's," he'd reply.

"What is Mr. Sample like?" they'd ask.

"Oh, he's a great, great guy," Sample would reply.

Although Chautauqua was one place where Sample didn't take his work (he was, however, elected the Chautauqua Institution's president in 1953), the family cottage bore plenty of evidence that he knew where his nickels and dimes came from. When a Murphy's store near Chautauqua was remodeled, Sample had the old soda fountain installed in the cottage and he amused the children by playing "soda jerk" and making milkshakes and ice-cream cones. The house was renovated under the direction of Murphy architect Ralph Barlow. Unbeknownst to the Samples, Barlow commissioned custom window shutters, each decorated with a "V" and an "X"—the Roman numerals "five" and "ten." Installed as a surprise, the shutters delighted Paul Sample to no end.

Sample's humor and Shaw's gumption were needed in the early postwar years because the variety-store industry was struggling despite the booming consumer market. For one thing, five-and-tens were labor intensive at a time when payroll expenses were rapidly increasing. They also were located in downtown areas while the population was moving to suburban residential developments where supermarkets, chain drug stores, and branch locations of big department stores were selling many of the same products as variety stores. Even with U.S. prosperity "swelling beyond all belief," said *Forbes* magazine, "the five-and-ten store lost its franchise." *Business Week* reported that variety stores were rapidly losing market share and were "unable to keep pace with the increase in the nation's disposable income." Frankly, the five-and-ten format itself was becoming stale; its basic operation and appearance hadn't changed much since the turn of the century. Merchandise was still sold from the tops of heavy wooden counters with a clerk standing behind each to ring sales. Despite spending millions of dollars on renovations—$5 million in 1948 alone—and doubling the size of locations such as Store No. 103 in Fort Wayne, Indiana, and Store No. 175 in Erie, Pennsylvania, G. C. Murphy Company still had many small stores with wooden floors, tin ceilings, and no air conditioning. Cash registers rang a maximum purchase of $5. Ron Templeton, who started at Store No. 203 in Linton, Indiana, in 1952, says that if a customer bought more than $5, the sale was rung twice and recorded by hand on a special register tape. It was hardly an enticement for customers to make large purchases.

The Murphy attitude toward personnel was also becoming fusty and old fashioned, and some practices were downright discriminatory. As was the case with nearly all publicly traded corporations in the 1950s, the G. C. Murphy Company had no African American executives and only a few women (mainly as merchandise buyers). But fundamentalist John Sephus Mack had tacitly barred other groups from promotion as well—the manager of one store in northwest Pennsylvania was replaced because a district manager felt that having a Catholic in charge hurt sales. All management employees also were required to abstain

FIG. 29
Murphy's in-store graphics and signs were considered some of the best in the industry; most were produced by artists at the company's extensive sign shop, shown here in a Jan. 27, 1953 photo. The shop was located next to the McKeesport, Pa., distribution center.

from alcohol, even when they weren't at work. Ed Davis, who started working in the Sharon, Pennsylvania, store in the early 1950s before moving to the home office to work in public, employee, and labor relations, remembers finding files full of handwritten letters from prospective store managers promising to forsake "demon rum."

Other practices were just as intrusive or unenforceable. As a new assistant manager in the 1950s, nineteen-year-old Roy Fowler Jr. asked for a day off so that he could get married. "I won't allow it," his manager said. "You're too young." Fowler told the manager his parents had already approved the wedding and he was taking the day off regardless. His attitude was typical of a new breed of more assertive workers, many of whom spent time in the service during World War II or the Korean Conflict and were ready to fight for their independence on the job when they got back. Davis entered Westminster College in 1945 but was drafted during the fall semester. When he returned to campus a few years later, "the whole culture had changed," he says. "When I left, the freshmen had to wear dinks and bow down to upperclassmen and all of that. The veterans that were coming back were guys who were fighting on Guadalcanal, and they weren't about to put up with that bull." Changes thus came to the personnel handbook of the G. C. Murphy Company, albeit slowly.

Other things changed, too. In 1954, Murphy's became the first variety-store chain to advertise on television when it sponsored a daily fifteen-minute exercise program called "It's Fun to Reduce" on Pittsburgh's WDTV Channel 3. The achievement was a bigger coup than it sounds. As the city's only television station for several years, WDTV enjoyed a virtual monopoly on the nation's eighth-largest market (one estimate said that 94 percent of all televisions in the Pittsburgh area were tuned to Channel 3; the others were trying to watch signals from places such as Johnstown). And as one of only about one hundred licensed VHF television stations on the air (the Federal Communications Commission froze applications during the Korean War as it tried to decide whether to license color television), WDTV's signal was largely free of interference, meaning that it could be received across large portions of western Pennsylvania, the Ohio Valley, and northern West Virginia—the heart of Murphy's sales territory.

Viewers of *It's Fun to Reduce* snapped up more than 300,000 exercise booklets from G. C. Murphy stores, and host Margaret Firth, a former physical education teacher from Sewickley, Pennsylvania, was soon receiving a thousand fan letters per month. A companion record album went on sale at Murphy's as well, and a ratings service reported that *It's Fun to Reduce* even outdrew Arthur Godfrey's morning show. Radio was fading under video's steadily increasing glow, but Murphy's didn't ignore it either. One store manager remembers that WCVI in Connellsville, Pennsylvania, broadcast a daily newscast from the window of Store No. 201, while another recalls a game show called *Dialing for Dimes* sponsored by G. C. Murphy Company on McKeesport's WEDO.

Many of the new television sets were being installed in the suburbs where developers were rapidly erecting new housing plans. Murphy's followed them in 1951, opening its first shopping center locations in Brentwood, Pennsylvania, south of Pittsburgh; West Erie Plaza in Erie, Pennsylvania; and Indianola Shopping Center in Youngstown, Ohio. They sported light-colored plastic trim instead of the dark mahogany that characterized Murphy's old downtown locations and had tiled floors instead of wood, but a Murphy girl still staffed each counter. The biggest expansion yet of the G. C. Murphy Company came on October 30, 1951, when it purchased Morris 5 & 10 Cent to $1.00 Stores Inc. of Bluffton, Indiana, for 207,500 shares of stock, valued at more than $10 million. The seventy-one-store chain was founded in 1903 by a young clothing-store clerk named George S. Morris, who mortgaged his house to pay the rent on his first location in Bluffton.

Morris stores were located primarily in Illinois and Indiana—areas where Murphy's had long been competitive—but there was little overlap between the two companies. Morris and Murphy's competed head to head in only seven towns (five in Ohio, two in Indiana), and the purchase extended the McKeesport company's reach deep into southern Illinois and up to the lower peninsula of Michigan. But the Morris stores were much smaller than most Murphy locations, which is evident from their comparative sales: Murphy's averaged $741,000 per store in 1951, while Morris stores averaged about $202,000—the volume that Murphy's was handling thirteen years earlier during the Depression.

"They were little tiny stores—terrible," says Fannin, who was transferred to Bluffton in 1954 to help upgrade the Morris stores to Murphy standards. "None of them was air-conditioned. They didn't believe in maintenance. Everything was run down. They just milked them dry." He was particularly amused by the attitude of the former Morris personnel in

FIG. 30
Morris 5 & 10 Cent to
$1.00 Stores Inc., based
in Bluffton, Ind., had sev-
enty-one locations when
Murphy's purchased it
for $10 million in 1951.
Though Morris's stores
were smaller and less
modern than Murphy's,
the acquisition allowed
the G. C. Murphy Com-
pany to dominate the
variety-store business in
much of Indiana.

Bluffton. "The Morris people kept saying they 'merged' with the Murphy Company. They didn't merge. We bought 'em." Fannin spent five years in the four states that composed Morris territory, putting more than fifty thousand miles annually on his car while converting Morris stores and helping remodel older Murphy's stores. Still, the Morris stores were located in small towns—often they were the only variety store in a community of a few thousand people—and nicely fit G. C. Murphy Company's long-established strategy of bypassing big cities. Templeton, who wound up managing a former Morris location, Store No. 449 in Vandalia, Illinois, says many of them turned out to be "good profit stores" for Murphy's.

Absorbing the small, underperforming Morris locations sent the company's per-store sales down nearly $50,000 in 1951. But, by 1952, with only thirty-five of the seventy-one Morris stores remodeled to Murphy standards, the average was back up to $623,950 and overall sales were at $184 million. In April 1953, Sample noted that the Morris acquisition had an unexpected side benefit: A prolonged strike in the steel industry had depressed sales in Murphy's territory of western Pennsylvania and West Virginia, but the new stores in Illinois and Indiana were insulating the company from the brunt of the resulting recessionary conditions. The cost of improving the Morris stores drove earnings per share down to 24¢, but Sample expected the remaining locations to be remodeled by the end of the year.

It actually took until 1955 to rebrand all of the Morris locations, and Sample, sadly, wouldn't live to see it. He had long suffered from high blood pressure, and after a mild heart attack in 1952, his doctors warned him to slow down. Sample made a few concessions—he began taking the elevator rather than the stairs at the home office—but otherwise kept a full schedule, often traveling several days a week by car or train. On nice days, he walked to the office; otherwise he drove himself, going home for dinner at 6:00 P.M. and working into the night in his study. On Tuesday, December 8, 1953, Sample gave his secretary and another employee a ride home before heading home himself. Once there, he told his wife, Helen, that he wanted to take a nap before dinner. He never woke up.

The Sample family was devastated, as was the community. Two McKeesport department stores took ads in the *Daily News*, lauding Sample as "a gentleman of sterling character, of deep religion that influenced his every act," and an editorial noted that the city had lost "one of its best-liked and most valuable citizens." The company closed the home office and McKeesport distribution center at 12:30 P.M. on December 11 while Sample was buried in Pittsburgh's Mount Royal Cemetery. *Chain Store Age* editor Ben Gordon, who attended the funeral along with James C. Penney and Sebastian and Stanley Kresge, remembered Sample as "not so much a boss, as a mentor" who left "a legacy of hundreds of disciples who have learned at his hand the profit of love for fellow man."

A week later, G. C. Murphy Company directors elected John Sephus Mack's son president. No mere nepotism was involved since thirty-eight-year-old James Stephen Mack came with qualifications that would have made him an attractive candidate for an executive position at any corporation. Mack liked to call himself a "simple country boy," but he was no rube. A 1935 graduate of the College of William and Mary, where he earned his bachelor's degree in less than four years, Jim Mack also held a Harvard MBA and had studied for a year at the University of Toulouse in Paris. He was "terrifically smart," says his widow, Barbara Mack Reister, and a voracious reader of history books and biographies, maintaining an extensive library at his home in McKeesport and on the family farm in Indiana County. The two met at Harvard, "and he just wooed me with a lot of persistence," she says. "He swept me off my feet. He told me afterward that when he first laid eyes on me, he knew he was going to marry me."

A relentless worker, Mack rarely had more than four hours' sleep, read several newspapers daily, and often came home with a folder of correspondence six or eight inches high. He began his career at Murphy's as a twelve-year-old helper in the stockroom of Store No. 1 in McKeesport and his rise through the company after college was steady. After an apprenticeship in the real estate and construction departments, Mack went back into the stores as an assistant manager, manager, and district manager before being named a vice president of real estate and construction. Impatient at times and occasionally brusque, some old

Murphy hands found him intimidating. Mack arrived at one store to find the stock boy locking the door. "I'm sorry, sir, but you can't come in," he told Mack. "Why not?" Mack asked. "We close the store at ten minutes to five," the boy replied. Mack quickly dressed down the manager: "I didn't know your sales were so good that you could close early."

Others say that what appeared to be rudeness was actually shyness and that Mack could be exceedingly kind. When Murphy's bought its first corporate aircraft in the mid-1950s, Harry Pfister was hired as the chief mechanic. On his way out of town for a business trip, Mack would pull up to the hangar at Allegheny County Airport near Pittsburgh in his Chrysler convertible and toss the keys to Pfister. "Now, Harry, you'd better use it once in a while to keep it in good shape," he'd say, smiling. Gloria Rodgers, Mack's secretary in the late 1940s and early '50s, remembers when she received her first vacation at Murphy's—her first paid time off from any job. She and a friend decided to go to New York City for a weekend, and Jim Mack overheard her discussing her plans. "I came in one morning and found a note and an envelope," Rodgers says. "It had a $20 bill inside. The note said, 'Here's a little something extra you didn't expect.' I kept that note for a long time."

Not yet eighteen when she joined Murphy's, Rodgers says she was in "awe" of Jim Mack, who took a fatherly interest in her progress. "Do not say, 'OK,'" he instructed her. "Say, 'All right.'" "Do not say, 'Yeah,' say, 'Yes.'" But she was well aware of his perfectionist streak. It was Rodgers's job to watch the clock and every so often run outside to put coins into the parking meter where Mack had left his car. Other duties included reading the *Wall Street Journal* each day and clipping out items of interest, and whenever Mack left his glass-top desk, Rodgers would dash in and wipe away the fingerprints. When she later became a secretary for an executive at U.S. Steel Corporation, she continued working with the same diligence: "He said I was driving him nuts!"

At the time of Paul Sample's death, Mack had just been named executive vice president of the G. C. Murphy Company. "He was always working on about five different things at the same time," Barbara Reister says. Mack's father had indeed instilled a demanding work ethic. Combining his father's drive and intelligence with a top-notch formal education should have provided Murphy's chief executive with an unbeatable combination of skills, but in hindsight it becomes obvious that Jim Mack badly misread the market in several ways. Perhaps his earliest misstep was his refusal to convert Murphy's labor-intensive operation to self-service. F. W. Woolworth Company was experimenting with supermarket-style check-out lines as early as 1952; by the middle of the decade, practically all variety-store chains were trying them. Not Murphy's, which kept a clerk behind practically every counter until 1960.

Mack believed personal service made G. C. Murphy Company stores stand out from their competition. "We sell the same merchandise, display the same products, have the same storefronts as the others," he told *Forbes* magazine. "The real difference is our organization." His son, Sephus Mack, says Jim Mack had a sense of "responsibility" to both the employees who worked as clerks and to Murphy's customers. Maintaining a full-service

FIG. 31
James Stephen Mack, son of former Murphy chairman John Sephus Mack, became the company's president after Paul Sample's death. Well read and Harvard educated, Mack combined his father's determination with a top-flight formal education, but many subordinates found him intimidating.

operation "wasn't done because it was profitable," he says. "It was done because he had a sense of obligation." But keeping a girl behind each counter also kept Murphy's personnel costs high and ate up valuable display space in the stores. Murphy's did experiment with something called a "quick service" station, which clustered registers from several counters in one place with a prominent sign overhead. Neither fish nor fowl, it was no substitute for a high-volume, low-overhead checkout system. Bill Anderson, a longtime manager and district manager who eventually became a Murphy's vice president, calls it "half-assed." Jim Mack "wouldn't do anything that was considered 'progressive,'" he says. "I don't think he knew that much about the business."

Unlike its competitors who learned that customers were inclined to spend more if they could "buy now and pay later," G. C. Murphy Company also refused to issue credit cards or accept any of the new bank-sponsored revolving charge plans for fear that administrative costs and bad debts would eat up any profits. As W. T. Grant Company and S. S. Kresge Company added big-ticket, high-margin items such as furniture and appliances, Murphy's kept most of its items under $1. "We're a variety store and we're going to stay that way,"

Mack said. *Forbes* called him "cheerfully out of step," adding "Mack and his Murphy managers have been mavericks, ignoring some of the basic rules of the game."

To be sure, plenty of things were going right for the G. C. Murphy Company under Mack's leadership. Even with the former Morris locations still selling about one-third the volume of the Murphy stores, sales were high, and the company crossed the $200 million mark in 1956, its fiftieth anniversary year. *Forbes* rated G. C. Murphy Company's management among the best in the industry, noting that during a period when most variety stores were losing market share, Murphy's boosted its sales 41 percent, while Woolworth, which was "closing as many stores as it opened," had grown only 20 percent and Kress had added an "uninspiring 4 percent." No doubt some Murphy stores continued to be successful because they were the biggest stores (in some cases the only stores) in small Appalachian and midwestern towns, but the company also was stepping into larger markets such as Cincinnati, Philadelphia, and Louisville, Kentucky, and almost all its new stores were going into suburban malls and shopping centers.

Such was the company's reputation as the darling of the dime-store business that a signed lease from G. C. Murphy was all that many mall developers needed to get a loan from a bank, says Jack Walsh of the real estate department, because the guarantee of rent from Murphy's was as good as collateral. As always, Murphy's was cautious before pledging any money toward a new shopping center, says Judson Ellis Jr., who joined the department in 1957 after several years in the sales division. "The stores were getting bigger then, and you had to evaluate the tenants that were going to be going in with you," he says. "If you had a Sears and Penney's, well then, hellfire, you knew that was going to be a good location."

Though the operation of the stores was slow to modernize, the merchandise was keeping pace with the times, especially with television as a driving force. With 34 million Americans owning at least one television set by 1954, nationally advertised brands became more important than ever. The biggest advertisers included toy companies such as Mattel, Ideal, Kenner, and Remco. Murphy's and other stores were at first reluctant to handle "TV toys" because discount stores were selling them in large volume at low profit margins, says Bill Kraus, who came to the home office as a toy buyer in the late 1950s. Murphy management said, "'We won't carry them,'" he remembers. "Well, you had to carry them, because that's what people wanted!"

Kraus convinced the company to set up ten stores in the Pittsburgh area to handle brand-name toys such as "Chatty Cathy" and "Barbie" dolls, the "Johnny Reb" cannon, and the "Give-a-Show" cartoon projector. He demonstrated the latter to G. C. Murphy executives on the merchandise committee by putting on an impromptu slide show in the only place he could find at the home office that was completely dark—a men's room. The projector cost Murphy's $2.37 and after a trial run was being sold throughout the chain for $2.99. "We were Kenner's number one customer for that projector that year," Kraus says. "We got behind Mattel merchandise and were their eleventh-best customer." The results were so good that first Christmas that many stores started running out of hot-ticket toys by mid-December only to find that the warehouse in McKeesport refused to ship any more because workers were doing inventory. A frustrated Kraus strapped cartons of toys to his 1956 Chevrolet and delivered them himself.

Television also pushed thousands of copies of the record "Let Me Go, Lover" out of Murphy stores when it debuted on the November 15, 1954, installment of CBS's anthology series *Studio One*. "The next day everybody wanted to buy the record," says Dave Backstrom, an assistant manager at Store No. 23 in Irwin, Pennsylvania. The little store sold 150 copies the first week and the song, recorded for CBS's Columbia Records by actress Joan Weber, went to number one on the *Billboard* magazine chart by the end of the year.

Other technological forces were moving the G. C. Murphy Company into the future as well. After laboring in the Baltimore district for ten years, Robert Dowie had just been promoted to manager of Store No. 174 on Harford Road in Baltimore and was attending his first meeting at the home office when Murphy vice president Ken Paxton tapped him on the shoulder. "Do you know Carl Schatz?" Paxton asked. Schatz was Murphy's treasurer. Dowie said no. Paxton took him downstairs to introduce him.

"What do you know about computers?" Schatz asked. "I know when I get my paycheck every month, it's got holes in it," Dowie replied, "but I thought that was you guys stepping on them with your golf shoes." Luckily for him, the other men laughed.

"What do you know about the Coats & Clark system?" Schatz asked. Coats & Clark thread was among Murphy's most popular items. Dowie knew the thread company had gone to an automatic reordering system; boxes of thread were packed with IBM punch cards indicating the quantity, color, and other details. When a box ran short, stores sent back the punch cards and the computer automatically shipped replacement merchandise. Paxton and Schatz sent Dowie back to the managers' meeting after directing him to take a test at IBM's office in Baltimore as soon as possible.

Months went by. In the meantime, hot-tempered Dowie had blown his stack at someone from the district office, who complained to his boss, who reprimanded Dowie, who got angry all over again and fired a letter back to the district office mincing no words. Dowie was summoned to report to McKeesport the following Monday and expected to be fired. Instead, he was shown to Schatz's office, where he learned that Murphy's had purchased the biggest computer that IBM then made—a System 7070 mainframe that cost more than $2 million—making it the first variety-store chain to buy one. It didn't come with any software or operating system, and no one at Murphy's knew anything about computer programming. But Schatz decided after seeing Dowie's test results that he was the person to oversee the installation. It would be a year before IBM could ship the machine, so Dowie and the "four Js"—Judy Clark, JoAnne Foreman, Janice Dunn, and June Cuffin from Murphy's finance department—began learning the fundamentals of computer operation first at IBM and later in a conference room at the home office.

Schatz and the rest of Murphy's financial arm wanted a computer to keep track of benefits and payroll and perform other accounting tasks, Dowie says. "Then somebody said, 'Hey, but we're a retail company!' So they decided they'd better do something with the warehouse, too." The computer would be used by stores for reordering merchandise and a special twenty-two-column punch card was designed for Murphy's by IBM. The cards were packed with merchandise as it was shipped from the warehouses to the stores. When the stores hit their "reordering points" for those items, they sent the cards back to the home office. There, the computer tabulated the cards and automatically punched out orders for replacement merchandise—a simple idea now, it was revolutionary at the time.

"Everybody else in the company was deathly afraid of it," Dowie says. When the 7070 finally arrived, it took up much of the first floor in the Ruben Building, forcing two other departments to relocate. With the computer came a printer that could output 150 typewritten lines per minute, a punch card reader, memory that could hold either five thousand words or forty thousand numbers, and six tape drives to store programs. While the machine was being installed, sales manager Walter Shaw Jr. came down to have a look around. As he left, he clapped Dowie on the shoulder. "I'm glad it's you and not me," he said. The sober, conservative Schatz and the outspoken, ebullient Dowie got along well, though there were some "terrible arguments" at times, Dowie says.

Despite tapering off a little during a nationwide recession in 1958, sales continued upward and Murphy's ended the decade with volume of $239 million—swelled by nearly $16 million over the previous year in part due to the acquisition of the ninety-two-store Morgan & Lindsey Company variety chain of Monroe, Louisiana. With locations mainly in Louisiana, Texas, and Mississippi, Morgan & Lindsey gave Murphy's a foothold in the rapidly growing southwest, though the smaller, rural locations dropped the company's per-store sales from $647,000 to $571,000. It would take nearly a decade for G. C. Murphy to get its average above $600,000 again. Still, it was easily $100,000 more than the sales average of Woolworth's 2,100 North American stores. *Forbes* called Murphy's nearly 12 percent return on stockholders' equity "a good cut above any other variety chain," describing Jim Mack as "the man to beat" in the field.

That same year, Murphy's expanded into Minnesota in a big way—literally. Its 100,000-square-foot location at the new Apache Plaza Mall near St. Paul was reportedly the largest variety store in the world at that time, and the shopping center itself was one of the most exciting retail developments in the country. Although he hadn't designed the world's biggest shopping mall (that came to Minnesota decades later in the form of the Mall of America), architect Willard Thorsen did create one of the most imitated and admired, featuring a center court with soaring cathedral-style ceilings and stained glass windows. It was only the second indoor shopping plaza in the state at the time, and as a writer for the Minneapolis *Star Tribune* years later said, it was "hot stuff." Some of the biggest names in American retailing vied for a place in Apache Plaza, including J. C. Penney Company, Montgomery

Ward, and Woolworth. Murphy's new variety store was right there alongside them as an anchor tenant.

"Nobody believed that we could do it, but we did it," says Terry Stadterman, who worked as an assistant manager at Store No. 270 in St. Paul, sent there from Store No. 26 in Marion, Ohio. With the high cost of space in an enclosed shopping mall, especially for a store as large as the one in Apache Plaza, the new Murphy's would have to be a roaring success right out of the gate. But it wasn't. For one thing, the company had outgrown its supply lines. Since there were no other Murphy locations in Minnesota at the time, the Apache Plaza store was forced to bear all the costs of distribution and advertising in the market, and Murphy's desperately needed advertising in St. Paul because it was all but unknown in the state.

Store personnel gamely pressed on. A promotions man got singers such as Johnny Cash and the Lennon Sisters of television's *Lawrence Welk Show* to visit, which attracted crowds. Dancers from the Ice Capades made a special appearance at a "winter carnival" sponsored by Murphy's, as did performers from the circus. Loss leaders drew some customers into the store; Stadterman remembers ordering an entire truckload of yarn and selling it for 99¢ a skein. The addition of more name-brand merchandise helped, too.

Yet, with slow sales, a lack of name recognition, and high overhead, it was all but impossible for the store to make money, Stadterman says. Not accepting credit cards when competitors such as Woolworth and Kresge were also hurt Murphy's. Plus, instead of moving into higher-ticket items that would generate larger profit margins, such as furniture or appliances, Murphy's was selling the same kinds of merchandise it sold in small neighborhood stores but in bigger quantities. "You can't spread tubes of toothpaste out over thirty feet," Stadterman says. At Apache Plaza, the G. C. Murphy Company found the upper limits of its tried-and-true techniques, but instead of retrenching it pushed ahead. That attitude was going to cost the company dearly in the next few years.

Fly the Murphy Skies

Variety chains existed with more stores than G. C. Murphy Company or with stores in bigger cities—some might claim there were even better variety chains, though Murphy loyalists would beg to differ. But there was one area where Murphy's could defeat every five-and-ten chain from F. W. Woolworth Company down to Neisner Brothers. Only Murphy's, if necessary, could have called in an air strike on its competition, since only Murphy's owned its own genuine World War II vintage B-26 bomber. Sure, it was converted to civilian use with seats and windows in the back, but it was a bomber just the same. Jim Mack wanted the bomber, says former home office employee Luther Shay, who calls it a "widowmaker" that was "too hot for anyone to fly." The Douglas B-26 Invader registered as *N510X* (for "five and ten") was one of the first planes in what eventually evolved into what employees laughingly called the "Murphy Air Force," a fleet of five aircraft based at Allegheny County Airport near Pittsburgh and at the Monroe, Louisiana, airport, next to the Morgan & Lindsey division's warehouse.

In years past, Walter Shaw Sr. had thought nothing of piling into his Cadillac and roaring off on a weeklong inspection tour of Murphy stores. Many of his trips included stops at antique stores where Shaw added to his collection of unusual glass paperweights, eventually amassing a unique menagerie that's now on permanent exhibition at the Southern Alleghenies Museum of Art in Loretto, Pennsylvania.

By the mid-1950s however, as the G. C. Murphy Company opened outlets in Minnesota and Florida, car trips were no longer expedient and air travel was a quicker way for district managers and home office personnel to keep tabs on stores around the country. But commercial aviation in those days was heavily regulated, expensive, and not always convenient. Murphy president Jim Mack began taking flying lessons at Allegheny County Airport from Ashland, Kentucky, native and instructor Jim Jordan. Soon he purchased an orange-and-white Beechcraft Bonanza for longer trips and a Bell helicopter that he used to commute to the family farm in Indiana County on weekends. Mack quickly concluded that an airplane would be a timesaver for Murphy's as well.

"The board of directors wasn't going to go along with it," says Harry Pfister, one of the first full-time aircraft mechanics hired by Murphy's. "But J. S. said 'to hell with you, I'll buy it myself.' So they relented." In 1956, Jordan was hired as the company's chief pilot and Murphy's purchased

two twin-engine Beechcrafts and a single-engine Cessna 180 Skywagon. In 1959, the L. B. Smith Aircraft Company of Miami, Florida, began running ads in *Flying* magazine promoting what it called the Tempo II, a civilian conversion of war surplus B-26s equipped with two 2,800-horse-power Pratt & Whitney engines and capable of speeds up to 240 miles per hour. It didn't take much for a man of Mack's ambition to want one for Murphy's. In 1959, he sent Jordan down to pick one out and fly it back to Pittsburgh.

"It had six seats in the back and three up front," Pfister says. "There was a small kitchen and a lavatory, but the wingspan went right through [the fuselage], and you had to crawl through a hatch to get from the front to the back." The *N510X* was equipped with almost every navigational aid and electronics device that could be installed in the early 1960s, he says, but because the ex-bomber wasn't pressurized, it couldn't fly above 10,000 feet or so. That kept it below the weather and made for some bumpy rides.

FIG. 32
As stores began opening farther from McKees-port and outside easy driving distance, the G. C. Murphy Company acquired a fleet of private airplanes. One of the most memorable was the ex–Air Force B-26 bomber shown here at Allegheny County Airport in Pittsburgh with crew-members and mechanics, including pilot Jim Long (far left, back row), then–chief pilot Jim Jordan (third from left, back row), and chief mechanic Harry Pfister (front row, far left).

Jordan considered the B-26 "his" airplane, and Mack allowed him to take the bomber on personal flights to Kentucky to visit his family at Christmas. "One time, they were going to have the plane worked on in California, so dad took us all to Disneyland," says his daughter, Jennifer Jordan Justice.

The B-26, unfortunately, wasn't so accommodating to Jordan. Twice in a single week in 1962, while on a trip to Florida with Murphy vice president Ken Paxton, Jordan was flying the *N510X* when one of the engines failed, forcing him to make emergency landings both times. "Ken Paxton just had a fit," Justice says. "He kept saying, 'I've got a bad heart! I've got a bad heart! You could have killed us all!'" Inside one of the pistons, a mechanic found a loose metal shard left behind after an engine rebuild, but the incidents destroyed Jordan's confidence. He spent several days walking the beach in Florida before collapsing with a nervous breakdown. After he told his doctors that "God was telling him not to fly," his pilot's license was revoked.

"I think it almost killed him," Justice says. "He was fine after that, but what got to him most was that the FAA told him he couldn't fly. He wanted to fly so bad." Jordan stayed on as manager of the G. C. Murphy hangar at Allegheny County Airport for two years before reluctantly returning to Kentucky. The B-26 was gone, too, after other incidents convinced the Murphy flight crew that it was a jinx. In one accident, a pilot was pulling *N510X* into the hangar at Pittsburgh when the propellers refused to "feather" and the plane banged into the back wall. Sold in 1967 to a German company, it continued to vex pilots and mechanics, crashing once in Stuttgart in 1970 when the landing gear refused to descend and again in Zurich, Switzerland, in 1973. That was the last straw, and aviation enthusiast publications report that an airport fire crew burned the old bird during a training exercise.

It was replaced as Murphy's top plane first by a Douglas DC-3, then by a British-made Handley-Page turboprop Jetstream, and finally by a Hawker-Siddeley HS125 jet. All carried the *N510X* registration and were decorated in blue and white with the Murphy's logo on the door. The DC-

FIG. 33
The G. C. Murphy Company's purchase of the Morgan & Lindsey variety-store chain, located in the southeastern United States, led to the opening of a new aviation base at the Monroe, La., airport. Pilot Al Rossbach, Chuck Howard of the construction department, and R. L. Barnes get ready to depart for a trip sometime in the 1960s.

3 was an early twin-engine commercial airliner that was being bumped in the 1960s to charter services, commuter lines, and private use. After the jet was purchased, Luther Shay tried to trade the DC-3 to television talk show host and casino owner Merv Griffin and flew with the plane to Las Vegas. "He looked at it and decided he didn't want it," Shay says. "Then we spent a couple of hours in Liberace's house. We didn't meet him, but we got to see his pianos." The DC-3 was eventually swapped for another twin-engine Beechcraft.

All the planes got a lot of use, Shay says, especially in the 1970s when the company was opening Murphy's Marts discount stores at a breakneck pace. With its smooth, quiet operation and a cruising speed of more than 450 miles per hour, the HS125 quickly became the favorite of home office executives. Emery Fannin of the construction division was in Fort Worth, Texas, one afternoon with then–chief pilot Jim Long just after the company acquired the jet. "We're going to be home before dark," Long told Fannin as they prepared for takeoff.

"I don't believe it," Fannin replied.

"Nope, I checked the weather," Long said. "We've got a strong tailwind." After cruising to Pennsylvania at five-hundred-plus miles per hour, the HS125's wheels indeed hit the runway at Allegheny County Airport before sunset.

Riding in the cockpit was a privilege many Murphy executives—those not afraid of flying—enjoyed exercising. Fannin was riding up front with pilot Al Rossbach one afternoon while three less-sanguine travelers were in the cabin. As the plane leveled off, Fannin called out, loudly, "You want me to take over, Al?"

"Those three guys in the back wanted to jump out," Fannin says.

Another frequent passenger of the Murphy Air Force was chief photographer Jack Loveall, who remembers taking aerial photos of the McKeesport warehouse in Jim Mack's helicopter one January. "It was so cold I basically only had one shot—as soon as I stuck my head out, my eyes froze," he says.

Since many Murphy stores were located in small Appalachian towns served only by tiny airports with grass or tar runways, several Murphy pilots were hired for their experience flying "crop dusters." Loveall flew with one of them from Pittsburgh to Fredericksburg, Virginia. "He came down so low that you could see people in swimming pools, smiling," Loveall says.

Another time, Loveall flew to Baltimore on the HS125 with a big group of Murphy executives, "but the only one going back was me," he says. "The two pilots grabbed me and said, 'Come on, Jack, we're ready to go.'

One of them grabbed my tripod and was carrying it. People were looking at me thinking, 'Gee, he must be some kind of a photographer—he's got his own jet!'"

Surprisingly, the fleet of planes took little abuse (though Loveall does remember being sent to Williamsburg, Virginia, to take aerial photos of chairman S. Warne Robinson's house), and the Murphy Air Force endured until the company's takeover by Ames Department Stores. As Ames dismembered the G. C. Murphy Company, the planes were sold off. The HS125 went to a charter operator in Texas and was retired after a crash at Houston's Hobby Airport in 1989. At last report, it was resting in a California junkyard. The hangar with the big "G. C. Murphy Co." lettering at Allegheny County Airport was also sold but presently survives, though it may yet be demolished as part of a planned expansion project.

Luther Shay says he's not sure the planes were economical but admits "that's hard to pin down." There's no question, though, they were a great convenience for a growing, far-flung retail company. And, after flying for thirty years without a serious accident or injury, the men of the Murphy Air Force could be proud of their service.

Even if they never did get to use the B-26 to make any bombing runs on Kmart.

THE
Pride
OF THE
Chain

With a squeal of metal against metal and a thump-thump-thump from the air compressors, Pittsburgh Railways' rusty orange streetcars growled to a stop every few minutes on Fifth Avenue in downtown Pittsburgh where the conductors called: "All out for Murphy's!" Not all the passengers were destined for G. C. Murphy Company's big Store No. 12 in the city's Golden Triangle, of course, but it sure seemed that way at times—especially at lunchtime when workers from the nearby office towers of Fortune 500 companies such as U.S. Steel, Rockwell, Dravo, Alcoa, and Gulf Oil mingled with cops and lawyers from the courthouse, panhandlers, prostitutes, and hucksters. Along with Store No. 166 in Washington, D.C., which took up a block of prime real estate between F and G streets on Capitol Hill, Store No. 12 was one of the company's flagships.

"For its time, No. 12 was the most advanced merchandising concept of any store in the country," says Bill Kraus, who worked at the downtown Pittsburgh store along with his father during the 1940s and spent nearly thirty years with Murphy's. There was a McCrory's across the street and a Woolworth about a block away, yet they paled in comparison

FIG. 34
Store No. 12 between Fifth Avenue and Diamond Street in Pittsburgh was the
G. C. Murphy Company's second attempt to open a location in the city's central
business district. The massive store was erected in record time during 1930. The
company's chief architect, Harold E. Crosby, sped up construction by connecting
several existing buildings with a new steel-framed structure.

to the beast that took up five buildings and most of a city block, which was "a nuthouse," he says, laughing. Lunch hours in Store No. 12 were "bedlam," adds Earl Rehrig, who managed the store in the 1970s. Fred Speidel, who became manager in 1984, says about 65 percent of the store's sales were made between 11:30 A.M. and 2:30 P.M. Before checkout aisles were installed in the 1960s, each counter at Store No. 12 was still staffed by clerks. During lunch hours, some counters might have four, five, or six clerks waiting on customers. "We had a captive audience there when people were on their lunch hours," Rehrig says.

That level of activity was one of many reasons people in the G. C. Murphy Company spoke about Store No. 12 in reverent tones. Only the best assistant managers from around the company were transferred to downtown Pittsburgh, and anyone who became the manager at "12" was almost surely destined for an executive post in the sales division or the home office. When fifteen-year Murphy employees arrived in Pittsburgh for their induction into the company's veterans' club, the chance to see Store No. 12 was one of the prime attractions. Everyone in the chain-store business knew about Store No. 12, too. Woolworth had more famous stores, such as the location on Powell and Market streets in San Francisco next to the cable car turntable, and Kress had more architecturally interesting stores. But with all due respect to Gimbels, which had a big store just a few blocks from Store No. 12, "nobody, but nobody," undersold Murphy's. By 1933, only three years after opening its doors for the first time, Store No. 12 was doing a million dollars' worth of business. Sales doubled four years later. During its best year, recessionary 1980, nearly ten million dollars' worth of goods left Store No. 12.

"Store 12 was a goldmine," says Jack Anderson, who was an assistant manager there. "Sales were great, profits were through the roof, everything we did was right." More than that, he says, the swirl of daily activity in the store was exhilarating. "I probably never worked harder in my life. Have you ever done anything so rewarding that it was just fun?"

Former Murphy vice president of sales Clair McElhinny, who managed Store No. 12 in the 1970s, tallied up the best-selling items of 1973. The volume is staggering: 800,000 nickel candy bars; nearly 200,000 twenty-five-cent greeting cards; enough cigarettes ($174,000) to send the surgeon general into apoplexy; enough pantyhose ($120,000) to outfit all the Pitt Panthers cheerleaders, past and present; and enough yarn ($119,442) to knit a slipcover for the U.S. Steel Building. "Store 12 was the best thing I ever had in my life," Rehrig says. "We had close to two or three hundred people working there. We had six floors—two floors of retail and four floors of stockroom—and it was great to go in there and see the amount of goods you could sell.

"We were the biggest bulk candy dispenser that E. J. Brach [and Sons] Candy Company in Chicago had," he says. "Whenever they had a new candy, they would call us first, and it was nothing for us to order forty or fifty thousand pounds of candy. . . . We had the same thing with hosiery manufacturers—they would call us to sell nylons at unbelievable prices." For Kraus, who had grown up poor during the Depression, the volume of merchandise

FIG. 35
During a Pittsburgh Pirates playoff run in 1975, Store No. 12 distributed women's headscarves, or "babushkas," decorated with the team's logo. The team thanked Murphy's with a special on-field promotion featuring Pirates broadcaster Bob Prince. Store manager Clair McElhinny (left), Pirates manager Danny Murtaugh (fourth from left), G. C. Murphy Company chairman S. Warne Robinson, and several unidentified members of Murphy's "Babushka Brigade" prepare to take the field at Three Rivers Stadium.

handled by Store No. 12 was "astounding." "We'd sell a thousand pounds of cookies in just a few days," he says. "Huge quantities of fabric—everybody used oilcloth for tablecloths. I can't remember what it sold for a yard, but we sold tremendous quantities of oilcloth. We carried over eight hundred styles of buttons." During a run by the Pittsburgh Pirates to the National League playoffs in 1975 (they lost to the Reds in three straight games), McElhinny ordered thousands of headscarves—Pittsburgh women call them "babushkas"—decorated with the team's logo. Most of them were silk-screened right in Store No. 12's sign-making department by longtime employee Joe Amoroso. Women old and young wore the scarves to Three Rivers Stadium to cheer on the Buccos, and legendary Pirates announcer Bob Prince called them the "Babushka Brigade." During "Mac's" tenure as manager, Store No. 12 also became one of the Pirates' first branch ticket offices. When the team went on a hot streak, fans lined the sidewalks outside the store to get their seats; soon other Pittsburgh-area Murphy locations became Pirates ticket outlets as well.

Though next door to National Record Mart, a Pittsburgh landmark, Murphy's Store No. 12 in the 1960s and '70s still sold more than sixty thousand 45-rpm records every year, many of them wrapped in cellophane on cardboard squares and sold at three for $1. Only the record on top was visible. Pittsburgh kids rummaged through the bins, paid for their selection with their hard-earned babysitting or lawn-cutting money, and then ran outside to tear off the plastic and see what the other two records were. Sometimes they were hits from the previous year, but often they were songs by new artists on their way up (who or what was Jefferson Airplane?) or one-hit wonders on their way down ("It's Up to You, Petula" by Edison Lighthouse). And their parents and grandparents had once enjoyed music played by a real, live piano player at Store No. 12. When most families still had a piano in their parlors or living rooms for entertainment, Murphy's did a booming business in sheet music. Customers who were thinking about buying a certain selection could hand the score to pianist Marie Moss, who would play it for them.

Downtown areas attract the commonplace and the crazy, and Store No. 12 was a magnet for oddballs at times. "Every day was Halloween," says Rehrig, who was there one a blisteringly cold, snowy day in February 1972 when "a big heavy-set gal" walked in, barefoot and clad only in a nightgown and a tiara. Jack Anderson was an assistant manager in the basement when another heavy-set customer fell backward down the escalator, tumbling end over end until she got stuck between the handrails at the bottom with the moving stair treads whacking her, one after the other. "You just couldn't get down there fast enough to reach the shut-off button," Anderson says. "Your whole life flashes before your eyes."

Another day, first assistant manager Ron Markwood came to Anderson with a customer complaint. "This lady says the escalator ate her son's rubber boots," Markwood said. Anderson thought it was a scam, but he gave the lady a new pair of boots from stock, and she went away happy. A month later, a serviceman was summoned to investigate a burning smell from the escalator and removed a mangled pair of rubber boots from its innards—it did eat the boots, but it couldn't digest them.

One Store No. 12 regular was nicknamed "The Duster" by employees because he walked around pretending to dust the shelves, says Speidel. "One night I got a call from the police that the alarm had gone off. I went down and there was old Duster. He said, 'I was in the bathroom and they locked me in.'"

Dick Scales, who eventually became head of Murphy's loss prevention department, was posted to Store No. 12 in 1950 to train as an undercover store detective with Jim Anglum, the only other security employee there at the time. All male Murphy's employees wore ties, but security personnel also had to wear hats, even indoors. "The idea was to keep you looking different from the other employees," Scales says. "In the winter it wasn't too bad, but in the summer you stuck out like a sore thumb." His first "collar" was a man who had palmed some costume jewelry. He wasn't prosecuted, and years later Scales was astonished to see the man's photo in the newspaper after he was picked to lead a council on international relations. "I thought, 'Boy, I picked this guy up for shoplifting in Murphy's and look at him now!'" Scales says.

Scales wasn't afraid to get physical with other customers at Store No. 12. One suspected shoplifter tried to hit Scales until he flipped him over and held him upside down by his ankles, telling him, "If you don't settle down I'm going to drop you on your head." Assistant manager Ernie Helmstadter could only shake his head and smile. "I don't know how you did that," he said.

Store No. 12 was as much an entertainment concept as a retail store, but afterall, the variety-store business had always depended on a certain amount of showmanship. "Tinseled, gaudy, and noisy," the *Pittsburgh Press* called five-and-tens in 1948. Candy, cosmetics, costume jewelry, glassware, toys—all were stacked theatrically in big pyramids under spotlights to give an appearance of abundance at bargain prices. By World War II, the G. C. Murphy Company was elevating dime-store "show business" to a high art, spending thousands of dollars to test various displays at Murphy's research and development lab in McKeesport, photographing the most attractive examples, and sending copies to all the stores to emulate. Except for Stores No. 12 and 166 in Washington who didn't imitate what other stores were doing—they set the pace. And if their merchandise was scenery and their sales methods were stagecraft, Murphy's flagships added actors and plots. The stars were the assistant managers who continually worked the public-address system, pitching products as carnival barkers do. The *Washington Post* transcribed one such rap at Store No. 166:

> Ladies, we're having a special on fitted bedspreads that we've just gotten in. And the little lady up front here isn't very busy, she'll style your wig while you wait. Chocolate bunnies—a full pound of pure milk chocolate—are on sale at the candy counter. While you're here, don't forget to have those extra keys made—house keys, garage keys, mail box keys, security box keys, luggage keys—we make them all, and the key man isn't busy!

Jack Anderson says that Ed Kohler, an assistant manager in the 1960s, was one of the best he had ever seen at using the PA system. "He would come on and say, 'Stop! Don't move!' We had people who would actually stop dead, afraid to move. Then he'd say, 'Don't move . . . until you see the special in the candy department,' on M&Ms or whatever, or he'd be pushing Matchbox cars at three for $1. We could move traffic around that store just by using the PA system. It was unbelievable." Murphy girls had roles, too, and not just on the "stage crew." Some days, there might be a fashion show, with the youngest and most lithesome clerks pressed into service as models.

The supporting cast at the flagships included the independent hucksters who worked the aisles with the G. C. Murphy Company's full sanction and blessing demonstrating knives, ballpoint and fountain pens, scrub brushes, "miracle" cleaning fluids, and kitchen gadgets. "There were demonstrations going on all the time—the kind of demonstrations you see now on TV," Kraus says. Customers gathered in little knots to watch the showmen

FIG. 36
One of America's first black female disc jockeys, Mary Dee of WHOD radio in Homestead, Pa., greets listeners during a live broadcast from Store No. 12 in the late 1940s. During the 1960s and '70s, Store No. 12 was one of the most successful variety stores in the United States, behind Woolworth locations in San Francisco and New York City. Hucksters, concessionaires, and appearances by local and national celebrities kept it hopping throughout the day.

display their wares, building sales floor traffic. Some people even took their lunch hours just to walk through Store No. 12, says former home office executive Luther Shay. Murphy's got a cut (up to 30 percent) of each sale made by the demonstrators and other concessionaires in Store No. 12, some of whom carved out handsome little niches for themselves, such as the fortune-teller named "Miss Chang," who held court each day above a stairwell on the Diamond Street side of the building. Though blindfolded, she would tell the fortunes of customers while unfailingly describing objects they pulled out of their pockets and handed to her associates. "I couldn't figure out how she did it, and, of course, they wouldn't tell me," Anderson says.

One of the best-remembered features of Store No. 12 wasn't run by the G. C. Murphy Company at all. The New Diamond Market took up one whole corner of the first floor and part of the basement selling fish, poultry, freshly butchered meat, produce, and any other comestibles on which the Glick family could get its hands, According to Kohler, it also made "the best corned beef ever." Diamond Street had been the center of Pittsburgh's wholesale grocery business almost since the city's founding in 1758, with farmers coming to town every morning to sell their wares from stalls and wagons. The first permanent market

FIG. 37
Operated by Pittsburgh's Glick family for six decades, New Diamond Market was a direct descendant of the open-air produce stands that once thrived in the city's Market Square. In this 1950 photo, customers compete for a chance at the market's outrageous bargains.

house was erected in 1794 and was replaced in 1853. The third and final market house was completed in 1914 and spanned both sides of the street with a brick archway.

By the 1950s, the old produce and meat vendors were moving to Pittsburgh's Strip District or being driven out of business by suburban supermarkets. The old Diamond Market House was torn down and replaced by a public park called "Market Square" in 1961. All that remained was the New Diamond Market, run by Sam Glick and his son Charlie on the Diamond Street side of Store No. 12—but what a place it was. "It was a tremendously promotional volume grocery store," Anderson says. "If the rest of the world was selling bananas for 29¢ a pound, they would find a deal on bananas and sell them for 5¢ a pound, and people would line up around the block."

The Glicks had a sixth sense for finding bargains in bizarre places. If a trailer load of food was damaged in an accident, Charlie Glick would buy the cargo, dispose of anything that had to be condemned for health reasons, salvage the rest, and sell it for pennies on the dollar. "I remember one time he bought a load of distressed beef," Ed Kohler says. "It was on a railroad siding and the refrigeration was gone. So they called Glick and he bought the whole goddamned railroad car and sold it for an ungodly price—I think it was 20¢ a pound. It was like a riot. People were banging on the windows." In 1973, with inflation running amok and produce and meat prices soaring daily, Glick sold 84,000 heads of lettuce for 7¢ each and marked all beef down to 1945 levels. Such stunts made the New Diamond Market beloved by customers, even when they had to push and shove their ways to the counters and listen to Mickey Glick yell at them to get out of the way so that more people could crowd in.

"He had some uncouth people working for him," Anderson says, "and people would cut in line, and things would get a little rough. They might hear words they would otherwise not hear. But nobody seemed to care—that was the New Diamond Market, and customers accepted it." And they were fiercely loyal to the Glicks. In the 1960s, activists protesting the mistreatment of migrant workers tried to stop the sale of grapes picked by nonunion farmhands. Led by a group of politically active Catholic priests and nuns, the group decided to picket the New Diamond Market. But many of Pittsburgh's immigrant families still made their own wine in the basement out of grapes they bought from Charlie Glick. The protesters were massing across Forbes Avenue (as Diamond Street was then named) when Glick picked up the phone and reminded a few local pastors that although the New Diamond Market was happy to support their food banks and soup kitchens, the donations would stop if his store couldn't sell grapes. Word reached the protest in record time, and the activists quietly dispersed. No picket line ever darkened the door of the New Diamond Market again.

New Diamond Market wasn't the only concessionaire selling food. Store No. 12 also hosted a retail outlet for Pittsburgh's Jenny Lee Bakery. "They took up a lot of space, but, boy, were they as busy as hell," Anderson says. "They'd stack loaves of bread in the window, and sometimes they'd get too many in there, and they'd roll away, break the window, and roll out into the street." While Jenny Lee Bakery survives in Market Square in another location, New Diamond Market faded in the 1980s as foot traffic in downtown Pittsburgh declined. It finally closed in January 1995 after McCrory Corporation, which took over Store No. 12 when it purchased the G. C. Murphy variety stores from Ames in 1989, refused to renew the lease. The market's manager told the *Post-Gazette* sales were down to $4 million—about one-third less than the previous year—although it remained profitable to the end.

The Glicks' "diamond in the rough," in the words of *Pittsburgh Press* feature writer Barbara Cloud, was located at the corner of Diamond Street and McMasters Way in one of two older buildings that were incorporated into Store No. 12 in 1930 by Harold Ellsworth Crosby, chief architect of the G. C. Murphy Company. It was Murphy's second try at a downtown Pittsburgh location, the original having been moved to Gallipolis, Ohio, shortly after Seph Mack and Walter Shaw took control of the company. The first store was a modest affair; the second was a monster with entrances on three different streets. The Pittsburgh contracting firm of H. Miller & Sons began work in April 1930 by demolishing

FIG. 38
Another of Store No. 12's busy concessionaires included a branch of Jenny Lee Bakery, based in McKees Rocks, Pa., which produced this wedding cake for a Murphy "Anniversary Sale" in the 1950s.

several nineteenth-century buildings between Fifth Avenue, Diamond Street, and McMasters Way, including a group of shops and offices collectively known as the Fifth Avenue Arcade. To take their place, Crosby designed a steel-framed, T-shaped building with handsome brick and terra-cotta facades on Fifth and Diamond and tied the new structure into two existing buildings on McMasters.

Miller was an old, established firm that had built such prominent Pittsburgh landmarks as Montefiore Hospital, the Irene Kaufman Settlement, and Taylor Allderdice High School, but Store No. 12 was perhaps the only one erected at a breakneck pace. New steel went up before the end of May, and the building was largely complete within seventy working days—"a record in speedy construction," according to one contemporary account. Perhaps the work went too quickly at times, for Crosby wasn't done with the blueprints and Murphy's frequently tangled with Miller & Sons over last-minute changes. "This work was not started or asked for until the plasterers had started work in the basement (July 15) and we finally received orders to proceed . . . Aug. 11," says a note from someone at H. Miller, written on a photo of the special plumbing required for a first-floor soda fountain. On a photo of a new floor, the same person wrote critically: "All this work could have been completed June 4 had plans shown details." Another note on a picture of a stairway stated: "First floor was in place before work was ordered. Wrecking for this stair was done entirely at night to speed up work and extra carpenters were placed on work . . . so as not to delay progress." The addition of an extra office to a stairwell on Diamond Street caused "at least a week's delay," Miller told Murphy's while reporting that changes to the facade held up a plastering crew ten days.

By mid-September, counters were going in, and the store opened for business on October 16. Newspapers reported the cost as $250,000, but reports from the construction division indicate the company spent at least $661,000, including $164,000 on fixtures alone. From there, Store No. 12 kept growing, first taking over a floral shop on McMasters Way in 1935, then adding the six-story Bedell Building on Fifth Avenue in 1940. The latter purchase increased the sales floor by 30 percent and gave Store No. 12 five new floors for storage. Crosby tied the Bedell Building and his 1930 structure together with a new, streamlined front of salmon-colored tile.

Between 1931 and 1950, at least ten remodeling projects were completed at Store No. 12. While the sales floors looked cohesive enough, it was a crazy patchwork behind the scenes. Floors sloped unevenly to connect old buildings together. One of the stockrooms had started life as a bowling alley and in a few places the ceiling was only five feet from the floor; scores were still chalked on the wall long after the last pins had fallen. There were two different dumbwaiters and three different freight elevators. Bill Kraus remembers watching one car sink straight to the basement under heavy loads. "It just bounced on the springs when the up button was pushed," he says. Given the enormous sales volume at Store No. 12, it made sense for Murphy's to expand whenever and wherever it could, but the combination of new and old buildings owned by several different landlords created a maintenance nightmare, and the rental contracts required the company to replace the old walls if it ever vacated the premises. "If we had to restore everything we tore out, it would have cost several million dollars," says E. J. Fannin, who worked in the company's maintenance department. Tom Hudak, who started as an accountant at Murphy's and eventually rose to chairman of the board, pegs the 1985 cost of putting back the walls at upward of $12 million. Murphy's real estate department made repeated, unsuccessful attempts to purchase all the buildings outright.

Despite its physical quirks and limitations, Store No. 12 was a known proving ground for future Murphy executives. One of the first managers was Edgar L. Paxton, a stocky young man who joined Murphy's in the 1920s when it acquired the Trick Brothers stores around Indianapolis. By 1946, Paxton was a Murphy vice president. While Paxton's tenure at Store No. 12 was relatively short, but other employees, such as Amoroso, a wiry Italian American who worked in the sixth-floor sign shop, stayed for years. "He smoked cigars, and he got married when he was about fifty," Kohler says. "He was a treasure—one of the treasures of the Murphy Company." Rumor had it that a young Pittsburgh art student named Andy Warhol had also worked in the Store No. 12 sign shop before taking a job trimming windows at a nearby department store. After Warhol's death in 1987, a few employees swore that he was haunting the store. Since Warhol conspicuously avoided returning to Pittsburgh throughout his life, it seems a bit unlikely that he'd return to Murphy's, but Speidel admits "there were some strange things happening on the sixth floor."

Other longtime Store No. 12 denizens of a more corporeal kind included the two parrots living in the downstairs pet department and who were named "George" and "Murphy" for the company's founder. Both became permanent residents in the 1960s and lasted at least until the 1980s. "People would come down all the time to talk to the birds," Speidel says. "They'd say, 'Hello, how are you?'" Someone bird-napped George and Murphy in the 1970s, but the parrots were quickly recovered on the city's North Side and restored to their perches in Store No. 12. Come lunchtime, a different flock perched on the stools at the two first-floor lunch counters in Store No. 12. With 120 seats, it wasn't the largest food-service operation in the G. C. Murphy Company, but it was by far the busiest, says Ellison "Al" Boggs, who ran the restaurant division for nearly twenty years. Up to sixty employees kept the two long lunch counters and two smaller snack bars buzzing from seven o'clock in the morning until the store closed—9:00 P.M. on Mondays and Thursdays—serving mostly breakfasts, "blue-plate lunches," and convenience foods such as hot dogs and hamburgers. As with many of Murphy's other restaurants, pressure from fast-food chains hurt Store No. 12's lunch counters; in 1984 and '85 they were losing $7,000 per week.

The company's other flagship, Store No. 166 in Washington, D.C., was one of only about a dozen G. C. Murphy locations that were unionized. But it "was a tremendous store," says one-time manager Clair Trost, who credits the employees for keeping the block-long sales floor the second busiest in the chain. "We had one hell of a crew there. That size store requires more assistant [managers] and a higher quality of personnel. We were doing $6 million to $8 million in sales—that's a lot of five- and ten-cent items." Negotiating his first contract with the clerks' union proved to be an eye-opener for Trost, who managed the store for three years. He attended the meeting with Murphy labor attorney Ed McGinley, who told Trost, "[Y]ou should come along for the experience and see how they operate."

"Like a dummy, I said, 'Isn't any of the rank-and-file membership going to be here for this meeting?'" Trost recalls.

The union president replied: "Hell no! We don't want them here. We'd never get anything done."

"You talk about running it through the mill," Trost says. "The union president said, 'We want this, this, and this, we want optical, dental, et cetera.'" The union also wanted Murphy's to collect dues automatically from workers' paychecks because too many members weren't paying. "McGinley said, 'You're nuttier than hell—you can't get that,'" Trost says.

Just four blocks from the White House, the Washington store spanned F and G streets between Twelfth and Thirteenth avenues with sales areas on the first floor and basement and three floors of stock space. As with Store No. 12, Crosby created a new store using

FIG. 39

Store No. 12 eventually grew to incorporate several neighboring buildings; a handsome streamlined facade designed by Crosby tied the Fifth Avenue storefronts together. Behind the glitter, however, was a patchwork maze of mismatched floors and doors.

parts of two older structures on the property, and just as it had for Store No. 12, Murphy's rented the space from several landlords. Construction began in February 1930 and Store No. 166 opened for business in May. With more than 21,000 square feet of sales area, Murphy's billed it as one of the ten largest dime stores in the country. "The place was alive," says William Anderson, who worked at Store No. 166 from 1936 to 1942.

Unlike other urban locations, which went into decline as downtown areas became less important, No. 166 improved with age, thanks in large part to the completion of the D.C. subway, or "Metro," in the 1970s. The new Metro Center, intersected by three subway lines, was located almost directly beneath the store, and several transit stops were within sight of Murphy's. Washington office workers thronged No. 166 during their lunch hours and on their way home at four o'clock; the restaurant in the early 1980s did an annual sales volume between $800,000 and $1 million. Seating was in such demand at the restaurant that the manager would force customers to share booths, says Andy Duris, an assistant manager of Store No. 166 in the 1960s. "All of those government people had nothing else to do during lunch hour, and it was so busy you couldn't hardly walk through the aisles. At some counters we had two or three girls and we pulled out all of the nonselling help—office people, stockroom people—and had them come down on the floor."

As did Store No. 12, Store No. 166 had a meat market and other concessions on the premises. "We got fresh chickens from Amish country twice a week," Trost says. "They'd arrive at six o'clock in the morning, iced-down—they had just been killed. We'd sell fresh chicken, fresh eggs, turkeys, rabbits." Local jeweler Nate Gendel leased space to sell watches, rings, earrings, and bracelets in the store for nearly forty years. A concessionaire known to Murphy employees as "Nick" sold candy, nuts, and ice cream, while a locksmith rented space under the basement stairs to sell keys. "He did something like $100,000 per year in keys and locks, and paid us 33 percent," Trost says. Demonstrators were a constant feature at Store No. 166, too. Gus Mahoney sold knives, while another man whom people called "Footsie" sold medicated foot powder. "Rug cleaners, slicing and dicing vegetables, any new products they wanted to push," Trost says. "The ballpoint pen guy would do a couple of grand per week selling those pens."

And as had Store No. 12, Store No. 166 became a training ground for future Murphy executives. Future Murphy chairman Kenneth "K. T." Paxton became manager of Store No. 166 in 1937 while his brother Edgar was still managing No. 12. Bill Anderson says the two frequently called each other long distance to compare notes, issue friendly challenges, and engage in some good-natured teasing. "Everything at Murphy's was always 'No. 12, No. 12,' but we actually beat No. 12 in some departments," Duris says. "They made more sales than us, but sometimes we came out with more profit. We were always trying to beat each other." Despite being located in a city full of sculptures, monuments, and memorials, the Washington store became a tourist attraction in its own right, thanks to a second-floor gallery featuring charcoal renderings of all the U.S. presidents. The current president's portrait was always kept on display in the front window in a white, colonial-style frame. "When Reagan was elected, I had to get the portrait done," Trost says. "I hired an artist out of White Flint [Maryland]. I think she charged us $800 or $1,000, but she did an excellent job." The portrait of outgoing president Jimmy Carter then needed to be moved upstairs. Trost needed three new frames in all and contracted with a local shop to do the work. When the framer presented a bill for $1,200, Trost thought he would die. "I was reluctant to call the office," he says, but they paid. It was the cost of maintaining a Washington landmark.

More so than at Store No. 12, celebrities—especially of the political kind—were a frequent occurrence at Store No. 166. In the 1950s, Mamie Eisenhower bought foundation garments at Murphy's Store No. 166 and later became a customer of the Gettysburg, Pennsylvania, location when she and Ike retired to a farm there. In the 1970s, presidential daughters Tricia Nixon and Amy Carter stopped traffic when they arrived with Secret Service agents in tow. Murphy general counsel Bob Messner says the store also became a favorite of senators, congressmen, and their aides, which provided the company with valuable Washington contacts when legislation was proposed that might impact the retail business.

In addition to being one of the company's flagships, Store No. 166 also was the largest of nearly a dozen G. C. Murphy Company stores in the District of Columbia and by the 1960s served an increasingly important African American population. Just as it successfully customized its merchandise mix in other communities, Murphy's learned to tailor its operations to a black, urban clientele as well, hiring residents of nearby neighborhoods as salesclerks and management trainees and stocking products that customers couldn't find elsewhere at the time, including a large selection of makeup, shampoo, and conditioners for ethnic and minority customers. Posner Cosmetics, one of the first beauty product companies to reach out to African American consumers, told Murphy's the store was its second-largest client in the United States. Jazz artist Natalie Cole and other celebrities made personal appearances on the store's behalf.

Perhaps for those reasons, Store No. 166 was one of the few D.C. stores spared by looters and vandals when riots swept the city following the assassination of civil rights leader Dr. Martin Luther King Jr. A smaller G. C. Murphy Company store not far away at 3128 Fourteenth Avenue NW wasn't so lucky and became a tragic footnote to the three days of violence that began on the night of Thursday, April 4, 1968. Just after eleven o'clock the following morning, rioters began breaking shop windows along Fourteenth Avenue NW, including those at the Murphy store. A fire broke out inside, but firefighters combating blazes throughout the city were unable to respond before the building was fully engulfed. When emergency workers finally searched the wreckage on Saturday morning, they discovered the bodies of two teenagers: eighteen-year-old George Neely was a senior at Phelps Vocational High School; the other victim was a young man of about fourteen who was never identified.

As did other Washington, D.C., area Murphy locations, Store No. 166 also catered to the area's sizable international population, which led the Capitol Hill store one year to buy forty thousand yards of fabric from a mill in New England on behalf of Middle Eastern and Indian women who made their own robes and saris. "Not every store could do that," Trost says. "They gave me a lot of leeway to do that sort of thing because we had a tremendous amount of traffic." In a 1972 profile of the store, a *Washington Post* reporter praised Murphy's for what she called "dime store couture" and called it "one of the greatest shows on Earth," comparing a walk through the hucksters at Store No. 166 to a stroll up Paris's Left Bank. "For the fashionable woman of modest means, of whimsy, or of iconoclastic urge to thumb her nose at the whole haute 'signature' scarf syndrome, the five-and-ten can provide . . . handsome accessories," Jeannette Smyth wrote. "As a matter of fact, Murphy's does have signature scarves, signed with an illegible scribble which, upon careful eyeballing . . . turns out to be 'Gundflab.' If anyone asks, you can tell them that Gundflab is a new rock string quartet from Sweden which also designs scarves. Or you could tell them that you got it at Murphy's for a dollar, and they'll think you're putting them on." It wasn't all praise; Smyth called some of the fashions on display at Store No. 166 "magnificently, galumphingly, cataclysmically ugly."

Store No. 166 survived galumphingly ugly fashions, the Depression, World War II, and the 1968 riots, but Washington, D.C.'s transformation from a sleepy backwater in the 1930s (when some foreign governments listed it as a "hardship post") to a great world capital doomed the store. The property that Murphy's leased for $2 million in 1929 eventually became too valuable and in 1986 was sold to The John Akridge Company, a Washington developer. A four-story 1913 office block called the Homer Building at the corner of Thirteenth and F streets was to become the base of a twelve-story office tower, and Akridge wanted to erect a matching structure next door. The final day of operations at Store No. 166—Washington's last downtown five-and-ten—was January 24, 1987. The *Post* called it a "symbol of a bygone era in city retailing" and reported that Ames Department Stores, which took over the G. C. Murphy Company in 1985, was not finding jobs for ninety-one employees, some of whom had worked there for thirty or forty years. "The attitude is 'take it and get,'" Frances Henderson, the store's personnel director, said. Store manager Wilbur Browning told the newspaper that Store No. 166 remained one of the most profitable G. C. Murphy locations, but its time had apparently passed.

In Pittsburgh, Store No. 12 fared a little better, avoiding the wave of closings that swept the variety stores after the Ames takeover and enduring until the G. C. Murphy division itself was sold to one-time competitor McCrory. But McCrory's had serious financial problems, and Store No. 12 was no longer the biggest and best showplace of a proud local chain—it was just one of many urban locations of a far-flung company saddled with debt and perpetually flirting with bankruptcy. Out came the restaurant, the concessionaires, and the demonstrators; in came a long period of decline.

"Every day it seems another fissure has developed in the strip of red paint behind the gold 'G. C. Murphy' letters," columnist Diana Nelson Jones wrote in the *Post-Gazette* in

1998. "The offerings are sparse on some of the shelves. Mid-days downstairs . . . have the dead feeling of a vault." The manager put on a brave face, telling Jones that McCrory's was shifting to a "dollar store" concept, reducing both price and variety. But as Jones noted, it just looked "depleted." Trost, who left Murphy's following the Ames takeover, was asked to come back and oversee Store No. 12 in the late 1990s. The merchandise that McCrory's was sending was garbage, he says—when a store somewhere else would close, its leftover merchandise was sent to Store No. 12 for liquidation. It was more than Trost could take, and he resigned again. "When you see a store that was run well and done right, and they're just bastardizing it, you don't want to do that," he says. The general deterioration of Pittsburgh's central shopping district, which accelerated when longtime department stores Gimbels and Joseph Horne Company went out of business, didn't help Store No. 12—the middle-class office workers who once thronged Market Square at lunchtime had been replaced by vagrants and drunks.

In September 2001, McCrory Stores filed for chapter 11 bankruptcy and two months later announced it would liquidate its remaining 193 stores instead of reorganizing. The merchandise left on the shelves at Store No. 12 was enough to make a longtime Murphy man cry. By its final days of operation in February 2002, the store that was once the pride of the G. C. Murphy Company was dirty and poorly lit, selling a shabby assortment of Chinese-made plastic knickknacks, off-brand toys, and household products. Pigeons flitted through upstairs windows that were broken or thoughtlessly left open.

For several years it stood empty, leaving a gaping hole in Pittsburgh's commercial core. Eventually, it was purchased by the city's Urban Redevelopment Authority (URA), which floated various concepts for retail stores, performance space, or condominiums. Several developers were stymied by the difficulty of matching the different floor levels inside the five buildings that made up Store No. 12—the legacy of all those walls that were torn down by Murphy's so many years ago. Worse yet, a lack of repairs under McCrory management allowed severe water leaks to develop throughout the store, damaging the interior and contaminating parts of the building with mold, according to URA officials. McCrory's "wasn't interested in keeping any of the maintenance up," Wayne Potter says. "That wasn't their theory."

In 2006, city officials approved a proposal by Washington, Pennsylvania, developer Millcraft Industries to convert the old store into a mix of loft apartments and shops with a parking garage in the basement. When the plans are completed, Store No. 12 should once again be alive with shoppers, but the atmosphere inside won't be one-tenth as exciting as it was when G. C. Murphy Company was running a three-ring retail extravaganza in downtown Pittsburgh six days a week.

"There's nothing like it today," Bill Kraus says. "I've tried to compare it to Wal-Mart, and people have tried to tell me it was like a Wal-Mart, but it was more than that. It was a circus."

Memories of Store No. 12

Born in 1955, I was raised in Castle Shannon, Pennsylvania, and as a small boy I remember numerous trips to downtown Pittsburgh with my mother and my two older brothers. Most of the time, the purpose of our trip was to see a movie. Now, I can't remember the movies we saw, but I do remember that it was a ritual to have lunch at Murphy's counter (a hamburger with yellow mustard for me) after which we browsed for a while before making a final stop at the cookie counter to stock up on snacks before the movie.

So when I hear or see the name G. C. Murphy's, I still think of those bus trips from over forty years ago with my mother, the requisite stop at the "five-and-ten," and best of all, the windmill cookies! I don't know if you can find them anywhere, but even if you could, I'm sure they wouldn't taste the same.

Today, my office is in Oxford Centre in downtown Pittsburgh, and sometimes when I walk past the old G. C. Murphy's I can remember walking in their doors . . . . I can remember how busy it always was, the noises, and the smells. I can remember safely holding my mother's hand as we walked around . . . and I can still remember those windmill cookies!

—Jim Jarrett
McMurray, Pa.

I guess you could say I grew up with Murphy's. My grandfather, father, mother, uncle, and aunt all worked there in different capacities, and I remember going with my dad on many occasions to all the local stores in the Pittsburgh area. When I got older I worked for Murphy's myself in the home office in McKeesport.

Going to No. 12 in Pittsburgh was a real treat! New Diamond Market was located in the store bordering Market Square. Ah, those wooden plank floors, the lunch counter, the bulk candy counter. . . . I work in the executive offices at PNC Bank now in downtown Pittsburgh and every time I go past that empty Murphy store I could cry, knowing what it used to be and seeing what it has become.

All of us old ex-Murphyites who lost our jobs because of the Ames takeover say we'd still be there if Murphy's was. We'd never have left— what a great job we had!

—Patricia Smith
Elizabeth, Pa.

No one went to town without stopping at Murphy's. I bought sheet music there when it was three for $1. In the 1930s and '40s, my mother and I always ate lunch at their counter and it always ended with their apple pie. We never went home without a purchase, even if it was just a pair of socks.

My mother told me she bought my older brothers "sneakers" there for about 50¢ when they went to school (Depression years), and she warned them not to get them wet because once they were soaked through, that was it for the shoes. I was the baby—and the only girl—and she bought me dresses for 75¢ to a dollar.

I still have six pink Depression-era glass sherbet dishes, for which my mom said she paid a nickel or dime before I was born in 1929. I also have clear glass "bread and butter" plates bought at Murphy's for a dime each. They are just as precious as anything bought at Neiman Marcus or any other store.

—Lorraine Lefler Beadle
Crafton, Pa.

When we were growing up in the late 1940s and early '50s, Murphy's was one of our favorite places to stop. Back then you could spend a nickel and still get quite a lot. I don't have pictures of it, but I can still see it in my mind.

—Margie McCauley Klinger
Pittsburgh

I lived on a small farm in McMurray, Pennsylvania. One of the highlights of my life as a child was going to Murphy's in downtown Pittsburgh and on Second Avenue in Hazelwood where my mother's family lived.

We could walk to the store when we were as young as nine years old and Dad would give us a few dollars to shop. I bought all my Christmas presents there as a child—a dollar went a long way then and I could buy everyone on my list a gift. As a teenager, I spent my babysitting money there on clothes and makeup.

I especially liked the downtown store because it had a fountain. Whenever my mom and I would go to town, we would stop and have a hamburger plate. (I guess kids always liked hamburgers.) This was the days before frozen fries, when they were made from real potatoes, and they tasted great!

—Linda Bear
Sewickley, Pa.

McKEESPORT YANKEES *in* Dixieland

For most of the G. C. Murphy Company's first fifty years, what *Chain Store Age* whimsically called "the borders of Murphy-land" never stretched more than about three hundred miles from McKeesport. John Sephus Mack and Walter Shaw often opened new locations only a few miles from existing ones. As late as 1950, with 219 Murphy stores spread from St. Joseph, Michigan, to Stamford, Connecticut, more than 20 percent of the company's business was still transacted within twenty-two miles of the home office—the better for stores to share advertising and delivery expenses. And although merchandise varied from region to region—Murphy stores at the Jersey shore sold beach wear while ones in West Virginia stocked batteries for coalminers' lanterns—the G. C. Murphy Company was at its heart a five-and-ten chain specializing in stationery, sewing notions, toiletries, candy, and other staples. Murphy's sold value, not fashion.

So it was a shock to G. C. Murphy employees and competitors alike when the company suddenly expanded into Texas, Louisiana, Arkansas, and neighboring southern states. From 1959 to 1962, Murphy president Jim Mack went on a buying spree, grabbing the ninety-two variety stores of Morgan & Lindsey, Inc., and more than forty department stores in Texas. Suddenly, the reliable, slightly stodgy, and very northeastern G. C. Murphy Company was selling cowboy boots to Texas oilmen and cocktail dresses to their wives. Tacos were being served alongside burgers in Murphy restaurants. At times, Murphy's found itself in deep and unfamiliar water, unable to tailor its merchandise mix to its new clientele and unfamiliar with southern customs and traditions. It also moved south just as the civil rights era was in full flower and became caught up in the sometimes-painful process of integration. On the other hand, Murphy used its new variety stores to experiment with things such as catalogs and credit, while its department stores allowed the company to improve its apparel and fashion lines. "Murphy-land's" rapid growth finally propelled it from a regional retailer to a national force.

Longtime employees disagree on why Murphy's made the move in the first place. A few say that Jim Mack had vowed to build the largest chain of variety stores in the United States, surpassing even Woolworth. Others claim that Mack and Walter Shaw Sr. enjoyed traveling through the southern states and opening stores gave them the excuse they needed to escape northern winters. Mack even had a ranch in Arizona, but Shaw was a far more inveterate snowbird. As early as the 1930s, Shaw was vacationing in Florida, always staying on the eighth floor of St. Petersburg's famous Princess Martha Hotel. Among other regular guests, he attained the unofficial status of "floor captain" and his dinner and conversation companions regularly included such notables as Baseball Hall of Fame member and Philadelphia Athletics manager Cornelius "Connie Mack" McGillicuddy.

Aside from Walter Shaw's and Jim Mack's personal attachments to Dixieland, the G. C. Murphy Company had plenty of reason to eye the southern states as an area for possible expansion after World War II. The South's old agricultural economy—badly damaged by the Depression—was giving way to heavy industry and high technology as major manufacturers opened factories to capitalize on the availability of inexpensive labor and low taxes. The increasing popularity and affordability of air conditioning made southern summers tolerable, while mild winters meant there was little snow or ice to disrupt distribution. New economic opportunities in the Sunbelt enriched millions of southerners and enticed millions of northerners below the Mason-Dixon Line, all of whom needed basic staple items that variety stores provided.

More important, although the northern states and New England were fairly well saturated by Murphy, Woolworth, Kresge, and other chains in the 1950s, the South presented one of the few growth opportunities left for variety-store operators. Woolworth had locations throughout the region, and so-called "sectional" chains such as North Carolina–based Rose's were well established, but there was plenty of room for a company like Murphy's, which was flush with cash, largely free of debt, and small enough to move quickly when it spotted an opening.

As with so many of its corporate moves, Murphy's didn't launch its southern expansion without thinking about it for years. For more than a decade starting in the late 1940s, Shaw

FIG. 40
The G. C. Murphy
Company's 1959 acquisi-
tion of Morgan & Lindsey
Inc. based in Monroe, La.,
added nearly one hun-
dred variety stores in the
fast-growing southeast-
ern United States. Many
were small-town stores in
rural farming communi-
ties, but a few, such as
Store No. 4102 in Dallas,
Texas, were in suburban
shopping centers. The di-
vision retained a separate
identity until 1978.

had eyed Morgan & Lindsey. Relatively young among the country's variety-store chains, it had grown throughout the Deep South despite operating in many impoverished communities. Morgan & Lindsey was born not far from the Louisiana border in Jasper, Texas, where the main industries in the early twentieth century were timbering, poultry, and dairy farming, but the dusty east Texas town lacked such basic amenities as paved streets and natural gas, according to a 1950 article in *Chain Store Age*. Electricity was supplied by a power station at the sawmill and shut off "promptly at nine o'clock every evening." Jasper also lacked a dime store. So in 1921, brothers Bronson and O. A. Morgan and their friends Cyril V. and B. G. Lindsey set out to rectify that. With another man, the Morgans and Lindseys borrowed $7,500 and opened their first store in Jasper on April 30; within a few months, they opened another store in Oakdale, Louisiana, and then a third in Timpson, Texas. By the 1950s, Morgan & Lindsey stores were located in small communities throughout Texas and Arkansas and clear across to Georgia, including the hometowns of two future presidents— Hope, Arkansas (Clinton), and Plains, Georgia (Carter). To get closer to the center of its distribution area, the company relocated its warehouse to Monroe, Louisiana, in 1940; the headquarters office stayed in Jasper for the time being.

By the 1940s, Morgan & Lindsey's founders were looking toward retirement, and in 1947 Murphy's first considered acquiring the company. It's not clear whether Murphy's or Morgan & Lindsey made the initial approach, but Walter Shaw thought it was a bad deal at the time. After analyzing several other G. C. Murphy Company purchases, including its takeover of Baltimore's Tottle Stores in the 1920s, Shaw concluded that Morgan & Lindsey wasn't a good investment. "According to what Morgan & Lindsey want, we would have to pay them $1 for every $2 worth of sales," he told Paul Sample.

That wasn't the end, of course. Jim Mack's son, Sephus, says he was told that Morgan & Lindsey had offered to sell the company to several variety-store chains, but Murphy's was the winning bidder in part because his father agreed to keep the name "Morgan & Lindsey" on the stores. "They had done a lot of work to build it up, and they had a lot of pride," says Sephus Mack, who at age nineteen accompanied his father to a bank in downtown Monroe as he closed the deal late one night in 1959. The sale was announced on April 13. For an undisclosed amount of cash (though Murphy's did take out a $10-million loan to finance part of the cost), the company acquired ninety-two stores in Louisiana, Mississippi, Arkansas, and Texas, along with leases for seven additional Morgan & Lindsey locations. Morgan & Lindsey chairman Cyril Lindsey told reporters it was a "splendid opportunity for our organization to progress at an even faster pace."

Murphy's brought more to Morgan & Lindsey than Morgan & Lindsey ever produced for its new parent company, including the money to build a 154,000-square-foot warehouse in Monroe in 1962. For one thing, the Morgan & Lindsey stores were considerably smaller than most of the G. C. Murphy stores. The biggest Morgan & Lindsey store at the time of the takeover was a 12,000-square-foot unit in Monroe, recalls longtime Murphy man Paul Hindes, who worked in sales promotion at the McKeesport home office from 1956 until 1959, when he was sent south to help Morgan & Lindsey. The smallest was Store No. 3026, an 1,800-square-foot unit on North Maple Street in Arcadia, Louisiana. "It wasn't as big as the first floor of my house, and yet it made money," Hindes says. "There was a woman who ran that store with only two other employees." Morgan & Lindsey's old No. 2 store on East Sixth Street in Oakdale was only wide enough for one counter against each wall and another in the center aisle. Sales at Morgan & Lindsey stores were commensurately smaller than at Murphy's as well; in 1958, they averaged $175,000 versus $646,000 at 324 G. C. Murphy locations. Though overall Murphy sales went up 14 percent in 1959 and 2.8 percent in 1960, per-store sales (always a strong point for Murphy's) dropped to just $525,000 in 1963, dragged down by the older and smaller Morgan & Lindsey outlets.

Murphy executives sent to inspect Morgan & Lindsey stores often felt they had entered a time warp. Many of the locations were in tiny rural towns and even the suburban locations were in small shopping centers with few other tenants. Older stores had wooden floors, tin ceilings, and wooden counters like the ones that had been phased out in Murphy five-and-tens a decade earlier. In towns where the Morgan & Lindsey store wasn't large enough to sell wearables, often an independent clothing store had opened next door. Morgan & Lindsey operated on tight profit margins and used its shoestring budgets to erect small stores on small lots; some of them weren't even built with blueprints. Bob Beyer, who worked in the real estate and construction division in McKeesport, remembers being sent down with two other Murphy draftsmen to go from town to town and document the mechanical and electrical systems and floor plans of each Morgan & Lindsey store.

The merchandise and the sales methods weren't up to Murphy standards either. Auditors found items for sale in one Morgan & Lindsey store that were eight to twelve years old. Morgan & Lindsey stores, often serving a fairly cash-poor and rural clientele of sharecroppers and farmers, conducted business on a different basis than Murphy's was used to. Hindes remembers visiting a Morgan & Lindsey store where more than three hundred electric blankets were on layaway because customers could afford to pay only a few dollars on them at a time. It was more electric blankets than he had ever seen on sale at any G. C. Murphy store, much less on layaway. "They used to do a tremendous business in [fabric] down there," Hindes says, because so many Morgan & Lindsey customers made their own clothes. But instead of bolts of new fabric, Morgan & Lindsey carried odd-shaped cast off pieces, "and they sold tons of them, absolutely tons of them," he says.

There was surprisingly little resistance by Morgan & Lindsey personnel to the Murphy management, perhaps because the division retained many of its old managers and a certain degree of autonomy as a wholly owned but separate subsidiary of G. C. Murphy Company. Even Morgan & Lindsey president Elzie E. Latham stayed on in the same capacity after the takeover, while Cyril Lindsey remained on the division's board of directors. Hindes says that some people at the Monroe office were surprised and maybe a little disappointed that Murphy's didn't do more to change Morgan & Lindsey. "They were hoping for updates for the stores, more merchandise, better merchandise," he says. "I think they hoped that we would broaden their base."

A few executives in Monroe also apparently hoped that the Morgan & Lindsey name would be dumped, but true to Jim Mack's word, Murphy's kept the name and opened more variety stores under the Morgan & Lindsey banner, adding another twenty during the 1960s and even a few Murphy's Mart–style stores in the 1970s under the name M&L Discount. The only hints of Murphy ownership came in the form of small gilt lettering in the windows and tiny type at the bottom of newspaper ads that read "A Division of G. C. Murphy Co.," along with the appearance of Murphy private-label merchandise, such as Carolina Moon hosiery and Big Murph jeans, on the shelves. The Morgan & Lindsey name soldiered on until 1977 when regional manager Clair McElhinny was sent down from McKeesport to oversee the conversion of all Morgan & Lindsey stores to G. C. Murphy Company locations at a cost of $1 million. At least some customers, he says, wanted to know if G. C. Murphy Company was owned by El Dorado, Arkansas–based Murphy Oil Company, which operated gas and oil wells and refineries throughout the region. They were reassured that the two companies were of no relation.

If there was any standoffishness, it may have been directed at the Morgan & Lindsey employees by a few G. C. Murphy people, says Dick Gibson Sr., who was sent to Spring Branch, Texas, in 1964 to manage a Morgan & Lindsey store. "Some of the Murphy guys kind of formed a clique," Gibson says. "We felt like we had the expert training and that we knew how to run stores better than anyone down south." At some meetings, he says, "Murphy guys" would sit on one wall and "Morgan & Lindsey guys" would sit on the other. Other Murphy managers didn't want to be transferred into Morgan & Lindsey territory for fear that their co-workers up north would forget about them. By and large, however, Murphy people liked their Morgan & Lindsey colleagues and Gibson says Morgan & Lindsey people were hospitable to people from Murphy's: "They were glad to have us come down there."

While Morgan & Lindsey employees welcomed the Murphy men, things didn't always go smoothly in the small towns where they lived. "Some of the Deep South people were not very open to outsiders," says Hindes, who lived for a time in Jasper. If a neighbor held a cocktail party, for instance, they would sometimes send three different sets of invitations—one for 5:00 to 7:00 P.M., another for 7:00 to 9:00 P.M., and the third for after 9:00 P.M. Only people the host considered friends received invitations for the third part of the evening, Hindes says. "If you got invited to the first [event], you were just being invited to be polite."

Other Murphy employees found Morgan & Lindsey people accommodating but couldn't find accommodations in Morgan & Lindsey territory. Some towns were so small they lacked apartment buildings or motels, says Martin Schultz, who worked in Murphy's construction division and moved with his wife from town to town as Morgan & Lindsey stores were remodeled. "In Bunkie, Louisiana, we couldn't find a place" to live, he says. They finally rented a room above a garage. "In Amite, Louisiana, we had to rent [a room] from an old lady in town. In Crowley, we rented a little house for $35 a month." Schultz's wife, Ilene, who worked in several Morgan & Lindsey stores during their tour of the South, says she found the people "really friendly and really nice. After they got to know you, they were just nice. If you had a friend, they were really good friends."

If Yankees from Murphy's struggled to learn about southern hospitality, they were utterly floored by the civil rights struggle that was exploding just as the company made its big move into Dixieland. African Americans—some of them college-educated northern transplants; others natives of the South—were demanding an end to segregated education, public transportation, jobs, and restaurants. Proponents of the old Jim Crow system liked to say that blacks had "separate but equal" facilities to whites, but in practice, they were anything but equal. African Americans were taught in overcrowded public schools using hand-me-down supplies from white facilities. When traveling, they rode at the back of buses or in converted baggage cars on trains. Many white-owned restaurants either wouldn't serve them or made them eat in the kitchen.

In fairness, though it operated most of its stores above the Mason-Dixon Line, the G. C. Murphy Company hadn't always been a shining beacon of racial equality. As late as the 1940s, blacks were not allowed into the upstairs dining room at Store No. 1 in McKeesport, and a construction division report from 1950 dryly notes that the "restrooms for colored employees" at Store No. 12 in Pittsburgh were remodeled. Many Murphy stores in West Virginia and Virginia also had separate "colored" and "white" facilities; one Murphy manager distinctly remembers seeing "colored" water fountains at the downtown Richmond, Virginia, store, for instance.

By the 1950s, there were a handful of black management trainees in inner-city stores, but most African American men who applied for a job at Murphy's were lucky to be hired as janitors, and there were no black executives at the G. C. Murphy Company until the early 1970s. Still, Murphy's made good faith efforts to abolish segregation. In September 1952, the last segregated lunch counter in the G. C. Murphy Company chain was eliminated at Store No. 166 in Washington, D.C., a flagship location near Capitol Hill. Admittedly, the move was made under duress—civil rights activists were picketing the store—but there would be no more "separate but equal" treatment of Murphy customers as a matter of company policy. That didn't set well in the South, especially when Murphy's started putting food service in larger Morgan & Lindsey stores and many new locations opened under its own name in Florida, Georgia, Alabama, and Louisiana. "They're all right to sleep with, but you don't eat with them," one man in Decatur, Alabama, told Ellison "Al" Boggs, who was southern district manager of Murphy's restaurant division in the mid-1960s. Boggs was flabbergasted.

Variety-store clerks had long been willing to wait on any kind of customer—the only color they recognized was "green"—but lunch counters were a different matter. Dime-store lunch counters would serve them, but they couldn't sit—they had to stand or take their food "to go." Segregation at five-and-ten lunch counters met its Waterloo in 1960, and as with so many things, F. W. Woolworth was the pioneer, though hardly by choice. On February 1, four freshmen from North Carolina A&T College went into the Woolworth's on South Elm Street in Greensboro, North Carolina, sat down at the counter, and ordered coffee. "We don't serve Negroes," the waitress told them. They stayed until the store closed. The next morning, thirty-one students from A&T arrived, were refused service, and stayed until the store closed. Before the week was out, four hundred students sitting in shifts were occupying the stools at the lunch counter. The Greensboro Woolworth's held out until July when three African American students were finally served. But managers of the chain's other stores refused to budge, and sit-ins were soon in progress at lunch counters in fifty-four cities, including Nashville, Tampa, and Hampton, Virginia. Some protests turned violent; in Nashville, a mob of white demonstrators pulled blacks from their stools and beat them.

Murphy's was determined not to repeat Woolworth's experience, but, just like the bigger company, it had a hard time convincing some of its managers to desegregate. In 1965, Boggs arrived at a store in Rome, Georgia, just as a sit-in was getting underway. "It's the sickest I ever got in my life," says Boggs, still visibly shaken by the memory. "It's kind of hard to talk about it." The manager ordered the lights over the lunch counter to be turned off. Out came the waitresses with tubs of hot, soapy water, which they proceeded to slop

onto the seated customers. Another Murphy executive remembers that one restaurant manager removed the seats from all the stools along the lunch counter in his store—rather than allowing blacks to sit with whites, everyone would have to stand. Murphy officials put out the word that any restaurant employees who refused to serve black customers should quit immediately, though few did. One girl sadly handed her resignation to Boggs with the words, "My daddy won't let me wait on colored people."

The opening of Store No. 297 in Gadsden, Alabama, with an integrated lunch counter brought angry protests from some segregationist whites. Murphy management asked representatives from the U.S. Justice Department to coach employees on how to handle the demonstrations. "It was a mess," Boggs says. "I didn't get them to change their ways. If [Bobby] Kennedy couldn't do it, I couldn't do it." Mindful of the need to keep the peace, Murphy officials preparing to open a store in Texarkana, Texas, told the police department there that it would be fully integrated. "The police told us, 'All right, we'll be around, but don't call us inside your store [in case of trouble] because we're not going in,'" Boggs says. "What kind of police are that?"

FIG. 41
Store No. 296 in Decatur, Ala., greets customers on opening day, May 2, 1963. While other chains were converting to self-service and checkout lines, G. C. Murphy Company insisted on keeping a girl behind each counter until the 1960s. The failure to simplify operations cost Murphy's dearly.

After opening Store No. 296 in the Gateway Shopping Center in Decatur, managers went to a nearby restaurant to celebrate. Boggs knew the town was dry but couldn't resist having some fun with the waitress. When she asked what he wanted, he said "a bourbon Manhattan—I know I can't have one, but that's what I want." She laughed and brought out the manager.

"Are you people from Murphy's?" he asked.

Yes, the Murphy crew responded.

"How did you make out serving those n——rs today?" he said.

Nonplussed, Boggs replied that if black customers came in and sat down, they would be served.

"Not me," said the other man. "I'll lock the doors. I'd rather go out of business."

"You know the thing we found out about that guy?" Boggs says. "He was from West Virginia. He went down there and opened up a restaurant and decided he wasn't going to serve 'colored' people."

Tensions faded over time, but new G. C. Murphy Company stores in the South faced other fundamental problems. "It was an unknown name," says Wayne Potter, who worked in the construction division. "I don't think they ever made money [in the South]. If they did, it was very little." Some locations did succeed, though. Store No. 306 in Huntsville, Alabama, home to a big NASA research center during the glory days of the space program, was one of the best locations of its size in the company at the time. "Woolworth was no competition, but they had a store," says Jeffery Fussell, an assistant manager there in the early 1960s. "McLellan's had a store in the same shopping center, but they were a joke. We didn't even check them for competition because if you walked in there it was empty."

But the Huntsville store may have been an exception—perhaps it was successful because so many transplanted northerners working for NASA were familiar with Murphy's. Other Murphy stores in the South were struggling, sometimes because what they were selling was out of touch with the market. "We were sending Kalamazoo Sleds into Alabama," says Roy Fowler Jr., a home office buyer in the 1970s. "And in lawn and garden we were sending snow shovels and ice melters. The shrubs you used up North were trash down South—they wouldn't grow there." A store manager in Georgia called Luther Shay in the home office's merchandise investment control department when he was shipped a load of pine cones at Christmas. Through his laughter, the manager explained that Georgia was known for pine trees and his customers would not pay for something they could pick up off the ground.

In time, Murphy's was able to adjust its merchandise mixes appropriately, but it couldn't do anything about the cost of advertising, which sapped profit from the thinly spread southern stores. In Pennsylvania, West Virginia, Ohio, and Indiana, where Murphy's stores often were clustered in neighboring communities, stores shared the cost of advertising, circulars, and other publicity. With only a handful of widely scattered G. C. Murphy stores in the

South, each was forced to bear the entire cost of any advertising that it ran. Pity the poor managers of the six G. C. Murphy stores in Texas, the two stores in Tennessee, or the single lonely location in North Carolina in 1966.

At times, even the advertising the stores could afford didn't do much. Clair Trost was the manager of Store No. 316, a 40,000-square-foot unit right across from a busy Sears, Roebuck & Company store in the new Central Park Mall in San Antonio. "When we would advertise, people would call up and say, 'Where are you?'" he says. They hadn't noticed Murphy's across from Sears. "Bealls was a local chain. Winn's was in all of the one-horse towns. People knew them. They didn't know us." It didn't help that Morgan & Lindsey, despite being well established, was an also-ran in the region. Fussell learned the hard way when he was sent to manage a store in Jackson, Mississippi. "It was one of the most dismal stores I've ever been in," he says. "It was dirty. The windows were dirty. It hadn't been merchandised. They had like eight footballs in the toy department—and that was the end cap feature." One customer complained that the music department didn't have any music; another came into the store, took a quick look around, and told Fussell, "I don't know how you can stand to work here." Then he walked out. After first planning to close the store, the home office decided to make a fresh start and change it to the G. C. Murphy Company name. As they were taking down the Morgan & Lindsey sign, a little old lady came in and asked, "Aren't you going to be TG&Y any more?" TG&Y was a competing southern variety-store chain.

"That spoke volumes," Fussell says. "You could bring in a marketing expert and have him talk for twenty minutes about branding and penetration and that one little old lady could have told him everything he needed to know."

Murphy managers tried their best to build sales. Trost was able to take advantage of a loophole in the ordering system to stock higher-cost—and thus higher-profit—items that few variety stores handled. The loophole was the new in-store catalog created by Murphy's in 1965 so smaller stores could list garden sheds, swing sets, and other large items they didn't have room to carry. Customers at Morgan & Lindsey locations would order these big-ticket items from the Monroe warehouse and have them delivered. Technically, store managers were only supposed to ask for these expensive items if they had an order in hand. Trost decided he could sell more of them if they were on display, so he faked orders for catalog merchandise and hoped it would sell. Luckily, it did.

As were other Murphy managers, Trost was allowed to make "local buys" of products that weren't on the company's order books. He took advantage of Dallas's status as the number 2 city in the United States for women's fashion by making deals for brand-name apparel at bargain-basement prices. "We had fur coats come in one time as a special buy, $50 and $100 a coat," Trost says. "There was a manufacturer downtown who cut and sewed men's pants and suits. He might bring in five thousand in all colors and sizes." Artificial flowers were in vogue at the time, and one of the biggest manufacturers—Teter Floral

FIG. 42
Murphy's had a difficult time integrating more than forty department stores it purchased in Texas in the early 1960s, including the small Terry Farris chain, based in McAllen, Texas. Terry Farris Store No. 5412 was located on West Jackson Street in Harlingen, Texas.

Products—was in Dallas. Trost decided they'd build traffic, so he ordered four times the typical amount of merchandise for a store of his size and put it on prominent display at the entrance. Just collecting everything he needed required multiple trips in his personal station wagon, but the giant spread of brightly colored flowers had great eye appeal, he says.

Not all Trost's promotions went smoothly. Though he can't remember exactly what the product was, he remembers heavily promoting a special buy in anticipation of a holiday sale. Trost ordered an entire trailer of merchandise that never arrived. "I called the warehouse [in Monroe] and said, 'If my assistant and I come up there, will it be on the dock? We can't disappoint these people.'" Trost and an assistant manager rode all night on a bus from San Antonio to Monroe, rented a truck, loaded it with merchandise, and drove back to the store. "It was an awful drive," he says. "You can bet we never ran another ad without sitting on the merchandise. You can't sell promises!" By the time Trost was transferred from San Antonio, the store at Central Park Mall was doing $1.2 million in sales. It was the store's best year yet, but because it was paying high rent and the cost of all its own advertising, that wasn't enough to put it into the black. The manager who followed Trost had a heart attack not long after taking over in San Antonio; he'd come from a smaller store and couldn't handle the stress.

Through a disciplined training program, rigorous cost controls, and creative merchandising, Murphy's had honed the operation of successful variety stores to a science by the 1950s, yet the company was having a hard time running five-and-tens in Texas. It seems obvious now that successfully incorporating more than forty department stores into the Murphy system would be a real challenge, but under Jim Mack's ambitious expansion program, G. C. Murphy Company was going to have to learn how—and fast. In November 1960, Murphy's acquired Cobb Department Stores' four locations in Odessa, Levelland, and Lubbock, Texas; three months later, it swallowed McAllen-based Terry Farris, Inc., which had seventeen stores. In 1962, Murphy's bought the twenty-eight-store Bruner's Department Stores chain in San Antonio and thirteen Morris Department Stores around Dallas. The new acquisitions were merged into a new Terry Farris Division of the G. C. Murphy Company. Mack was scrambling the careful "growth through concentration" policy that his father had laid out thirty years before. Murphy's was now in unfamiliar territory both geographically and philosophically, and its years of expertly selling large quantities of variety-store merchandise turned out to be a liability. Confronted with fashion-conscious shoppers who were more interested in high styles than low prices, Murphy's made serious missteps.

The Terry Farris stores were "junior" department stores compared to "real" department stores such as Macy's. As did their bigger brethren, they sold men's and ladies' apparel, housewares, and linens, but they were smaller (typically about 10,000 square feet) and slightly less expensive. The chain was founded in McAllen, Texas, just after World War II by O. A. Terry and Carlton Farris and had expanded east and west along the Rio Grande River. Because Terry Farris was heavily involved in apparel sales, a menswear buyer named Bob Snell was sent to Texas to check out the chain before Murphy's bought it. "[Snell] came back and said he thought it would be a mistake, and he was right," Paul Hindes says.

Terry Farris specialized in "Western" wear, such as boots and jeans, and catered to families who worked on oil wells or cattle ranches—or wanted to look as though they did. Well-meaning Murphy's executives insisted on installing gondolas (freestanding shelves made of pegboard and metal) in Terry Farris locations and filling them with toiletries from the variety stores. While it made some sense to sell hairspray and combs alongside the jewelry and accessories Terry Farris already carried, it cheapened the stores' image. "They were clothing stores, and [Murphy's] didn't know anything about clothing stores," Schultz says, adding that the company's executives also didn't understand the importance to Texans of maintaining Terry Farris's "Western" heritage.

There were other problems that no one foresaw. Department stores carried many nationally advertised name brands, such as Levi Strauss jeans, that weren't then sold to discount chains. When Murphy's took over Terry Farris, Bruner's, Cobb's, and Morris, some manufacturers refused to sell to those stores any more for fear their products would be diverted to the parent company's five-and-tens. Murphy's responded by sending its own

private-label brands into the department stores, which "more or less ruined them," Schultz says. "They were high-class stores, selling a lot of name-brand stuff, and they sent them a lot of Murphy's 'Big Murph' stuff. That didn't go over too well."

Bruner's and Cobb's had been more upscale than Terry Farris, and the damage to their images was consequently more severe. Bruner's "was like a [J. C.] Penney's, not as big, but a Penney's-type store," says Wayne Potter, who worked in maintenance for Murphy's for more than thirty years. "That changed after Murphy's bought them. They started putting our merchandise into them, and they went downhill. It was a medium-grade store, and we took it down."

The department stores had their defenders in Murphy management. Some executives argued with justification that the expertise the company gained in apparel was improving "soft lines" throughout the chain. Textiles were becoming an increasingly important part of Murphy's business in the mid-1960s, with 30 percent of the company's sales coming from housewares and 35 percent from clothing. And with customers placing more emphasis on trendy and "fad" clothing, the Texas department stores became training grounds for Murphy buyers and sales personnel to experiment with fashions. Larger Murphy stores

FIG. 44
Though Murphy's opened several new Terry Farris and Bruner's locations, such as Store No. 5422 in San Antonio, Texas, shown here, only a handful of the department stores remained by the 1980s.

copied window trim and display ideas from the department stores and brought in several higher-priced clothing lines after first trying them out in Terry Farris. All that experience proved useful in the 1970s when the company began opening Murphy's Marts, which devoted much of their floor space to apparel.

The Terry Farris Division also gave Murphy's its first experience with credit cards. Existing credit plans at Cobb's and Terry Farris were expanded and promoted, and by the 1970s shoppers could use their Cobb's or Terry Farris charge cards at many G. C. Murphy locations in Texas. No doubt the promise of "buy now, pay later" lured some Cobb's and Terry Farris customers into the unfamiliar new G. C. Murphy variety stores that were opening in Texas. The southern stores also were among the first in the G. C. Murphy Company to enroll in credit plans run by banks, such as Master Charge. By 1970, virtually all Murphy stores were accepting bank credit cards and the company soon rolled out its own chain-wide "Murphy Charge" card.

Overall, though, the Terry Farris Division was never more than an interesting experiment for Murphy's—and the interest quickly faded after Jim Mack's untimely death in 1968. The company's annual reports don't break out exact sales and revenue figures for the Texas department stores, but surviving executives are adamant they never produced much return on Murphy's investment. After opening four new Terry Farris stores in 1967 and 1968, the division went into a long, slow decline, and locations began closing year after year. In July 1968, Murphy's sold the remaining ten Morris Department Stores around Dallas to Myers Department Stores, a competitor in neighboring Fort Worth. By the mid-1970s, all that remained of the department stores were sixteen Terry Farris and Bruner's locations and two Cobb's stores in Odessa. The entire division dwindled to just nine stores by the time Murphy's was taken over by Ames in 1985.

Martin Schultz, who spent most of his Murphy's career working in the South, says the department store experiment can be summed up in one sentence: "You can't run a store in Texas out of McKeesport."

"We Always Went to Murphy's"

As a child, Murphy's was my favorite store in Dixie Manor Shopping Center in Louisville, Kentucky. It was (and still is) a long L-shaped strip center with about forty stores, built in the mid-1950s. It had two department stores, and there was another five-and-ten, Woolworth's, but my family rarely went there. We always went to Murphy's.

That's where I bought most of my toys. There was a lunch counter and a sandwich lady. If you go to Subway and get the cold cut combo and don't get it too fussy, you can get close to the Murphy's submarine taste. They were fairly plain! And they were quite small. I remember the shredded lettuce.

The toy department had counters with little ledges so kids could examine the toys closer to eye level. I went around the three aisles of toys so many times I can still see it in my head. The books were in one corner, but the comics were on a stand by the lunch counter. Murphy's was directly next door to a Walgreen's, which had a competing restaurant that usually was more popular, but Murphy's managed to keep theirs going. I believe the store closed sometime in the late 1970s.

—Scott Santoro
Louisville, Ky.

If the G. C. Murphy Company was the darling of the variety-store industry in the 1950s, then S. S. Kresge Company was the dud. Unlike Murphy's, Kresge followed F. W. Woolworth Company into major cities, and with their downtown shopping areas in serious eclipse by suburban malls, Kresge was paying the price with flat earnings and slow sales growth.

McCrory's was in even worse shape than Kresge. After changing ownership several times in a series of nasty takeover battles, the chain was forced into two shotgun weddings, first with McLellan Stores and then with H. L. Green Company. Hundreds of McCrory's locations were losing money, morale was sinking, lawsuits were flying, and the parent corporation failed to turn a profit in 1962 or 1963. In a four-year period between 1960 and 1964, it had four different presidents and one acting president.

Alas, Kresge didn't even have boardroom intrigue to liven things up. Though approaching one hundred years old, founder Sebastian S. Kresge was still chairman of the board. His son Stanley, the vice chairman, said later the company and the industry were in the doldrums: "We were doing about as well as the other variety stores, but we were all doing very poorly." In 1957, Kresge's affable sales manager, Harry B. Cunningham, was given the nebulous title of "general vice president" and directed to study Kresge's competitors and the retail industry and then devise a plan for pushing the corporation out of its rut. He spent two years traveling the country and became excited by one emerging segment of retailers—discount department stores.

Discount merchandisers had been around in one form or another since the 1930s. Many made their reputation by purchasing odd lots of discontinued merchandise and selling it with little markup from locations with low overhead—converted warehouses and factories or stores abandoned by other retailers. To keep personnel costs low, there was little service and customers were left to fend for themselves. Department- and variety-store veterans looked at them askance but didn't think these fly-by-night operations were a threat until they began selling name-brand, nationally advertised merchandise such as Parker pens, Lionel trains, and Remington shavers below manufacturers' suggested retail prices. The big chains, long accustomed to comfortable 20 and 30 percent markups, complained to the manufacturers, who responded by refusing to sell to discounters or suing to stop their products from being sold at below-list prices. Each lawsuit brought free publicity to the discounters, whom the public began viewing as champions of the consumer. The courts eventually threw out much of the litigation as unfair restraint of trade. The king of the discounters was Eugene Ferkauf, whose E. J. Korvette's grew from one luggage store on the second floor of an old building in Manhattan to a half-billion-dollar chain in ten years.

But Korvette's was run haphazardly by people with little retailing experience. Many of the other early discount stores lacked reliable distribution channels, trained staff, and experienced promotion and advertising departments. Cunningham realized that S. S. Kresge Company had distribution centers around the country; hundreds of experienced back-office personnel to handle buying, accounting, and advertising functions; and a well-run training program similar to that of G. C. Murphy's. If a discounting operation could be built on the existing Kresge framework, the company would blow away Korvette's and all its imitators. In 1961, Kresge converted three money-losing variety stores into discount houses under the name Jupiter. When the experiment proved successful, it opened eighteen new high-volume, low-margin discount department stores the following year under a new name: Kmart.

Cunningham, who later became president and CEO of Kresge, wasn't the only person to see the potential of discounting, and Kresge wasn't the only old-line retailer to try its hand in the field. L. S. Ayres, an Indianapolis-based department-store chain, launched its Ayr-Way discount outlets in 1961, while Minneapolis's Dayton Company created Target in 1962. Mighty F. W. Woolworth Corporation launched its first Woolco store in Columbus, Ohio, in June of that same year, and in July 1963 even punch-drunk McCrory was able to open Mc-Crory Village, an 80,000-square-foot discount department store in Poughkeepsie, New York, featuring clothing, appliances, auto accessories, shoes, jewelry, and a garden shop.

In fact, among the big national chains jumping into the discount field in the 1960s, one name was conspicuous in its absence: G. C. Murphy Company. Instead, Murphy president Jim Mack put out a dictate: The company would not use the word "discount" on any signs, advertising, or correspondence. "I don't think anybody in the company agreed with him," says Bill Kraus, a toy buyer in the home office. "You could feel the change in the marketplace. Discount was the biggest selling tool to hit the market—we were dead." Rather than moving toward a discount operation, Murphy's purchased the Morgan & Lindsey chain and dozens of Texas department stores, moves—particularly the acquisition of Morgan & Lindsey, which had many small, rural stores—that left Murphy executives scratching their heads. "I had trouble making sense of it," confesses Jud Ellis Jr. of the real estate department. Murphy's needed a Cunningham; instead, it had taken a big step backward.

Though Walter Shaw Sr. remained chairman of the board and was vigorous into his late seventies, he was leaving more of the company's operations to the younger generation (including his son Walter Shaw Jr., then Murphy's vice president of sales), and Jim Mack was firmly in command. Some suggest Mack wasn't the only G. C. Murphy Company executive reluctant to plunge into discounting; perhaps he's unfairly blamed for stifling innovation. Ellis, for one, found Mack soft spoken and even a little shy at times but intelligent and open to suggestion. "You have liberty to come down here and talk to me about anything at any time," Mack once told him. "You will find that I am responsible for 'disapproving' of many things I never heard of." It's also possible that longtime Murphy hands were unwilling to turn their backs on the dime-store field in which they'd spent their entire careers and may have purposely misdirected Mack. "My uncle is not a very good judge of people," his nephew John Mack once said.

Bob Messner, whose father was a Murphy hardware buyer, joined the company as its first in-house attorney in 1968 and says it was led astray in part by its own research. As early as the 1950s, Murphy's was running focus groups to predict trends and improve service and merchandise. Time and again, customers told Murphy's they preferred to have a girl behind each counter, Messner says, "but they kept going to Kmart." In 1960, Kresge posted sales of $419 million versus Murphy's $246 million. But as Kmart took hold, the gap widened dramatically. Eight years later, Kresge sales were up 300 percent to $1.7 billion while Murphy's had gone up only 48 percent to $365 million.

In the meantime, Walter Shaw Sr. was directing his energy toward philanthropy. McKeesport Hospital received $850,000 in cash, stock, and other contributions from Shaw in the 1950s and '60s, not including the addition of an entire wing—the two-hundred-bed Shaw Building—in 1952. McKeesport's Boys and Girls Club also moved into a handsome new headquarters thanks in large part to Shaw, while at Westminster College in New Wilmington, Pennsylvania, he funded construction of a dormitory for 158 women students and an infirmary. In all, Shaw gave away more than $3 million in the late 1950s and early '60s—the equivalent of roughly $20 million in 2006 dollars. And though Mack was running

FIG. 45
A customer feedback panel in Erie, Pa., describes what they like and dislike about the G.C. Murphy Co. on May 24, 1956. Murphy's was among the first variety-store chains to research consumer preferences through focus groups.

the G. C. Murphy Company, Walter Shaw Sr. remained its public face, especially after the death of his wife, Una, in 1954. Saturday nights found Shaw sitting at the front of Store No. 1 in McKeesport talking to customers and passing out anti-Communism pamphlets to the adults and candy to their children. It also wasn't unusual for him to pack a sandwich, an apple, and his loyal secretary, Chuck Shaw (no relation), into his Cadillac and light off at top speed for some far corner of Murphy territory. People who rode with Walter Shaw Sr. said they witnessed more than a few close shaves on narrow mountain roads. Chuck Shaw joked that he "kissed the ground" when they returned to McKeesport: "Every time we get back, that Cadillac is a little narrower."

The impromptu store tours came to an end in late 1961 when Shaw began feeling ill and headed to Florida for his annual vacation, hoping the sunshine would revive him. It didn't. On January 10, 1962, little more than a week after turning eighty-one, he died at St. Petersburg's St. Anthony Hospital. As with Sephus Mack's death more than twenty years earlier, there was a genuine outpouring of grief. The *Daily News* called Shaw McKeesport's "most popular citizen." On January 16, hundreds of people crammed into the city's First Methodist Church for his funeral where Westminster president William W. Orr credited Shaw's success to "love of work, love of people and country, and humbleness. . . . It takes a fine quality to love people generally, but this man was thorough and genuine in his love for people. If any of you has ever walked down a street with him, you know just what I mean. Time and time again . . . you had to stop while he talked to his many acquaintances." Twenty-five honorary pallbearers accompanied Shaw's casket from the church, and a procession led by two motorcycle policemen and ten limousines carried "the engineer" of the G. C. Murphy Company to Mt. Vernon Cemetery in Elizabeth Township, Pennsylvania.

With Shaw's death, Jim Mack added "chairman of the board" to his duties. Friends and family say that Walter Shaw Jr., though bright and articulate, didn't have his father's love of the business, and the relationship between Jim Mack and Shaw Jr. was strained at best, which affected the way he was treated by the Murphy board of directors. "I don't think they ever gave him a chance," says Bill Anderson, then the Baltimore district manager. "They didn't have the confidence in him that they had with Mr. Mack. They made a hell of a mistake."

Unlike his father, who shared the burden of leading the company, Jim Mack would guide Murphy's alone, which was too bad because Murphy's could have used an extra hand at the tiller as it struggled to incorporate Morgan & Lindsey and the Texas department stores into its operations. A dizzying array of management and organizational realignments—many of them related to the southern expansion—ate up energy that could have been directed toward a discount operation or updating the variety stores. "We scattered ourselves around too much," says Terry Stadterman, assistant to a regional manager whose territory stretched from Ohio to the Georgia state line. "We had too many committees and we didn't update fast enough."

Murphy's did bow to some inevitable marketplace trends. It began converting stores to self-service with checkout counters in the early 1960s; by 1963, 183 of the company's 512 locations had switched, with most of the rest using quick service stations. A few older stores—some of them dating to the company's earliest years, such as Store No. 25 in East Pittsburgh—were closed as the move into the suburbs continued in earnest. Anderson traveled the Baltimore area with the real estate department, scouting new locations, sometimes trying to imagine how an empty field would look after it sprouted a Murphy store. Days counted in the race to saturate the suburbs, and as a store in Hillandale, Maryland, was being erected, Walter Shaw Jr. called to make sure it would open on time. "Mr. Mack was worried we were going to work [the construction] people on Sundays," Anderson says. "I said, 'How in the hell do you think I'm going to get it done?'" He finally reached a compromise so the Sabbath wouldn't be violated—the construction crews would work "right up until midnight on Saturday night."

Sometimes, Murphy's could hardly keep up with the pace. At Store No. 280 in Olympia Shopping Center near McKeesport, the parking lot still wasn't paved a week before the official opening, says Dave Backstrom, the first manager. While crews came in with flamethrowers to dry the clay so that asphalt could be laid, trucks trying to make deliveries kept getting stuck in the mud; bulldozers towed them to the store's back door. "That store just scared me to death," says Backstrom, who had been running the tiny California, Pennsylvania, store. "I came home and told my wife, I can't take it, it's too damned big." The Olympia store was a headache, but not because of its size—as the closest shopping center location to the home office, Murphy executives liked to visit and show it off to out-of-towners. "Every Saturday after they played golf, they'd be in about one o'clock, so I couldn't take Saturdays off," Backstrom says. "Walter Shaw Sr. was in there all the time. All of the buyers who lived up on the hill were in there all the time." Each night before he left, Backstrom would stand in the parking lot and study the store through the front windows to make sure nothing was out of place.

The modernization trend didn't affect many traditional practices, as Clair McElhinny found out while he was managing Store No. 167 in Jamestown, New York. Though Murphy's wasn't open on Sundays, most of the new discount stores were. When a Jamesway opened on the outskirts of the city, McElhinny decided he'd better respond. Without telling the home office, he placed ads in the Jamestown *Post-Journal* and ran commercials on the radio announcing that Murphy's would open on Sunday as well. Bob Grove, an assistant manager, says the store did an "unheard of" $3,000 worth of business on the first Sunday it was open, but Jamestown officials fined Murphy's $300 for violating the city's so-called "blue laws" and McElhinny says he caught "all kinds of hell" from the home office. After three Sundays and $900 in fines, the experiment ended, though G. C. Murphy Company stores located inside shopping malls were eventually forced to open on Sundays by covenants in their leases or by competition.

On Sunday sales and in other areas, Murphy's no longer innovating, it was being forced further into changes. In 1966, for instance, customer demand and slipping market share finally compelled Murphy stores to accept credit cards and a group of fifty-eight stores near Pittsburgh joined a bank charge plan—more than a decade after Woolworth and Kresge. That G. C. Murphy Company remained profitable might have had something to do with store managers such as McElhinny who were willing to break rules. Murphy managers retained an extraordinary degree of autonomy into the 1960s, including the freedom to order items that weren't normally stocked. Earl Rehrig added furniture to his store in North Ridgeville, Ohio, when a distributor offered to sell him sofas and reclining chairs for $99 per set. Then he talked a General Electric jobber into supplying him with hi-fi equipment. That went well, too. Riding lawn mowers finally got him into hot water; a dealer offered a tractor-trailer load at $125 each, and Rehrig put a full-page ad in the local newspaper offering them at $149 the following weekend.

Rehrig called the home office buyer in charge of garden equipment Monday morning. "Ollie, I have a problem," he said. "I sold $3,600 worth of goods."

"What were they?" the buyer asked.

"Riding lawn mowers."

The buyer went "ballistic," says Rehrig, but adds, "You've got to stick your neck out every now and again." Such rule breaking was tolerated because it usually improved sales,

FIG. 46
The G. C. Murphy Company followed its customers out to the suburbs, and by the late 1960s, nearly all new stores were opening inside shopping malls instead of downtown urban areas. This modern store equipped with checkout lines opened in May 1967 at Greece Town Mall in Rochester, N.Y.

thanks to the education that store managers received in the Murphy Executive Training Program, which had evolved into what *Chain Store Age* called a "graduate course of retailing." It turned out "mini-merchants," says Ed Kohler, an assistant manager in the 1960s who later became a manufacturers' representative for a cosmetics company that supplied Murphy's and other chains. "After I left, I knew many people from Kresge and F. W. Woolworth because I sold to them, but they couldn't touch Murphy's," he says. Headed in the 1960s by Chuck Lytle, a protégé of Paul Sample, most employees entered the training program the day they started with Murphy's. (Most *male* employees, that is. The first women weren't admitted to the program until the early 1970s. College educated or not, they all started work as humble stock boys with an employee handbook and a procedure manual. After a twelve-week correspondence course, including homework assignments, multiple-choice quizzes, and short essays, they received a written test on what they'd learned. Some were paid extra money for grading other people's tests. Luther Shay received 25¢ for each test he graded: "Extravagant," he says with a laugh. If they passed, they progressed to the next set of assignments on sales and service and counter operation and then through twenty-six lesson plans covering topics from employee relations to cash handling to advertising and allocating shelf space. "You came out of there knowing how to run a store," says Pete Shuppy, who started with the company in 1958 and whose father was also a Murphy manager.

FIG. 47
Vic Lauerman of the Murphy employee relations department; director of employee, public, and labor relations Ed Procious; and Procious's assistant, Edwin Davis, conduct a sales class for clerks in 1968. Refined for more than thirty years, the G. C. Murphy Company training programs had evolved into what one trade publication called "a graduate course in retailing" when this photo was taken.

A few people washed out and were doomed to spend forever as assistant managers, but the rest graduated following a weeklong series of examinations and interviews at the home office under the watchful eyes of Murphy executives. Thirty to forty assistant managers, most in their late twenties or early thirties, composed each graduating class. "You had better know what you were talking about before you go in there," Shuppy says, "because you were in competition with everyone in that room." Fred Speidel remembers studying for a month with four other assistant managers before taking his exams. "It was hell week, basically," Roy Fowler Jr. says. "You were away from home for a full week and it was just one thing after another." Most graduates were assigned to manage their own stores shortly after graduation, but others were tapped for home office assignments.

The confidence earned in the training program bred a certain competitiveness among Murphy personnel. When Bob Bishop was assistant manager of the Eastgate Shopping Plaza store in Indianapolis, he was responsible for seasonal merchandise. On the day before Halloween candy and costumes were to go on sale, Bishop decorated thirty feet of counters, which included cutting the glass dividers that still trimmed each Murphy's display—a time-consuming and potentially painful job. He left that night proud that his counters were neatly trimmed and ready. He returned in the morning to find every piece of glass missing—the other two assistants had hid it. Bishop stormed into manager Jake Spannuth's office: "What kind of an operation are you running here?"

Spannuth leveled his gaze at him and said, patiently, "Bob, you've got to take care of your own battles."

Bishop waited until the other assistant managers were gone for the night. Then he methodically removed every single piece of glass from every one of their counters and hid them. "I never had any trouble after that," he says.

Sharp elbows were thrown sometimes too during "assistant managers' sales" at Murphy's stores, held whenever store managers went to the home office for sales meetings. Assistants competed for prize money that was awarded to the stores with the biggest one-day sales increases. At the Eastgate store one year, Bishop, Ron Templeton, and Bob Baxter decided amongst themselves that the winning assistant manager there would also get a free meal from the other two. The day before the assistant manager's sale was to begin, Templeton lined up racks of housedresses that his department would feature but made the fatal mistake of going home before the store closed. Baxter took over the PA system to announce a massive sale on housedresses. Templeton arrived the next day to find row after row of empty dress racks—and because they'd been sold before the contest began, the sales didn't count toward his total.

The roughest tactics were reserved for competing stores. In the 1960s, Ed Kinter ran the restaurant at Store No. 165 on Market Street in Harrisburg, Pennsylvania, across the street from a Kresge store and next door to an H. L. Green. "We were all friends," he says. "If I needed a gallon of Coke [syrup] or something, I could run over to them and borrow it, and then bring it back." The truce evaporated when a big parade was scheduled to pass down Market Street where Kinter was planning to sell submarine sandwiches from the front window for 39¢. That morning Kresge's had an ad in the newspaper featuring subs for 29¢.

"Hey, lookee, what's the big idea?" Kinter asked the manager of Kresge's restaurant. "Why are we giving sandwiches away? Neither one of us can make any money at 29¢. This is a big day. The hay is ripe. We can harvest it!"

"I told them we shouldn't do this," the Kresge man said, but his district manager wanted to undersell Murphy's.

"You know I can't let you get away with it," Kinter replied. Then he went back to his store and made a new sign for the front window with a red bull's-eye on it: "Submarine Sandwiches: 25¢."

"Next thing I know, across the road they're selling submarine sandwiches for 23¢," Kinter says. "I grabbed another bull's-eye: 'Submarine Sandwiches: 19¢.'"

That brought the Kresge district manager across the street to complain. "Let's be reasonable," he told Kinter.

"Okay, let's all go back to 39¢," Kinter said.

"We can't," the Kresge district manager said. "We've already got it in the paper at 29¢."

"Okay," Kinter said, "we'll both go to the price you put in the paper, but you pay me 12¢ difference for every one I sell."

The Kresge district manager exploded. "We can't do that!"

"Well, that's fine," Kinter told him, "but I will not be undersold. I got another sign downstairs, and if I have to, I'll give 'em away for free. If I'm going to lose money, I'll lose big!"

The battle ended in a draw as Kresge's and Murphy's both went to 29¢. "The restaurant manager apologized to me up one side and down the other," Kinter says. "The district manager never talked to me again." Even that doesn't compare to what happened before another big parade in Harrisburg when Kinter arrived at the store early in the morning to find that someone had parked a hot-dog cart in front of Murphy's. Kinter hitched the wagon to his car, drove it to the outskirts of town, and abandoned it in a parking lot.

"Murphy's guys were pretty sharp guys when it came to retailing," Shuppy says. "You didn't want to go toe to toe with them."

Beyond simple pride, Murphy managers were pushed by financial incentives, including healthy year-end bonuses based on their store profits and annual contests to see who could sell the most paint, light bulbs, or toiletries. With financial assistance from major suppliers such as General Electric and Colgate-Palmolive, Murphy's advertised seasonal sales on certain products and then offered prizes to managers in each district who moved the most merchandise among stores of similar size. Murphy's house-label paint, Super-Tex, remained a key profit center through the 1960s. One manager of a tiny West Virginia store won the annual contest by stocking virtually nothing but paint and supplies for the month of the competition. Another at Store No. 18 in Moundsville, West Virginia, won after contracting with the nearby state prison to supply all its paint for the year.

Despite managing an old, wooden-floored Murphy store in Frankfort, Indiana, directly across the street from a Woolworth, Bob Bishop won two muscle cars, a Chevy Camaro and an Oldsmobile 4-4-2, during the annual Con-Tact shelf paper sales contests. "We have to rig the sales up," he told his clerks. "We can't give any discounts on anything, but push it." They responded by suggesting Con-Tact paper to every customer who walked through the door—one even held a "Con-Tact party" in her home. Victorious managers knew enough to the share the spoils with their staff. When Dave Backstrom won a $1,000 cash prize in the General Electric light-bulb contest, he split the money with a clerk. (She used her share to buy false teeth.)

Still, all the gimmicks, tricks, and contests in the world couldn't change the fact that Murphy's was falling behind the industry. In 1963 and 1966, the company closed more stores than it opened. As S. S. Kresge racked up 25 percent sales increases in 1964 and 1965, Murphy's gained only 5.1 and 6.1 percent, respectively. For the first half of 1966, G. C. Murphy Company sales showed a handsome 7.3 percent increase, but the national average among chain stores was 11.5 percent. Among variety stores, only Neisner and Newberry turned in a worse performance than the G. C. Murphy Company. Meanwhile, Kresge was up 36 percent and even Woolworth, whose Woolco stores were struggling, was up 9 percent. Bill Anderson says Murphy's was at least "ten years behind the competition" by the mid-1960s, which became obvious when Kresge erected Kmarts at all four compass points around Pittsburgh, encircling Murphy's home turf. "That didn't happen by accident," he says. "They knew it was easy pickings."

Publicly, Jim Mack remained contemptuous of discount stores, saying they were "blowing their horns, exploding big firecrackers," and setting prices to confuse shoppers. "They have nothing that we can't compete against and do even better," he said. Memos from Mack to senior personnel from the mid-sixties drip with scorn: "Discount stores attained success originally because of their duplication of five- and ten-cent origin practices," he wrote in one. "By overdoing it on low margin and poverty image, they have been forced to retreat." In hindsight, Mack seems dangerously out of touch. New discount stores were opening on a weekly basis in Murphy's markets. If Kmart, Hills, Zayre, and the rest of the discounters were "retreating," they didn't show it. One memo noted that families were shopping at night and that Murphy's should consider keeping "some of its stores" open late. Kmart was already advertising that every store was open from 9:00 A.M. to 9:00 P.M.

But Mack clearly recognized that Murphy's needed a fresh direction. In early 1966, he assigned Murphy's sales manager George McCormick, merchandise vice president Edgar Paxton, regional sales manager Hal Sebra, and other home office executives to come up with a plan to compete. The result debuted in October at Store No. 103 in downtown Fort Wayne, Indiana. Murphy's called it "the A-A store."

Much about the Murphy A-A (pronounced "double A") concept was sound, and it was a good start toward reinventing the variety-store format. As did most dime-store chains, Murphy's had always purchased merchandise by departments that bore little rhyme or reason to how products were actually used. Worse yet, stores were organized the same way. In Fort Wayne, for instance, women's fashion accessories and jewelry were on the first floor, but women's clothing was in the basement. Tie racks weren't with ties, they were in housewares, but paper plates weren't in housewares, they were in stationery.

The A-A program broke down artificial borders between departments by organizing products into themed groups. The "Entertainment Center" included not just records, radios, and television sets but books, magazines, craft supplies, musical instruments, and cameras. Sporting goods and menswear were next to auto accessories and hardware to catch the eye of male shoppers. In some locations, merchandise groups were enclosed on three sides to create a "boutique store" feeling; wider aisles guided shoppers around A-A stores, while prominent displays featured special bargains. Where Murphy's traditional stores had high profit margins and extensive selections at the expense of low turnover, A-A stores were "hotline" locations with larger budgets for seasonal and fad merchandise. Theoretically, they were able to jump on trends and advertise prices lower than their competition's with the aim of building profit through volume.

It was revolutionary enough in the variety field for *Chain Store Age* to devote most of its December 1967 issue to profiling the G. C. Murphy Company as one of America's "great retail institutions." The cover photo showed Jim Mack, Walter Shaw Jr., and other executives poring over a blueprint of what the caption called Murphy's "store of tomorrow." "G. C. Murphy's on the Move Again!" read the headline.

Yet the A-A program was less than the sum of its parts. G. C. Murphy Company always prided itself on carrying something for every need. Managers kept customer "want lists" of products they didn't stock. And under Jim Mack's leadership, Murphy's was advertising itself in newspapers and on radio as "The *Complete* Variety Store." But A-A stores dropped all varieties except the top sellers, axing 20 percent of the items carried in health and beauty aids and hardware, for instance. Suddenly, the "complete variety store" was promoting lack of completeness as a virtue, which didn't fly.

Take sewing notions, for instance, which were a strong point at Murphy's since the early days. Lose a shirt button, and chances are Murphy's could provide an replacement. Tear a sleeve, and Murphy's had a rack of Coats & Clark thread in every color of the rainbow. Clair McElhinny was at the Jamestown store when management converted it to the A-A format, which meant that slower-selling colors of thread in each store had to be dropped.

"What's going to happen to the racks?" McElhinny asked a home office man.

"The manufacturer will make new ones," the man replied.

"Maybe I'm stupid," McElhinny said, "but if all of the A-A stores are different, how is the manufacturer going to make different racks for every store?"

"Are you disputing what the company says?" the home office man demanded.

"No, no, I'm just asking," McElhinny said. What should he do with the empty slots on the rack? Leave them empty until the new racks arrive, he was told. A few months later, the home office man was back to say that Coats & Clark was not going to make special racks for Murphy's A-A stores: "Put all of the colors back in."

Though the program allowed stores to carry high-profit lines of appliances and furniture that were driving discount-store sales, too many Murphy A-A stores simply spread out their old merchandise over a bigger area, says Bishop, who worked at a 60,000-square-foot store in Carmel, Indiana, north of Indianapolis, when it was converted. "If we had five feet of jeans [in a conventional store], we went to fifteen," he said. "If we had five feet of shoes, we went to fifteen. We doubled and tripled the amount of product, but we didn't change the mix." Sales didn't double or triple—volume was actually about two-thirds lower than the home office estimated the A-A program would generate.

Perhaps most damaging was the "flexible pricing" at stores, which allowed A-A managers to sell goods at lower prices than their competitors. In many places, A-A stores were also undercutting other Murphy stores. Since both types of stores carried the same external

G. C. Murphy Company signage (A-A stores added two capital-As to their facades), customers had a hard time telling them apart. Complaints poured in. Murphy customer relations person Ed Davis remembers fielding a call from a woman who couldn't understand why a downtown A-A store sold skirts for $8.98 while a suburban store had them at $9.98. One manager was asked why cashews at his store were $1.29 while a nearby Murphy A-A store had them for 73¢. "Mine are a little bit better," he said.

Even the company's executives had a hard time explaining the differences. After a writer for *Sales Management* magazine attended a press conference announcing plans to convert forty-one stores to A-A in 1968, he called Murphy's "Adrift in Concept Land":

> "For simplicity's sake, may I call them bigger and better variety stores?" a reporter asked. "I suggest you call them a new retailing concept," one of several vice presidents answered. The reporter hinted that he liked his phrase better. "Well," said another vice president, "why not call them 'the stores of tomorrow'?" "No," another executive objected, "I like 'out-discount the discount stores.'"
>
> That misfired, too, and was followed by "trade-up stores," "entire-family stores," "self-service stores," "general merchandise stores," "break-out-of-line stores," and "tailored to their communities stores," at which point it was obvious that when you're dealing in semantics, it may be better to be in the old-fashioned and uncomplicated five-and-ten-cent store business.

The home office wasn't amused. "Quote and misquote, real garble," sniffed Walter Shaw Jr. to Ed Paxton. Ken Paxton told Ed Davis, "I think this writer is a 'concept' himself."

There were a few A-A successes. Jack Gordon was sent from Store No. 58 in Farrell, Pennsylvania, to manage Store No. 175 in downtown Erie, Pennsylvania, when it was converted to the A-A program. The Erie store had been "the laughingstock of the Murphy Company," he says. "Our volume was pathetic." One year, the store lost $100,000—an eye-popping amount when some small Murphy stores were doing about that in sales. Under the A-A program, Gordon was allowed to do more advertising, carry better grades of merchandise, and expand his clothing selection. The aisles were expanded into "midways" with bargain tables, including a few items sold at cost. During Gordon's final year in Erie, the store was within a few hundred dollars of breaking even. The A-A program "was crappy," Gordon says, "but it worked for me."

If nothing else, the A-A program finally gave Murphy's experience in high-volume, low-margin retailing—just as the discounters were doing. Given some time, G. C. Murphy Company would be able to iron the kinks out of the A-A program. But it didn't get the chance. Support for the A-A conversions was lukewarm even before Walter Shaw Jr. was pushed out of his position as senior vice president of sales in 1968, though he remained a major stockholder and retained his seat on the board of directors. The official word was that Shaw wanted to pursue his other interests, including extensive service to the Chautauqua Institution, and that he had retired. Shaw was a relatively young fifty-six-years old, and few people were fooled. Insiders say that long-simmering tensions between Jim Mack and Walter Shaw Jr. came to a head over the latter's divorce and remarriage to a former home office secretary and that Shaw finally tired of the stress. "He wanted to be a success for my dad's sake," adds his sister, Betty, "but I don't think he had the love for it that my dad did."

The Mack and Shaw rivalry was no secret, and perhaps Shaw's departure from management wasn't a surprise, but what happened on May 21, 1968, was a shock. That night, an ambulance rushed Mack from Indiana County to McKeesport Hospital where he died a few hours later at age fifty-four. Weeks earlier, doctors had diagnosed aneurysms in his brain and heart and operated successfully to repair them. In one of his last messages to Murphy staff, Mack joked that he had "used up a few of my lives for our good company, but they were worth it, for I know that we will move onto greater heights than ever before." But Mack contracted hepatitis in the hospital and was recuperating at the family farm when his condition suddenly deteriorated.

Colleagues were crestfallen. Senior vice president Edgar Paxton called the loss "difficult to reconcile." Services were held a few days later at Indiana's Greystone Presbyterian Church and Mack was laid to rest in the family plot at nearby Greenwood Cemetery. At the time of his death, Paxton said, Mack "was on the verge of witnessing the accomplishment of great personal plans" for the company, but whatever he envisioned died with him. Mack's son Sephus will say only that his father was working on a strategy for the 1970s, but his death "cut it short."

Luckily, Murphy's had acquired two of its most able executives in the 1920s with the purchase of Trick Brothers in Indianapolis, and the board of directors elevated Edgar Paxton to the Murphy presidency and his older brother Kenneth to chairman. Both were exceedingly well liked—the elder Paxton had been vice president of personnel, while the younger was vice president of merchandising —and few doubted their ability. Still, for the first time since 1911, neither a Mack nor a Shaw was in charge. It was a discomfiting feeling for many Murphy veterans, perhaps none more so than the first assistant manager of Store No. 103 in Fort Wayne, John Mack. He was headed to law school before his Uncle Jim had started saying, "You owe it to the family to go with Murphy's." Jim Mack's son Sephus worked as a store manager for a few years before resigning frustrated, he says, that "bean-counters and attorneys" had taken his father's place.

While Sephus Mack's view might not be shared by everyone, it's true that the company's direction did shift rapidly. After 10 percent of G. C. Murphy's more than five hundred stores had been switched to the A-A program, the conversions suddenly came to a halt. Something new was in the works. Regional sales manager Bill Anderson found out what was up early in 1969 when Ken Paxton called him to his office. Paxton knelt on the floor, rolled out a blueprint, and asked Anderson to get down there with him to inspect it. The

DECEMBER 1967

CHAIN STORE AGE

GREAT RETAIL INSTITUTIONS STUDY NO. 5

J. S. Mack and his top management team sift out some of the ideas
that will emerge in Indianapolis next year when their first all-
new "store of tomorrow" opens—another signal to a watchful industry that . . .

G.C. MURPHY'S ON THE MOVE AGAIN!

FIG. 48
Murphy's efforts to diversify into department store operation and its new A-A concept for modernizing its five-and-tens led *Chain Store Age* to dub the company a "great retail institution." Most of the magazine's December 1967 issue was devoted to the company's history and operations. The cover depicted vice president of personnel Ken Paxton, senior vice president of sales Walter Shaw Jr., president and chairman Jim Mack, vice president of merchandise Earl Paxton, and vice president of real estate and construction Earl McClune examining plans for a A-A store in Indianapolis. Within a year, Shaw was forced into early retirement and Mack was dead.

plans were for a defunct complex in Bethel Park, Pennsylvania, south of Pittsburgh, called The Mayfair. It wasn't quite a discount department store; instead, the owners had gathered a variety of different shops operating in the style of a shopping bazaar under a single roof. Pittsburghers were unimpressed and The Mayfair bombed, leaving empty a big, modern, 100,000-square-foot building at the intersection of several major thoroughfares.

Murphy's real estate division pounced on it and a parcel north of Pittsburgh near the Pennsylvania Turnpike's Harmarville interchange. Few within G. C. Murphy Company realized that despite Jim Mack's protestations, some of their co-workers were quietly walking around inside Kmart, Woolco, and Zayre's taking notes. Behind Mack's back, they were planning a discount division for Murphy's.

After a few minutes of looking over the plans, Paxton stood up. "Okay, sweetheart," he said to Anderson. "It's all yours."

"How in the hell are we ever going to fill that?" Anderson thought.

Chasing the Checkered Flag

As the man from the Indianapolis Motor Speedway approached G. C. Murphy Company executives Phil Rogers and Bob Thorniley, it was obvious that he wasn't happy.

Eager to promote its entry of the first-ever "G. C. Murphy Special" in the 1965 Indianapolis 500, the company had printed up a big batch of "Indicators"—paper scorecards that fans could use to record the times of the cars participating in the qualifying runs. Then Murphy's hired a group of "temp girls" from the Manpower agency to stand outside the gates of the Speedway and hand out the Indicators. The problem was that sales of official programs had tanked, and the Speedway had a good idea why.

So at eleven o'clock that night in the north turn of the fabled Brick-yard, the remaining Murphy scorecards were piled up and burned under the watchful eye of Speedway officials. It was one of the first lessons—but hardly the last—that Murphy's learned during its seven-year involvement with big-time auto racing. Long before Kmart, Target, Home Depot, and other retailers realized that sponsoring a race car plastered their logos on sports pages around the world, Murphy's was fielding its red, white, and blue open-wheel racers on the Indy car circuit. And though none of the Murphy Specials won at Indianapolis, the cars provided a wealth of publicity for the company and a great rallying point for employees.

G. C. MURPHY STORES INDIANAPOLIS '500'

Member RACE TEAM

1965

The G. C. Murphy Race Team was the creation of Thorniley and Rogers, two employees of the research and development department at the McKeesport warehouse. Avid racing fans, they attended the 1964 Indianapolis 500 under somewhat specious circumstances. Rogers had relatives in England, and as the race approached he talked one of his U.K. connections into writing to the Indianapolis Motor Speedway and requesting media credentials for two "reporters" (himself and Thorniley) who were supposedly going to cover the legendary five-hundred-mile race for a British publication. The pit passes were duly issued and the duo was admitted to the inner sanctum of the speedway during Memorial Day weekend.

In those days, the cars were the stars and were customarily referred to by the name of their primary sponsor—1964's entrants, for instance, included the Kaiser Aluminum Special, the Vita Fresh Orange Juice Special, and the Diet Rite Cola Special. As Thorniley and Rogers watched the race, they realized that more than 300,000 fans had seen or heard the names of the race car sponsors over and over again.

Murphy's had a major presence in Indiana, including seven stores in Indianapolis, and in twenty-one other states where the company did business, millions of race fans and potential Murphy's customers were following the "greatest spectacle in racing." Why shouldn't Murphy's have a race car, wondered Rogers and Thorniley?

By the time they returned to McKeesport, both men were dreaming of a Murphy race car flying around the most famous track in the United States. Soon they had computed the cost of sponsoring a race car and any possible company liability in case of an accident, and were honing a pitch to make to the company's top executives. That fall, they wrote

FIGS. 49, 50 (next page) Bumper sticker distributed to employees working on the G. C. Murphy Race Team in 1965 and a detail of one of the first G. C. Murphy Specials.

to the official employee suggestion program recommending that the company team with Pittsburgh attorney and race car owner Gil Morcroft to field a G. C. Murphy Special. Any publicity needs could be handled through Murphy's public relations department, and the cost would be minimal. No one remembers the exact number, but it was less than $20,000, a tiny fraction of today's Indy car sponsorship.

"A lot of people were really opposed to it," says Ed Davis, then assistant to Ed Procious, Murphy's director of employee and public relations. Vice president of sales Walter Shaw Jr. thought it was "an idiotic idea." But Murphy president Jim Mack liked it, and vice presidents Ken and Ed Paxton—both Indiana natives—needed no convincing. Word came down to Thorniley and Rogers that Murphy's would sponsor a car in the 1965 Indianapolis 500. Davis was assigned to handle promotions, while Rogers would negotiate with Morcroft, who would run a roadster built by A. J. Watson and powered by an Offenhauser engine.

Murphy's hired a part-time publicity man in Indianapolis to begin spreading the word. "His name was Bill Marvel, and he became a 'marvel' for us because he knew all of the press people, print and TV," Davis says. To get maximum exposure in towns where Murphy's had stores, four or five old racecars were painted up as G. C. Murphy Specials and towed to various shopping centers. The clapped-out old cars were obsolete and had as much a chance of winning a five-hundred-mile race as grandma's Rambler Classic, but for people who didn't know anything about auto racing, they were impressive.

Bob Wente was to drive the first Murphy Special, which was finished by January and placed third in New Jersey's Trenton 100 that April. At Murphy's annual sales meeting for store managers held at Pittsburgh's William Penn Hotel, the car was proudly displayed in the lobby. Each manager posed with the car for a photo. The pictures, distributed to small-town newspapers, garnered "great publicity," says Davis, who decorated a bulletin board at the home office with clippings and pictures.

Murphy's also held a reception for the media at the Speedway Motel in Indianapolis, distributing little sterling silver replicas of the car—tie tacks for men, bracelet charms for women. "I learned you don't put those out on the table before the [dignitaries] get there because every waiter and waitress will have one," Davis says.

It was Rogers and Thorniley, too, who dreamed up the idea for the Indicators. More than eighty cars had entered the thirty-three-car race, but not all would qualify. The Murphy scorecard had spaces for the name of each driver, their cars, the owners of the cars, and columns for the average speeds. Printed in the home office, the backs of the scorecards advertised Murphy private-label brands such as Big Murph overalls, Carolina Moon hosiery, and Pelham underwear.

The Indicators worked like a charm, putting Murphy's on the minds of all the race goers. When Wente spun out in one turn, the track announcer quipped, "There goes Wente, and I wonder what happened to his Pelham shorts." The experiment was a roaring success until the Speedway demanded the programs be destroyed. Even that wasn't quite the end of the idea. As soon as the thirty-three cars qualified, the home office sprang into action again, cranking out more scorecards and distributing them to Indianapolis-area stores as souvenirs to be stuffed into shopping bags.

Alas, Wente and the Watson-Offy car weren't as successful. The more he drove in the qualifying laps, the slower the car went; it turned out that the exhaust headers were coming apart. Another driver, Art Malone, took it out for a qualifying run and came back to the pits disgusted: "I couldn't get anything out of it," he said. Murphy's made a quick deal to put its name on the Central Excavating car with Mickey Rupp behind the wheel. That car finished sixth, earning Rupp and car owner Pete Salemi nearly $19,000.

Advised that if you're going to race at Indy, you'd better get the best car you can afford, Murphy's teamed with wealthy Atlanta businessman Lindsey Hopkins. Besides owning a series of Indy racers, Hopkins also had a stake in the Atlanta Falcons football team. For the next three years, Roger McCluskey drove the G. C. Murphy Specials, which were powered by Ford engines for three years and an Offenhauser in 1968. As with most experienced Indy car owners, Hopkins entered more than one car to improve his chances of qualifying and provide protection in case the best car was damaged.

McCluskey's first year with Murphy's race team was also his best finish behind the wheel of a Murphy Special—he placed thirteenth with an average speed of 159 miles per hour. But his best chance at a trophy might have been in 1969 when he averaged more than 168 miles per hour (better than eventual winner Mario Andretti) and at times battled with A. J. Foyt for the lead. "After a couple of laps, Foyt was first and McCluskey

FIG. 51
Driver Roger McCluskey pilots his Ford-powered No. 8 G. C. Murphy Special out of the pits at the 1966 Indianapolis 500. Though none of Murphy's cars won at Indy, the race team generated excitement among customers and employees during its seven years of operation.

was second," Davis remembers. "All of a sudden, Foyt was still first, but McCluskey was nowhere to be seen. He had run out of fuel and had to be towed in. Of course, he lost a lot of time." McCluskey ended up running the car so hard that he blew the engine and didn't finish.

Still, the Murphy race team received lots of attention wherever the company had stores. Nearly all the local newspapers in towns that Murphy's served printed photos of the car, though the *Erie Times-News* airbrushed the Goodyear logos off the tires (it turned out they had an advertising deal with Firestone). Murphy's was less successful in getting the Pittsburgh media interested. In the days before NASCAR and Formula 1 contests were nationally televised, many reporters felt that auto racing was a far lesser sport than baseball, college football, and golf. The sports editor of the *Pittsburgh Press*, says Davis, "didn't know a race car from a racehorse."

Although the Murphy Specials didn't win any races with Hopkins and McCluskey, Davis calls them "great years" in terms of building the company's image. "Hopkins was a great ambassador for racing, we got good coverage every single year, and we met tons of people," he says. The stores got into the act, too, holding Indianapolis 500 sales each Memorial Day weekend and selling toy plastic Indy cars decorated with G. C. Murphy logos. The partnership with Hopkins ended when Coca-Cola decided it was going to run a car at Indianapolis for its Sprite-brand soda, and the businessman, who sat on Coke's board of directors, went with them. For 1969, Murphy's teamed with Foyt, who fielded three of his Ford-powered Coyotes as G. C. Murphy Specials, though he drove at Indianapolis for a competing race team. McCluskey returned for his final year as Murphy's driver.

In 1970 and 1971, Murphy's joined Milwaukee-based Leader Cards, Inc., whose race cars won the Indy 500 in 1959, 1962, and 1968, to campaign two G. C. Murphy-Leader Cards Specials. Leader didn't repeat its first-place finishes in those years, though driver Mike Mosley did score front-page coverage when he crashed at Indianapolis in 1971 during a qualifying run. The next day's *Chicago Sun-Times* sported a picture of the wreckage flying through the air—including the all-important Murphy's logo. Mosley had better luck driving one of the Ford-powered Murphy Specials to victory at Trenton in April 1971, averaging 132 miles per hour in the two-hundred-mile race.

It was the last hurrah for the G. C. Murphy Race Team, which closed up shop with the cancer-related death of its biggest booster, Ken Paxton, in July. Paxton's brother Ed had left Murphy's two years earlier with heart problems. "I'm sure it was a great thing for Ken Paxton to be able to go back to Indianapolis, a few miles from where he was born, and be an executive in charge of a race car," Davis says. The last time Davis saw Paxton was after a weekend trip to Indianapolis where Mosley and a G. C. Murphy Special had just qualified for the 1971 race. Two months later, Paxton was dead.

One of the reasons that Murphy officials cited for eliminating the racing program was the opening of the new Murphy's Marts. All available energy and assets were going toward promoting the fledgling discount-store division. In retrospect, perhaps the cars might have been renamed Murphy's Mart Specials. By staying in auto racing, Murphy's would have been far ahead of its competitors, including archrival Kmart, and could even have expanded its sponsorship to the stock car circuit. Having a presence in NASCAR would certainly have helped the company build its image in the South where Murphy's was struggling to establish itself.

But it didn't happen. And none of the G. C. Murphy Specials were preserved, though you can still see McCluskey and Mosley wheel them around the Brickyard in Indy 500 highlight films, and the toy replicas occasionally pop up on Internet auction sites.

Since retiring from Murphy's in 1985, Davis has carefully preserved a few choice pieces of the G. C. Murphy Race Team, including jacket patches, photos, and checkered flags. They're mementos of seven high-octane years when G. C. Murphy Company wasn't the largest variety-store chain, but it was the fastest—at least on Memorial Day weekends.

Happy HOLIDAYS

When songwriter Meredith Willson penned his immortal lines about those glimmering five-and-tens bedecked with candy canes at Christmastime, he wasn't necessarily talking about the G.C. Murphy Company, but he might have been. One of the chain's radio jingles in the 1970s sang "nobody but Murphy's," and in many towns, "nobody but Murphy's" held the attention of small children during the holidays. On Wednesday night before Thanksgiving, the windows of a Murphy five-and-ten held boring necessities—winter coats and scarves, shampoo, and soap—but two days later, as if by magic, they were full of train sets and dolls, Christmas trees and lights, ornaments, and holiday cards, all laid out in white cotton "snow" flecked with silver glitter.

It wasn't magic, of course. The managers and assistant managers were up most of Wednesday night stripping the windows and bringing out the Christmas merchandise and on Friday were still picking pieces of white glue and glitter off their fingertips.

Inside, the transformation was even more exciting. The stores smelled of peppermint candy mixed with old wood and cleanser but looked like Santa's Workshop. Bicycles and coaster wagons were assembled, bedecked with bows and ribbons, and suspended from the ceiling above the toy department. Even the lunch counters looked festive, with small artificial trees and twinkle lights strung in and among the boxes of cereal and cans of soup on the shelf that lined the back walls. Counters held gift sets—matched handkerchiefs, striped "rep" ties, boxes of perfume and cologne—priced just inside a preteen's budget. Many children who saved up quarters from allowances, paper routes, or babysitting bought all their Christmas presents for mom and dad at Murphy's.

"Little children could come in and for $5, buy something for dad, mom, grandfather, grandmother," says Millie Reiland, who grew up in North Braddock, Pennsylvania, during the Depression and worked for Murphy Store No. 25 in nearby East Pittsburgh for twenty-one years. "Ninety percent of your Christmas shopping was done at the five-and-ten," adds Cece Gallagher, who grew up in Elizabeth, Pennsylvania, three blocks from Murphy Store No. 46 and later worked there as a clerk. "It was probably one of the first places I was ever allowed to go by myself."

Christmas was a magical time for children in hundreds of towns with G. C. Murphy Company stores. But for the men and women working behind the scenes, the last week of November marked the start of a month of exhaustion that wouldn't abate until the year-end inventory was completed on New Year's Eve. "I will never forget my first Christmas," says Bob Bishop, who started with Murphy's at Store No. 81 in Columbus, Indiana, in 1961. "I spent probably ninety hours a week in the store. You didn't have anyone else to do these jobs. I had to [decorate] the windows. I had to get the merchandise into the stockroom and put in on the floor."

At times, store personnel were fighting both the crowds and Murphy bureaucracy. When Bishop was made manager of his first store—a 10,000-square-foot unit in Frankfort, Indiana—he filled the display windows with tricycles and toolboxes and small appliances wrapped in white paper with red bows. "These were items that were in the back of the store and didn't get a lot of advertising," he says. District manager Bob Smeltz blew his top when he saw what Bishop had done.

"You're missing the boat!" Smeltz said. "This looks like a hardware store! Where are the cards? Where is the gift wrap?"

"How long has this store been in this town?" Bishop asked.

"Thirty years," Smeltz said.

"Well, they know we have gift wrap and boxed cards, but they don't know we've got these other things."

Smeltz wasn't swayed and demanded the windows be changed. "I decided, it's November," Bishop says. "How many times will he come back between now and Christmas?" He didn't redecorate, but he held his breath for a month for fear Smeltz would return.

Most former Murphy's employees remember holidays with fondness. "I loved to do Christmas windows," Gallagher says. Pat Potter, who worked at Store No. 201 in Connells-

FIG. 52
Murphy president Paul
Sample and chairman
Walter Shaw Sr. examine
a toy race car sometime
in the late 1940s. At
Christmas time, says one
former clerk, G. C. Mur-
phy Company's variety
stores were the "Toys 'R'
Us of their day."

ville, Pennsylvania, while attending college in the 1950s and '60s, liked working on the toy counter: "It was such a lively time. We had about twenty-five feet of toys, plus a wall of bicycles and stuffed animals and bigger toys. It was the Toys 'R' Us of its day." Murphy's flagship Store No. 12 in downtown Pittsburgh did a "tremendous job in toys" at Christmas, says Earl Rehrig, a manager there in the 1970s. "It was a madhouse for thirty days." Still, he remembers getting burned on one item—a toy airport. "I can't think of the name of the company, but again I stuck my neck out and said, 'We ought to buy about eight hundred of those because I think they're going to sell,'" Rehrig says. "I got stuck with about two hundred of them."

One traditional staple of Christmas shopping that has been almost forgotten in the age of credit cards was the layaway. In 2006, Wal-Mart, the nation's largest retailer, discontinued its layaway service altogether, while other chains such as Target and Circuit City either long ago stopped offering layaways or never had them in the first place. But in the small factory and farming towns where G. C. Murphy did much of its business, working-class customers

simply couldn't afford to buy their Christmas presents all at one time and couldn't get credit. With a 10 percent deposit and a $1 service charge, Murphy's would hold any item worth $10 or more for as long as ninety days, as long as customers agreed to make regular payments on a schedule. Most stores set aside a special area of the stockroom to safeguard layaway merchandise, which was supposed to be claimed at least three days before Christmas. It didn't always work that way, says former manager Dick Gibson Sr.: "Always we'd get a call on Christmas Eve that someone forgot their layaway, and we'd have to go down and open the store."

One tradition that might have been exclusive to Murphy's was "Family Christmas Night." On a Sunday evening before the holiday, each store would open for a special sale by invitation only where cookies and punch were served and guests received 10 percent off all purchases. "There was no end to the lines," says Marianne Molnar, a clerk at Store No. 321 in Belle Vernon, Pennsylvania, and later manager of the Elizabeth store, "and on the old registers, you had to figure out the 10 percent discount by hand. We had one table just for layaways, and it never stopped. You had everybody in the store that night, and you even asked people to bring in their relatives to help bag."

During one Family Christmas Night at Store No. 12, Murphy's was featuring imported flannel shirts at two for $3. Manager Don Duncan approached Jack Anderson, assistant manager responsible for menswear, before the sale.

"See those shirts out there?" Duncan asked. "Do you have enough of them?"

"I've got fifty dozen up in the stockroom," Anderson said.

"You get all of those shirts down here and push them," Duncan said. His instincts were 100 percent correct—when the doors opened, shoppers grabbed them as soon as they hit the shelves. "During the night, I would just get boxes of them and reach over people and dump them over the counter," Anderson says. "You couldn't even get a [hand] truck through. I had a lady who stocked underwear for me—it was stacked up to the [ceiling]—and we wiped out that counter on Family Night. We offered value, and there is absolutely no question about it."

Store employees were supposed to reserve invitations for close relations, but sometimes liberties were taken. While Pete Shuppy was working as an assistant manager at Store No. 72 in Seymour, Indiana, he resolved to win the district's contest for best sales on Family Christmas Night. "They were going to give out some crappy award," he says. "I told the manager I'd like to win this thing, and he said, well, do whatever you can." The store was tiny—only 7,000 square feet—but Shuppy went through town passing out invitations to every "Tom, Dick, and Harry," and on the night of the sale, it was jammed from wall to wall. "It took a half-hour to walk from one side of the store to the other," Shuppy says. "It was packed."

The manager grabbed him afterward and pointed out the damage that had been wreaked on the displays, the counters, and the shelves, which would take hours (if not days) to put into order.

"Look at the sales!" Shuppy cried.

"Look at the damned store!" his manager replied. "This place is a piece of ——!"

Indeed, when it came to holidays, the best-laid plans of mice and Murphy's occasionally went astray. In the early 1960s, as an assistant manager for Store No. 270 at Apache Village Mall near St. Paul, Minnesota, Terry Stadterman was in charge of bringing Santa Claus to the shopping center to kick off the Christmas season. He arranged for Kris Kringle to arrive via helicopter. It was a novel idea that caught the attention of the local television stations and was eventually copied by other Murphy stores. At the appointed time, everyone gathered in the parking lot to await the chopper's arrival. "All of the kids were there, and the news cameras were there," Stadterman says. "Every time a plane went over, all of the kids would look." But Santa didn't appear, and small children who had been waiting for a long time in the cold Minnesota air began crying.

With a Christmas dream about to turn into a public relations nightmare, Stadterman called the helicopter company. "They said, 'Oh, no, not this week, next week,'" he says. "I thought, 'Oh my God, what are we going to do?'" A quick-thinking publicity man called the fire department and talked them into sending a ladder truck to pick up Santa Claus. Tears were dried, noses were wiped, Christmas lists were delivered, and no one was worse for the wear. "It's funny now, but it wasn't funny at the time," Stadterman says.

While managing Store No. 280 at the Olympia Shopping Center in McKeesport, Dave Backstrom imitated Stadterman's helicopter promotion, but this time Santa was going to

FIG. 54
Santa Claus greets children at Store No. 40 in Sidney, Ohio, on the day after
Thanksgiving 1948.

parachute into the mall. The results were almost as bad as when Stadterman first tried the stunt. The first year, Santa leapt from the helicopter above the parking lot but landed on the opposite side of a four-lane highway. The following year, he nearly landed in the middle of traffic. "I decided I had better quit before I killed Santa Claus," Backstrom says.

Christmas wasn't popular with the wives and husbands of Murphy employees. Nancy Mack, whose husband was an assistant manager and manager in the 1960s and '70s, says that between Thanksgiving and Christmas Eve, John Mack left home each day before 7:00 A.M. and returned after 11:00 P.M. "By the time Christmas Eve got here, he had had it," she says. Sometimes, the only way she could see her husband was to visit him at the store. Some Murphy employees also dreaded Christmas because of the lengthy year-end inventory that was necessary to calculate each store's annual profits (and the manager's all-important bonus). In the days before computers could automatically calculate inventory based on the price tags being scanned at the cash registers (an innovation that didn't arrive at the G. C. Murphy Company until its final years), the annual inventory was labor intensive and intense—inventory didn't start until December 26 but had to be complete before December 31.

"Between Christmas and New Year's, everything had to be counted, and I mean everything," says Gertrude Geisler, who worked a notions counter in the Tarentum store in the 1930s. "I had needles and threads and everything, and I had to count all of them by hand." It took "forever," Molnar says. "You had these little yellow pads, with one slip for each item, and you would take one of the carts and go down the aisles. Even if you only had one item, you still had to make out a slip. Then you sorted them by department and by price and you totaled them." Automated systems that Murphy's began installing in the 1960s and '70s did the final tabulations, but the handwritten information had to be entered onto sheets that could be scanned into a computer. "I can remember sitting up in the office with an adding machine for ten or twelve hours" at a time, Molnar says.

One New Year's Eve, everyone in the Tarentum store had completed their inventory, except for the woman who sold pots and pans. "The manager said, 'Sorry, girls, you all have to stay until Loretta gets hers done.' Well, we had all just about had it with Mr. Waldron. I was mad! It was New Year's Eve, I was twenty years old, and I had a date!" In a fit of rage, she picked up shoes from one of the counters and began throwing them across the store. When Geisler ran out of shoes, Waldron, the manager, approached her.

"You are fired," he said. "Go across the street and have a sandwich. But when you get back, if all of those shoes are picked up, you are rehired."

"Looking back now," Geisler says, "he wasn't the ogre I thought he was then."

Inventory literally wrecked the health of at least one manager who fretted over the figures that showed how much "leakage"—merchandise lost to thieves or damaged and unsellable—their store suffered each year. Mo Lambert, longtime manager of Store No. 1 in McKeesport, became so tense and nervous over the leakage figures each year that his entire digestive system shut down. "It took a long time because the girls were using adding machines and comptometers," remembers Bill Kraus, an assistant manager there in the 1950s. "When the girls told him it was less than one-half percent, he said, 'Oh, thank God! I'm going to go to the bathroom!'"

No sooner was New Year's Day past than it was time to start thinking about Easter, an important holiday in Murphy's many ethnic communities where residents joked that they had as many churches as they did saloons (or was it the other way around?). Candy was a big seller at Murphy's at any time of the year but particularly at Easter when many Christians who had observed Lenten fasts by sacrificing sweets finally indulged themselves. A week or two before Easter Sunday, entire counters were devoted to jelly beans, chocolate rabbits, and candy eggs with walnut, fruit, or cream fillings. "You also got a lot of hollow chocolate Easter bunnies, and they all had to be separated and checked for breakage," says Luther Shay, who managed several stores before taking a job in the home office.

A little creativity on the part of a Murphy manager and his salesgirls turned standard items into Easter-themed candies. Dave Backstrom remembers taking two Snickers bars, pinning them together with toothpicks to form a cross, and then covering them with icing. "We'd put them in a basket with little rabbits and stuff on it and sell them for 59¢," he says. "They were 5¢ candy bars, so that was a big money maker." Today's stringent health codes and worries about tampering would probably forbid any store from copying the practice today, while liability concerns would stymie another Easter promotion that Backstrom cooked up while he was managing Store No. 31 in Monessen, Pennsylvania. He called it the "chewing gum scramble."

"We blocked off Donner Avenue and I had ten thousand sticks of Beech-Nut chewing gum," Backstrom says. "I took handfuls of it and threw it off the roof. We'd give prizes out for the kids who got the most sticks."

Many Murphy's stores put together ready-made baskets to sell to customers. "You'd do it whenever you had a slow period of time," Backstrom says. "We'd have them all stacked up and make a place for the girls to decorate them. We even went to the trouble of taking metal [toy] trucks, filling the back up with Easter eggs, and selling the trucks as Easter baskets." Gert Geisler remembers it well. "Everybody had to help," she says. "They would give us straw and baskets and candy, and we had to put those baskets together. They didn't waste any of your time!" Sometimes the children of managers and assistants would get recruited to help make up baskets, too, says Shay, whose father ran Murphy stores in Ohio, West Virginia, and Pennsylvania. "There were eight children in our family, and on holidays we all worked for free for my dad," he says.

One-time Murphy manager and buyer Roy Fowler Jr., whose father was also a store manager, remembers assembling "hundreds and hundreds" of Easter baskets for his dad's store. "I also had the job before Christmas of assembling all of the bicycles and tricycles," he says. That practice ended at the G. C. Murphy Company after a child going downhill on his new bike crashed when the handlebars came off. "Someone sued and got a $2 million settlement, and that was the last time we assembled a bicycle," Fowler says. "From then on in, we [had] professional services with liability insurance."

Flowers were another seasonal staple. "All of the women wore a corsage or something for Easter," Backstrom says. "We might also sell fresh orchids in vases." But talk of Murphy's at Easter invariably causes customers to remember the "peeps"—little ducklings or chicks that were sold as pets and sometimes even dyed in pastel Easter colors. Murphy's finally stopped selling them in the 1960s because of stricter laws governing animal cruelty and the keeping of livestock in city stores. Few salesgirls were sad to see them go. "The ducks were terrible," says Esther Weatherton, a clerk at Murphy stores in Greensburg and Latrobe, Pennsylvania. "They were filthy. You'd smell them as soon as you came in the store—before you could hear them."

While the chicks were cute on Easter morning, few children realized that they were invariably male. Farmers wouldn't knowingly sell hens to Murphy's because they could lay eggs and produce revenue when they matured. The cute little peeps grew up to become ornery, noisy roosters, and many Easter pets wound up either given away to farmers, sold to poultry markets, or slaughtered in the backyard to the chagrin of their youthful owners. "I can remember putting them in the windows and then cleaning the[mess] out," says Jack Gordon, who says the practice of selling peeps didn't end "soon enough."

Some Murphy's stores went further than chickens and ducks. "I was talking to someone who had rabbits," Shuppy says. "The rabbits cost me a buck, and I was going to sell them for $2.99, so we were going to make some money. A week before Easter, I got one dozen, and boom! I sold them right out. I ordered twelve more, and boom! I sold them right out." The following year, one week before Easter, Shuppy called the same breeder, ordered two dozen, and again sold out. He called the man back: "How many you got?" Seventy-five, came the answer. "Bring 'em in," Shuppy said.

"What are you going to do with them?" the breeder asked.

"I'll keep 'em in boxes up in the stockroom," Shuppy said. The day they arrived, he sold four or five rabbits. The following morning, he arrived at the store and was confronted by a terrible stench. The frightened rabbits had evacuated themselves all over the room and each other, and their fur was matted down in foul-smelling clumps. "I mean everywhere," Shuppy says. "It was so rank in there."

"I told the manager, 'We've got a problem. It's those rabbits.' He said, 'We've been selling a lot of them.' I said, 'Yeah, but we aren't going to be selling any more.'" Shuppy had bought the rabbits for a dollar and wound up paying the breeder $1.25 each to remove them. "You want to talk about ticked," he says.

Anderson had better luck when he was at Store No. 258 in a shopping center near Pittsburgh one Easter. "We made a big display and we must have sold two hundred white rabbits," he says. "Business was great. I was running out of rabbits so I called the vendor and said I needed some more. He said, 'Well, they're not quite as white.'" Anderson

wasn't happy when the rabbits were delivered—"not quite as white" turned out to be "solid brown."

Gallagher was hired into the Elizabeth, Pennsylvania, store during the spring of 1980 to help with the Easter rush. "My first day, I must have unpacked five hundred bags of Easter grass," she says, "and the man who was the manager came over and wanted it all displayed according to color. Mr. Clark said it had to be green and yellow and pink, and I probably did that for the better of that eight-hour day."

Religious holidays weren't the only special occasions at Murphy's, and regional and local tastes played a factor in which events stores promoted. George Washington's birthday, for instance, was a big deal at Store No. 166 on Capitol Hill in Washington, D.C. Assistant managers selected ten big-ticket items, such as area rugs and portable televisions, and marked ten of each to be sold for 99¢. Ads in the *Washington Post* and *Star* heralded the bargains. "We'd open up at nine o'clock and we had to have two big stockroom guys to hold the doors because people would just run when we unlocked them," says Earl Fenton, an assistant manager at Store No. 166. "One year we did over $74,000 in sales on George Washington's birthday."

Even in its small stores, Murphy's had a talent for creating "excitement," perhaps because cramming them with merchandise kept shoppers' adrenaline levels high. On the Saturday before Mother's Day, Murphy stores sold corsages in the "hundreds of dozens," Kraus says. "On Father's Day we had a full thirty-foot counter, both sides, filled with men's shirts—short-sleeved, long-sleeved, and dress white. It would be so crowded we would have to reach over the heads of customers and throw replacement stock on the counter."

Another beloved Murphy promotion was "Old-Fashioned Bargain Days," and each June the local manager of each G. C. Murphy store was expected to put the arm on neighboring businesses to participate. Sometimes an antique car parade or show would be organized to promote the Murphy sale, while the stores would be decked out in a "gay '90s" theme, with male employees wearing straw hats, striped shirts, and bowties, and women clad in bonnets and gingham dresses or shirt-waists. Gibson remembers going to all the antique stores in his town to borrow "beds and dresses and gowns" and setting them up in his stores. Earl Nottingham got a player piano for Old-Fashioned Bargain Days at Store No. 52 in Salem, Ohio. Jack Anderson would have been happy with a piano when he worked at Store No. 12; instead, one of the other assistant managers brought a horse into the store. "The only thing that saved me was that I was in the basement," he says, wrinkling his nose at the memory.

Murphy's Holiday Memories

My husband and I both immediately thought about the peeps or baby chicks for sale before Easter each year. When you entered G. C. Murphy's in Wilkinsburg, Pennsylvania, from the Penn Avenue door you immediately smelled sawdust, cornmeal, and peeps. When you went down the marble stairs with the large gold handrails to the lower level there was a huge display of colored peeps.

It was our tradition to buy one for each of the kids in my family and take them home and house them in a cardboard box. Sad to say, the chicks never lived to tell their stories. (Some things have changed for the best.)

Believe it or not, all six of us could go to G. C. Murphy's with $1 to purchase a Christmas gift for our mother—and still have some change for the Salvation Army kettle outside. I remember buying cookie cutters for 10¢ each one year. Another time I remember buying a tube of lipstick from the cosmetic counter. (I was born in 1947—the time frame would have been about 1955 or so.)

—Nancy Fritsch
Pittsburgh, Pa.

Holidays were special at Murphy's. At Easter the entire store was decorated [with] baskets of all sizes (some of them were huge) with crinkly, colored cellophane wrapping around the outside of each. Inside each basket were one or two huge, solid chocolate bunnies. Here and there on the floor were pieces of the colored grass used in the baskets. It was quite clear that the Easter Bunny had already been here and dropped off plenty of goodies!

Christmas was no different, with garlands draped over the tops of displays and down the poles throughout the store. Some areas had old glass Christmas tree lights strung over and around the displays, and every year the Lionel train was on its track and on prominent display. Toward the back of the store, employees decorated a large Christmas tree with beautiful glass bulbs and lights, the angel topping the tree, and every branch covered with silvery icicles (the real foil ones, not the plastic ones we have today) dangling everywhere. Near the tree sat Santa on his big, red, velvet chair, and he'd take every baby and child onto his knee for the annual picture with Santa.

Shelves throughout the store had boxes and boxes of trains, glass bulbs, angels, garlands, and wreaths. And, of course, the Salvation Army bell ringers with their distinctive buckets were always outside of Murphy's every year (or just inside the door on bitterly cold days).

—Judith Florian
Girard, Ohio

The Dog That Shopped at Murphy's

Murphy's was the place to go back in the "Good Old Days" when Washington, Pennsylvania, had a downtown. I was on sick leave nursing an ulcer in the '60s. Part of my therapy was to take relaxing walks. So almost every day, my Scottie dog, Scotia, and I would head for downtown Washington and the campus of Washington & Jefferson College. Scotia absolutely refused to wear a collar, but she stayed reasonably close (for a Scottie) to my side.

Once or twice, I went into Murphy's and down the steps to the pet supply counter. Each time, Scotia got a squeakie toy. The next time we went walking, Scotia left Washington & Jefferson's campus and went up Beau Street and down Main Street straight to Murphy's. Without hesitation, she marched inside and straight down the stairs to the pet department—with me huffing along behind her. She stopped only when she got to the squeakie toys display.

She studied them for a while, then picked out one and pulled it down. Ignoring me, she went to the register and stood there for a while. When she thought the time had been sufficient, she tore the wrapping from the toy, left it on the floor, and took her toy toward the stairs. Needless to say, there was some commotion by now. This slowed her down long enough for me to pay for the toy, but that was too long for her. I caught up with her at the intersection of Beau and Main (where we always had to stop for traffic).

Scotia did this at least three or four times a week as long as I was on sick leave, which was one semester. It got a wee bit expensive, but people in town still remember the Scottie dog who did all her shopping at G. C. Murphy's!

—Sue Vacheresse
Washington, Pa.

HOME RUNS
and A few ERRORS

It wouldn't be fair to say that Ron Templeton "wrote the book" on the new Murphy's Mart stores. Templeton didn't become operations manager at G. C. Murphy Company's first discount store in Bethel Park, Pennsylvania, until a month after it opened when his predecessor, teetering on the edge of a nervous breakdown, asked for a transfer back to the less-hectic life of a variety store. But Templeton was one of the employees who helped rewrite operations manuals on the fly during the first few months after the new Murphy's Mart opened in the summer of 1970. "We had to get rid of antiquated five-and-ten things that you didn't need in the discount business," he says. "It was mind-boggling."

Take paperwork, which had become a cherished part of life in the G. C. Murphy Company by the end of the 1960s when literally hundreds of different forms were flowing to stores from the print shop in McKeesport. Did customers want to layaway some merchandise? Record the transactions on an "S-12," remind them to retrieve their layaways with an "S-54," and if they no longer want the items, refund their money with an "Audit 8" slip and log all the transactions on the weekly "Audit 102" report, deducting the cost from "Account No. 94-15" in the cash book. Chuck Breckenridge, who eventually became director of internal audit for Murphy's, once conducted a show-and-tell presentation at the home office to demonstrate the excessive paperwork required to sell items in the stores from start to finish. Executives watched with sickening fascination as a flurry of forms filled the room.

Every transaction created a paper trail that enabled what Murphy's called the merchandise investment control department to track profits and losses to the penny. *Chain Store Age* said Murphy's had the best cash-control policies in the five-and-ten business. But the paperwork was a relic of the days when Murphy's had clerks at each counter, and in a high-volume discount operation such as the first Murphy's Mart, Store No. 802, it was a nightmare. Recording the standard 10 percent employee discount required two different slips, with one taken to the office for approval and the other kept at the register, but clerks couldn't close a busy checkout line just so a fellow employee could save 9¢ on a pair of tube socks. Templeton wanted to deduct the discount at the register, so when sales manager Bill Anderson visited the store, he was dragged to a back room where the procedure was rewritten on the spot.

Despite the company's experience running large, downtown operations in Pittsburgh, Washington, and other cities, many Murphy's employees were used to "little country stores," Templeton says, and convincing them to put aside long-established practices was a struggle. "That was the hardest year of my life. You were always there before the store opened and you were always there after the store closed. You were always fixing something and rewriting something. We had never sold lottery tickets before. We had never sold a half-million dollars of cigarettes [in a single store] before. We never had to worry about snow removal before—but if you have a big parking lot, what happens if the guy doesn't show up? It was a whole different world."

It wasn't just the size of the store that boggled the mind. The first Murphy's Mart sold a different mix of merchandise and attracted a different kind of customer from the variety stores. Templeton, for instance, came from Store No. 221 in nearby Whitehall, Pennsylvania, where his most expensive items were priced at $29. Murphy's Mart sold jewelry and console television sets running up to $300. Though all Murphy locations were accepting credit cards by 1970, charge sales at the mart were three times the company average because higher-ticket items enticed customers to pay with plastic.

The manager, Chuck Henderson, was a veteran of Murphy's giant Store No. 166 in Washington, D.C., whose take-no-prisoners style got the experiment moving in the right direction. "They couldn't have picked a better guy to manage our first mart because he knew how to get the sales," says Fred Speidel, one of four assistant managers responsible for different "zones" inside Mart No. 802. "It took a good year to get things right, and Henderson was the kind of man who did things on the fly." Yet, his ability to make things up as he went combined with a perfectionist streak made his orders seem capricious at times, and his tirades were one reason the first operations manager was driven to the breaking point.

One night, Henderson discovered that the racks near the cash registers had run out of peppermint Life Savers—one of many "checklist" items all Murphy's stores were expected to keep in stock and, more important, Henderson's favorite candy. He'd quit cigarettes and was using the mints as a substitute. When the store closed that night, Henderson gathered the assistant managers in the parking lot to harangue them for at least two hours on the importance of peppermint Life Savers. Another time, Henderson decided he didn't like a sign advertising parakeets in the pet department. He told assistant manager Bob Bishop he wanted it changed before he got back from lunch, but the sign painter needed more time. When Henderson returned, he blew his top.

"I give you a job and you can't do it!" he said, shaking with rage. Customers stared as Henderson ripped the sign down, tore it to pieces, and jumped up and down on them. Still furious, he went looking for his next victim and spied an easy going assistant manager by the name of Fred Fennell. "Get your pad," he growled, then marched Fennell from aisle to aisle, criticizing each of his displays. Finally, Fennell had enough.

"You know, I've never done anything right, have I?" he said, throwing the pad so hard it skipped across the floor and bounced off of the far wall of the store.

Henderson smiled and put his hand on Fennell's shoulder. "I knew I'd get to you some day," he said, then turned and went back to his office.

His abrasive manner eventually caught up to him. When he was promoted to district manager, some employees boycotted his going-away party. He later lost the post because store managers who worked under him kept quitting. But Bishop, Speidel, and others credit Henderson with the Bethel Park mart's successful start. "He was probably the best manager I ever worked for as far as getting excited about items and selling merchandise," Bishop says, adding that Henderson could be quite pleasant away from the store. "All of the wives of the people who worked for him thought he was the nicest guy. I'd say, 'You don't have to work for him!'"

In its first four days of operation, Mart No. 802 did more than $450,000 in sales. "The place was packed and jammed," Anderson says. "We had sixteen checkouts and an annex, and we couldn't let anyone else in." Mart No. 801 in Harmar Township, north of Pittsburgh, was the first Murphy's designed from the ground up. Its opening sales of $295,000 "more than fulfilled our expectations," Murphy chairman Ken Paxton and his brother, Murphy president Ed Paxton, told employees. "Customers and knowledgeable specialists in our industry have commented that Murphy's Mart has the image of high-level, quality stores with merchandise offered at discount prices."

Some credit for the high-quality look of the early Murphy's Marts belongs to vice president of construction and chief architect Ralph Barlow, who started with the company in 1935 and was nearing retirement when the mart program began. While surveying other discount stores, Barlow, an architect trained at Carnegie Institute of Technology in Pittsburgh and the Fontainebleau Schools in Paris, became discouraged by their industrial, warehouse-like appearance. Discount stores needed large, open sales floors and didn't have many windows, but Barlow decided he could distinguish Murphy's Marts through their use of color. Inside, he painted the marts in deep, rich shades of green, gold, and orange; outside, the facades received deeply sculpted metal panels in the same bold colors. As a result, Murphy's Marts looked nothing like the plain-white Kmarts. By the end of 1972, six additional Murphy's Marts had opened near Pittsburgh and two more near Youngstown, Ohio. More than two dozen were up and running in 1974 and forty-four were open by 1975. That year, although marts represented fewer than 10 percent of the company's 529 locations, they were responsible for 36 percent of its $554 million in sales; ten marts in Pennsylvania produced nearly a quarter of Murphy's profits in the state.

Unfortunately, one of the biggest boosters of the mart program wasn't alive to see it succeed. For the second time in three years, an untimely death claimed the chairman of the board of the G. C. Murphy Company when Ken Paxton died at home on July 16, 1971, at just sixty-four years old. He had been diagnosed with cancer several months earlier. In the classic tradition of Murphy executives, Paxton started his career on the floor of a five-and-ten, climbed to regional manager by 1942, and became vice president in charge of personnel by 1946. It was a job for which Ken Paxton was ideally suited. By all accounts, he loved dealing with people and was something of an inveterate "joiner," being an active leader in the Methodist Church, the Boy Scouts, the Pittsburgh and McKeesport symphonies, and the district council of the Masons where he held the fraternity's highest honor, a Thirty-Third Degree.

Tom Hudak, who was hired by Murphy's in 1968, was impressed by both Ken and Ed Paxton during his initial job interview. He remembers asking them why a "career-oriented junior executive" would want to work for the G. C. Murphy Company. "Boy, they just dug into their files and pulled out papers on the mart program and the double-A stores, and what they were doing and what they had plans to do," Hudak says. At a meeting in New York, Hudak watched with admiration as Ed Paxton went one on one with a top official from Moody's Investors Service. "They talked like two brothers who hadn't seen each other for years. Ed was able to talk nuts and bolts about the business and individual products and how they sold. . . . Any time we did anything you could see the pride that they had in the company."

In the wake of Ken Paxton's death, Edgar Paxton became chairman (a position he held until January 1975) and helped elevate his friend Fred Greenleaf, a merchandise buyer from Murphy's New York office, to the presidency. But Ed Paxton had a serious heart condition, and there was a widespread feeling that he didn't have what one executive calls his brother's "burning ambition." Several old hands say Ken Paxton's death was the most serious misfortune to befall Murphy's in the 1970s because it left the company without a strong leader when it most needed one. Greenleaf's promotion meanwhile, wasn't an entirely comfortable fit for either him or the company. Already unhappy at trading the hustle and bustle of Manhattan for McKeesport, Greenleaf found that the cigar-chomping, earthy style that had served him well in the Garment District didn't translate at the home office, where he was out of step with the people around him. Murphy general counsel Bob Messner remembers sitting next to Greenleaf at meetings of the board of directors, one of whom was Reed Albig, the white-haired, courtly president of McKeesport National Bank. After the third or fourth meeting, Greenleaf pulled Messner aside to report that Albig was "pretty damned strange. He gets up like he's thinking, and then he goes into this goddamned closet, and after a little while he comes out. What the hell is he doing?" Messner didn't know how to explain that Albig was simply using the executive washroom that Greenleaf hadn't noticed.

One thing Greenleaf did know was merchandise. The marts were selling 60 percent more per square foot than the five-and-tens—partly because of the big-ticket items, but also because they moved volumes of merchandise that astonished longtime Murphy's employees. Ordering mass quantities of product was "very foreign to the five-and-tens," says

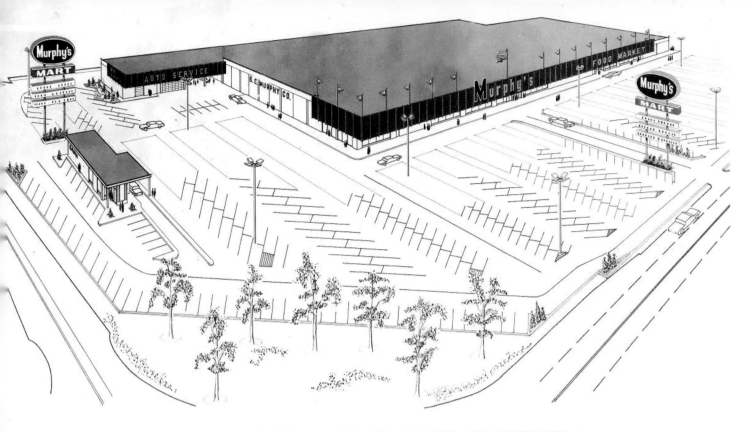

··G.C. MURPHY CO. STORE No. 801·· ··ROUTE No.28·· ··HARMAR TWP., PENNSYLVANIA··

Templeton, who remembers selling five tractor-trailer loads of antifreeze in Mart No. 802 over one Labor Day weekend. Bishop was summoned to the office when 52 crates of bath towels arrived unexpectedly. He hadn't ordered them, but to teach him a lesson, Henderson told him to put all the merchandise out for sale. There were 144 towels and 72 washcloths in each crate, which Bishop kept putting out until they were gone. But the manufacturer had mistakenly sent the towels, which had been intended for dozens of stores, not just one, to the mart instead of the McKeesport distribution center . Although Murphy's was forced to cancel a chain-wide sale on towels advertised that week, the incident proved that the marts could produce record volumes.

Terry Stadterman was at Bethel Park when a salesman for Nordic Ware, a Minnesota-based supplier of pots and pans, paid a visit. Nordic Ware was having great success in the upper Midwest with new donut-shaped cake pans it called "Bundt," for which the Pillsbury Company had created a special cake mix. Would Murphy's Mart be interested? Stadterman knew that shipping charges from Minnesota were exorbitant unless he made it worth the store's while, so he asked for twenty-four dozen. "We stacked them in the midway and they just walked out the door," Stadterman says.

Talk to Murphy men and women who worked in the stores in the 1970s and conversation invariably turns to the colorful vice president of sales Richard T. "Dick" Tracey, an

FIG. 57
Designed by Murphy's chief architect A. Ralph Barlow Sr., the new Murphy's Mart on Route 28 north of Pittsburgh distinguished itself from competitors through the use of rich, bold colors inside and out. Moving from small variety stores to large new discount stores required longtime employees to rewrite selling procedures, sometimes on the fly.

army captain during World War II who had risen through the company's ranks to become manager of Murphy's big Store No. 166 in Washington, D.C. In the seventies, Tracey was a district and regional manager with a no-nonsense attitude many swore by. "Tracey was outstanding," says Dick Gibson Sr., who managed several stores, "by far the number one guy. He didn't take any [crap] off of anyone. But I never knew him to hold it against anybody. I thought well of him." Tracey had a "natural instinct for merchandise," says another store manager, Clair McElhinny, who followed him as a vice president of sales. "He could just look at an item and know whether or not it would sell." Tracey motivated employees through a combination of praise and profanity, often treating subordinates to ostentatious outbursts in the afternoon and elaborate dinners a few hours later. His secretary, Carolyn Gibson, remembers a softball game between the home office and the Baltimore-area Murphy's Marts. When one of the Baltimore workers learned that Gibson worked for Tracey, he genuflected. "At the name of Tracey, every knee shall bend," he said.

Some people in the company found Tracey abrasive, uncouth, and arrogant. Even those who admired his salesmanship occasionally chafed at his style. One afternoon while having lunch with Stadterman in Bethel Park, Tracey launched into a monologue. When Stadterman interrupted, Tracey snapped at him: "You be quiet and I'll tell you when to talk." Finally, Tracey asked Stadterman a question. The younger man remained silent for a minute or so, then replied: "Oh, can I talk now?"

And Tracey knew his limitations. One day he had the manager of an urban variety store in his office in McKeesport along with the district and regional managers. "Why do you have these big [expletive] boxes of Tide in that store?" Tracey shouted, his voice blasting through the door and echoing in the hallway. "People ride the bus to that [expletive] store, get that big [expletive] box of Tide, and then they can't buy anything else because they have to get back on the [expletive] bus." Cringing, Gibson stepped away from her desk until the three men crept out of Tracey's office. Finally, Tracey also emerged and sat on the edge of Gibson's desk. "What did you think about that?" he asked her. "You had to leave, didn't you?"

Pushing the sales volume that Tracey was demanding through the marts required a different mindset for people buying merchandise and tracking budgets at the home office, says Paul Hindes, who was overseeing infants' wear for the company. "They didn't want to give us the money that we needed," he says. "I'm not sure they knew how much we were going to need in that Bethel Park store." Murphy's conservative budgeting was a thorn in the side of aggressive managers who were discouraged from ordering too much merchandise. Bishop was managing the Frankfort, Indiana, store when he got a call from Luther Shay in the merchandise investment control department, which kept a tight leash on the inventory stores could carry.

"Bob, you've got way more merchandise in that little store than you can get sales for," Shay said. "You should just light a match to that store and burn it." Over the phone from Indiana he heard a "pffft!" sound.

"What's that?" Shay said.

"I just lit a match and I'm burning it down," Bishop said.

Ed Kohler, who left the company to become a salesman for a cosmetics firm that sold to Murphy's and other chains, puts it bluntly: "The problem with Murphy's was that they would feed you like a bird and expect you to [defecate] like an elephant. Murphy's was still in the dark ages. . . . Woolworth was the best because they made it simple—when something new came out, they would jump on it. They would buy quantities that would stagger Murphy's."

Merchandise investment control was designed to keep managers from tying up capital in items that got dirty, were out of date, or were otherwise unsellable, Shay says. Each store received a purchasing allowance based on its sales figures and those of similar Murphy locations. Managers planned future volumes based on factors such as population increases or changing demographics. "It was exquisite to a fault," says Shay, who became head of the merchandise investment control department and tried to simplify the system after seeing what competitors were using. "It was very good, but it was too complicated," he says, noting that many managers ignored their allowances anyway.

More than just quantities of merchandise, the marts also caused a sea change in the things Murphy's sold, putting it into the apparel business in a big way for the first time. Though Murphy's had sold house dresses, work clothes, and children's wear since the 1930s, along with hosiery and underwear, only a few of its variety stores were large enough to display or carry much clothing. "We were good at selling hammers and toothpaste and all of those kinds of things," Templeton says. "We were not good at apparel." Suddenly, Murphy's was buying clothing "in tonnage," he says. The typical Murphy's Mart carried "ten thousand pairs of men's pants. We hardly carried men's pants in a five-and-ten."

Much of the new apparel was being sold for the first time under Murphy's own name. Chain stores had long before figured out that instead of buying from wholesalers and passing the markup onto customers, they could have goods manufactured to their own specifications, sell them under their own name, and pocket a higher profit margin. Hard lines, such as appliances and tools, were being sold under "private labels" by the 1930s—the best-known examples were Sears, Roebuck & Company's Kenmore and Craftsman brands—and by the 1960s department-store chains were doing the same with clothing. In 1963 and 1964, Murphy's greatly expanded its private-label clothing lines, introducing Pelham men's and boys' underwear, Murtag men's shirts, Carolina Moon women's hose, Murfimade lingerie, Patti Jo clothes for girls, and Carole Joanne ladies' shoes. But there was little rhyme or reason to the branding (for example, why was cold cream sold under the Murcrest name while the facial tissue used to remove it was labeled Regal?) and few of the fourteen different labels had any obvious relationship to Murphy's. And without the marketing might of Sears, it was unlikely that any of the names would stick in the public memory as Kenmore and Craftsman did.

Rebranding the clothing and other merchandise under Murphy's own name was the suggestion of Earl Nottingham, an assistant manager in several Ohio stores in the 1960s, and was championed by Phil Rogers, manager of the research and development department. At the time, Murphy's private-label clothing "wasn't that stylish," admits Nottingham, who was recruited to oversee the Murphy private-label program. "They were stronger in work clothes, sport shirts, underwear, things like that." Nancy Mack, whose husband was a Murphy manager, used to sneak their children over to a Hills store to buy school clothes. Murphy's was going to have to start selling more fashionable clothing in a hurry if it hoped to attract younger, more style-conscious customers. Children's wear buyer Paul Hindes says Murphy's asked suppliers to make their clothing to the same design and quality specifications as J. C. Penney Company, knowing the larger firm had more experience in fashion but was conservative enough not to jump too quickly into fads. Unlike department stores that marked clothing up as much as 300 percent to insulate themselves from fashion blunders, Murphy's Marts sold garments on much thinner margins—as little as 40 percent—and had less room for error.

To keep costs competitive, Murphy's joined a growing number of retailers that were buying clothing from factories in Asia. It was a bitter pill for some executives to swallow, says toy buyer Bill Kraus, but Murphy's was "paying through the nose" for goods that competitors were getting from importers. So he got the go-ahead from Greenleaf to make a buying trip to Japan, Korea, and Taiwan. Dealing with a foreign culture proved by turns frustrating and frightening—Kraus cooled his heels in one office for an "interminable amount of time" while a clerk laboriously figured out every price using an abacus—but his troubles were well rewarded. He returned having sourced toy trains, stuffed animals, tea sets, and inflatable beach balls at $110,000 less than Murphy's was paying stateside. Paul Hindes and menswear buyer Bob Snell were among the next two Murphy executives sent overseas. They started their first trip in Osaka, Japan, and visited Taiwan, Hong Kong, Manila, and New Delhi in a whirlwind two-week tour, finally returning to the United States via England because Snell wanted to say he had "flown around the world."

Murphy buyers also learned some lessons about dealing with Asian manufacturers—namely, that some bargains were too good to be true. Electronics buyer Roy Fowler Jr. made a deal with Sharp to purchase one million dollars' worth of black-and-white portable televisions at 50¢ less per unit than anyone else. The first shipment never arrived. Neither did the second shipment. The Sharp factory was pushing Murphy's order to the back of the pile to first take care of customers who were paying more. "I found out you could overnegotiate," Fowler says.

All the new merchandise wasn't going to do G. C. Murphy Company any good if it wasn't getting into stores, but Murphy's distribution centers were turning into major bottlenecks. Construction of the Monroe, Louisiana, distribution center in the early 1960s to serve the southern states was followed by a major expansion of the McKeesport facility that more than doubled the floor space, along with the addition of a new "fashion center" to distribute apparel in Jersey City, New Jersey, within sight of the Statue of Liberty. A new distribution center was added in Indianapolis in December 1971. But Murphy's distribution problems weren't lack of capacity—they were antiquated handling practices that slowed the movement of goods from factories to stores, along with management-labor relations that ranged from neglect to outright hostility. One set of problems fed the other: Many warehouse workers were frustrated because their jobs were dull and tedious, and they took out their frustrations by doing sloppy or slow work.

When products arrived at Murphy's distribution centers—mainly by tractor trailer in the 1970s, though bulky paper products and some other items still arrived by rail—laborers unloaded them using hand trucks and forklifts and sorted them into numbered bins. When stores placed orders, home office computers generated lists of merchandise to be picked from each bin. The items were placed on carts and towed from place to place by a clanking metal chain that hung from the ceiling, making a continuous circuit through the building. In the shipping area, the carts were disconnected from the chain and orders were consolidated into loads for each store, usually with several stores being shipped on a single truck that made numerous stops. It was mindless, repetitive drudgery, and the rapid increase in sales the marts were generating made the jobs more grinding than usual. Gary Sexton, who started work at Murphy's Indianapolis center shortly after it opened, studied job satisfaction among co-workers while he earned a master's degree in human resources at Indiana-Purdue University. They described their work as "boring" and "not stimulating" and rated their job satisfaction levels a full seven points below what a common formula said would be a "neutral" score.

The tedium didn't encourage the team spirit that characterized life in the stores. Worse yet, Murphy's distribution centers seemed to take a perverse pride in hiring dysfunctional managers and stubbornly standing behind them when employees complained. The easy camaraderie that existed in the McKeesport distribution center when it opened in the 1940s was absent in Indianapolis from the very first day, says Sexton, who went on to a career as a personnel director at Ford Motor Company. "They didn't treat people with respect. They weren't good listeners. They really had poor supervision," he says. "They didn't understand the impact of the quality of their management on the workers. They didn't put much thought into the selection of their management. They brought in a 'personnel manager' who had been a payroll clerk at one of the stores in Indianapolis. They brought in a supervisor from Monroe who struck me as illiterate—he reminded me of Junior Samples from *Hee Haw*." The manager of the Monroe distribution center also had a well-deserved reputation as a "hard-ass," says one home office executive. The Indianapolis center opened as a nonunion shop, but by 1973 frustration reached a breaking point and employees voted 92 to 14 to join the Teamsters. Sexton was elected one of the stewards. Rudimentary attempts by the company to reach out to the rank-and-file, such as an employee bowling league, swiftly ended as Murphy's hunkered down and workers who tried to talk to managers were told, "See your union representative."

The G. C. Murphy Company was stridently antiunion, partly because of its founders' conservative political leanings and also because upper management genuinely believed that the company was a family—and no family likes to air its dirty laundry in front of the neighbors. After joining Murphy's in 1970, attorney Ed McGinley spent many days running antiunion campaigns at stores, trying to convince employees that management had their best interests at heart. The advent of the mart program "elevated the profile of the company," he says, and increased union activity throughout the chain. Teamsters put informational pickets in front of the Connellsville, Pennsylvania, Murphy's Mart for more than a year as they tried to organize employees. An effort by the United Steelworkers to unionize clerical personnel at the home office failed by only seven votes. But where home office secretaries or even store employees might regard themselves as white-collar workers who didn't need collective bargaining, employees in the rough-and-tumble warehouses felt kinship with industrial trades, especially in McKeesport where the Steelworkers' union was founded in the 1930s. Workers at the McKeesport distribution center joined the Retail, Wholesale, and Department Store Union (RWDSU) in 1956 and then switched to the Teamsters in 1970. Strikes closed the center for a month in 1969 and three times in 1972.

One of Murphy's few attempts to get on the same side as its unions in McKeesport resulted in a landmark federal court case that set a precedent for women's rights. In 1969, laborer Joanne Glus tried to apply for a job running a forklift—a plum position that paid more than twice her $85 per week salary and allowed her some freedom to move around the plant. The foreman laughed. So did the union. "I worked hard and long and got nowhere," she told the *Chicago Tribune*. "Men had all of the high-paying jobs. A woman could be there thirty years and be lucky to make $2.87 an hour. A man there with one year experience would make $2.90. It just wasn't fair." When Glus and other female employees questioned the disparities, Murphy management and union leaders patiently replied that women lacked the upper-body strength to handle more strenuous jobs. But that didn't explain why women weren't allowed to drive forklifts—little more difficult than driving a car—or why there were different pay scales for men and women performing the same work. Nor did it explain why women employees didn't have the same seniority protection as male employees.

After failing to get satisfaction from the Equal Employment Opportunity Commission, Glus contacted the National Organization for Women, which helped her file a federal discrimination lawsuit against Murphy's and the RWDSU under the Civil Rights Act of 1964. The next three years were miserable for Glus, as co-workers taunted her and supervisors made it clear they were watching her every move. But the National Organization for Women leafleted Pittsburgh-area Murphy stores to keep up public pressure. In August 1972, *Glus v. G. C. Murphy Company* was settled out of court. Murphy's agreed to pay up to $4,300 each in back wages to Glus and 245 other female employees at the McKeesport distribution center. Separate job classifications and seniority lists disappeared, and Glus went to work as a forklift operator at $190 per week.

Murphy's sued the RWDSU to recover its costs while mistrust between warehouse workers and the company deepened as allegations flew back and forth, including accusations of deliberate sabotage. In McKeesport, a series of ramps connected the original two-story 1940 warehouse with the 1960s addition. A few strategically misplaced freight carts colliding at those ramps brought the towline grinding to a halt and shut down operations for hours at a time. "The Teamsters were just horrible—nasty," Nottingham says. "They'd do so many things at that warehouse to screw it up. . . . What did they care if ten trucks didn't go out? They hurt us so much."

Theft was a continuous problem as well. When Polaroid introduced its new automatic SX-70 instant cameras in 1973, retailers could barely keep up with demand for film. But in the G. C. Murphy Company's case, part of the problem was that shipments were being sent to stores light. Murphy security director Dick Scales called in the FBI to help bust an interstate theft ring that was stealing merchandise out of the McKeesport distribution center. A crucial break came when Scales, out for a ride in the country with his wife and children, spotted a truck from Murphy's parked behind a private residence—the driver had stopped to see his girlfriend on his way to dispose of the loot. To thwart theft of high-priced merchandise in the warehouses, Murphy's began locking it in security cages. One McKeesport laborer was seriously injured when he tried climbing a cage to steal transistor radios; then he asked for workers' compensation.

But again and again, heavy-footed management only pushed labor farther away from the company. In 1974, the Indianapolis center was experiencing a serious theft problem, and employees soon fingered the prime suspects. Instead of working with the union to root out the thieves, Murphy's put a plainclothes security officer in the warehouse as a temporary worker, and it didn't take long for the union to realize he was a plant. The day after a laborer was nabbed by police with a carload of stolen calculators, the company made its move. One by one, seventeen employees were called to the office, questioned briefly by Murphy security, and fired. Sexton says it was a "seminal experience" that permanently damaged morale among the rank-and-file. The union filed formal grievances against fifteen of the firings; thirteen were overturned when the detective admitted he had mixed up the names of the suspects.

"I wouldn't put the whole onus of the problem on Murphy's," says Sexton, who blames in part the climate of the post–Vietnam War era when everyone was primed to question authority. In August 1976, Indianapolis warehouse workers walked off the job for fifty-four days even though union leaders had recommended they accept a new three-year contract with a built-in $1.90-per-hour raise. "It was a grudge strike," Sexton says. "There was this pressure in the bargaining unit to pressure those 'sons of bitches' and get more money." One veteran on the picket line had to be dissuaded from bringing a gun and taking some shots at management. The strike was finally settled in federal mediation when Murphy's offered another 10¢ per hour, but the impulse by employees to "screw the company" remained. Guerrilla warfare by workers, combined with Murphy's labor-intensive system of unpacking, sorting, and repacking merchandise in the warehouses, was a recipe for chaos. "In McKeesport we lost a million dollars every year in inventory," says Ed McCandless, who worked with distribution, data processing, and merchandise investment control to try to straighten out the mess. "At the end of the year I would go in to [check] inventory that the computer said was there and it wasn't. It was horrible. Other times you were overstocked with [outdated] merchandise you couldn't sell."

Frustrated by inefficiency and labor problems, Murphy's began threatening to close one or more of its warehouses, especially after opening a new 220,000-square-foot facility in 1974 in Fredericksburg, Virginia—an area with less union activity. But the threats made workers more defiant, Sexton says: "Management didn't have much credibility." Employees in McKeesport thought it was a negotiating tactic when Murphy chairman S. Warne Robinson announced in September 1976 that the distribution center would be shuttered on October 31 due to its age and the "unfavorable labor climate." The Teamsters and Murphy's were engaged in their triennial contract negotiations and, as usual, both sides were deadlocked over union demands for higher wages and stronger job protections.

Robinson called the Teamsters' bluff by laying off ninety-seven people—about half the McKeesport center's workforce. Employees became more concerned when McCandless starting shipping out inventory as fast as railroads could supply boxcars to put it in. Many of those railcars, ironically, were routed to Indianapolis, which, of course, was having labor problems of its own. Though McKeesport officials begged Murphy executives to change their minds, only a skeleton crew and a handful of packing crates remained in the cavernous facility by October 29 when Murphy's announced that it had reached a tentative contract agreement to save the warehouse. Workers in Indianapolis weren't so lucky. McGinley was bargaining a new contract in 1979 when he called Robinson to report the union's latest proposal. "I say we close the son of a bitch," McGinley said. Robinson agreed. The distribution center's managers were as flabbergasted as the Teamsters. About one hundred employees lost their jobs and stores serviced by the Indianapolis center were divided up among McKeesport, Monroe, and Fredericksburg.

At the end of the 1970s, an uneasy détente developed between Murphy's and its warehouse unions (possibly due to weariness more than anything else), and a new effort by the company to improve efficiency helped. In 1968, Murphy's had recruited industrial engineer C. Lee Breakwell from time-and-motion consulting firm H. B. Maynard and Company to run the McKeesport warehouse. After being elevated to assistant vice president for distribution and traffic in 1976, Breakwell brought in Maynard to set efficiency and performance standards for each distribution center. Union stewards were invited to participate in the planning process and attend the training sessions. If the company made more efforts like that, Sexton believes, many of the problems—at least in Indianapolis—might have been mitigated. "I have spent most of my career trying to avoid unions," he says. "You talk to people and you listen to people and you hear their concerns. Murphy's never did that—they just dug in."

Aside from the warehouses, the G. C. Murphy Company's rapid transformation was straining other parts of the chain in unexpected ways. The decision to call the discount stores "Murphy's Marts" was a mixed blessing that gave the division instant credibility in areas where G. C. Murphy stores had long been reliable community fixtures, but it also muddied the company's image. "I think we made a huge mistake with the name 'Murphy's Mart,'" Bill Anderson says. "We were more concerned with 'should the logo be straight print or fancy writing'? They never stopped to think what the name 'Murphy's' would do."

FIG. 59
G. C. Murphy Company vice president of sales William Anderson breaks ground on the first Murphy's Mart in the Baltimore, Md., metropolitan area in 1974. In its race to catch up with S. S. Kresge Company's Kmart division, Murphy's went on a buying spree in the 1970s. The most rapid expansion program in the company's history would have serious consequences in a few years.

At Store No. 46 in Elizabeth, Pennsylvania, one of Murphy's oldest and smallest locations, Marianne Molnar was constantly trying to placate shoppers who were angry that they couldn't return items they had purchased at Mart No. 808 just a few miles away up Route 51. "They would buy it at the bigger store and then insist that you take it back," she says. "I'd tell them, no, no, no, I don't have that here." Anderson contends the low-volume, high-margin Murphy variety stores also were hurt because they couldn't meet the marts' low-margin, high-volume prices. The variety and discount stores shared advertising; customers were left wondering why G. C. Murphy Company was charging different prices on the same items—did lower prices at the marts mean the variety stores were overcharging?

Murphy's further confused the issue by creating a new 600-series store for towns such as Waynesboro and Greenville, Pennsylvania, that weren't large enough to support a Murphy's Mart but had outgrown their downtown five-and-tens. The new stores were hybrids that resembled Murphy's Marts and carried many of the same items but marked the prices up to traditional variety-store levels. It was the A-A debacle all over again. One of the important lessons of the Kmart experience, argues Anderson, who retired in 1975 as Murphy's executive vice president of sales, was that S. S. Kresge Company distanced its discount division from its variety stores by giving it a different name. "People went for a long time without realizing that 'Kresge' and 'Kmart' were the same company," he says.

There was another important factor in Kmart's success that Murphy's couldn't copy. Kresge purchased sites for Kmarts in the 1950s and '60s before the fuel crises of the early 1970s pushed inflation and interest rates into double digits. Murphy's was paying too much for many of its new locations. In its mad rush to catch up with Kresge, the G. C. Murphy Company launched in November 1975 what Robinson and recently installed president William T. Withers called the most "aggressive expansion program" in its history, issuing $15 million in bonds to fund construction of thirty-one new locations in 1976 and twenty-five new stores the following year. Work gangs of employees were dispatched from throughout the company wherever a new Murphy's Mart was about to open and spent two to three weeks stocking the shelves, readying the offices, and hanging the signs.

Management made the trips enticing to get store employees to leave home and live in a motel for several weeks, says Clair Trost, who supervised set-up crews in the 1970s as an assistant to northern regional sales manager Jack Franklin. "You worked hard and you played hard," says Trost, who relied on a core group of "good, hardworking people" that he knew would cooperate and meet a tight deadline. "It was a lot of fun and a lot of hard work," says Emmeratta McDonough, a Murphy traveling auditor who helped set up several marts. "There were some pretty wild parties, and some of those people got carried away." Reports of dalliances between younger employees were exaggerated, but a few did occur. In Franklin's territory, which comprised core Murphy states such as Pennsylvania, Ohio, West Virginia, and Kentucky, Trost says Murphy's Mart grand openings were "a madhouse. Every one of them was so well received. Every one that I ever saw, you couldn't even get in the place—it was so jammed."

But it wasn't a great time to borrow money or buy real estate. When Murphy's tried to save money in 1976 and 1977 by purchasing forty existing discount stores from the bankrupt W. T. Grant Company and other floundering retailers, it wound up with a bunch of lemons. While Murphy's got the locations cheap, they had already failed once under previous owners. Worse yet, many of the stores were in markets where the company either wasn't well known or its variety stores were still operating under the Morgan & Lindsey banner. Though sales went to $615 million in 1976 and $665 million the following year, operating costs were rising quickly and profits were flat. In the summer of 1976, Legg Mason put Murphy's on a list of companies whose cash positions were deteriorating. A year later, Moody's downgraded the company's bonds, citing low earnings.

Murphy's responded as it had to every crisis, including the Depression—by trying to stimulate higher sales—but field personnel felt the home office was sending mixed messages. For years, Murphy store managers earned their annual bonuses based on profits, and to protect the bottom line they disguised losses by raising prices on "safe" items where they faced little competition. Although officially discouraged, top executives accepted the practice as the cost of doing business. In the cutthroat world of discounting where a Murphy's Mart might be competing with a Kmart, a Woolco, and a Zayre in the same vicinity, every

FIG. 60
Murphy president Bill Withers, an unidentified store manager, Murphy chairman S. Warne Robinson, and vice president of store planning and construction Eugene Grissinger celebrate the opening of Store No. 711 in Huntsville, Ala. Some of the new Murphy's Marts in the southern United States were locations abandoned by the defunct W. T. Grant Company and other retailers; several of them turned out to be duds.

penny counted and there were no safe items. So, managers were now told that bonuses would be paid on volume, not profit. The home office hoped managers would lower prices, attract more customers, and improve their volume, but the trick worked too well. "It was crazy," Stadterman says. "They were ordering truckloads of Coca-Cola and giving it away." In other areas, Murphy's was still too cautious. By 1976, more than two hundred of the company's 545 stores were finally open on Sundays but only from noon until 5:00 P.M. Although Sunday sales accounted for 20 percent of the week's total in some locations, Murphy's dragged its feet. "We won't open on Sundays unless forced into it by competition—we're never the first," Withers promised. "We'd rather see employees take the time off."

Individually, the warehouse snafus, overexpansion, inflation, or soaring interest rates might have been manageable, but together they were disastrous and the bottom finally fell out. In the first half of 1978, Murphy's reported a loss of more than $634,000 and the company's stock, which traded as high as $23 per share a few years earlier, skidded to $13. That was the end for Withers, who in October was placed on "indefinite leave of absence" by the board of directors. He wouldn't return. Many saw Withers as a fall guy taking the blame for bad decisions made by the board itself.

S. Warne Robinson must have known the G. C. Murphy Company was in treacherous water. A graduate of the College of William and Mary, he had spent nearly forty years with Murphy's, most of them overseeing the company's finances, including twelve years as director of merchandise investment control before becoming vice president and treasurer in 1970. *Chain Store Age,* which ten years earlier had devoted an entire issue to praising Murphy's, now blasted what it called "a decade of substandard industry performance" and blamed the company's "inability to absorb the intricacies of large store operations." One unnamed observer told the magazine that Murphy's didn't have the "depth of qualified store management personnel" necessary to run the new marts it was opening—particularly, the troubled former W. T. Grant Company locations.

People at Murphy's were watching the W. T. Grant saga closely. As Murphy's had been, the W. T. Grant Company was founded in 1906. And, just as Murphy's had, it expanded rapidly to catch up with Kmart, adding 376 stores between 1969 and 1973. Also like Murphy's, Grant's had added big-ticket merchandise it wasn't used to handling, including appliances and clothing, enticing customers to buy with the promise of easy credit. But bloated inventories and uncollectible credit-card debts wound up sinking Grant's, whose October 1975 bankruptcy filing was one of the largest in American history. If the G. C. Murphy Company didn't want to have something else in common with Grant's—liquidation—Robinson needed to turn things around quickly.

Home, Sweet Office

Sure, the Woolworth Building has been an icon in New York City since 1913, and Chicago's Sears Tower is among the world's best-known skyscrapers, even though its namesake has moved to the suburbs. But as handsome as those retailers' famous office buildings might be, they weren't a patch on G. C. Murphy Company's palatial world headquarters at 531 Fifth Avenue in beautiful downtown McKeesport, Pennsylvania. Or were they?

"The executive offices were very nice," says Thelma Sharpe, who began work at Murphy's in 1948 and wound up as a secretary to several top officials, "but the rest of the place wasn't."

Company public relations man Ed Davis's five-by-eight-foot office was carved from another office's reception area using walls made of plywood and two-by-fours. Visiting journalists would cast a hairy eyeball around the tiny cubicle—just large enough for two chairs and a desk—and remarked on the "austerity" of the dime-store business. "Well, we've got a nice office in the back for the president," Davis would reply. "It's got carpet on the floor." Privately, some Murphy executives grumbled that store managers had nicer offices than they did.

Generations of female students from McKeesport High School, many of whom were recruited for secretarial jobs, toured the Murphy home office just before graduation. Carolyn Gibson nearly walked away from a Murphy career after visiting the building in 1969: "It wasn't very impressive. There wasn't much that matched in there. It really brought to light how down-to-earth the Murphy people I worked with were."

Rose Cafiero, who began work in the home office in the 1940s, is diplomatic. "It didn't have to be fancy," she says. "It made you realize different things about Murphy's—how to be frugal, for instance."

"Frugal" is a charitable way to describe the G. C. Murphy Company's nerve center: an agglomeration of mismatched buildings that grew from George Murphy's first five-and-ten to eventually incorporate a church, a livery stable, a hardware store, and the old Montgomery Ward store across the alley. According to John Barna, a Murphy staff photographer and history buff, the oldest structure in the complex was the Cumberland Presbyterian Church, erected in 1882. The neighboring Wernke Carriage Works followed a few years later.

Murphy's first five-and-ten in McKeesport was located on the first floor of the five-story Ruben Building, with office and storage space on the upper floors. After purchasing the company from Murphy's heirs in 1911, new owners John Sephus Mack and Walter Shaw Sr. moved out of the Ruben Building and bought the church down the block, gutting it to create a second floor inside and erecting a false brick storefront along Fifth Avenue. The Wernke building was added a few years later and the three-story Moskowitz Building (between the church and the Ruben Building) followed in 1934. In 1940, Murphy's repurchased the Ruben Building and remodeled the upper floors after World War II to add an auditorium. The neighboring five-story Hartman Hardware building was added a few years later, as were the offices of the real estate and construction division in the "home office annex" above the old Monkey Ward's.

"It was a hodge-podge," Barna says. "The second floor of the Hartman building didn't match up with the second floor of the Ruben Building; consequently, any time you went from one to the other through the common wall, you had to go up two steps or down two steps, or even up a ramp." A few hallways either went or seemed to go nowhere, and years of remodeling projects created all sorts of other strange nooks and crannies. Earl Nottingham of the research and development department says one conference room had a small door at the back that led into a storage area only three or four feet high. Nottingham once went into that "half room" to retrieve something only to find that someone had locked the door behind him as a practical joke. Cries for help went unanswered and he finally forced the door open with his knee. "I never did find out who did it," Nottingham says, "probably one of the secretaries."

It wasn't unusual for newcomers to get hopelessly lost. Visitors entered in the storefront of the old church—the buttresses were still visible out in the alley—but there was no lobby. Instead, they went upstairs to a big reception room that featured a grandfather clock that had once stood in the living room of Murphy president Paul L. Sample. To one side, a bank of telephone operators answered calls on a manual switchboard that was an antique even in the 1960s.

At many companies, upper management was treated to offices on the top floor; at Murphy's, they worked on the "executive floor" above the old livery stable. Many employees came in through an entrance next to the loading dock, and woe betide those who showed up after the official 8:00 A.M. starting time. Barna, who says he "invariably" got to work just as

FIG. 61
Switchboard operators answer phones at the G. C. Murphy Company home office in the 1970s. Though the stores were being transformed rapidly in the '70s and '80s, life changed slowly inside the home office, which was a mismatched collection of nineteenth- and twentieth-century buildings on McKeesport's Fifth Avenue. The down-to-earth surroundings lent a collegial atmosphere and tied employees and executives alike into a tight family.

the door was being bolted, remembers leaning on the door buzzer to get someone from the nearby printing department to let him in.

Buzzers and bells were a part of life for more than nine hundred employees at the Murphy home office. Executives pushed buzzers to summon secretaries and chimes rang all day long—first to signal the start of work, again at 10:00 A.M. and 2:00 P.M. for ten-minute coffee breaks, at 11:30 A.M. to mark the beginning of lunch, and at 12:30 P.M. to call people back to work. When it was time to head home at 4:30 P.M., workers were dismissed again by the bell. "Everyone used to laugh about the bells," Sharpe says. Anyone who didn't work there thought it sounded like grade school: "The bells, the bells, the bells, how do you put up with that?" they'd ask. Vice president of employee relations Ed Procious finally put a stop to the bells in the early 1970s.

Other customs at the home office were almost as rigid. Men were addressed as "mister" and wore suits and ties; women as "miss" and wore skirts or dresses. Eventually, women were allowed to wear pantsuits, but a male buyer who passed an executive in the hallway while wearing a sport coat and a tie instead of a suit learned that certain standards were still expected. "I'm sorry to hear you're leaving us," the senior man said.

"I'm not leaving," the buyer said, confused.

"If you wear a sport coat again, you will be," the senior man said, continuing down the hallway.

For all the ritual, the atmosphere in the home office was far from stuffy—perhaps because the ramshackle surroundings kept those in charge from putting on airs. Gibson remembers one of the first letters she typed for Luther Shay, head of merchandise investment control. "I had never, ever heard this word before, so I typed, 'The crust of the matter is. . . .'" Never raising his voice, Shay quietly fixed the mistake and sent the letter back to Gibson: "I thought, 'Oh, he's going to think I'm an idiot.'" Another secretary, Audrey Puko, remembers seeing Bill Verlander of the maintenance department racing down the hallway trailing flames. Someone had dropped a match in his wastepaper basket and set it ablaze.

The earthy surroundings in downtown McKeesport kept people's feet on the ground too. The windows in the executive suite looked out on U.S. Steel's National Works with its blast furnaces and Bessemer converters belching black smoke and red iron oxide into the air, while the trains of the Baltimore & Ohio Railroad ran just past the home office's back door, dividing the business district and snarling traffic several times an hour. The railroad also provided a favorite excuse for employees who had trouble getting back to work on time after lunch since the restaurant at Murphy's Store No. 1 was on the opposite side of the tracks. "I had to wait for a train," the tardy employees would humbly say to their skeptical bosses.

If they weren't eating at Store No. 1, you could often find employees in one of the shot-and-beer taverns and hole-in-the-wall lunchrooms that catered to steelworkers. One of them was the *Beer Barrel,* located next to the home office annex. One night while working late, Puko went to the Beer Barrel for a sandwich and a Coke to go.

"How about a rum and Coke instead?" the bartender asked. "I'd love to have one, but I have to go back to work," Puko said.

She got back to the office, sat down at her desk, took a big swig from the cup, and found out the drink was half rum anyway. Puko finished her "Coke." If anyone noticed, they didn't say anything.

Pizza was a favorite treat, of course, though maybe not the one that Puko sent to buyer Frank Dziabiak. One night she was with a group of employees that was planning a trip to a famed Pittsburgh-area pizzeria, Vincent's in nearby North Braddock. "Dziabiak kept going on and on about how he liked pizza," Puko says. "But when it came down to it, he didn't want to go with us. Every time we saw him after that, he would say, 'You never take me out for pizza.'" Finally, Puko's mother was getting ready to throw away a mummified frozen pizza that had been forgotten in the freezer. Instead, Puko took it to work, stuck it in an envelope, and mailed it to Dziabiak.

FIG. 63
Home office personnel get ready for the Pittsburgh Steelers' appearance in Super Bowl XIV against the Los Angeles Rams, January 1980. The Steelers won 31–19.

"I waited and waited and waited, and I didn't hear from him for the longest time," she says. "Finally, my phone rang one day and he said, 'I like pepperoni on my pizza.'"

Other than the bells, few things triggered action faster than news of a "sample sale" starting in the stairwell, during which merchandise that had been sent to the home office for evaluation was sold off cheap from atop a big wooden box that employees nicknamed "the coffin." "It was like grand theft, depending on what you were looking for," Barna says. "I remember after Christmas I used to go down and clean up on [model] train stuff. You didn't care what it was—you knew it only cost you 50¢."

Working at the home office had other advantages. From the front windows, for instance, employees had a bird's-eye view of parades. Puko was watching one parade when Oscar Mayer's famed "Wienermobile" made an appearance: "I got a phone call and said, 'I can't talk right now, there's a big hot dog driving down the street.'"

It wasn't all fun and games, for workloads could be crushing at times, especially during the end-of-year inventories and audits when page after page of sales figures had to be manually collated and sorted or during the 1970s when dozens of Murphy's Marts were opening each year. But the combination of unrelenting paperwork, rituals punctuated with silliness, and the dingy surroundings bonded home office employees into a family. "When you made a friend at Murphy's, you made a friend for life," Sharpe says. "I met a girl in the invoice department [in 1948] and to this day, we're still friends."

More than a family, it was a sisterhood since so many home office employees were young women hired right out of high school. And, despite low pay, efforts to unionize the secretarial staff went nowhere. The fact that roughly half the home office staff consisted of young, single women wasn't lost on male employees. "At lunch time, all of the guys used to stand on the street and watch the girls come out because it was just a parade of girls," Sharpe says.

Barna certainly enjoyed it: "Here I was, a single guy, twenty-six years old, working in a building with four hundred women, most of them young and single," he says, laughing. "I enjoyed what I was doing. It was fun." He's also quick to add that he enjoyed his work, too, which usually consisted of taking pictures for Murphy's newspaper ads and circulars with old-fashioned, German-made large-format cameras. "I don't know if Murphy's was 'cheap' or 'stingy' or whatever, but I always thought I was pretty well treated," he says. "I remember Ken Swauger [another photographer] saying to me one time, 'You know what, John? We're never going to have a job this good again.' And you know what? He was right."

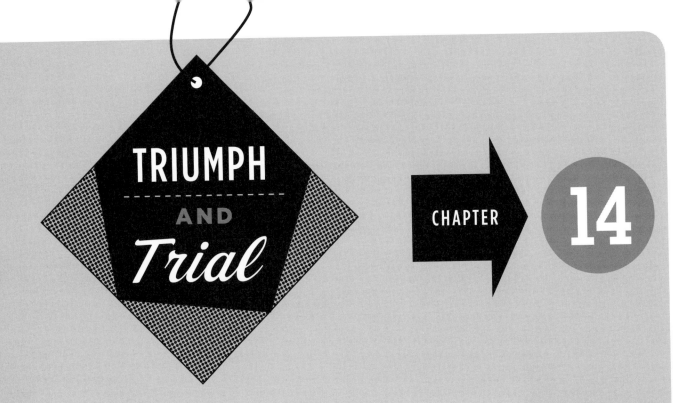

CHAPTER 14

TRIUMPH AND *Trial*

If G. C. Murphy Company employees knew nothing else about their new president, they knew he liked Charlie Brown.

After a yeoman-like effort by Murphy's clerks and managers to cut costs and boost sales, a surprisingly strong performance in the fourth quarter of 1978 enabled the company to show a profit—albeit only 5¢ per share—for the year. At the end of 1979, profits were back on track at $2.50 per share. Chuck Lytle, who was named the company's president in February, ordered several cases of greeting cards featuring the hero of Charles Schulz's *Peanuts* comics strip. "Thank you from the bottom of my socks," the cards said. "Somehow, 'thank you from the bottom of my heart' didn't seem deep enough!" Lytle sent hundreds of the cards to store managers, supervisors, and other personnel and wrote a short, personal message inside each.

"It really does something for one's morale, and I speak for myself as well as my men," Philadelphia district manager O. D. Lloyd wrote back. "I thank you for it, and I want to add, the response from my managers has been the same."

Whatever problems Murphy's faced at the end of the 1970s, a lack of dedicated, loyal employees wasn't one of them. Tom Hudak, who became chief financial officer and senior vice president for finance in the wake of Withers's departure, arrived at work one morning to find his secretary shaking her head. "A lot of girls are talking about how unfair it is not to bring those three women in," she told him.

"What three women?" Hudak asked. Three store employees with fifty years' service each were not allowed to attend the upcoming G. C. Murphy Veterans Club banquet. Hudak called Phil Rogers, the new vice president of employee, public, and labor relations, to find out why. "Geez, Phil, what are you doing?" Hudak asked him.

Rogers replied that eligibility for veterans' club events stopped at forty-five years' service—few anticipated that someone would stay with Murphy's for a half-century—and he was trying to follow the rules. Besides, he said, "I thought it might be too hard on them to travel."

"At least give them the chance!" Hudak replied, laughing.

Although Warne Robinson remained chairman of the board, Lytle and Hudak were two of the key players tapped to turn the company around by shedding money-losing operations, streamlining office procedures, and giving Murphy's its first comprehensive strategic plan in years. Robinson called them his "Young Turks," and as with Mack and Shaw or Shaw and Sample, the partners' talents complemented each other—Lytle admired Hudak's financial acumen, while Hudak liked Lytle's easy way with people. They were "beautifully balanced," in Robinson's opinion. Their backgrounds seemed a little incongruous: Lytle, an heir to Pittsburgh's Heinz fortune, began his working career not at the H. J. Heinz Company but in the stockroom of a G. C. Murphy five-and-ten; Hudak, who grew up in the steelmaking town of Donora, Pennsylvania, worked as an auditor for Industrial Nucleonics and AT&T's Western Electric division while earning his MBA from the Ohio State University College of Business.

Lytle's uncle, Paul Sample, inspired him to join Murphy's. After the untimely death of Lytle's father, Harry, Sample stepped in to provide a positive male role model. "Chuckie" became part of his extended family, providing his daughters with the brother they never had. Like nearly everyone else, Lytle couldn't help but be impressed by Sample's honest and ebullient personality. In 1952, not long before his uncle died, Lytle gave up a likely executive position at Heinz to work for Murphy's unloading trucks at Store No. 167 in Jamestown, New York. Minus two years in the army, Lytle spent the next eleven years at various Murphy stores working his way up to assistant manager and manager.

Lytle was utterly without airs. One of Thelma Sharpe's enduring memories from her career as a home office secretary remains seeing Lytle, president of the then $800-million G. C. Murphy Company, walking down Fifth Avenue in McKeesport with a cup of McDonald's coffee and an Egg McMuffin in his hand, memos and papers tucked under his arms, and his shirt tail hanging out. "He was too cute for words, and you could not get mad at

FIG. 64
Murphy assistant secretary Joe Haggerty, assistant vice president and treasurer Gerry Prado, senior vice president and finance and chief financial officer Tom Hudak, and president Chuck Lytle celebrate a birthday at the home office in the late 1970s. Stung in 1978 by operating losses and slow sales, the G. C. Murphy Company board forced Bill Withers out of the presidency and tapped Lytle and Hudak to lead the chain's turnaround; Robinson called them his "young Turks."

the man," Sharpe says. "His wife would buy him these wonderful briefcases and he would carry all of these papers just under both arms."

"Oh my, yes, that was Chuck," says his widow, Ann, laughing at the story. Lytle's family and colleagues remember him as many things—deeply religious, deliberate, diligent, and extremely conscientious—but "neat and organized" isn't one of them. "He would think of nothing but wearing a jacket and tie to the office, but coming in at the last minute, with stacks of papers under his arm—she's exactly right," she says.

Sharpe became Lytle's secretary when he replaced Bill Sweet as Murphy's vice president of personnel in 1975. "You would go into his office and there would be papers everywhere—all over the tables, all over the desks," she says. "I thought I was going to be a big help, so I put everything away. That was the wrong thing to do—he couldn't find anything."

As a member of the home office personnel staff since 1964, Lytle knew practically every manager and assistant manager in the company. Hudak hadn't worked in the stores and was viewed with suspicion by some people as an "outsider." But an outside perspective was exactly what Murphy's needed, says buyer and later vice president of merchandise Bill

Kraus, who became close to Hudak after they started carpooling (both owned Volkswagen Beetles). He began bending Hudak's ear about the need for more automated systems to track sales and inventory. Though other stores were collecting point-of-sale information directly from their cash registers, Murphy's was still ringing sales manually, which didn't allow the home office to easily track which products were selling and which were flops.

Though he hadn't started in a Murphy's stockroom, Hudak did have retail experience from working at several small stores while in high school and college. And like Lytle, he wasn't afraid to work long hours, having put in fifty-six hours per week at Western Electric while carrying two graduate-level courses per semester at Ohio State. At Western Electric, Hudak bought AT&T's first million-dollar computer (an IBM mainframe with 128 kilobytes of memory), using it to streamline inventory and record-keeping at the Columbus plant, which manufactured telephone-switching equipment. He quickly came to agree that Murphy's systems were behind the times, and capturing point-of-sale information became one of his top priorities.

Mike Dujmic, who was hired as a Murphy auditor in 1972, says Hudak was one of the few people in the company who intimidated him. "He was a nice guy, but I felt like when I was in his office talking to him, it was almost like he could read my mind—he was that intelligent." Under Hudak's prodding, Murphy's began preaching turnover instead of profit margin, which was almost anathema. During one meeting a few years earlier, Luther Shay had told managers to keep an eye out for items they could reduce in price while selling in higher volume. "The vice president of merchandise raised hell," he says. "We were very, very margin conscious."

Some Murphy old-timers felt that if they didn't have strong competition in a market, they should hold out for whatever prices the traffic would bear. But with interest rates in double digits, Murphy's could make more money with its capital in investments than in stale inventory. Hudak rankled the old guard by telling them to move more merchandise at lower prices. "Take cigarettes—they're a low-margin item, but they're high turnover," Dujmic says. Plus, smokers might return to Murphy's twenty or thirty times a year to buy their cigarettes, adding traffic.

More painful than lowering margin was the decision to close more than sixty-eight variety stores in 1978 and eleven in 1979, shuttering locations in places such as New Kensington, Ford City, Turtle Creek, and Tarentum that dated to the early days of the company. In some cases, says district manager Earl Rehrig, stores that closed were in small business districts that had been deteriorating gradually but steadily. "Oakmont, for instance, was originally a good store, but [sales] kept dropping and dropping," he says. "The others were profitable, but not nearly generating the profit that should have been generated." Steel industry layoffs that were putting thousands of men and women out of work around Pittsburgh and Youngstown were also crippling newer Murphy's stores in shopping centers such as the Kenmawr Plaza west of Pittsburgh, which also closed. In many cases, it may have been sentiment that kept failing stores open. Perhaps, too, some people thought the declines were just a natural business cycle that would eventually be reversed.

"It requires a certain amount of confidence to say, 'Hey, this store's not making any money, it's lost money for three years, let's close it up,' especially if you had anything to do with putting it there," says Bob Messner, Murphy corporate secretary and general counsel.

Other executives were reluctant to close locations for fear that Murphy's would incur stiff penalties for canceling decades-old leases that had years left to run. But, as Hudak notes, Murphy's could have declared bankruptcy and exited most of those contracts by paying only two years' rent. Instead, the real estate division met with landlords and explained the bankruptcy option while noting that Murphy's was paying Depression-era rents as low as $3 per square foot when surrounding properties were worth $10 per square foot. Put in those terms, many owners were happy to cancel Murphy's leases in exchange for cash settlements. For cases in which landlords wouldn't allow Murphy's out of its rental agreements, the company created a new chain of stores called Bargain World, which operated with fewer employees and sold closeouts and discontinued merchandise. Minimal staffing and low inventory levels kept costs low, and by operating the stores under a different name, the company didn't dilute the G. C. Murphy brand. By selling limited assortments as cheaply as possible with little or no service, the Bargain Worlds hearkened back to the early days of the five-and-ten business and predated the dollar-store boom of the 1990s. More than two dozen small Murphy stores were converted between 1979 and 1981.

Surprisingly, it wasn't just five-and-tens being closed. Although the ninety Murphy's Marts were generating almost as much in sales as Murphy's 374 other stores, marts were shuttered in markets such as Jacksonville, Florida; Virginia Beach, Virginia; and Richmond, Virginia, where three stores alone lost a combined $2.5 million in one year. The company had spread too far too fast, says Terry Stadterman, who became sales manager for Murphy's Marts in November 1978. "In West Virginia we did well. In Pennsylvania we did well. But we had some of them that didn't make money." Wherever Murphy's didn't enjoy the market saturation of its traditional territories, marts were struggling. "People didn't know Murphy's," says Bob Bishop, merchandise manager of the Murphy's Mart in Pekin—at the time, the only one in the state of Illinois.

In other parts of the Midwest, such as Indiana, which had more than thirty Murphy stores, the marts continued to do a land-office business. "Northern Indiana was one of the best districts in the whole Murphy Company," says Jack Anderson, who ran the Plymouth, Indiana, Murphy's Mart, one of the W. T. Grant takeovers. "I was doing about $5 million per year in sales, at 11 or 12 percent [profit], and that was the fourth-highest profit in the district. . . . I had great personnel, great assistant managers, and when you have an organization like that, you have nothing to worry about." Ron Templeton, who went from managing Mart No. 904 in Dunbar, West Virginia, to running an entire district, remembers completely turning over the inventory in the store between Thanksgiving and Christmas. "It was a gold mine," he says.

Also in late 1978, Murphy's finally addressed a fundamental problem by separating five-and-ten and mart operations. "Crossover" stores that mixed variety store and discount store signs would disappear and no longer confuse consumers by sharing advertising but pricing items differently. Each group finally received their own district and sales managers, who could focus on the unique problems each type of store faced and would receive explicit and direct marching orders. G. C. Murphy variety stores would sell "complete lines of merchandise closely tailored to fit the local market . . . at higher margin levels," while Murphy's Marts would be "high-volume, mass merchandising stores which sell general merchandise at discount prices." Murphy chairman Warne Robinson diplomatically called it "a modification" of operating philosophies that he admitted had become "somewhat blurred." Templeton was tasked with separating personnel and policies across the chain, which didn't make him popular, especially when he assigned two employees to travel from town to town and check prices on a thousand different items sold in Murphy's Marts. If they weren't competitive, managers were forced to lower them. "I was probably not the most friendly person," he says.

Things were starting to go right again by February 1981 when Robinson retired from the chairmanship and handed his duties over to Hudak. "I've had my stay," he said, adding that it was time "that the old boy gets out and lets the young fellows go to work." *Chain Store Age* wrote that Robinson had brought Murphy's out of a crisis "if not high and dry, then perhaps only slightly damp." Those who worked with him say Robinson had the common touch. "He was a real gentleman," says Luther Shay, who worked closely with Robinson in the company's finance arm and became a Murphy vice president. "Warne was a little guy, but very smart and very good with people. He accommodated rather than intimidated people. He could have been a father to me." If Robinson was at a meeting, he happily got up to pour the coffee, and no pilot of a Murphy plane ate alone if Robinson was along for the trip. "Warne would feel comfortable going into any store and talking to any clerk and making them feel as if they knew each other," Hudak says. "He knew them, he knew their families, and he really, really cared about people. But he could also sit on a bench at Laurel Valley Country Club overlooking the eighteenth green and talk with the chairman of the Chase Manhattan Bank." When things went wrong, Hudak says, Robinson "took the responsibility, but when things went right, he complimented everybody. He was a very, very unusual person."

Earnings were steady in 1980 as sales went to $803 million chain wide. Fiscal year 1981 wasn't as good. Though sales were up, runaway inflation meant that actual volume in constant dollars had gone down slightly. But conditions were lousy across the United States in the face of the so-called "Reagan Recession," the worst economic slowdown to hit the nation since World War II. With the prime interest rate above 15 percent, credit dried up, consumer spending plummeted, and retail stores were hit hard. And the steel industry contraction that began in the 1970s was accelerating, slamming Murphy's in core markets such as Pittsburgh and Baltimore. By Christmas 1981, 20 percent of all steel industry employees were either laid off or working reduced hours. U.S. Steel, which was at 50 percent capacity, shut down two plants near Pittsburgh and fired a third of the employees at its Fairless Works near Philadelphia. The following spring, the unemployment rate topped 9 percent nationally and approached 30 percent in parts of Pennsylvania.

Closing unprofitable locations and refocusing the stores were enough to return the company to financial health, but competing in a bad economic climate required Murphy's to improve the quality of the merchandise and the stores themselves. The bright, bold colors that decorated the early Murphy's Marts, for instance, had become passé, and the merchandise—never that fashionable to begin with—was further behind the times. District manager Dave Backstrom remembers joining a bunch of home office executives, including Lytle, to watch from behind a one-way mirror as shoppers were quizzed about Kmart, Hills, and Murphy's Mart. The Murphy representatives were squirming. "No one can see us and I'm telling you right now, some of those people were just cutting us apart—'it's a bunch of crap they're carrying out there, their prices are high, they're not competitive,'" Backstrom says.

Lytle got the message loud and clear. Murphy's "did not have a particularly strong image" in the areas of "price, quality, and fashion," he said later. Just as variety stores hit their limits in the late 1950s, the discount-store formula of moving large quantities of cheap merchandise from barn-like stores had run out of steam. Traditional mid-price department stores such as Sears and Montgomery Ward were discounting, while discounters such as Kmart were adding higher-priced, brand-name merchandise. Murphy's fought back on several fronts. Marketing consultant Blair J. McRae was recruited from Ohio's Lazarus department store chain to become Murphy's vice president of corporate planning and revamp the interiors of the variety stores and the marts. Out went the fake wood, the fluorescent-orange signs, and the green and yellow walls that Lytle called "garish and carnival-like." In came a subdued color scheme of earth tones in pastel shades. The old chipboard and bare steel fixtures, a staple of discount stores since the 1960s, were replaced with brushed aluminum, chrome, and glass, while wider aisles and better lighting encouraged shoppers to linger.

With the new layout, just piling massive quantities of items onto gondolas and listing them at rock-bottom prices wouldn't be enough. A new emphasis was placed on offering more fashionable, trendy clothing. And with other merchandise changes it became clear that Murphy's was aiming for more sophisticated shoppers and was now willing to move quickly to cash in on fads. In the late 1970s, manufacturers such as Atari and Coleco had introduced the first arcade-style video games that could be played at home, and Murphy's and other stores carried them in the toy department. Now Atari, Texas Instruments, and other companies were introducing ready-to-use home computers. Murphy's jumped into the fray, featuring large displays of the new machines along the aisles of most Murphy's Marts by the end of 1982. Computer paper and floppy disks appeared in the stationery department alongside ballpoint pens and envelopes.

When federal regulators split up the Bell System at the end of 1983 and allowed customers to buy their own telephones, some discounters held back, fearing that AT&T's "Phone Center" stores would dominate the market. Not Murphy's Mart, which quickly rolled out a selection ranging from traditional Bell models to the brand-new cordless phones just being developed. In July 1984, Murphy's Mart became the second discounter in the country to sell $2,000 to $3,000 home satellite dishes in rural areas not served by cable. The first was a regional chain based in Arkansas named Wal-Mart.

The variety stores weren't neglected. In 1980, vice president of sales Dick Tracey directed his regional sales managers to break the five-and-tens into five working groups ranging from the biggest shopping-center locations, which would carry the best selections, to the smallest downtown stores, some of which were in declining areas where the G. C. Murphy store was one of the few major retailers left. Murphy's would turn those urban locations from deficits into assets by stressing convenience and "hometown shopping." And they would dominate traditional dime-store categories such as cosmetics, sewing notions, stationery, and candy that smaller stores could handle as effectively as large discounters. At the same time, slow-selling items that small Murphy stores couldn't easily carry, such as clothing, were dropped.

Two years later, director of construction Fred Lantz and Clair McElhinny, newly installed as assistant vice president for sales, reached into the company's history to redesign the five-and-tens. An old-fashioned logo that recalled turn-of-the-century signs replaced the mishmash of 1950s, '60s, and '70s Murphy emblems that persisted in many of the 260 remaining variety stores. Black-and-white photos of Murphy stores from the 1900s through the 1940s were enlarged and hung along the walls. Storefronts received new red-and-green-striped canvas awnings or decals inside the windows that looked like awnings. Larger stores got special kiosks that highlighted variety-store staples such as candy and toys in nostalgic settings that recalled the days when Murphy girls worked behind each counter.

The new merchandising direction was a realistic approach to the variety-store business in the 1980s that worked. Former Murphy assistant manager Ed Kohler, then a top sales representative for Sally Hansen cosmetics, remembers installing four display racks of a new "wet look" lipstick at Store No. 174 in the Monroeville Mall near Pittsburgh. He moved $3,000 worth in a single weekend. Lytle beamed with pride as he took reporters on a tour of that store in late September and showed off the renovations. "Gone are the tight checkout areas . . . that may have seemed more like a barricade than an entrance and exit location," reported the McKeesport *Daily News.* "And the seemingly cluttered, narrow aisles have disappeared also. Instead, there is an open entrance area [with] colorful displays and wide aisles." The second remodeled variety store, No. 8 at the Washington Mall south of Pittsburgh, opened two weeks later. Stripped of slow-selling merchandise, given an infusion of popular items, and treated to Murphy's most comprehensive remodeling program since World War II, the variety stores proved they could still produce as sales per square foot went up 7 percent. "The redesign really stimulated the variety stores—it was quite a turnaround," Lantz says.

Overall, 1983 proved to be the G. C. Murphy Company's best year in history with sales at $872 million and profits per share up to $4.56. Adjusted for inflation, it was the strongest earnings performance for Murphy's since the glory days of the mid-1950s and early 1960s. One man who was part of the turnaround wasn't around to enjoy it, however, as Dick Tracey was asked to retire in February 1982, ending a forty-two-year Murphy career. In the end, his abrasive, flamboyant style finally aggravated too many people on the board of directors. Some say the last straw came when Tracey refused to rein in his expense account, while others contend he was spending too much time visiting stores and not enough time helping eliminate old, outdated practices at the office. "Personnel didn't like him and finance didn't like him," McElhinny says, "but he got results, and isn't that what you're in business for?" Retailing was too ingrained in Tracey's character for him to sit still for long; with his sons, he opened three small variety stores in the Pittsburgh area.

To most observers, the G. C. Murphy Company seemed to be out of the woods with $116 million in working capital and only $34 million in long-term debt, but some people at the home office were starting to get an uneasy feeling that Murphy's was—to use one executive's words—"sitting on our assets." Murphy shares traded on the New York Stock Exchange for under $20 for most of 1982, though the company itself was valued at nearly $37 per share. Put bluntly, if some outside investor gained control, they could easily liquidate Murphy's for more than they paid.

Quietly, the home office started trying to make the company less attractive by taking on debt. An experiment with pharmacies in a handful of Murphy's Marts had proved somewhat successful, so Murphy executives inspected drugstore chains as possible acquisitions, including Rite Aid, based in Camp Hill, Pennsylvania, and Fay's Inc., which had about a hundred stores mainly in Syracuse, Rochester, and Buffalo, New York. Other retail outlets, including auto parts stores, were examined as well. "It seemed like every three or four weeks we were going away somewhere, but we never bought any of them," Lantz says. "A couple of them looked very attractive to me. Unfortunately, we turned all of them down." Someone proposed replacing the mismatched buildings of the home office in McKeesport with a modern office tower, which besides incurring debt might have increased efficiency at headquarters and generated rental revenue. Company photographer Jack Loveall took pictures of one prospective site on several acres near the Pennsylvania Turnpike outside of Irwin, not far from Murphy's Mart No. 807.

Yet remnants of the inertia and reluctance to change that characterized Murphy's in the 1960s still lingered. At one point, Luther Shay and others were appointed to the "cor-

FIG. 65
A redesign program spearheaded by director of construction Fred Lantz in 1982 gave Murphy's variety stores a fresh look that recalled the halcyon five-and-ten days of the teens and 1920s. Slow-selling merchandise was removed and at larger locations, such as Store No. 174 in the Monroeville Mall near Pittsburgh, special kiosks highlighted variety-store staples such as candy.

porate planning" committee, but, as he wryly notes, Murphy managers "didn't want to be 'corporate-planned.'" A prime example of corporate foot-dragging was the stalled attempt to update the antiquated process of marking merchandise for sale in the stores. Competitors had cash registers that automatically recorded each purchase and fed the information back to company headquarters where computers kept track of sales and inventory. Wal-Mart, for instance, invested $24 million in 1983 to connect cash registers in all its stores via satellite to computers at the company's Bentonville, Arkansas, headquarters.

Murphy's had opened its own fairly sophisticated computer center in 1976 a few blocks from the home office with more than one hundred data-processing employees—some recruited from IBM and J. C. Penney Company as well as from colleges and universities—who were linked to the company's distribution centers via leased telephone lines. Nearly all ordering was automated, along with payroll and accounting, and complicated reports that once took weeks to produce were being done in days, says Bob Dowie, who became vice

FIG. 66
Murphy's purchased its first computer in the late 1950s at a cost of more than $2 million. By 1976, the increased need for data-processing capacity led the company to open a new computer center near the home office in McKeesport. Leased phone lines linked the ibm System/370 mainframe with distribution centers in McKeesport, Fredericksburg, Va., Indianapolis, Ind., Jersey City, N.J., and Monroe, La.

president of computer services in 1981. But in Murphy stores, clerks still marked each item with individual yellow price tags and rang up purchases on massive metal cash registers. When Murphy's finally tested computerized checkouts in sixteen stores in 1983, they didn't use the bar codes that manufacturers were already applying to consumer products. Instead, clerks scanned a special proprietary price tag designed by Murphy's in cooperation with the label-making company Dennison.

Since only a tiny percentage of Murphy's stores were using point-of-sale technology, merchandise buyers and managers called one another long distance to find out what products were hot sellers. "The company was very, very good to Bell Telephone," mart manager Pete Shuppy says. "You'd talk to other guys three or four times a week—what's going on over there? What's good? What's hot? They'd say 'We sold twelve of these.' You'd go out on the floor to check yours out. It was that kind of merchandising that people were willing to do." It was time consuming, but attempts to convert the company more quickly met with resistance, and Lytle was reluctant to force the stores to do something they didn't want to do. "Chuck Lytle was a good man, but he had trouble making up his mind," Jud Ellis contends. "You'd come to him with a proposal and it would seem like it took forever, and by the time he did, all of the things in the proposal had changed." Others say Lytle wasn't indecisive, but he was concerned about building consensus before taking drastic action.

In the meantime, Murphy's was trying to keep as many of its four million shares of stock in friendly hands as possible. Though the company had been publicly traded since

1927 and listed on the New York Stock Exchange since 1936, a perception remained that most of the shares were still held by the Mack and Shaw families. Through the 1960s, Jim Mack did nothing to discourage that belief, releasing as little information as possible to the press or Wall Street. As Kmart boomed, Wall Street's spotlight drifted away from G. C. Murphy Company and its stock was modestly traded. It steadily paid dividends—$1.28 per share through the 1980s—making it an ideal "widows and orphans" stock for conservative investors who held their shares for many years. Many company employees also held small stakes of G. C. Murphy stock, which were given as bonuses for anniversaries or purchased through payroll deductions. In the 1980s, about 40 percent of the shares were held by current or former employees or their families.

But that was a relatively small stake, and assuming that control could be maintained by the Mack and Shaw families or by former employees was dangerous. The investment community had drastically changed since the 1960s, spurred by early corporate raiders such as James J. Ling of LTV Corporation, who spun a tiny electronics company into a billion-dollar conglomerate by borrowing money to purchase control of weaker firms; among his victims had been Pittsburgh's Jones & Laughlin Steel Corporation. Another corporate raider was Meshulam Riklis, who controlled Murphy's erstwhile competitor in the variety-store business, McCrory Corporation. Riklis built his Rapid-American Corporation in the 1960s and '70s by pledging the assets of one company to borrow money to purchase another. In the mid-1960s, though already a Wall Street whiz kid, he returned to college to complete his MBA at Ohio State, where one of his classmates was Tom Hudak. , and where his thesis was on the "effective non-use of cash" in mergers and acquisitions.

To Hollywood gossip columnists, Riklis was notorious for his 1977 marriage to diminutive starlet Pia Zadora, more than thirty years his junior. To financial analysts, he was more infamous for the complicated maneuverings that allowed him to control such famous brand names as Schenley Distillers, Faberge cosmetics, Culligan water softeners, and Samsonite luggage while investing relatively little of his own money. They called his conglomerate "Rancid-American." Syndicated financial columnist Allan Sloan offered three bits of advice to readers: "Don't do big home repair jobs when the hardware stores are closed. Don't spit into the wind. And never, never, never become Meshulam Riklis's junior partner." Riklis and others were aided by a new breed of investment banker such as Michael Milken of Drexel Burnham Lambert, Inc. Where traditional bankers had been conservative capitalists who raised money for businesses to grow and expand, younger and more aggressive bankers such as Milken were making millions by arranging takeover deals.

It was a "wild environment," says Messner, who as general counsel and corporate secretary was responsible for investor relations. While most publicly traded companies were trying to get their stocks in the hands of big institutional investors such as mutual funds that were easier to track, Murphy's was catering to mom-and-pop investors who might be less likely to sell large blocks of shares to speculators. One innovative program was called

"Superbuys for Shareholders," which allowed owners of Murphy stock to purchase hot-selling toys, gifts, designer cookware, and electronics at wholesale prices; it was even written up by *McCall's* magazine. Besides keeping these stockholders loyal to Murphy's, it also provided the company with valuable information. To qualify for Superbuys, stockholders had to provide their real names and addresses, not just the names of their brokers. Murphy's also moved to protect itself legally from unwanted Wall Street attention. Along with Lancaster-based Armstrong Cork and Philadelphia-based Scott Paper, the G. C. Murphy Company successfully lobbied the Pennsylvania General Assembly to change the state's corporation laws in December 1983. Previously, companies incorporated in Pennsylvania were allowed to consider only the financial benefits of takeover proposals. Now, directors could reject takeover offers they felt weren't in the best interests of employees, suppliers, and other stakeholders. Though some powerful investors grumbled that the law was an unfair restriction on shareholders that favored the corporate status quo, the survival of individual Pennsylvania corporations would still depend on the types of takeovers that were attempted—and the willpower of their boards of directors to resist them.

They were good attempts, but Murphy's stock was already moving in the market. Trade publications for the discount store industry reported on the turnaround at the G. C. Murphy Company, attracting the attention of magazines such as *Financial World* and *Business Week*, which wrote of "tantalizing leverage opportunities" at Murphy's. Rumors spread that the company was investigating a merger with Hallmark Cards or Wal-Mart. To head off a hostile takeover, Murphy directors proposed an amendment to the corporate bylaws that would require an 80 percent vote of shareholders to remove anyone from the board or merge the company with another. The amendment forced one of the Wall Street's sharks to surface as New Jersey financier Arthur Goldberg—whose later activities supposedly inspired portions of the Oliver Stone movie *Wall Street*—filed a form with the Securities and Exchange Commission on May 10, 1984, declaring that he had acquired 7.5 percent of outstanding G. C. Murphy Company stock. Two weeks later, he announced a proxy fight to defeat the so-called "shark repellent" amendment.

As newspaper ads and letters from Goldberg's firm urged Murphy shareholders to reject the proposed amendment, Joe Haggerty, Murphy's assistant general counsel, organized an effort to place personal phone calls to investors urging them to vote for it and against Goldberg. Murphy executives made the calls using names and addresses gathered in the Superbuys program. Another member of Murphy's legal department, Bill Cullen, persuaded the U.S. Labor Department that the company was entitled to vote a large share of stock held in its retirement plan. Before 1984, most Murphy shareholder meetings had been quietly held in the assembly room at the home office or in the nearby computer center, but the June 12, 1984, gathering was a raucous gathering in a Monroeville, Pennsylvania, hotel ballroom attended by five hundred people, many of them attorneys, public-relations experts, and financial analysts. Over Goldberg's loud objections, shareholders approved the amendment, though the final tally took weeks as every ballot was examined and contested by one side or the other.

Frustrated by the rebuff, which reportedly cost him more than $2 million, speculation grew that Goldberg was "greenmailing" Murphy's—that he would go away if the company agreed to buy his 380,000 shares at a premium price. Several large publicly traded corporations were fighting off greenmailers in 1984, including Texaco, which bought out Texas's billionaire Bass family for $1.3 billion; the parent company of Warner Brothers, which paid Rupert Murdoch $181 million to prevent a takeover; and Walt Disney, which gave financier Saul Steinberg $325 million for his 12 percent stake in the movie and theme-park giant—a $32 million premium. Pittsburgh's Gulf Oil Corporation, one of the fabled "seven sisters" of the global petroleum business, was frantically trying to block a bid by T. Boone Pickens Jr. Defenders of corporate raiders and greenmailers said they forced companies to sell unprofitable or marginal operations and drove up stock prices, creating "value" for investors. Indeed, Murphy shares that traded at $15 in 1980 were worth $42 in 1984.

Although greenmailing wasn't illegal, it had an air of impropriety. One broker told *Time* magazine the Disney deal was like "watching your mother get ravaged by New York thugs." Several people close to Murphy president Chuck Lytle advised paying off Goldberg, but the board of directors refused. Messner says Lytle was swayed by arguments that it was wrong for one shareholder to profit at the expense of others; some pundits were also saying that executives who caved into greenmail were only trying to protect their own jobs. "Chuck Lytle was a very, very moral, religious, principled guy, and the moment someone said it 'wasn't right,' it probably put him on the other side," Messner says. "I, on the other hand, thought he was a wonderful guy, trying to play by the Marquis of Queensberry rules when we were in a knife fight in a dark alley."

In late September, as Goldberg confirmed that he wanted to sell his G. C. Murphy shares, Rapid-American approached board member Malcolm Anderson, a one-time confidant of Jim Mack's, and asked if the company was interested in a merger. Murphy's demurred, and by October 8, Hudak, Messner, and Murphy treasurer Gerry Prado had arranged for several investors friendly to the company to purchase about 300,000 of Goldberg's shares. But he grew tired of waiting for a deal on the other 80,000, and the other shoe dropped as Goldberg sold them to one of the most notorious wheeler-dealers of the 1980s, Minneapolis investor Irwin Jacobs—called "Irv the Liquidator" for his habit of buying asset-rich companies and carving them up for parts. Jacobs, whose holdings included Pabst Brewing, ITT, Kaiser Steel, and Phillips Petroleum, also controlled a direct-marketing firm called Fingerhut, which sold kitchen gadgets and other novelties through catalogs and circulars in Sunday newspapers. An October 16 article in the *Wall Street Journal* contended that Jacobs became interested in Murphy's after hearing about the Bargain World division—the low-buck stores designed to burn off unprofitable leases—and deciding they were a potential outlet for unsold Fingerhut merchandise. With Goldberg's stake and other shares bought on the open market, Jacobs and several investment partners had acquired 803,700 shares of the G. C. Murphy Company, or about 19 percent of the common stock. The day of reckoning had arrived.

Lytle, Hudak, and others quickly began planning to buy Jacobs out and take the company private through an employee stock ownership plan (ESOP) and engaged the investment-banking firm Kelso & Company to arrange financing. ESOPs had strong merits—a steel mill in Weirton, West Virginia, had just been saved from closure when workers purchased it from National Steel Corporation through an ESOP. But there were serious obstacles to the Murphy proposal. Unlike Weirton Steel, which had "hard" assets such as rolling mills and railroad cars that could be used as collateral, Murphy's assets consisted largely of inventory, favorable leases on real estate, and goodwill—not items that lenders can seize and easily resell in the event of bankruptcy. Several New York lenders agreed to underwrite the debt, but Pittsburgh's Mellon Bank, which long held many of Murphy's accounts, turned the company down flat. That was no surprise; Mellon was also taking abuse in Pittsburgh for turning down steel mill ESOPs. Mellon's reluctance made smaller banks hesitant about investing in the Murphy ESOP, Hudak says. Worse, because Murphy's was essentially mortgaging its own assets, the company would have to retire all its existing debt before buying the stock. While an outside investor could simply assume those debts as part of the purchase, says Hudak, "the hurdle was a lot higher for the employees to buy the company."

Other problems were less tangible but still serious as Murphy's learned that there were problems in its own takeover defense team. Murphy's had long used the investment banking firm Goldman, Sachs & Company, a partner of which, John C. Jamison, sat on the company's board. Goldman had recommended that Murphy's retain the New York law firm Skadden, Arps, Slate, Meagher & Flom to help fight takeover attempts. As Murphy management worked with Kelso, however, both Goldman Sachs and Skadden Arps made it clear they were against an ESOP; coincidentally or not, they also sharply increased the fees they were charging Murphy's. Skadden Arps also had a potential conflict of interest: on behalf of one of its other clients, it was challenging the Pennsylvania Shareholder Protection Act that Messner and others had worked so hard to get through the legislature. Within hours of secret strategy sessions by Murphy executives in McKeesport and Pittsburgh, Messner started receiving calls from Wall Street analysts who knew details of the meeting. He and others concluded that someone working on the ESOP was leaking the information. In November, Murphy executives quietly engaged the Pittsburgh law firm of Kirkpatrick & Lockhart, whose attorneys Charles Smith and Michael McLean had structured other ESOPs, to work on the process away from Wall Street's prying eyes.

Amazingly, despite the turmoil roiling the company, store employees were still focused on sales and redesigned the Murphy's Marts for the second time in four years. The new layout called for an even stronger emphasis on high-quality clothing in expensive-looking

displays lit with baby spotlights. Store interiors were done over in sleek, corporate white with red and blue accents and simple, handsome signs—in fact, their appearance was startlingly similar to the store design Target would use decades later. Murphy's called it "FIND" for "Fashions in New Dimensions." Mart No. 830 near the Greater Pittsburgh International Airport was the first to be remodeled, followed quickly by other stores. Sales for 1984 hit $913 million—5 percent over the previous year's record—with the 119 marts generating 70 percent of the total. The volume in the 230 variety stores was up again too after another fifty-one were renovated. Only fifty remained to be upgraded to the new design that had debuted in 1982.

Even during the darkest hours of the fight to save the company there was time for a little farce. Jacobs had been calling Lytle on almost a daily basis to get assurance that his stock would be purchased soon. Over the winter of 1984–85, he decided he wanted to see the retail company in McKeesport, Pennsylvania, in which he now held a 19 percent stake. Greg Lehner, an employee in Murphy's security department, rented a van and Lytle and Hudak met Jacobs to take him on a tour of a few "typical" G. C. Murphy Company properties. Actually, they were anything but typical. To motivate Jacobs to sell to Murphy's at a price the company could afford, the home office called the manager of Store No. 88 in

FIG. 67
The Fashions in New Dimensions (FIND) program of 1984 moved both the appearance and the merchandise selection inside Murphy's Marts up in the market. Store No. 809 on state Route 60 near Pittsburgh was the prototype for what was supposed to be a chain-wide remodeling program. Only a few dozen marts were converted to FIND before the company was taken over by Ames Department Stores in 1985.

Clairton, Pennsylvania—one of the company's oldest locations, which was in an economically depressed urban shopping district—and told him that visitors were coming but that he was not to clean up. The manager of a nearby mart received a similar message. Jacobs, Hudak, and Lytle arrived to find the stores in chaos. "Then they took him to the warehouse in McKeesport, which had that old clankety-clank [chain-driven] conveyor belt—it was not a modern distribution center at all," Messner says. "He must have gotten on the phone to his people and asked them what they had gotten him into."

As weeks turned into months, Hudak and others lined up enough financing to purchase the company's stock for $42.50 per share, but Jacobs wanted $46.50. In April 1985, he got tired of waiting. On April 13, Ames Department Stores, Inc., of Rocky Hill, Connecticut, announced that it was buying an option on Jacobs's shares for $44.25 each and that it intended to acquire the G. C. Murphy Company.

Jaws dropped throughout the Murphy empire—a canary was swallowing a cat. Founded in 1958 in Southbridge, Massachusetts, by brothers Herbert, Milton, and Irving Gilman, Ames had 180 discount stores mainly in New England, Pennsylvania, and Maryland and sales in 1984 of $821 million—less than Murphy's. The stores were also something less than Murphy's. In northeastern markets where Murphy's Mart and Ames went head to head, the latter was regarded as no competition. "Ames' [prices] were as much as 20 percent higher on merchandise than Murphy's," Hudak says. "They were operating in New England in small towns where they didn't have to worry about Kmart or Wal-Mart and their price structure was entirely different." While Murphy's Marts were trying to move up in the market by improving selections and reducing prices, Ames hewed to old discount store formulas, moving piles of off-brand merchandise in bare-bones stores. One Murphy executive cracks that Ames stores were "honky-tonk operations." Murphy buyer John Mack visited an Ames store while on vacation at the Delaware shore and was shocked by what he found. "A mess," his wife Nancy says. "A terrible store with terrible merchandising." Another buyer, Paul Hindes, says Ames had a bad reputation among vendors and customers as a tough company to deal with. "Obnoxious would be a good word," he says. "We should have been the one to take Ames over."

But that wasn't about to happen. There were two board meetings to consider the Ames offer. The first was held on Wednesday, April 17; the second, which sealed the company's fate, began Monday afternoon, April 22, but dragged into Tuesday morning—fifteen hours in all, and few who participated would ever forget it, in part because they had a hard time staying awake. Chuck Breckenridge, Murphy's director of internal audit, remembers Hudak disappearing at one point for a short period of time and learning later that he had gone to church to pray—"just as the company's founders may have done," Breckenridge notes. After last-minute negotiations with several banks, the Murphy executives leading the ESOP team offered $46.50 per share, but Ames counteroffered with $48, and the Murphy group was tapped out. Two Murphy directors—Walter Shaw Jr., whose father had helped purchase the company from the G. C. Murphy estate back in 1911, and Martha Mack Lewis, a daughter of J. S. Mack's cousin Edgar Mack—staunchly refused to vote for the buyout. So did former board chairman S. Warne Robinson. The five directors who were current employees—Hudak, Lytle, Ellis, Rogers, and Dowie—had to abstain because of conflict-of-interest provisions. But Murphy's external directors—Anderson, Jamison, J. Wray Connolly of the H. J. Heinz Company, and John F. Oates Jr., a coal-company executive—were in favor. It seemed the vote would be four to three for the takeover until Dowie and Ellis announced that effective immediately, they were retiring from the G. C. Murphy Company, which would make them outside directors and eligible to vote, thus making the results five to four against the Ames offer.

Pandemonium ensued as Connolly and Jamison stormed out to call their attorneys, who threatened Dowie and Ellis with lawsuits. Anderson, whose firm had for years been Murphy's principal outside legal counsel, declared that he was "outraged" that Lytle and Hudak were working "to take this company private for themselves rather than maximizing return for the stockholders." ("That was Malcolm's position," retorts Hudak, "but he was dead wrong.") Oates, who held 20,000 shares of Murphy stock, told Hudak he couldn't accept the ESOP under any circumstances. He had calculated the difference between the ESOP and Ames's offer and wanted the additional $50,000 he would get at the higher price. "I would have liked to have said at the moment, 'John, we'll give you the $50,000,'" Hudak says. But that wasn't legal, and the courts might have also frowned on Dowie's and Ellis's last-minute decisions to retire. Again they recused, and the remaining seven directors voted. As expected, they agreed to the takeover four to three.

"You think about it every day of your life," Hudak says. "You look back at that and say, 'What could we have done differently to achieve a different result?' And the answer is 'nothing.' We took it to the eleventh hour and the fifty-ninth minute. We fought the fight. We just had all of the debt in addition to all of the equity, and we couldn't get over that hurdle and make it work." Messner calls the takeover a product of the times, noting that much larger companies, including Gulf, eventually succumbed as well. "I don't think there are any easy answers," he says. "I think that Chuck and Tom did everything that they thought could possibly be done to save it."

Gloom settled over the G. C. Murphy Company, though one especially nasty event a week later had nothing to do with the Ames buyout. Just after ten o'clock on the night of May 2, Richard McClelland, the manager of Murphy's Mart No. 706 on Churchland Boulevard in Portsmouth, Virginia, locked the store and headed to his car. He didn't see twenty-five-year-old Coleman Gray and his friend Melvin Tucker waiting in the parking lot. Gray's wife had recently been fired from the store and Gray swore to friends that he was "going to get" the manager. As McClelland drove away, Gray and Tucker followed in their vehicle. When he stopped at an intersection, the two men blocked his path and forced him at gunpoint to return to the store. They made McClelland remove $12,000 from the safe, then drove him four miles north on Route 135 to Tidewater Community College where they pushed him to the ground and shot him six times in the head with a .22-caliber revolver. Both men were arrested and indicted for McClelland's murder. Gray was sentenced to death while Tucker turned state's evidence and went to prison.

In lieu of their independence, Murphy executives spent the following weeks trying to salvage something for employees. Few of them had severance agreements ("Murphy's never laid anyone off," Messner says), so workers from the legal and human resources departments went from office to office getting people locked into contracts that provided compensation if they were let go. "Chuck Lytle, Tom Hudak, Bob Messner, and Phil Rogers tried very hard to make sure that as many people as possible were given some level of protection," Breckenridge says. "They were genuinely more concerned with taking care of people at lower levels than those in executive positions." When Ames chairman Herb Gilman magnanimously said he didn't want the acquisition to be a "hostile takeover," Murphy's used that as leverage and got him to agree to keep the McKeesport office open for at least three years, honor all employment contracts, pay severance to store clerks, and create a one-million-dollar fund that could be disbursed to laid-off employees by Lytle and Hudak as they saw fit. Ames also would assume Murphy's pension and insurance plans.

Some at Murphy's hoped their fate would be better in a merger with Ames than if the company had been dismembered by Goldberg, Jacobs, or some other investor. After all, Lytle and Hudak were being added to the Ames board of directors where hopefully they could watch out for their old employees. The former would oversee the new "G. C. Murphy Company division" and run the variety stores, while the latter had an offer to become Ames's chief financial officer. Tensions eased when Gilman called a meeting of Murphy employees at the home office and told them not to worry about their jobs. "You're a billion-dollar company, and we're a billion-dollar company, and we plan to add another billion dollars in sales," he said. "We need all of the Ames executives, we need all of the Murphy executives, and we're going to add a lot more people." Hudak went home that night feeling slightly better. "Maybe this is going to work out after all," he told his wife, Dot.

The following Tuesday, Hudak boarded one of Murphy's airplanes and flew to Rocky Hill to meet with Gilman. He had barely sat down when the Ames chairman stood up, walked over, and tapped him on the knee. "Tom, go back and start making plans," Gilman said, handing Hudak a list of 120 Murphy stores that were to be closed as soon as possible. "We're going to keep a skeleton crew in McKeesport, but I want you to let all of the buyers go and transfer the accounting people up here."

Hudak was flabbergasted. "Herb, you just got through telling everyone that they've got a job," he finally said. "What's happened in two days?"

"Well, what did you want me to tell them?" Gilman said. "We need 'em through the transition. We don't want them out looking for jobs." Then he paused and smiled. "But don't worry, Tom," he said. "We'll take care of you."

Hudak stood up. "Herb, thank you very much," he said. "But you don't have to worry about me." He asked an Ames employee to drive him back to the airport, returned to McKeesport, and called a meeting of the Murphy operational staff and told them what happened. Actions like that and his insistence on speaking his mind at Ames board meetings didn't endear Hudak to his new employer, and he was gone by the end of the year. The axe fell on Murphy variety stores from New England to Texas, including some opened by George Murphy himself in Greensburg, Uniontown, and Brownsville and other western Pennsylvania towns that were already suffering from steel industry layoffs. Not even the McKeesport store was spared. Manager Russell Phillips locked the doors of Store No. 1 for the last time on Christmas Eve in 1985. The money-losing Texas department stores were sold to Shoppers World Stores Inc., based in San Antonio.

There were plenty of long faces on Tuesday, August 6, when Murphy's board of directors met for the last time in the ballroom of a McKeesport hotel to conclude the company's affairs. Only a few stockholders rose to complain, including Raymond Roebuck of nearby White Oak, Pennsylvania, who called on the Securities and Exchange Commission to regulate takeovers. "It seems to me the people who get hurt are the employees and the shareholders," he said. "They get it right in the neck." Accountants tallied the shareholders' votes on the merger—a largely academic exercise since Ames now owned 95 percent of the outstanding stock. At 10:07 A.M., Hudak brought down the gavel, closing the meeting and the existence of the G. C. Murphy Company. Everyone knew that Ames didn't really want the variety stores—it didn't have any of its own—but it coveted the highly profitable Murphy's Marts, so a group of home office employees wore T-shirts parodying the recent hit movie *Ghostbusters*. "Murphy's Mart Busters," they said, with the stores' logo slashed out.

Murphy loyalists would need a sense of humor to get through the next few months as hundreds of store employees—many with twenty or thirty years of service—went through the sad process of liquidating inventory and selling fixtures. Decades-long friendships fractured as some employees went to Ames, others stayed in the Murphy division, and hundreds more were let go. Men and women who had spent entire careers with the company suddenly faced the prospect of starting over at age fifty or fifty-five in parts of Pennsylvania, West Virginia, and Ohio that had high unemployment rates. At the home office where a collegial atmosphere had always prevailed, laid-off employees were coldly escorted from the building by Ames security personnel.

Lytle was walking down a hallway in the home office one day when a secretary suddenly snapped and turned on him in a rage: "You did this to us! This is your fault!" she shouted before being led away by co-workers. Friends and family say the gentle, spiritual, soft-spoken Lytle felt sick over his inability to stop the Ames buyout. "The day the company was taken over, Chuck died a little," says his wife, Ann. "I hate to say he lived for that company, but it was his whole working life." Lytle lasted less than two years as head of the Murphy division before being forced out by Ames. Hudak says Lytle could have retired with a modest "golden parachute" but felt an obligation to stay and protect as many G. C. Murphy employees—many of whom he personally hired or trained—as he could. "I think it did break his heart," Messner says. "It certainly took all of the joy out of his life and made him feel very guilty."

Some terminated employees were driven to depression, drink, or worse. In December 1985 on the day a large group of home office employees were about to be let go, stationery buyer Eddie Lautner arrived despondent at work for his last day. "You know, my family would be better off if I died," he told someone. Minutes later Lautner collapsed, stricken with a massive heart attack. An ambulance rushed him to McKeesport Hospital a few blocks away, but doctors' attempts to revive him were futile. Kraus walked into the office, learned of Lautner's collapse, and walked back out again, never to return. He had tired of Ames's sarcastic and hostile attitude toward Murphy's anyway: "I had to go up every Monday to their office and meet with them. We got a lot of flip and smart answers." Other Murphy employees who stayed were soon eager to join him on the unemployment line. "Ames just beat the [hell] out of Murphy's," says Harrisburg-area Murphy's Mart manager Pete Shuppy. "They thought they knew everything there was to know about retailing. You were looked at as a dinosaur. You had all of the knowledge in the world, but they never tapped it." He lasted two years before quitting Ames in disgust during the busy Christmas shopping season.

Another Murphy's employee remembers attending a meeting at Ames headquarters and following one of the executives into the hallway to suggest a promotional idea. The Ames man stopped him in mid-sentence. "What the hell would I care what you have to say? We bought you, remember? If you were any good, you would have bought us." Such conversations had a demoralizing effect on Murphy personnel. Ames also decreed an end to the popular G. C. Murphy Veterans Club. About 140 employees, including four with forty-five years of experience, gathered on May 19, 1986, at the Pittsburgh Hilton for one last fling. They tried to smile at the end of the night as they adjourned the forty-sixth and last meeting by singing a version of the World War I–era tune "'Til We Meet Again" with special words by former club president Harry Altman: "Friends we've made and friendships grown / Once again our neighbors known. . . . May you in God's grace abound / 'Til we meet again."

Though Ames wanted the G. C. Murphy Company solely to gain control of the Murphy's Marts, they proved difficult to integrate into the parent company's systems. The biggest contributing factor was Ames itself. The upscale décor and fixtures installed by Murphy's a few years earlier were ripped out and replaced by cheap-looking Ames signs and racks that practically screamed "bargain basement." Murphy's inventory and accounting systems had served the company well for decades, but they were labor intensive. When the employees who maintained those systems were fired, the processes collapsed and Ames had nothing ready to put in their place. Murphy's Marts soon were receiving merchandise

they didn't need, shipped by Ames buyers who averaged fewer than two years of experience. Product lines that were sales dynamos for Murphy's Marts, such as the house-brand paint, were dropped while Ames saved a few pennies by switching to lower-quality items. In rural Appalachian towns, complaints were loud and long when marts stopped carrying funeral wreaths on Memorial Day and "Pick-a-Mix" assortments of Brach's candy. To Ames, they were niche items that didn't fit the new merchandise mix, but they were important to customers who had been fanatically loyal to Murphy's for years. Those shoppers went elsewhere.

Ironically, the variety stores fared better at first, perhaps because Ames's lack of interest in the five-and-ten business left the stepchild division in McKeesport in a state of benign neglect. Though Lytle was removed in 1987, a procession of Ames-appointed executives came and went with little impact on a core group of G. C. Murphy Company veterans who went about their jobs running the stores as best they could despite a much-diminished personnel roster. Store No. 1 in McKeesport even reopened on August 6, 1987. Though it was now a Bargain World, it made old Murphy hands happy to see the store in use again. "We made money and we contributed substantially to the bottom line," says Ed McGinley, the former Murphy labor relations attorney who became the Murphy division's vice president of distribution, administration, and human resources. "We sold merchandise in the five-and-ten-cent stores that had a high markup, and Ames left us alone for the most part."

With 130 remaining variety stores producing steady profits, the Murphy division even expanded, creating two new chains of specialty stores. Murphy's "Crafts and More" offered a deeper selection of variety store staples like hobby supplies, artificial flowers, and sewing notions, while the "Office Shop Warehouse" capitalized on the G. C. Murphy Company's years of experience in selling stationery. Early successes were promising enough for Murphy's to plan an Office Shop Warehouse "superstore" with furniture, paper products, and other supplies for the growing number of people who were working from home. That market was predicted to hit $150 billion by 1989, and for once Murphy's would be on the ground floor—a new chain called Office Depot was reporting $33.7 million in sales from fifteen stores in the southeast United States, while a company called Staples had just opened its sixteenth store in New England.

Yet, no matter what successes the G. C. Murphy Company could report, the fact remained that Ames had no interest in the variety-store business or any spin-offs. By November 1988, financial writers were speculating that the division was for sale. Ames had recently paid $838 million for the failing Zayre Department Stores division of Zayre Corporation and was frantically trying to raise money to cut its debt load. Along with new Murphy president Gary Brown, McGinley and other executives made pitches to Prudential-Bache Securities and other investors to attempt a leveraged buyout that would have made the G. C. Murphy Company independent again. Negotiations with Ames continued almost until the announcement in August 1989 that the Murphy division and its 155 stores were being sold to the parent company of Riklis's McCrory Corporation for $80 million.

McGinley suspects Ames never had any intention of selling Murphy's to its employees and that it entertained the offer simply to extract a better deal from McCrory's. "I can truly say that as an entrepreneur, I was a failure," he says with a little self-deprecating humor. Ames transferred the Murphy division to McCrory, based in York, Pennsylvania, on December 20, 1989, and 135 remaining employees in McKeesport cleaned out their desks in the home office. McGinley had the dubious honor of locking the door for the last time.

In its eighty-three-year history, the G. C. Murphy Company had embodied some of the best traditions of American entrepreneurship while struggling with many of the serious problems inherent in any large bureaucracy. It weathered two world wars, a global depression, and several serious recessions; adapted itself more or less successfully to changing consumer tastes and demographics; and seemed to be on the verge of reinventing itself again when it was blindsided by financial maneuverings that few people could have predicted would ever touch a company such as Murphy's. As a retailer, the "G. C. Murphy Company" would survive now only as one of several brand names on McCrory's patchwork of thirteen hundred variety and discount stores.

But a funny thing happened on the way to obscurity. The G. C. Murphy Company had made a point of planting deep roots in the communities it served, and those roots wouldn't be eradicated quite so easily. Although the company was gone, the people who made the company a local legend in American small towns survived, and while the name "G. C. Murphy" was fading from store windows, they were not about to disappear so easily.

AFTERMATH
AND
Legacy

It's early spring and the trees and flowers aren't yet in bloom, but J. S. Mack Community Park in Indiana, Pennsylvania, still looks beautiful. Local attorney Jonathan Mack is proud to show off this rare gem—a free community park open from 7:00 A.M. to 10:00 P.M. daily that's also privately owned. Other than the occasional grant from state or local governments, Mack Park's swimming pool, playgrounds, farm show arena, and other amenities operate at no cost to the taxpayers of Indiana County, just as they have since the land was purchased by John Sephus Mack and his cousin Edgar McCrorey Mack more than seventy years ago.

"It's an unbelievably well-used asset in this community," says Jon Mack, grandson of Edgar McCrorey Mack and the current president of the foundation. Run by the J. S. Mack Foundation, the charity set up by the G. C. Murphy Company's chairman and president shortly before his death, Mack Park is the home of the Indiana County Fair, fireworks on Independence Day, football and softball games, horse races, and countless picnics and celebrations. "Mack Park has for decades been the central gathering place of this community, and that's what J. S. Mack provided," Jon Mack says. "We're still enjoying the legacy of what he created. Just think of the hundreds of thousands of people who have used this park over the years." No new money has been donated to the Mack Foundation since Seph Mack's death in 1940, so Jon Mack and other board members know that keeping it solvent and vital is a continuing challenge. But they have every intention of making sure that Mack Park will be available for many years to come—the grandstands around the horse track were rebuilt a few years ago, a new skateboard park was recently dedicated, and the swimming pool is about to be completely renovated.

In Pennsylvania and more than twenty other states where the G. C. Murphy Company once operated, descendants of the founders and former employees remain dedicated to their communities. For Murphy veterans, the constant reminders about "public service" that began in Seph Mack's day were more than mere words; they were a call to action. Some of the efforts have obvious links to Murphy's, such as Mack Park or the G. C. Murphy Company Foundation, created as the corporation's charitable arm in 1952. Since becoming an independent nonprofit entity in 1986, the Murphy Foundation has contributed more than $3 million to charities and educational institutions in cities where Murphy's had stores. It has also helped former Murphy employees whose lives were touched by chronic illnesses and natural disasters. Other parts of the Murphy legacy are less obvious. In the 1990s, for instance, a crew of former G. C. Murphy employees helped put Pittsburgh's Goodwill Industries on the path to self-sufficiency by redesigning its thrift stores.

More than two decades after the Ames takeover, employees of many Murphy stores still keep in touch and hold summertime reunions, though the youngest attendees are now in their forties and fifties. For many years, several hundred ex-Murphy workers kept in touch through a group with the tongue-in-cheek name "SMERF"—Society of Murphy Employees Retired and Fired. It says something about the abiding affection for the G. C. Murphy Company that more tangible evidence remains of its existence than of the two corporations that outlasted it, Ames and McCrory, which disappeared almost without a trace—except for their lengthy files in federal bankruptcy court.

Ames's slide to oblivion began with its disastrous 1988 purchase of the Zayre discount chain. Founded in New England in 1956, Zayre was one of the discount industry's success stories of the 1960s. But in the 1980s, Zayre's parent company focused on its fast-growing apparel chain, T. J. Maxx, and the discount stores suffered years of neglect and deferred maintenance. In the first two quarters of 1988, 388 Zayre stores located mostly in declining urban areas lost $70 million and the Zayre Corporation was happy to unload them onto Ames. Former Murphy regional manager Dave Backstrom, then working for Ames, was nearing retirement when he was asked to straighten out four struggling Zayre locations near Pittsburgh. He was appalled at their condition: tractor-trailers in the parking lots were crammed with merchandise that had no waybills or inventory sheets, while stockrooms were filled to the rafters with out-of-date, unsellable merchandise. The situation was similar at Zayre stores throughout the Northeast. A writer for the *Boston Globe* who visited one in Roslindale, Massachusetts, seven months after the Ames takeover found "filthy floors, cartons in the aisles, jumbled merchandise, and gap-toothed shelves."

After losing $228 million in 1989, largely as a result of the Zayre acquisition, Ames filed for Chapter 11 bankruptcy. It emerged in 1992 after closing dozens of stores and the former G. C. Murphy Company distribution center in McKeesport and declared that Ames would distinguish its stores through personal service and a commitment to serving small and rural towns where larger retailers wouldn't go. If Ames's new direction sounded familiar, it should have—it was the same business plan Murphy's had followed successfully for eight decades. After several profitable years, Ames purchased the failing Hills Department Stores chain based in Canton, Massachusetts, and entered bankruptcy for the second time in 2001. This time, citing its inability to compete with more aggressive rivals such as Wal-Mart and Target, Ames announced that it was liquidating its remaining three hundred stores and going out of business. Seemingly as one last affront to former G. C. Murphy Company employees covered by its retirement plan, Ames tried to cancel their life insurance coverage. Murphy employees sued to protect what they could of those benefits.

The remaining variety stores that carried G. C. Murphy Company signs were doing little better as a brand name on the dwindling and dispirited group of five-and-tens that started out as the McCrory, McLellan, and Green chains but eventually included nearly every one of their competitors except Woolworth. Since 1960, McCrory and its affiliated companies had been controlled by financier Meshulam Riklis, whose enemies accused him of draining McCrory and other companies of their assets to finance his personal philanthropies, often at the expense of those who invested in their stocks and bonds. Servicing its heavy debts eventually wiped out McCrory's profits and pushed the chain into bankruptcy in 1992. The constant turmoil at the top left the company without any effective leadership or marketing strategy. "McCrory would ship all of this merchandise that we couldn't sell," says Marianne Molnar, who was managing the G. C. Murphy store in Elizabeth, Pennsylvania. She remembers McCrory's sending dozens of plastic toy shopping carts to the tiny store one Christmas. She had soon filled the entire wall of the store with them, but more were still coming in. As McCrory's lurched from crisis to crisis until its final liquidation in 2001, life within the company became chaotic, says maintenance supervisor Wayne Potter, another Murphy veteran, who was fired in the parking lot of Greengate Mall in Greensburg, Pennsylvania. "The day [McCrory's] let me go was the happiest day of my life," he says.

Fred Speidel was managing Murphy's old flagship Store No. 12 in downtown Pittsburgh when Riklis visited. He greeted Speidel by complaining that the store had too many "fat" and unattractive clerks. Not long after, frustrated by McCrory's insistence that he accept a demotion to a smaller store, Speidel quit. Former Murphy district manager Earl Fenton quit when McCrory's changed the criteria for annual bonuses just one month before they were to be dispensed. "I lost about $135,000 in wages and a $35,000 Cadillac," he says. "I told my regional manager, 'You guys screwed me out of my bonus.' He said, 'Oh, it happened to everybody.' I said, 'It doesn't make it right.'"

After a brief stint at Wal-Mart, Fenton got a call from former G. C. Murphy housewares buyer Jim Turner. "Do you know anyone who would like to be sales manager for Goodwill?" Turner asked. "How much money do you want?" Fenton joked.

Goodwill Industries was founded in Boston, Massachusetts, in 1902 by a Methodist clergyman who collected cast-off clothing and household items and then hired disabled and mentally handicapped people to restore and repair them for resale in second-hand stores. His "employees" learned skills and trades while earning money, which enabled many of them to lead independent lives for the first time. A Methodist minister in Pittsburgh started the city's first Goodwill workshop in 1919, and by the 1950s, local businesses were hiring Goodwill workers as subcontractors on their products. But cutbacks in state and federal subsidies in the 1970s and '80s forced Goodwill Industries of Pittsburgh to look for ways to become more self-sufficient.

In 1989, Goodwill president and CEO Robert S. Foltz decided the agency should lean more heavily on its thrift stores for revenue. To help lead the charge, Goodwill turned to one of the many Ames refugees in the Pittsburgh area. Jim Turner, a recently laid-off thirty-five-year G. C. Murphy Company veteran, joined Goodwill as a "procurement specialist," using his old contacts among Murphy's old vendors and manufacturers to track down discontinued, damaged, and surplus household goods that could be profitably sold through the thrift stores. "Retail was his cup of tea," says his widow, Midge Turner. Within a few years, Goodwill of Pittsburgh had twenty-four stores in Western Pennsylvania and West Virginia. While there was plenty of "gently used" second-hand clothing and furniture at the back of those locations, the front had shelves of brand-new cosmetics, packaged foods and candy, sewing notions, stationery, and toys—items that were mainstays at G. C. Murphy Company variety stores.

It was no coincidence. As Goodwill added stores, Turner kept recruiting other Murphy hands such as Barbara Balawajder, another former home office buyer, and former district manager Bob Grove. It also helped that Luther Shay, Murphy's former vice president of administrative services, was on the Goodwill board of directors. Even though Goodwill staffers started laughing about the "Murphy mafia," the results they obtained were no joke. By 2006, Goodwill's Pittsburgh-area stores were generating roughly half the agency's income. "Murphy people had a good work ethic," says Grove, now retired. "We didn't have to be told how to start, how to stop." Balawajder, who purchased paper goods and household cleaners for Murphy's, says buying for Goodwill required her to learn a different way of merchandising. While Murphy's had a list of standard items that were always in stock, Goodwill had to be creative, snapping up odd and out-of-season items from bigger retailers. If she was offered twenty-five cases of plastic Easter eggs in the middle of summer, she bought them but had to put them away for the following spring. Although Goodwill's Pittsburgh stores currently only do about 12 percent of their business in new goods, the five-and-ten-style items generate traffic by allowing customers to grab essentials they need while looking for other bargains. In 2006, $18 million in revenue generated by the stores helped fund job training, literacy education, senior citizen programs, and other services for more than sixty-two thousand people in Pennsylvania and West Virginia.

Other residents of Western Pennsylvania benefit in more direct ways from the G. C. Murphy Company's legacy. In the company's final years, employees saved as much of its history as possible, sometimes smuggling photos and documents out of the home office in briefcases or purses to keep them from being thrown away. No one had a pocket big enough to hold the grandfather clock that once belonged to Murphy president Paul Sample and his wife, Mae, and which stood in the reception area at the McKeesport headquarters. When an Ames executive noticed the clock and mentioned how nice it would look in that company's Connecticut offices, Murphy loyalists knew they had to act quickly. Surreptitiously, they hid the clock in an elevator shaft and in the dead of night moved it to the library of Penn State University's McKeesport campus in a hearse loaned by a friendly local funeral director. The Sample clock now chimes the hours and quarter-hours at the McKeesport Heritage Center, a museum and home for genealogy research that also houses the G. C. Murphy Company archives.

The Heritage Center is one of many beneficiaries over the last twenty years of grants from the G. C. Murphy Company Foundation, another piece of Murphy's history that was quietly slipped out from under Ames. The Connecticut discounter didn't have a charitable arm, but Murphy's had established one with a grant of $500,000 back in 1952 at the suggestion of vice president Jim Mack. (Company treasurer Carl Schatz had pointed out that Murphy's was otherwise subject to the Excess Profits Tax of 1950 and would owe the federal government about $410,000 if it didn't make a large charitable contribution.) Allegheny County Common Pleas Court granted the foundation's charter on December 30, 1952, authorizing it to make donations to "charitable, religious, and educational agencies" and to offer assistance to employees or former employees in the event of "financial reverse," illness, or "untoward circumstances." According to former Murphy public relations man Ed Davis, for most of the foundation's first thirty years, its primary activities included regular grants to hospitals, community chests, colleges, and other charities in cities where the company had stores. Though it was a relatively minor part of the foundation's overall activites, many employees have fond memories of the G. C. Murphy Company Foundation Scholarship, administered through the National Merit Scholarship Corporation and awarded annually to employees' children. Two female students and two male students received scholarships each year. The first were awarded on May 19, 1967, to Patricia Ann Lytle of Ocean City, New Jersey; Richard K. Freeman of Fort Worth, Texas; Jean Ann Trotter of Pontiac, Michigan; and Stanley Karrs of New Kensington, Pennsylvania. The last were awarded June 27, 1985, to Greg O. Lang of Tiffin, Ohio; Susan Breth of Kent, Ohio; Jennifer Waschak of Greenville, Ohio; and Scott A. Franklin of St. Joseph, Michigan.

When former Murphy general counsel Bob Messner reorganized the Murphy Foundation in April 1986, board members had to set a new direction. Davis, who now serves as the foundation's part-time administrator, says the directors decided to focus their efforts on

McKeesport and nearby communities where the G. C. Murphy Company had a high number of former employees. One of the first recipients of a grant from the renewed Murphy Foundation was Chatham College in Pittsburgh, which at Chuck Lytle's request began offering career counseling and classes in résumé preparation to laid-off Murphy employees. Former Murphy chairman S. Warne Robinson served as the first president of the foundation, but the position now rotates from board member to board member each year. The scholarship program was reborn as the G. C. Murphy Company Foundation Scholarship at Penn State McKeesport (now Penn State Greater Allegheny). The foundation's endowment provides financial support to students whose grandparents or parents worked for Murphy's or who are from Allegheny, Washington, and Westmoreland counties in Pennsylvania.

Regular grants also support groups such as the Greater Pittsburgh Community Food Bank in Duquesne, Pennsylvania, which in 2006 distributed 19.5 million pounds of food to 120,000 needy people in an eleven-county area. "There aren't many organizations like the Murphy Foundation that will give annually and will give general operating support, and those things are very important," says executive director Joyce Rothermel, adding that some other donors attach restrictions that make it difficult for the food bank to use the money where it's most needed. Founded in 1980, the food bank spent fourteen years in a warehouse near Murphy's McKeesport distribution center before moving to a new facility in 1999 where volunteers sort, pack, and disburse food to the hungry. "Knowing that the Murphy Foundation has been there for us has given us the ability to grow the work that we do," Rothermel says. "The generosity, the flexibility, and the sustaining nature of the annual gifts have made their support extremely valuable."

Laurie MacDonald, executive director of the Womansplace shelter in McKeesport, says annual grants from the Murphy Foundation enable her thirty full- and part-time employees to assist five thousand abused women and their children each year. Open twenty-four hours a day, seven days per week, Womansplace has provided victims of domestic violence with emergency housing and medical and legal advice since 1976. "The G. C. Murphy Company Foundation has always been a good friend to Womansplace," MacDonald says. "We do get some state and federal funding, but we rely on private foundations because they provide us with consistent funding—and it's community dollars going to community projects."

The G. C. Murphy legacy has touched the LaRosa Boys and Girls Club of McKeesport in several ways, says executive director Tom Maglicco. Besides regular operating grants from the Murphy Foundation, in 2000 the club added a new youth activities center thanks to a gift from Betty Shaw Gamble, daughter of Walter Shaw Sr. Named for founder Sam LaRosa, an inspector at Westinghouse Electric, the club was a favorite charity of Shaw, his son Walter Shaw Jr., and Elmer Lowery, whose E. J. Lowery Trucking Company held a lucrative contract to deliver merchandise from Murphy's McKeesport warehouse to stores in several northeastern states. The elder Shaw donated more than $50,000 toward the construction of the club's first building in 1956 and used his considerable influence to rally other prominent businessmen to the cause. His son also was an active supporter until his death in 1989.

The wing added with Gamble's donation includes several classrooms, a multipurpose assembly room, an arts and crafts center, and a computer lab with ten brand-new PCs. With poverty levels in McKeesport above 20 percent and 13 percent of children being raised by only one parent, the LaRosa club is an invaluable city asset. According to Maglicco, more than six hundred boys and girls are members and take advantage of services such as homework help, teen counseling, mentoring, and tutoring, in addition to youth sports including basketball and softball. Continued support from the Murphy Foundation and Betty Shaw Gamble has helped ensure the club's success, Maglicco says. "It warms my heart that she stays in touch with us," he says. "She knows so much about the community and wants to see the community succeed. It's part of her family history." The original building was long ago dedicated to Walter C. Shaw Sr. The new wing was recently dedicated to his daughter.

Though some Murphy stores have been torn down, others are still busy and productive. At Store No. 120 on State Street in St. Joseph, Michigan, tourists can rent beach houses along Lake Michigan. Store No. 130 on West Pitt Street in Bedford, Store No. 117 on Franklin Avenue in Aliquippa, and Store No. 202 on Lincoln Avenue in McDonald, all in Pennsylvania, are being used as artists' studios, while Store No. 45 on Clay Avenue in Jeannette, Pennsylvania, is an antique store. Some reuses have been quite creative. Architects Jeffery Smith and Michael Holly received an award from the State of Louisiana in 1997 for transforming Store No. 521 in Hammond into the Morgan & Lindsey Apartments. Store No. 172 on Main Street in Fairmont, West Virginia, is a centerpiece of a multimillion-dollar downtown rehabilitation project. Renovated for office and retail space, the store is now known as the Veterans Square Building, but the rich red, gold, and green trim chosen by the architects can't help but remind visitors of its G. C. Murphy Company heritage. One of the company's larger locations, Store No. 123 on Indianapolis's Fountain Square, now houses an antique mall, several galleries, and performance space for dancers and musicians. It's been renamed (appropriately enough) the Murphy Art Center.

Not every Murphy location led such a charmed life after the company's demise, of course. After the home office closed, McKeesport real estate agent Nancy Mack received a phone call from Ames headquarters. They wanted her to sell the building for them. Mack, whose husband had been laid off after the takeover, nearly fell out of her chair. She reluctantly agreed to tour the complex with several Ames representatives only to find that the company's failure to maintain the buildings had left them a mess. "I think you should tear it down," Mack told them. Ames eventually found a buyer—a moving company that wanted to use it for storage—and sold the entire complex in 1993 for $42,780, less than the price of a single-family home. The name "G. C. Murphy Co.," proudly painted in eight-foot-tall letters on the west and east sides of the building, disappeared under a coat of ugly brown paint that quickly chalked and peeled. (Apparently, it wasn't Murphy's "Super-Tex.") At one point, Davis tried to salvage the "G. C. Murphy Co." sign from the employee entrance, but the new owners hung up on him. "I was never treated so rudely in all my life," he says.

On the other hand, if "location" means everything in business, it's a testimony to the skill G. C. Murphy employees had in selecting sites that many former stores are still being used by major chains selling five-and-ten-style merchandise. In Irwin, Pennsylvania, former Store No. 23 on Main Street is a Rite Aid pharmacy, while Store No. 197 on High Street in Morgantown, West Virginia, is a Dollar General. Store No. 68 in Beaver, Pennsylvania, continued operating almost intact until the summer of 2005, complete with the red, white, and green signs and "old-fashioned" paint scheme installed during the remodeling program of the early 1980s. Druggist Anthony Passeri and his wife, Jill, purchased the store from McCrory's and changed it only enough to add a pharmacy counter. Otherwise, the "Beaver 5 & 10" looked just like a G. C. Murphy store. Business was still good when Anthony Passeri, in his early eighties, decided that he wanted to cut back on his workload and sold the store, ending its life as a five-and-ten. But the old Murphy distribution center in McKeesport is back in operation for a company called Magic Creations, Inc., which manufactures and imports holiday merchandise, gifts, toys, and craft supplies for variety and discount stores throughout the country. The "clankity-clank" tow chain around the ceiling is long out of service, but the sprawling facility is packed to the rafters with many items that Murphy's would likely be selling today if it had survived.

What might have happened if the G. C. Murphy Company had successfully fought off the Ames takeover in 1985? Ask a dozen Murphy employees and you'll likely get a dozen different answers. The biggest question is whether Murphy's could have competed with Wal-

Mart, which became an international retail juggernaut in the 1990s and drove many smaller competitors out of business. In 1984, Wal-Mart had 640 stores and sales of $4.5 billion; it was just starting to go head to head with Murphy's in a few southern markets. Murphy's Mart manager Pete Shuppy is convinced the company would have held its own "probably better than most because of the management that ran the stores. The guys who ran the stores were merchants. They weren't following directions from the home office. They knew what sold and they knew what to have in the building." Former store manager and buyer Bob Bishop says both the Marts and the variety stores would have been able to adapt and compete. Murphy's excellent locations, including many in or near shopping centers, were a valuable asset in their own right, he says. "I truly believe we were a very viable company when Ames bought us," Bishop says. Others, like former home office executive Bill Kraus, argue that Murphy's would have followed Jamesway, Caldor, Bradlee's, and other regional discounters into bankruptcy in the face of Wal-Mart's giant "supercenter" stores and its policy of slashing prices to their bare minimums. Murphy's was too conservative to make leaps that Wal-Mart did, he says "The way to go was the big discount store, and it had to be a big, aggressive operation," Kraus says. "We had the infrastructure, but we needed more volume to support our fixed costs, and we were afraid of long-term debt."

Everyone seems to agree that Murphy's would have needed to streamline its distribution centers and convert all its stores to point-of-sale cash registers. Murphy distribution executive Ed McCandless remembers visiting Wal-Mart's Bentonville, Arkansas, headquarters in the early 1980s and being amazed by the quality and quantity of the data the company was able to get from its stores thanks to its rapid computerization and satellite communications system. McCandless and several computer analysts from Murphy's toured a Wal-Mart distribution center with an IBM salesman and found it equally impressive. "I never saw a warehouse like that—stuff was coming in one side and going out the other, bang!" McCandless says. "Nobody was pushing things around or doing a lot of manual labor. That was the way it ought to be."

Tom Hudak says the direction Wal-Mart took was the route that Murphy's was headed as well. "We were in the process of converting the marts from manager run to computer based, with buyers making the decisions," he says. "That was a total change, taking the authority away from the sales division, but it was the way we had to go. That fundamentally was the way Wal-Mart went. When you're dealing with that kind of volume, you can't have someone walking around saying, 'We're going to carry miniskirts,' or certain kinds of Fisher-Price toys. I would have liked to have had that opportunity to see it develop."

Speculating about what might have happened to the G. C. Murphy Company with the benefit of two decades' worth of hindsight is probably unfair. Perhaps the best-case scenario would have been if the Murphy's Mart Fashions in New Dimensions program had continued to develop and moved those stores further upmarket. Target Corporation and Wisconsin-based Kohl's Department Stores proved in the 1990s that there was plenty of space for "upscale discounters" in the territory between Wal-Mart and Kmart on one side

FIG. 71
More than six hundred youth and teenagers participate in athletics, educational, and mentoring programs at McKeesport's LaRosa Boys and Girls Club. Murphy chairman Walter Shaw Sr. led the fund-raising drive for the club's first building in 1956. The newest wing on the building is named for his daughter, Betty Shaw Gamble, who helped pay for its construction.

and traditional department stores such as Macy's on other. As for the variety stores, the burgeoning growth of low-end merchants such as Dollar General of Goodlettsville, Tennessee, which had more than eighty-two hundred stores in 2007, indicates that Murphy's was on the right track with its Bargain World division.

Kansas-based Duckwall-ALCO Stores Inc. is one regional retailer that has been able to survive in the Wal-Mart era. A. L. Duckwall opened his first five-and-ten in Abilene in 1901, just about the time George Murphy was establishing himself in McKeesport. In 1968, Duckwall opened its first ALCO discount store, only two years before the first Murphy's Mart. As Murphy's did in 1985, Duckwall currently operates a mix of variety and discount stores, most of which are located in smaller towns where the company can be the dominant retailer. In fact, Duckwall-ALCO has stores in some of the very same places as Murphy's, such as Hartford City and North Manchester, Indiana, and Delphos, Ohio. After what the company called a "disappointing" year in 2005 when it missed its sales targets, Duckwall-ALCO closed twenty-three underperforming stores, cut old inventory, and named a new president and CEO. Sales were up 6.3 percent in 2006.

If Murphy's had acquired a drug store chain or installed pharmacies in its existing five-and-tens, it might have grabbed a piece of the fast-growing market in prescriptions and health and beauty aids that allowed the Walgreen Company to practically double in size between 1990 and 2006. There remains an obvious niche being filled by drug store chains for stationery, cosmetics, candy, sewing notions, and other convenience items that Murphy's once carried. In 2006, nonprescription merchandise represented $17 billion in sales to Walgreen and $6.2 billion to Rite Aid. On the other hand, trying to service the debt necessary for Murphy's to complete an employee stock ownership plan or leveraged buyout might have drained it of profits, preventing it from growing. And even mighty F. W. Woolworth Company decided to exit the variety store business for good in 1997, closing its remaining four hundred red-fronts to focus on its seven thousand other stores, including the Foot Locker sporting goods chain.

Despite the tumultuous final years under Ames and McCrory ownership, there's little bitterness among former Murphy employees. "There was always a little bit of good with the bad, but there was a lot more good than bad," Bob Bishop says. In fact, hundreds of men and women retain what Pete Shuppy calls an "unbelievable" loyalty to the G. C. Murphy Company. "I don't know what it was, but I know they cared about people," he says. "The first house I ever bought they helped me buy. They gave me an advance on my bonus, and there aren't many companies that would do that. You were a family. I knew everybody and everybody knew me."

If former employees have any regrets, it's usually that they're no longer behind the counter of a Murphy store serving neighbors and friends. "We had a lot of good times, I enjoyed the people, and I enjoyed my work," says Betty Moats, who worked for forty-three years in the Mercersburg, Pennsylvania, store, her last sixteen as manager. "I was sorry when they closed, you know? A lot of people tell me they still miss Murphy's." They miss the G. C. Murphy Company in West Newton, Pennsylvania, too, says lifelong resident Sandra Kuch, herself a one-time Murphy girl. "People compare our new Dollar General to it all the time," she says. Kuch remembers the white cardboard containers of tropical fish that used to "follow" her sister home, much to their mother's chagrin, while her father was angry when Murphy's stopped carrying leather that he could use to repair his own shoes. Sandra Gallardo calls her Murphy store in Brazil, Indiana, "one of the special places of my childhood." She wound up marrying the assistant manager of the Brazil store, Larry Brown, and they moved from town to town as he took new assignments at Murphy's. Gallardo says the G. C. Murphy Company was a family, and she was proud to be a part of it. Though her husband passed away in 2005, Gallardo says her "pleasant memories continue on."

While serving as Murphy's chairman and president in the 1950s and '60s, Jim Mack earned a reputation, probably unfairly, as a stern and cold man. But he struck a powerful emotional chord in his speech to the G. C. Murphy Veterans Club in 1965. "When that great trial lawyer Clarence Darrow described a corporation as 'a legal entity, with no soul to feel,' he proved conclusively that he had never heard of Murphy's," Mack said. "The G. C. Murphy Company has a soul. You—our veterans. May your spirit spread." In the memories of customers and employees and in the communities Murphy's served, maybe it still does.

All direct quotes from living G. C. Murphy Company sources come from interviews conducted by the author between 2003 and 2007. Quotes from the deceased are taken from other sources listed below, including magazine and newspaper articles; unpublished memos and letters in the archives of the McKeesport Heritage Center, McKeesport, Pennsylvania; and speeches delivered to the G. C. Murphy Company board of directors, the G. C. Murphy Veterans Club, and elsewhere.

Earnings and sales figures, unless otherwise noted below, are from G. C. Murphy Company or Ames Department Stores, Inc., annual reports, available at the Carnegie Library of Pittsburgh, Downtown and Business Branch, Pittsburgh; the Historical Society of Western Pennsylvania, Pittsburgh; and the McKeesport Heritage Center.

Stock prices come from G. C. Murphy Company annual reports; the ledger of the corporation's secretary, on file at the Heritage Center; and New York Curb Exchange and New York Stock Exchange tables in the *New York Times* and the *Washington Post*.

General background material comes from "The G. C. Murphy Co.: 1925–1950," an extensive article in *Chain Store Age*, June 1950, pp. J14–J16, 103–111, and 244–247; as well as the special December 1967 issue of *Chain Store Age* devoted to the G. C. Murphy Company, which includes an in-depth history of operations, interviews with key executives, and articles examining every division of the company.

INTERVIEWS

Quotes from the following people are taken directly from interviews conducted by the author. They are listed in alphabetical order. Where available or appropriate, the location and date of the interview is included.

Jack Anderson, Pleasant Hills, Pa., May 2004; William Anderson, Bryn Mawr, Pa., Sept. 5, 2005; Dave Backstrom, Bethel Park, Pa., Aug. 31 and Sept. 7, 2004; Barbara Balawajder, McKeesport, Pa., May 3, 2004; A. Ralph Barlow Jr., telephone, March 2005; John Barna, West Mifflin, Pa., Jan. 6, 2005; Minnie Beckman, McKeesport, Pa., Nov. 2004; Robert Beyer, North Huntingdon

notes on sources

Township, Pa., Jan. 8, 2005; Bob Bishop, Bethel Park, Pa., June 2004; Ellison "Al" Boggs, Pleasant Hills, Pa., April 25, 2004; Rose Cafiero, White Oak, Pa., May 6, 2005; Edwin Davis, Elizabeth Township, Pa., numerous interviews and letters; Lloyd "Del" Davis, New Florence, Pa., Nov. 2004; Robert Dowie, York, Pa., Feb. 12, 2005; Mike and Marsha Dujmic, White Oak, Pa., Sept. 24, 2004; Andrew Duris, North Huntingdon Township, Pa., May 24, 2004; Andy Duris, North Huntingdon Township, Nov. 2004.

Judson Ellis Jr., Cape May, N.J., Sept. 5, 2005; Earl Fenton, Ligonier, Pa., July 8, 2004; Roy Fowler, Pleasant Hills, Pa., Oct. 27, 2004; Joseph J. Franklin, Hobe Sound, Fla., June 9, 2005; Roy Fowler Jr., Pleasant Hills, Pa., Nov. 2004; Cece Gallagher, Jefferson Hills, Pa., Feb. 10, 2005; Betty Shaw Gamble, Ligonier, Pa., May 28, 2005; Gertrude Geisler, Upper St. Clair, Pa., Nov. 2004; Carolyn Gibson, White Oak, Pa., Oct. 7, 2004; Dick Gibson Sr., Cassville, W.Va., Nov. 7, 2004; Bob Golby, Nov. 26, 2004; Jack Gordon, State College, Pa., May 7, 2005; Robert Grove, McKeesport, Pa., May 3, 2004; Rebecca Sample Habenicht, by telephone, Nov. 2004; Dorothy Sample Hill, O'Hara Township, Pa., Nov. 2004; Paul Hindes, Bethel Park, Pa., Oct. 22, 2004; Tom Hudak, Bridgeville, Pa., Nov. 6, 2004, and additional conversations; Jennifer Jordan Justice, by telephone, Nov. 2004; Ed Kinter, Portersville, Pa., June 6, 2004; Ed Kohler, Port Vue, Pa., April 27, 2005; Bill Kraus, Bethel Park, Pa., Jan. 2005, and letter to author.

Fred Lantz, North Huntingdon Township, Pa., April 30, 2004; Jack Loveall, Uniontown, Pa., Jan. 9, 2005; Barbara Reister Mack, by telephone, Jan. 25, 2005, and Bradenton, Fla., June 7, 2005; Nancy Baum Mack, Rostraver Township, Pa., Dec. 30, 2004; Jonathan Mack, Indiana, Pa., March 9, 2007; Joseph Mack, Penn Run, Pa., April 8, 2007; Sephus Mack, by telephone, Jan. 25, 2005, and Bradenton, Fla., June 7, 2005; Laurie MacDonald, by telephone, April 26, 2007; Tom Maglicco, McKeesport, Pa., March 2007; Ed McCandless, McKeesport, Pa., April 18, 2004; Emmeratta McDonough, Bellaire, Ohio, Nov. 28, 2004; Clair McElhinny, Greensburg, Pa., numerous interviews and letters; Ed McGinley,

Pittsburgh, Oct. 14, 2005; Robert Messner, numerous conversations and letters; Betty Moats, by telephone, May 5, 2005; Marianne Molnar, Feb. 10, 2005; Earl Nottingham, Naples, Fla., June 7, 2005; Alberta Onaitis, Jan. 29, 2005; Harry Pfister, Sebring, Fla., June 6, 2005; Sally Porterfield, Moon Township, Pa., July 18, 2006; Patricia Potter, Moon Township, Pa., July 18, 2006; Wayne and Lillian Potter, Acme, Pa., Dec. 2005; Audrey Puko, Trafford, Pa., Dec. 29, 2004; Millie Reiland, Forest Hills, Pa., March 2005; Betty Briggs Rehfeldt, Montgomery, Ohio, May 25, 2005; Earl Rehrig, Murrysville, Pa., July 11, 2004; Gloria Rodgers, Pittsburgh, Dec. 2004; Joyce Rothermel, by telephone, April 26, 2007; Arthur N. Rupe, by telephone, Aug. 17, 2006.

Dick Scales, Elizabeth Township, Pa., July 30, 2004; Thelma Sharpe, McKeesport, Pa., Dec. 13, 2004; Martin and Ilene Schultz, Pleasant Gap, Pa., May 7, 2005; Luther Shay, Edgewood, Pa., Jan. 10, 2005; Ed Sherman, McKeesport, Pa., June 6, 2006; Pete Shuppy, Highspire, Pa., Feb. 12, 2005; George Smillie, Mt. Pleasant, Pa., November 2005; Fred Speidel, Pittsburgh, Oct. 28, 2004; Terry Stadterman, Delray Beach, Fla., June 7, 2005; Ron Templeton, Upper St. Clair, Pa., June 7, 2004; Clair Trost, Carroll Township, Pa., Nov. 27, 2004; Midge Turner, by telephone, Nov. 6, 2004; Lena Togyer, McKeesport, Pa., December 2004; Jack Walsh, McKeesport, Pa., Jan. 3, 2005; Ed Whalen, Pittsburgh, Pa., Sept. 24, 2005.

CHAPTER 1

Many details about the opening of the Bethel Park Murphy's Mart come from a special advertising section published May 24, 1970, in the *Pittsburgh Press*. The quote from the unnamed executive is from Tom Mahoney and Leonard Sloane's seminal history of American retailing, *The Great Merchants: America's Foremost Retail Institutions and the People Who Made Them Great* (New York: Harper & Row, 1974), p. 355, and additional background on the discount industry is from pp. 355–372.

CHAPTER 2

Background material about stores of the nineteenth century comes from Mahoney and

Sloane, pp. 3–19. Information about Frank W. Woolworth's early life and the history of the F. W. Woolworth Company are from John K. Winkler, *Five and Ten* (New York: Bantam Books, 1957); John P. Nichols, *Skyline Queen and the Merchant Prince* (New York: Simon and Schuster, 1973), pp. 25–58; Jean Maddern Pitrone, *F. W. Woolworth and the American Five and Dime* (Jefferson, N.C.: McFarland & Company Inc., 2003), pp. 3–20; F. W. Woolworth Company, *Woolworth's First 75 Years* (New York: F. W. Woolworth Company, 1953), pp. 9–18. Details of the purchase of the first G. C. Murphy Company are in Winkler, p. 129; and Woolworth, p. 18. Information about the life of George C. Murphy comes primarily from his personal papers, including his last will and testament, loaned to the author by his granddaughter, Betty Briggs Rehfeldt, as well as from U.S. Census Records for McKeesport, Pa., 1900 and 1910; William Fell Smith, *The Greater Pittsburg Real Estate Reference Book* (1903); and Pittsburg & Allegheny Telephone Company directories. Quotes are from John Sephus Mack's letters to G. C. Murphy Company stockholders, Feb. 4 and Sept. 17, 1919; Walter C. Shaw Sr.'s letters to Edgar M. Mack, Sept. 11, 1943; Arthur Batty, August 20, 1946; and Paul L. Sample, April 14, 1953; and Paul L. Sample's speech to G. C. Murphy Veterans Club, May 13, 1946; and George Swetnam, "Dollars and Dimes," *Pittsburgh Press Sunday Roto,* June 19, 1960, pp. 6–7.

Details of the G. C. Murphy Company's early years can be found in *The Rebirth of the Murphy Company,* an undated, unpublished manuscript in the heritage center's collection. Stories of the early life of John Sephus Mack are taken from interviews with relatives as well as from "Indiana Hospital Gets Magnificent Donation," Indiana, Pa., *Evening Gazette,* Oct. 1, 1935; G. C. Murphy Company, *The Twenty-Fifth Anniversary of the G. C. Murphy Company,* February 1931; and the Mack family genealogical collection at the Historical and Genealogical Society of Indiana County, Indiana, Pa.

Walter C. Shaw Sr.'s biographical information is complied from interviews with relatives as well as from *This Is Your Life* and *Walter Carlysle Shaw,* privately printed by Youghiogheny

Country Club, McKeesport, Pennsylvania, 1958.

Details of Sebastian S. Kresge's early career and relationship with John McCrorey and George Murphy come from Stanley S. Kresge and Steve Spilos, *The S. S. Kresge Story* (Racine, Wis.: Western Publishing Co., 1979); Kresge, *The S. S. Kresge Company and Its Builder, Sebastian Spering Kresge* (New York: The Newcomen Society, 1958), p. 12; the Detroit Historical Society, which has a replica of Kresge's first store on display at its museum, 5401 Woodward Avenue, Detroit, Michigan; and The Kresge Foundation, 3215 West Big Beaver Road, Troy, Michigan.

CHAPTER 3

General details about the economic conditions of the 1920s come from John Kenneth Galbraith, *The Great Crash* (Boston: Houghton Mifflin Co., 1955), and Robert T. Patterson, *The Great Boom and Panic* (Chicago: Henry Regnery Co., 1965). Shaw quotes are taken from letters, Walter C. Shaw Sr. to Paul L. Sample, Nov. 12, 1947, Nov. 17, 1947, and April 17, 1953. Sample's quotes are from a speech he delivered to the G. C. Murphy Veterans Club, William Penn Hotel, Pittsburgh, Pa., May 13, 1946.

Other information comes from Ben Gordon, "From Five and Dime to Family Shopping Centers," *Chain Store Age,* June 1950, pp. J6–J8, J72; Godfrey M. Lebhar, "The Story of the Variety Chains: 1925–1950," *Chain Store Age,* June 1950, pp. J1–J5; Stewart Monroe, "Brother Team," *Indianapolis Star,* Aug. 1, 1948; an undated report titled "Distribution History," in the G. C. Murphy Company files at the McKeesport Heritage Center; *The Rebirth of the Murphy Company;* "Local Chain Stores," *Time,* Sept. 5, 1927; *G. C. Murphy Company Welcomes You to an Open House in Its General Offices, Dec. 15 and 16, 1947;* "Murphy Co.'s New Store Is Now Completed!" McKeesport, Pa., *Daily News,* May 11, 1921.

CHAPTER 4

Information about Depression-era conditions in Pittsburgh, Baltimore, and elsewhere is drawn from Brian Apelt, *The Corporation: A Centennial Biography of United States Steel Corporation, 1901–2001* (Pittsburgh: Cathedral Publishing, 2000);

Robert R. R. Brooks, *As Steel Goes: Unionism in a Basic Industry* (New Haven: Yale University Press, 1940); Stefan Lorant, *Pittsburgh: The Story of an American City,* 5th ed.(Pittsburgh: Esselmont Books, 1999); William Manchester, *The Glory and The Dream,* vol. 1 (Boston: Little, Brown & Co., 1974); Mark Reutter, *Sparrows Point: Making Steel—The Rise and Ruin of American Industrial Might* (New York: Summit Books, 1988); Vincent D. Sweeney, *The United Steelworkers of America* (Pittsburgh: United Steelworkers of America, 1956); Michael P. Weber, *Don't Call Me Boss: David L. Lawrence, Pittsburgh's Renaissance Mayor* (Pittsburgh: University of Pittsburgh Press, 1988).

Other G. C. Murphy Company and variety-store industry information is from Thomas M. Foristall, "The Inquiring Investor," *Wall Street Journal,* March 19, 1935, p. 6, and March 23, 1936, p. 6; Ben Gordon, "G. C. Murphy Marks 40th Anniversary," *Chain Store Age,* August 1946; Kenneth T. Paxton, speeches to G. C. Murphy Veterans Club, May 23, 1966, and May 20, 1968; George Swetnam, "Dollars and Dimes," *Pittsburgh Press Sunday Roto,* June 19, 1960, pp. 6–7; "Chain Stores," *Time,* Oct. 20, 1930; "Earnings," *Time,* Feb. 8, 1932; "December Sales of Chains Lag," *Wall Street Journal,* Dec. 17, 1932, p. 3; "52 Chain Stores Show Increase in Sales for First Nine Months," *Hartford* (Conn.) *Courant,* Oct. 14, 1930, p. 22; "5 & 10," *Pittsburgh Bulletin Index,* June 6, 1935, pp. 14–16; "43 Chain Stores Off 5.26 P.C. for 11 Months," *Hartford* (Conn.) *Courant,* Dec. 15, 1931, p. 21; "40,000 Shares of G. C. Murphy Offered Today," *Chicago Daily Tribune,* Dec. 23, 1935, p. 26; "G. C. Murphy Plans to Sell Preferred and Common Shares," *Wall Street Journal,* Dec. 2, 1935, p. 2; "Kindly Lights," *Time,* July 28, 1930; "1932 Chain Store Trade Under 1931," *Wall Street Journal,* April 12, 1932; "Sales of Chains About 15% Lower," *Wall Street Journal,* Jan. 2, 1933, p. 15; "Shadow of Panic," *Time,* Oct. 20, 1930; "20 Cents," *Time,* Feb. 29, 1932; McKeesport, Pa., *Daily News,* June 10, 1929, and Sept. 27, 1929.

Sources for the Henrietta Leaver sidebar include W. H. Barr, "Studio Cameras Get View of 'Miss Model America,'" McKeesport, Pa., *Daily News,* Feb. 1, 1936; Evelyn Burke, "I'd Rather Have a Job than Wear a Beauty Crown," *Every Week,* Nov. 3, 1935; Ron Schuler, "Miss America, 1935," *Ron Schuler's Parlour Tricks,* March 28, 2006, retrieved from http://rsparlourtricks.blogspot.com/2006/03/miss-america-1935.html; Miss America Foundation records; "Service Here Today for Miss America 1935," *Columbus* (Ohio) *Dispatch,* Sept. 21, 1993, p. 13C; "The Lady with the Torch," Columbia Pictures public relations department, undated; "Henrietta May Reconsider Her Stand Taken in Opposition to Nude Statue," McKeesport, Pa., *Daily News,* Nov. 2, 1935; "Local Beauty Wins Contest," McKeesport, Pa., *Daily News,* Aug. 9, 1935; "Miss America, Awaiting Stork's Visit, Reveals Secret Marriage in 1935," McKeesport, Pa., *Daily News,* Aug. 22, 1936; and "Miss America's Marriage to 'Johnny' Is Revealed," McKeesport, Pa., *Daily News,* July 18, 1936.

CHAPTER 5

Most information is drawn from the author's interviews, as well as from Barbara G. Allison, letter to the author, July 2005; Sandra Wilson Cramer, letter to author, Dec. 10, 2005; Dorothy V. Everetts, letter to author, July 2005; Tom Glenn, letter to author, undated; Adrienne Kapisak, letter to author, Jan. 7, 2005; Eva M. Miller, letter to author, July 2005; Wanda Wood, letter to author, July 2005.

Information about Murphy personnel policies is drawn from Ken Paxton, *Rules for Women Employees* (G. C. Murphy Company, 1950); *A Look at Your Job* (Morgan & Lindsey Inc., Division of G. C. Murphy Company, 1970); *Service with a Smile* (G. C. Murphy Company, 1929); *The Spirit of Service* (G. C. Murphy Company, 1947); *The True Spirit of Service* (G. C. Murphy Company, 1959).

Other details are drawn from "Five & Ten Girls," *Time,* Feb. 17, 1930; "Murphy Store Will Have Formal Opening Friday; 200 Clerks on Payroll," Connellsville, Pa., *Daily Courier,* Nov. 24, 1937, p. 3.

CHAPTER 6

Sources include author's correspondence with Public Affairs Office, Bob Jones University, Greenville, S.C., 2004 and 2005; Douglas Carl

Abrams, *Selling the Old-Time Religion: American Fundamentalists and Mass Culture, 1920–1940* (Athens: University of Georgia Press, 1991), pp. 56–57; Daniel Bloomfield, ed., *Chain Stores and Legislation* (New York: H. W. Wilson Co., 1939); Alfred G. Buhler, "Chain Store Taxes," *Journal of Marketing,* January 1937; Peter Carlson, "Taking the Bob out of Bob Jones U.," *Washington Post,* May 5, 2002, p. C01; William J. Hitchens Jr., "Bob Jones Opens Revival Here: Immense Crowds at Three Services Yesterday," McKeesport, Pa., *Daily News,* Jan. 3, 1927; William D. Hubbard letter to the editor, *Indiana* (Pa.) *Weekly Messenger,* June 7, 1936; Paul Ingram and Hayagreeva Rao, "Store Wars: The Enactment and Repeal of Anti-Chain Store Legislation in America," *American Journal of Sociology,* September 2004; John A. Krut, letter to G. C. Murphy employees, March 1, 1944; Godfrey Lebhar, *Chain Stores in America: 1859–1959* (New York: Chain Store Publishing Corp., 1959), pp. 101–283; Douglas J. Lucas et al., *Cornerstone of a Community* (McKeesport, Pa.: McKeesport Hospital, 1994); G. C. Murphy Company, *Service Sound-Offs,* March 1, 1944; Wright Patman, "Curbing the Chain Store," *The Nation,* Nov. 28, 1938; Paul L. Sample, *The Requisites of a Good Superintendent,* and letters to Murphy employees, June 27, 1942, Jan. 3, 1944; Walter Shaw Sr. letter to Edgar M. Mack, Sept. 11, 1943; Helen Woodward, "Pocket Guide: The Patman Bill," *The Nation,* Jan. 21, 1939; Nancy Beck Young, *Wright Patman: Populism, Liberalism and the American Dream* (Dallas: Southern Methodist University Press, 2000); Kimberly Young, "Brush Valley: Serenity and Secret Recipe Flavor Farm Community," Greensburg, Pa., *Tribune-Review,* June 9, 2002.

"Chain Store Fight Opened by Congressman Halleck in Two Addresses Here," *Indiana* (Pa.) *Weekly Messenger,* April 30, 1936; "Committee Working Hard for a Good County Fair," *Indiana* (Pa.) *Progress,* Aug. 11, 1937; "Council Heeds Citizens' Vote Against Parking Meters," *Gettysburg* (Pa.) *Times,* Jan. 26, 1938; "Dauphin Court Drafts Chain Tax Decision," United Press, Jan. 12, 1937; "Economist in Tax Statement Reveals Destruction of Benefits Under Proposal," Associated Press, April 11, 1938; "Files Answer in Chain Store Suits," *Charleroi* (Pa.) *Daily Mail,* Aug. 14, 1937;

"5 & 10," *Pittsburgh Bulletin Index,* June 6, 1935; "Folded Arms Close 4 Pittsburgh Stores," *New York Times,* March 21, 1937, p. 30; "G. C. Murphy Co. Will Reemploy Drafted Workers," *Washington Post,* Sept. 8, 1940, p. 5; "Grocers to Oppose Retail Federation," *New York Times,* April 24, 1935; "Highest Salaries Paid in Nation Are Listed by House Committee," *New York Times,* Jan. 9, 1938; "Indiana Hospital Gets Magnificent Donation," *Indiana* (Pa.) *Evening Gazette,* Oct. 1, 1935; "Indiana Hospital to Dedicate Memorial Building on Thursday," *Indiana* (Pa.) *Evening Gazette,* Sept. 20, 1939; "Inquiry Ordered on Retail 'Lobby,'" *New York Times,* April 25, 1935.

"Mack Memorial Is Presented to Local Hospital," *Indiana* (Pa.) *Evening Gazette,* Sept. 22, 1939; "Merchants of the Nation Organize to Act as Unit on Economic Issues," *New York Times,* April 17, 1935; "The MPR-330 Battle," *Time,* Sept. 27, 1943; "The Patman Bill Is Up Again," Monessen, Pa., *Daily Independent,* April 4, 1940; "Ruling Against Chain Store Tax Upheld," United Press, June 19, 1939; "Showdown Nears on Chain Store Taxation Tonight," Associated Press, May 10, 1937; "Shaw Hailed As District Benefactor," McKeesport, Pa., *Daily News,* Feb. 7, 1940; "Consuming Public Will Really Pay the Tax, Say U.S. Investigators," Monessen, Pa., *Daily Independent,* April 12, 1937; "This Is the Story the Radio Kept from You," Monessen, Pa., *Daily Independent,* March 27, 1937.

CHAPTER 7

Most of the information in this chapter comes from the author's interviews, with additional details from Ron DaParma, "Fight for Seats Ended; Murphy's to Close Up," McKeesport, Pa., *Daily News,* Feb. 28, 1980; "Murphy Food Service: More of It, More Service," *Chain Store Age,* December 1967, pp. 220–25; G. C. Murphy Company menus from 1934 to 1987, donated by Ellison "Al" Boggs and Ed Kinter; and *Eating at Murphy's,* an undated employee handbook published by the G. C. Murphy Company, available at the McKeesport Heritage Center.

CHAPTER 8

Information about American life in the 1950s is drawn from David Halberstam, *The Fifties* (New

York: Ballantine Books, 1993); William Manchester, *The Glory and the Dream: Volume 2* (Boston: Little, Brown & Company, 1974); Vance Packard, *The Hidden Persuaders* (New York: David McKay, 1957). Information about television-viewing habits in Pittsburgh is drawn from the author's own research and from Lynn Boyd Hinds, *Broadcasting the Local News: The Early Years of Pittsburgh's KDKA-TV* (University Park: Pennsylvania State University Press, 1995).

Additional quotes and information specific to the G. C. Murphy Company and the variety-store industry come from Edwin Beachler, "The Exercise Lady," *Pittsburgh Press Sunday Roto,* Sept. 5, 1954, p. 8; Louise Gephart, "Dolls Will Wear Heels and Nylons," *Washington Post,* Nov. 1, 1956, p. C24; Ben Gordon, "The Righteous Live Forever," *Chain Store Age,* January 1954; Walter C. Shaw Sr.'s letter to employees, April 1, 1946; "Country Boy," *Forbes,* Sept. 1, 1959, p. 31; "Experimenting with the Five-and-Dime," *Business Week,* Nov. 8, 1952, pp. 54–61; "G. C. Murphy Co. Growth," *Chicago Daily Tribune,* March 5, 1952, p. C6; "G. C. Murphy Co. Plans to Purchase Morris 5 & 10 Cent Stores Inc.," *Wall Street Journal,* Sept. 11, 1951, p. 9; "General Store Grown Up," *Forbes,* Jan. 1, 1960, pp. 41–44; "Murphy Co. Acquires Morris Stores Chain," *New York Times,* Nov. 1, 1951, p. 47; "South Hills Shopping Center," Pittsburgh, Pa., *Charette,* December 1950, pp. 16–17; "Steering the 5 and 10's," *Newsweek,* June 23, 1958, pp. 87–88; "The Tortoise Strategy Is Working," *Business Week,* July 26, 1952, pp. 38–42; "The $1 Billion Five & Ten," *Time,* Aug. 31, 1959; "Variety Chains," *Forbes,* Jan. 1, 1956; "Variety Chains Have Tough Time in Race for Consumer's Dollar," *Business Week,* Sept. 3, 1955, p. 34; "Variety Chains Put Brakes on Prices," *Business Week,* Oct. 16, 1948, pp. 65–69.

Details of Apache Plaza are taken from Jeff Anderson, "Apache Plaza: Farewell to the 'Center of the Community,'" http://ApachePlaza.com/, retrieved on Oct. 20, 2004.

"Fly the Murphy Skies" section: In addition to the author's interviews, sources for the disposition of G. C. Murphy Company's planes include the Warbird Registry at http://www.warbirdregistry.org/ and the Aviation Safety Network at http://www.aviation-safety.net/.

CHAPTER 9

Most details come from the author's interviews and from G. C. Murphy Company construction division reports in the archives of the McKeesport Heritage Center. Additional information comes from Barbara Cloud, "I Like It Because It Is Crowded and Pushy," *Pittsburgh Press,* Dec. 10, 1984, p. C1–C2; William Faust, "The Five and Ten . . . It's a Billion Dollar Baby," *Pittsburgh Press Sunday Roto,* Dec. 5, 1948; Frank C. Harper, *Pittsburgh of Today,* vol. 4 (New York: The American Historical Society, Inc., 1932), p. 377; Diana Nelson Jones, "Dime Stores Grow Rare and Precious," *Pittsburgh Post-Gazette,* Jan. 29, 1998; Walter C. Kidney, Pittsburgh History & Landmarks Foundation, letter to author Jan. 12, 2005; John Mintz, "Murphy Store Closing, Last Five-and-Dime Leaves Downtown," *Washington Post,* Jan. 7, 1987, p. C1; Mobile Access Networks Corp., "Case Study: The Homer Building," undated press release; Cristina Rouvalis, "Market on the Square to Close Doors this Winter," *Pittsburgh Post-Gazette,* Nov. 22, 1994, p. C6; Tim Schooley, "Grocer on Tap for Downtown Pittsburgh," *Pittsburgh Business Times,* Dec. 12, 2003; Ben Semmes, "Former G. C. Murphy's Building Sold," *Pittsburgh Business Times,* Dec. 14, 2006; Jeannette Smyth, "Dime Store Couture," *Washington Post,* March 26, 1972, p. G1; Albert M. Tannler, "Take a Closer Look at Art Deco Commercial Architecture in Pittsburgh," *Pittsburgh Tribune-Review Focus Magazine,* March 26, 2000; Hopkins Plat Maps of Pittsburgh, 1924; "Downtown Properties Rented for $2,000,000," *Washington Post,* Nov. 3, 1929, p. M14; "The January Meeting," Pittsburgh, Pa., *Charette,* February 1931, p. 9; "Milton (Mickey) Glick," *Pittsburgh Post-Gazette,* Jan. 23, 1997, p. C9; "Murphy Co. Plans Store Expansion," *Washington Post,* Jan. 18, 1933, p. 10; "Nathan Gendel, 62, Jewelry Wholesaler," *Washington Post,* March 12, 1977, p. D6; "Renovation Begins on D.C. Landmark," *Washington Post,* July 30, 1988, p. F8; Washington Metropolitan Area Transit Authority history retrieved from http://www.wmata.com/about/history.cfm on July 9, 2004.

CHAPTER 10

Details on the Woolworth sit-ins come from Pitrone, pp. 152–157, and Karen Plunkett-Powell,

Remembering Woolworth's (New York: St. Martin's Press, 1999), pp. 157–163.

Background on Morgan & Lindsey, Inc., and the Texas department stores was found in the G. C. Murphy Company archives, McKeesport Heritage Center; additional sources include "Carl A. Morgan Dies," Winnfield, La., *Winn Parish Enterprise,* July 15, 1948; "G. C. Murphy Acquires 4 Texas Outlets of Cobb Department Stores," *Wall Street Journal,* Nov. 17, 1960, p. 10; "G. C. Murphy Co.," *New York Times,* Feb. 12, 1960, p. 37; "G. C. Murphy Plans to Buy Terry Farris, Inc.," *Wall Street Journal,* Dec. 23, 1960, p. 5; "Jasper County" and "Jasper, Texas," *The Handbook of Texas* (Austin: University of Texas at Austin) at http://lib.utexas.edu/, retrieved June 3, 2004; "Morgan & Lindsey," *Chain Store Age,* June 1950; "Murphy Buys Store Chain," *Gettysburg* (Pa.) *Times,* April 13, 1959; "Murphy Opens Store Here Thursday," *Panama City* (Fla.) *Herald,* June 27, 1962; "Murphy Reports Income Higher," *Odessa* (Texas) *American,* Oct. 29, 1968, p. 11A; "Murphy Sells Morris Stores," Connellsville, Pa., *Daily Courier,* July 12, 1968; "Murphy's Buys Variety Chain," St. Joseph, Mich., *Herald-Press,* April 13, 1959; "Store Adopts Policy of Non-Segregation," *Washington Post,* Sept. 6, 1952, p. 3; "Terry Farris in the Mall Celebrates Anniversary," Harlingen, Tex., *Valley Morning Star,* Nov. 19, 1969, p. C6.

CHAPTER 11

Some quotes in this chapter are drawn from memos written by James S. Mack to G. C. Murphy Company staff on Feb. 2, 1962, Aug. 22, 1962, and Jan. 17, 1967, on file at the McKeesport Heritage Center.

Background on McCrory Corp. is from Isadore Barmash, *For the Good of the Company* (New York: Grosset & Dunlap, 1976); Clare M. Reckert, "Suit Says 3 McCrory Officers Violated Fiduciary Obligations," *New York Times,* Sept. 24, 1963, p. 68; Leonard Sloane, "New Round Opens in M'Crory Fight," *New York Times,* Oct. 11, 1963, p. 53; Sloane, "McCrory Meeting Short, and, for a Change, Sweet," *New York Times,* May 27, 1964, p. 49; "McCrory Corp. Reports Profit of 2 Million in Second Quarter," *New York Times,* Aug.

29, 1962, p. 57; "The Rapid Riser," *Time,* June 6, 1960; and various undated clippings and brochures in the McCrory archives at York County Heritage Trust, York, Pa.

Other information is from Robert Drew-Bear, *Mass Merchandising: Revolution & Evolution* (New York: Fairchild Publications, 1970); David Dworsky, "Chain-Store Volume for Half Shows 11.5 Per Cent Increase," *New York Times,* July 23, 1966, p. 45; Dworsky, "Sales Rise Slim at Chain Stores," *New York Times,* Feb. 22, 1967, p. 39; William M. Freeman, "Chains Outgrow 'Five & Ten' Label," *New York Times,* Aug. 30, 1959, p. F1; Myron Kandel, "Big Chains Adding Discount Stores," *New York Times,* Oct. 1, 1963, p. 1; Stanley S. Kresge and Steve Spilos, *The S. S. Kresge Story* (Racine, Wis.: Western Publishing Co., 1979); Tom Mahoney and Leonard Sloane, *The Great Merchants: America's Foremost Retail Institutions and the People Who Made Them Great* (New York: Harper & Row, 1974); G. C. Murphy Co., *Welcome to Murphy's A-A Team,* undated; Karen Plunkett-Powell, *Remembering Woolworth's* (New York: St. Martin's Press, 1999); "Adrift in Concept Land," *Sales Management,* Jan 15, 1968, p. 31; "Big Store Sales Rise in Quarter," *New York Times,* April 22, 1966, p. 57; "Demand for Discounters," *Time,* March 30, 1962; "Everybody Loves a Bargain," *Time,* July 6, 1962; "Funeral Rites Held for Walter C. Shaw," McKeesport, Pa., *Daily News,* Jan. 17, 1962; "Introduction to Society," *Time,* June 23, 1961; "Kresge Earnings Increase by 32%," *New York Times,* Nov. 25, 1967, p. 57; "Murphy Co. in Changes; Shaw Retires," McKeesport, Pa., *Daily News,* May 7, 1968; "McCrory Village," *McCrory-McClellan-Green News,* July 1963; "Murphy's A-A Store—A New Break-Through in Customer Service," *Chain Store Age,* November 1966; "Revolt at Kress," *Time,* March 3, 1958; "Sales of Leading Chain Stores Seen Surpassing All Records," *New York Times,* Dec. 16, 1965, p. 75; "Walter C. Shaw," McKeesport, Pa., *Daily News,* Jan. 11, 1962; "Women's Dormitory," Pittsburgh, Pa., *Charette,* March 1959, p. 22.

CHAPTER 12

All material in this chapter was developed from the author's interviews with the sources quoted.

CHAPTER 13

Some sales figures in this chapter are taken from an unpublished internal G. C. Murphy Company report compiled in 1974 by former vice president of sales William Anderson. Other sources include Donald R. Cooper, "Murphy Suit Settled for $548,000," McKeesport, Pa., *Daily News,* Aug. 24, 1972, p. 1; Cooper, "Murphy Hints Warehouse Closing," McKeesport, Pa., *Daily News,* May 15, 1974, p. 36; Charles J. Elia, "Despite Trend of Strengthening Liquidity, Weaker Firms' Positions Are Deteriorating," *Wall Street Journal,* Aug. 27, 1976, p. 25; James B. Johnson, "But Murphy Warehouse May Remain," McKeesport, Pa., *Daily News,* Oct. 29, 1976; Johnson, "Murphy Moves to Cut Losses, Makes Changes," McKeesport, Pa., *Daily News,* Oct. 4, 1978, p. 1; Johnson, "Murphy Says It Will Close Its Warehouse," McKeesport, Pa., *Daily News,* Sept. 27, 1976; Jack Markowitz, "Murphy at Highs, Marts Do It," *Pittsburgh Post-Gazette,* Feb. 11, 1977, p. 16; G. C. Murphy Company, *Murphy's Mart: A Special Report,* July 22, 1970; Gary W. Sexton, *A Case Study of Job Satisfaction: G. C. Murphy Company Distribution Center, Indianapolis, Indiana,* MBA thesis, Indiana-Purdue University at Indianapolis, 1978; Singer, Deane, and Scribner, "G. C. Murphy Company," *Research Report,* Oct. 18, 1972; William H. Wylie, "Murphy to Open 25 New Stores," *Pittsburgh Press,* Feb. 11, 1977; "Chain's Profit Drops During First Quarter," McKeesport, Pa., *Daily News,* May 15, 1974, p. 36; "G. C. Murphy Co.," *Chain Store Age,* November 1978, p. 47; "G. C. Murphy Co. Reverses Decision to Close Facility," *Wall Street Journal,* Nov. 1, 1976, p. 11; "G. C. Murphy Co. Says William T. Withers Resigned as President," *Wall Street Journal,* Feb. 8, 1979; "G. C. Murphy Directors Place President, 63, on Indefinite Leave," *Wall Street Journal,* Oct. 6, 1978, p. 35; "G. C. Murphy Planning to Close Warehouse at McKeesport, Pa.," *Wall Street Journal,* Sept. 28, 1976, p. 47; "G. C. Murphy to Close Facility," *Wall Street Journal,* Sept. 5, 1979, p. 16; "G. C. Murphy Will Pay 246 Female Employees $548,000 Back Wages," *Wall Street Journal,* Sept. 5, 1972, p. 8; "G. C. Murphy's Rating Reduced," *Wall Street Journal,* June 29, 1977, p. 21; "Grant Goes Under," *Time,* Oct. 13, 1975; "Grants Cut Back," *Time,* Jan. 27, 1975; and "Store Chain Offers Money in Bias Suit," *Washington Post,* Sept. 2, 1972.

Joanne Glus's quotes come from Carol Kleiman, "Joanne Glus: She Just Kept on Trucking," *Chicago Tribune,* Nov. 2, 1972, p. B5; additional details are from *Joanne Glus et al. v. The G. C. Murphy Company et al.,* United States Court of Appeals, June 27, 1980.

CHAPTER 14

Much of the information about the Ames takeover of the G. C. Murphy Company has never been published and comes from the author's interviews with Ed Davis, Tom Hudak, Bob Messner, and others. Additional information is drawn from Isadore Barmash, "Retail Chains Say State's Strong Points Help Retail Growth," *New York Times,* May 25, 1986, p. 1; Barmash, "Bankrupt Ames Hires a Turnaround Expert," *New York Times,* May 1, 1990, p. D5; Barmash, "Jacobs Has Stake in G. C. Murphy," *New York Times,* Oct. 10, 1984, p. D6; Eleanor Bergholz, "Store Means a Lot to McKeesporters," *Pittsburgh Post-Gazette,* Aug. 1, 1985, p. E1; Ron DaParma, "Murphy Company Ceases to Exist," McKeesport, Pa., *Daily News,* Aug. 6, 1985, pp. 1–2; DaParma, "120 Murphy Outlets to Go," McKeesport, Pa., *Daily News,* July 24, 1985, p. 1; Kenneth N. Gilpin and Todd S. Purdum, "Head of Ames Is Glad He Listened to Brothers," *New York Times,* April 26, 1985, p. D2; John Greenwald, "The Great Takeover Debate," *Time,* April 22, 1985; Robert T. Grieves, "Greenmailing Mickey Mouse," *Time,* June 25, 1984; Chuck Lytle's letter to store managers, Jan. 16, 1986; Arthur Markowitz, "Acquisition Wave Engulfs Chains; Some Public Firms Go Private," *Discount Store News,* Nov. 26, 1984; Clemens P. Work, "Greenmail: It's Legal, but Is It Right?" *U.S. News & World Report,* June 26, 1984, pp. 75–76; "Ames in Talks with Murphy," *New York Times,* April 16, 1985, p. D15; "Ames to Buy G. C. Murphy," *Washington Post,* April 24, 1985, p. F1; "Ames Will Dispose of 130 Units of G. C. Murphy," *Wall Street Journal,* June 13, 1985, p. 1; "Frantically Shopping for Suitors," *Time,* March 12, 1984; "G. C. Murphy Explores Employee Buyout Plan," *Washington Post,* Feb. 1, 1985, p. F1;

"G. C. Murphy Says Management Mulling Buyout by ESOP," Dow Jones News Service, Jan. 31, 1985; "Jacobs in Filing on Murphy Stake," *New York Times,* Oct. 16, 1984, p. D5; "Jacobs Increases Stake in Murphy," *New York Times,* Oct. 18, 1984, p. D4; "More Chains Devise Techniques to Block Unfriendly Takeovers," *Discount Store News,* June 25, 1984.

Information about recessionary conditions and steel industry layoffs is drawn from a variety of sources, including the author's own experiences, as well as John M. Berry, "State Unemployment Claims Breach 600,000 Level in Week," *Washington Post,* June 4, 1982, p. C9; Lydia Chavez, "U.S. Steel to Close Big Plant," *New York Times,* Dec. 31, 1981, p. D3; Clara Germani, "Pinched By Steel Layoffs, Pittsburgh Spins a Safety Net of Last Resort," *Christian Science Monitor,* Feb. 2, 1983, p. 3; Steven Greenhouse, "U.S. Steel Plans Closings, Loss of 15,430 Jobs," *New York Times,* Dec. 28, 1983, p. A1; Jerry Knight, "J&L to Close Youngstown Plant, Fiscal Crisis Threatens Community," *Washington Post,* Nov. 29, 1979, p. B1; Staughton Lynd, "Big Steel's Irony," *New York Times,* Dec. 1, 1981, p. A31; Rudolph A. Pyatt Jr., "There's Improvement, but Recession Lingers," *Washington Post,* Nov. 26, 1982, p. E8; Leonard Silk, "A Steep Slide into Recession," *New York Times,* Nov. 11, 1981, p. D2; Paul Van Slambrouck, "Shoppers Hang on to Wallets as Economic Slump Worsens," *Christian Science Monitor,* May 23, 1980, p. 3; "1,800 Get Pink Slips and a Blue Christmas," *New York Times,* Dec. 25, 1981.

In addition to interviews with Chuck Lytle's widow, Ann, and key executives in the G. C. Murphy Company, information specific to the company's problems and turnaround in the late 1970s comes from James B. Johnson, "Lytle New President at G. C. Murphy Co.," McKeesport, Pa., *Daily News,* Feb. 19, 1979, p. 20; Johnson, "Murphy Management 'Enthusiastic' Despite Setbacks, Sees Turnaround," McKeesport, Pa., *Daily News,* Nov. 22, 1978; Johnson, "Murphy Moves to Cut Losses, Makes Changes," McKeesport, Pa., *Daily News,* Oct. 4, 1978, p. 36; Chuck Lytle's letter to employees, Oct. 25, 1978; Jack Markowitz, "G. C. Murphy Not Slashing Dividends," *Pittsburgh Post-Gazette,* Oct. 17, 1978; John

R. McCarty, "First Quarter Good Sign for G. C. Murphy Co.," McKeesport, Pa., *Daily News,* June 3, 1980, p. 18; James Rankin, "Murphy's CEO Leaving, McKittrick Taking Over," McKeesport, Pa., *Daily News,* Feb. 4, 1987; S. Warne Robinson's letter to employees, Oct. 3, 1978, and Feb. 20, 1979; Claire Simmons, "Lytle Steers G. C. Murphy in New Marketing Direction," *Pittsburgh Business Times,* June 21–27, 1982, pp. 1, 21; William H. Wylie, "Sales Up, G. C. Murphy 'Aggressively' Hunts Store Sites," *Pittsburgh Press,* June 4, 1980, p. C-22; Wendy Zellner, "Lytle Steps Down as Head of G. C. Murphy Division," *Pittsburgh Post-Gazette,* Feb. 4, 1987, p. 13; "G. C. Murphy Earnings Up," *Pittsburgh Post-Gazette,* May 20, 1980; "Great Expectations: G. C. Murphy's Leverage Potential Is Tantalizing," *Financial World,* Nov. 15, 1982, pp. 33–34; "Lytle, Hudak Get New G. C. Murphy Posts," McKeesport, Pa., *Daily News,* May 20, 1980; "Murphy: Changing from the Top Down," *Chain Store Age,* February 1980, pp. 37–45; "Murphy's Moves Signal Transition," *Chain Store Age,* July 1980, p. 7; "Murphy Sales up Again; Mack Unit Reorganizes," McKeesport, Pa., *Daily News,* March 2, 1979; "Murphy Shuffles Execs to Plug Drain," *Chain Store Age,* November 1978, p. 47–49; "President with a Personnel Touch," *Chain Store Age,* April 9, 1979, p. 45; "Robinson Retires, Murphy's in Gear," *Chain Store Age,* February 1981, pp. 49–53; "Sears, Others Report Decline in Profits, but City-Based G. C. Murphy Bucks Trend," McKeesport, Pa., *Daily News,* May 20, 1980; "Top Brass Named at Two Chains," *Discount Store News,* March 12, 1979, p. 1.

Direct quotes from Lytle about the variety store reorganization and the FIND program at Murphy's Marts are taken from a tape recording of his June 12, 1984, speech to Murphy stockholders, available at the McKeesport Heritage Center, as well as from Ron DaParma, "New Look at Murphy Mall Outlets," McKeesport, Pa., *Daily News,* Oct. 1, 1982.

Besides the author's interviews, details about changes to the merchandise mix in Murphy stores comes from Brent Felgner, "Murphy's Mart set to Add Satellite Dishes, Receivers," *Discount Store News,* July 9, 1984; Felgner, *Discount Store News,* Jan. 9, 1984; Felgner, *Discount Store*

News, Feb. 6, 1984; "Blank Videotape Discounters' Biggest CE Traffic-Puller; Less Effective for Catalogers," *Discount Store News*, Jan. 7, 1985; "Computer Paper Invades Stationery Sections," *Discount Store News*, March 19, 1984; "Nationwide DSN Report," *Discount Store News*, June 11, 1984. The Crafts and More stores and the Office Shop Warehouse are described in Helen Huntley, "Workplace Looks Good on Paper," *St. Petersburg* (Fla.) *Times*, June 6, 1988, p. 7; "Ames Posts Sales, Profits Increase," *Discount Store News*, Sept. 12, 1988; "Crafts & More Stitches a New Niche," *Discount Store News*, May 8, 1989.

In addition to the author's interviews, details of the McCrory purchase of the Murphy variety stores come from Jim Gallagher, "Murphy Bought by McCrory's," *Pittsburgh Post-Gazette*, Aug. 8, 1989, pp. 13–14; Peter Hisey, "Ames Deals Variety Division to McCrory for $80M," *Discount Store News*, Aug. 21, 1989; James Rankin, "Ames Sells Murphy's to McCrory's for $80 Million," McKeesport, Pa., *Daily News*, Aug. 7, 1989, p. 1; Constance Walker, "McCrory Buys Murphy Stores," *York* (Pa.) *Daily Record*, Aug. 7, 1989, p. 1; "Managers of Murphy Unit Make Offer to Acquire It," *Wall Street Journal*, Feb. 17, 1989, p. 1; "2 Groups Interested in G. C. Murphy," *New York Times*, Feb. 17, 1989, p. D3.

The McClelland murder is documented in Laura LeFay and Robert Little, "Coleman Gray Put to Death by Injection," Norfolk, Va., *Virginian-Pilot*, Feb. 27, 1997, p. A1; and *Coleman Wayne Gray v. Charles E. Thompson, Warden, et al.*, U.S. District Court for the Eastern District of Virginia, June 28, 1995.

Wal-Mart information is drawn from Sam Walton with John Huey, *Sam Walton: Made in America* (New York: Bantam Books, 1993); the Wal-Mart point-of-sale computer system is described in pp. 270–273. Details of Meshulam Riklis and McCrory Corporation under his control comes from Abdalla F. Hassan, "McCrory's Nears Sale to Owner," *York* (Pa.) *Dispatch*, Aug. 1, 1997, p. 1; Allan Sloan, "Making Mischief with Riklis and His Partnerships," *The Washington Post*, July 31, 1990, p. C3; Sloan, "Riklis' New McCrory Maneuvers Could Be a Nightmare in the Making," *Washington Post*, Dec. 22, 1982, p. E3.

CHAPTER 15

Most of the information in this chapter comes from the author's interviews. Ames details come from Jennifer Babson, "Discount Retailer Ames to Acquire Hills for $330m," *Boston Globe*, Nov. 13, 1998, p. C1; Greg Gatlin, "Ames Misses Its Last Shot; Low-Cost Retailer Won't Emerge from Bankruptcy," *Boston Herald*, Aug. 15, 2002, p. 30; Teresa Lindeman, "Bankrupt Ames Hanging It Up," *Pittsburgh Post-Gazette*, Aug. 15, 2002, p. E1; Lindeman, "Wal-Mart Wins Again," *Pittsburgh Post-Gazette*, Aug. 18, 2002, p. E1; Teresa Chris Reidy, "Troubled Ames to Shut Remaining 327 Stores," *Boston Globe*, Aug. 15, 2002, p. C1.

The Ames takeover of Zayre is documented in David Mehagen, "Ames Jumps into the Big Leagues," *Boston Globe*, Sept. 18, 1988, p. A1; Mehagen, "Ames Looks Beyond Zayre," *Boston Globe*, April 18, 1989, p. 33; Mehagen, "Ames Loss Blamed on Zayre's Old Stores," *Boston Globe*, Jan. 11, 1990, p. 53; Mehagen, "Trouble in Rocky Hill: Old Zayre Stores Haunt Ames Discount Chain," *Boston Globe*, March 6, 1990, p. 25; Mehagen, "Zayre Sells Its Discount Stores for $800m," *Boston Globe*, Sept. 16, 1988, p. 1; Mehagen, "From Z . . . to A," *Boston Globe*, Feb. 3, 1989, p. 21; Lena H. Sun, "Zayre Sells Discount Stores to Ames; Defensive Action Follows Haft Interest," *Washington Post*, Sept. 16, 1988, p. C11; Todd Vogel, "'They Took Their Shot at Being a Giant'—And Missed," *Business Week*, May 7, 1990, p. 39; "Ames Gobbles Zayre Stores," Sept. 26, 1988, *Discount Store News*, Sept. 26, 1988.

McCrory details are drawn from Doug Desjardins, "McCrory Corp. to Go out of Business," *Discount Store News*, Dec. 10, 2001; Neal G. Goulet, "McCrory's Problems Cloud What's in Store," *York* (Pa.) *Daily Record*, Feb. 26, 1997, pp. 1, 7; and "McCrory Stores Calls It a Day," *Home Textiles Today*, Nov. 29, 2001.

Details of the current operations of pharmacy and general-merchandise chains are described in the 2005 and 2006 annual reports of Duckwall-ALCO Stores Inc. and the 2006 annual reports of Walgreen Company and Rite Aid Corporation.

photo credits

index

Page numbers in *italics* refer to illustrations.